HILARITY ENSUES

Also by Tucker Max

I Hope They Serve Beer In Hell

Assholes Finish First

Sloppy Seconds: The Tucker Max Leftovers

HILARITY ENSUES

TUCKER MAX

815-A Brazos Street
Suite 220
Austin, TX 78701

Manufactured in the United States of America

10 9 8 7

Library of Congress Cataloging-in-Publication Data

ISBN 978-1-61961-003-3

Contents

Author's Note

My real name is Tucker Max. All the events described in the following stories are true to the best of my recollection, though certain dates, characteristics, locations and other trivial details have been altered.

I hope you enjoy reading about my life as much as I have enjoyed living it.

The Cancun Stories

Occurred, Spring Break 2000

I worked in Cancun, Mexico for six full weeks during my second year at Duke Law School. I left Durham at the end of February, and then stayed down there for spring break season. You're probably wondering: How could I up and leave not just school, but the entire United States of America, while still enrolled in a top ten law school, with classes going on every day, and not have any negative consequences?

Because everything about law school is a complete fucking joke.

Yes, Duke is a top ten law school, but the only thing difficult occurred well before I ever set foot on campus; getting admitted. Once I actually arrived on campus, I realized that not only was the hardest part done, but *everything else was a complete joke.* The emperor had no clothes.

Going to class is a complete waste of time. The professors don't care about teaching; they either ramble endlessly about meaningless shit, or they spend the whole time telling you how important they are. The students are no better; the ones constantly raising their hands to talk (they're called "gunners") are all pompous suck-ups, and add nothing of value to the conversation. The work itself is a fucking joke; there's no daily homework, it's just reading and "considering issues"—and I would say that probably 90% of what you go over in class has no bearing on either your life or your job as a lawyer. Think about that—most of what you learn in class has *no application anywhere* outside of law school.

Grades aren't a problem either. Your entire grade is based on one final exam at the end of the semester. Law school professors all use the same basic test format and look for the same basic type of answers. If you crack the law school test "code" and write for what they are looking for, the tests are a cinch. If you're really smart, you don't even need to study. Just read through the book about a week before the test and you should be able to walk in and pull out at least a 3.0. You're not going to be top of your class doing this, but you can easily graduate in the middle. At a top tier law school, that's more than good enough to get a lucrative law firm job (at least it was when I was in law school . . . now, if you're in law school at all, you're just totally fucked regardless of where you graduate in your class. But that's a different discussion.)

By mid-first semester of my first year, I'd already stopped going to class. By second semester, I didn't bother buying my books. I spent that money getting drunk in Chapel Hill and fucking my way through a bunch of UNC sorostitutes. By second year, that was getting boring, so I looked for other ways to push the envelope. I decided I would go on vacation. During law school.

The problem is that I had no fucking money. But there are solutions to that. I could be one of those air couriers who gets to fly to Bangkok for like $50 if I don't bring any luggage and let the courier company use my allotted cargo space, but that requires responsibility and accountability—no chance. Then I thought—what about those companies that ship kids to various spring break spots? They have to have on-site staff, right?

I did a little research, figured out which companies were hiring, and started calling people. Getting a job overseas is pretty easy, especially at resort-type places. They're always desperate to find halfway competent help, and if you have a little intelligence and a lot of aggressiveness—I definitely have that—about getting the job, you're usually in. I just kept bugging every one of the travel services, making sure they knew how awesome I was until one hired me for the spring break season. Easy and obvious. When you spot market inefficiencies you don't tip your cap and go on your merry way. You ruthlessly exploit the fuck out of them.

So in the middle of the second semester of my 2L year, with all my law school classes still in session, I left North Carolina for Cancun. They paid me like $400 a week, plus expenses and accommodations . . . and my entire job was to party. I got paid to be me. I would show up at the day party, get hammered, go fuck some girl, take a nap, go to the night party, get hammered again, and fuck another girl. I woke up every morning sending out AMBER Alerts for my dignity . . . and I was getting paid for it.

If you've never been to Cancun or done this kind of "job," it's hard to understand what a fucking shitshow it is. You think your college partying days were bad? Not like Cancun. You may disagree, but you're wrong. You may have gone to the best party school in America, and you may think you threw down—and I am sure to some extent you did—but remember:

Cancun is where college kids go for vacation when they want to party EVEN MORE.

These are some of the funnier stories—at least the ones I can remember—from my time there:

WHY TO LEARN CPR

This incident happened at the famous bar Pat O'Brien's. There is a huge outdoor bar area that is grassy and hilly. It was relatively early in the day and I was bored and walking around checking things out when I saw a dude lying on his back, in the grass, way in the corner. Something about the way he was lying looked weird, limbs all akimbo, so I went to make sure he was OK.

He was not.

Dude had a vomit bubble coming out of one nostril. This is REAL bad; it's the first sign of asphyxiation, and means he is literally drowning on his own puke. I immediately roll him over, and give him the Heimlich. I know for CPR I probably should have given him mouth-to-mouth, but fuck that—if the Heimlich worked, I wouldn't have to put my lips on the puke-filled mouth of some random dude.

He immediately starts coughing and all kinds of shit comes spitting from his mouth and nose. That triggers some kind of violent spasm and he starts puking all over the place, making a complete mess of himself. Yeah, he ruined his favorite Señor Frog's t-shirt, but that's way better than fucking dying.

The Mexicans call the ambulance and they take him away to the clinic. After it was all over, it dawned on me: I just saved a dude's life. That's pretty fucking cool.

I was strutting around the bar, saying stuff like, "I saved a guy's life today. What'd you do? Jack shit probably." Now I know why doctors are so arrogant.

That was on a Tuesday. On Thursday, I saw the guy out with his friends.

Tucker "You back at it already? Brave man. Make sure and take it a little slower this time."
Guy "Uhh . . . OK."

It was obvious by his eyes that this dude was not registering who I was.

Tucker "You don't recognize me?"
Guy "Uh . . . not really."
Tucker "I'm the guy who saved your fucking life at Pat O'Brien's. You were choking on your own vomit, I gave you the Heimlich and called the ambulance."
Guy "Oh, yeah. I don't really remember that day much, but yeah I'm alive, so OK, cool, thanks."
Tucker "You don't remember it? You don't remember going to the hospital?"

Guy "Not really. I mean, I remember starting the day, and I remember leaving the hospital yesterday, but that's about it. But if you really saved my life, then thanks, I guess."
Tucker "You guess???"

Unappreciative fuck didn't even buy me a drink. That's why you don't try too hard to save the life of a University of Tennessee frat guy.

Boot and Rally

I know I said my only job in Cancun was to party, and that's the way it worked out most of the time, but ostensibly I was supposed to be doing actual things as well. Like make sure the kids who traveled to Mexico with our company went back to America alive.

So late one night in a club, I was watching this one guy who was in bad shape, making sure he didn't die before his friends came to get him. I was talking to girls at the same time, however, so I wasn't paying *that* much attention.

He was sitting on a couch and leaned over to puke, and as he did this, he pulled his hat off his head and threw up right into it. I probably should have called one of the busboys to clean it up, but in Cancun, this is pretty common. Plus, the girls and I were all having fun watching him.

He just sat there for what seemed like forever with his mouth open, drooling bile into his hat, which was completely full. Like a bowl of soup, except it was vomit. He eventually sat up, drank some water, and started to actually look like he had some life back in him. Then he got up, reached down for his hat and, having forgotten that he threw up in it, put it back on his head.

The dude didn't even flinch as the vomit oozed out the sides and down his face and head.

Of course, we all broke down laughing. He looked at us with one of the most pissed off drunk faces I've ever seen, and then walked off, without saying a word, vomit trailing behind him.

Give me two pair, I need two pair

I don't think it's that funny, but this story always cracks my friends up for some reason:

I left a club real late one night with a girl and went back to her hotel. By the time we were done fucking, it was like 6 or 7am. Even though I was exhausted and still really drunk, I decided to take the bus back to my hotel so I could sleep it off there and not have her bother me. I got on the bus, and even though I swore I'd stay awake, I promptly passed the fuck out.

I'm not exactly sure when I woke up, but it had to have been at least 10am. When I'd gotten on the bus, it was all Mexicans riding to work to start their shifts; now it was pretty much all young kids riding to various beach clubs to day drink. I'm not sure how many times I passed my hotel; the bus just runs in circles along the one road in Cancun, but I managed to stay awake until it got back in front of it again, and got off.

I must have been much drunker and more sleep deprived than I thought, because it wasn't until I walked out on the sidewalk that I noticed I was barefoot. How could that be? I remember putting my shoes on when I was leaving the girl's hotel room last night . . .

DID SOMEONE STEAL MY SHOES OFF MY FEET WHEN I WAS ASLEEP ON THE BUS?

Yes Tucker, someone did. Some dirt-poor Mexican realized that I was so deeply into a drunken stupor, they took my shoes off my feet. On a public bus.

WELCOME TO THE THUNDERDOME

Because the Cancun resorts are so nice and everything looks clean and neat, it's easy to forget that Mexico is NOT America. So when the vacationers would show up, I would take pains to explain this to them. Yes, being in Mexico is good because you can get as drunk as you want at 18. But there is a flip side to no rules: The American safety net isn't there to protect you from the consequences of your stupid decisions.

There are two things I saw that really drove this home for me.

The first happened when I was sitting out by the pool at my hotel one day, drinking and flirting with some girls. Some stupid frat guys were being idiots and jumping from the rocks into the pool, which the Mexican employees didn't like at all. Then, one of the guys got the brilliant idea that instead of jumping 10 feet off some fake cliffs next to the pool, he'd be the coolest guy in his group and jump off a third story balcony that overlooked the pool. He got up there, screamed for everyone to look, and dove in. Head first.

I won't go too far into detail, because it was gruesome, but the guy ended up paralyzed from the neck down. It was a bad scene, and I gotta be honest—I'm pretty sure the Mexican "paramedics" made it worse. I don't think proper spinal stabilization techniques involve jerking the victim around by the head. Of course, I'm not a doctor; I just watch a lot of "ER" and "House."

If there is a bright side, it was that he lived. Two weeks after that, someone died. Not even by doing something obviously stupid, like jumping in a hotel pool off a balcony, but by doing something they thought was safe.

There are two bungee towers in Cancun. One is made out of wood and built over water. It's as safe as anything in America. Even if the cord breaks, you just hit the water, no biggie. When I went bungee jumping, that's the one I used. It is far more expensive than the other bungee tower. Why?

Because the other one is a crane. Just a normal fucking crane, sitting in a parking lot right above the asphalt. I don't know if any official statistics are kept on that thing, but I can tell you that just in the time I was there, there was one near-miss accident with a kid who came with our company (the cord snapped and the safety line saved him), and another kid had the ropes secured improperly, and he fell out of the harness and died. I didn't see it, but it was all hushed up by the locals and everything went on as normal.

Sadly, he was not the only person to "die." I put that in quotes because I know of at least two people that went missing while I was in Cancun. They completely disappeared, and no one could find them. I never saw anything on the news about it in America because this was pre-Natalie Holloway, before the 24-hour news cycle figured out they could milk the disappearance of pretty white girls for money. I have no idea if they were ever found or not.

Sorry, that's not a very funny section. The Cancun hotel zone on spring break is like fucking Thunderdome. Go at your own risk. Especially if you're an idiot.

How Tucker Max became "Tucker Max"

Before I got to Cancun, I'd gotten my little pencil wet plenty of times, so I thought I knew how to get girls and I thought I understood women. I didn't. Cancun taught me that all my assumptions were completely, totally wrong.

I got laid and had fun before I went down there, but only in spite of myself, not because I knew what I was doing. Cancun taught me the two big life lessons that have guided me since, the two things I always tell people when they ask for life advice:

1. Be honest: I wasn't really a liar back in America, but I was no different than any other young stupid guy trying to get ass; I thought you had to "convince" or "persuade" women to fuck you, and it was their job to kinda resist and make you work for it.

In Cancun, doing anything other than being direct and telling the truth was a complete waste of time. In Cancun, everyone let loose and did the things they wanted to do—getting drunk, fucking, being a little reckless—but were afraid to do in America. They felt safe letting go because it was Mexico; as if it didn't count down there. Girls wanted to fuck, and here, as opposed to America, they were honest about it. Complete honesty worked *way* better than telling girls what you "thought they wanted to hear."

But it was more than that. Being honest wasn't just about telling the truth and being direct to girls—it was also about being honest *to myself,* and owning everything about who I was. I wasn't looking for anything serious at that point in my life, I just wanted to get drunk and fuck a bunch of different girls. Once I figured that out and admitted it to myself—which I hadn't done in America, but did do in Cancun—everything changed. By being honest with myself about what I wanted, it freed me up to be honest and direct with girls . . . and as a result, I got way more pussy with much less effort.

2. Don't worry about results, just have fun: There were so many girls in Cancun, it was hard *not* to get laid. Because I knew I had pussy locked down basically any time I wanted it, I stopped worrying about it. I didn't stop caring whether I got laid or not, but I did stop caring about any specific girl. By releasing my desire for any specific girl, no girl's pussy had a hold on me anymore, and as a result I had more fun and was more fun to be around. This took some practice at first—I'm not the fucking Buddha—but when I finally got the hang of it, a miraculous thing happened: I couldn't beat the pussy off with a stick. Ten times the girls with 10% of the work, all because I just had fun and didn't care what any specific girl (or person) thought or did.

Once these two things combined in me—complete honesty and not caring about the results—the world changed overnight. I remember the specific night where the combination of these lessons were burned into my head:

I was one of several dudes talking to this one really hot girl. She was the type that knew she was hot and was used to getting a ton of attention, and because all these guys were sweating her, she was bitchy to everyone, playing hard to get. Not even a month earlier, I might have fallen for that; I would've tried even harder, and worked to out compete the other dudes.

But barely halfway into my first week in Cancun, I'd already fucked like four hot girls. I didn't care about this girl anymore; I *knew* I was getting ass. Whether this *particular* girl wanted to fuck me had become irrelevant.

Released from any focus on the outcome, not caring about anything other than entertaining myself and having fun, I started fucking with her and saying completely ridiculous shit just to make everyone laugh and put her in her place:

- "My penis is going to be in something tonight. The more you talk, the less likely it'll be you."

- "When you talk, I have to block out what you're saying and replace it with thoughts of what you could be saying. That way, you're still attractive."

- "What do you think is more disgusting: what they put in hotdogs, or what a hotdog would taste like after it's been inside of you?"

- "I know this really sexy move you can do with your mouth. It's called 'shutting the fuck up.'"

- [in front of her, to a guy who was hitting on her] "Hey dude, make sure you wear a rubber with her. Lumberg fucked her."

- "I can be sensitive sometimes. Right up until I sleep with you. Then I inject all my sensitivity right into you, and it's gone."

- "No way you can convince me to hook up with you. If you do, I'll strip naked and let you take a picture of me punching a mule in the mouth."

- "I'm gonna drink until you're pretty, then fuck you until you're ugly again. I'm totally kidding, you aren't ugly. And I'm also kidding about fucking you."

- "If I decide to fuck you, I hope you're OK with me taping a picture of a hot girl to your back while I rail you from behind. You know, so I can stay hard."

Lo and behold, after spending an hour saying the most preposterous shit I could think of just to crack everyone up . . . she was not only still there, she was utterly, completely into me. All the guys sweating her . . . she didn't give a fuck about them.

Girl "So what are you doing tonight?"
Tucker "Didn't you say you had a boyfriend?"
Girl "Yeah."
Tucker "Shouldn't you be worried about what he's doing, not me?"
Girl "He's in America."
Tucker "Just like your dignity, right?"

We went back to her room and I knocked the bottom out of her.

Even though I'd hooked up with girls many times before by playing that type of game—the funny asshole game—it was that night where it all clicked for me, where I actually *understood* what was going on and why. I went from being an above-average guy, to being, well . . . me. Tucker Max. It's a very simple lesson, anyone can apply it:

To get what you want out of life, all you really need to do is be honest about it, don't be afraid to go for it, and have fun while you do it—and you'll eventually get it.

Girls are no different.

It's a Love Spot

When you are on-site staff in Cancun, you get a badge that hangs around your neck. It has your picture, your name, and the company you work for. It's basically an ATM card for pussy and alcohol. Alcohol, because the Mexicans who work on the island consider you a local and give you everything for free, and pussy, because you are an authority figure and thus every girl automatically trusts you. It's basically the perfect way to get laid.

It's not just their loins they trust you with. They also trust you with their secrets. This one girl let me in on the issue she was discussing with her friends because she wanted a male perspective.

Girl "Well, the guy I've been fucking all week was in my bathroom last night, and I think he saw my herpes cream in my toiletries bag. I don't have an outbreak now, and we use condoms so it's fine, but I still think he's freaked out. If this were just some random I wouldn't care, but he goes to my school."
Tucker "That's what you get for not fucking randoms."

Girl "Ugh no! Randoms are nasty!"
Tucker "You have herpes . . . and you're calling someone else nasty?"
Girl "It's different! Seriously though, help me. How do I deal with this?"
Tucker "Here's what you do: First, tell him you have AIDS and that he needs to get tested. After he freaks out, tell him you're kidding, you only have herpes. He'll be relieved. It's all about framing."
Girl "You think that'll work?"
Tucker "Did you not see my staff badge? This means that everything I say is right."

Cancun is so lawless, Mexicans walk around with chimps on a leash, and charge people for pictures.

The First Rule of Mexico

Everyone knows the first rule of Mexico: Don't drink the water (that's for tourists; for Mexicans, the first rule is 'move to America and become a busboy'). Not everyone heeds this rule, either because they are stupid or drunk, or both.

I was fucking this one girl doggy style, when she started farting. You know those nasty wet farts that come out so hard they smack your ass cheeks together, like you're kick-starting a dirt bike? Yeah, well, my hotel room sounded like the X Games.

You'd think since quieter farts usually smell worse that these would have floated by without much problem. Oh, no. These smelled like the Puerto Rican Day Parade. And when I say they smelled, I mean they were RANK. It was so bad, I had to stop fucking her.

Tucker "What the fuck is wrong with you?"
Girl "Sorry, I think I accidentally drank some Mexican water when I was brushing my teeth."

We were really drunk, so of course this was uproariously hilarious. Who's so sensitive that a little bit of toothbrush water turns their GI tract into a barrio sewage pipe? Apparently this girl. We're laughing our asses off . . . when all of the sudden her nose starts bleeding.

Tucker "Oh my God—you farted so hard it made your nose bleed!"

I almost pissed myself I was laughing so hard, as she ran into the bathroom to shit and clean up her face. If she'd have puked and achieved the hat trick of bodily fluids, I might have cared enough to go in there and help her. Instead, I passed out.

Finder's Fee

It was late in the week, and I was flirting with this girl that had fucked so many guys—just that week—that I probably should have put a condom on just to talk to her. As the case can be with a really slutty girl, there was something attractive about the way she handled herself. Her smile, her attitude, her . . . alright, I need to shut the fuck up. I wish I could justify my desire to fuck her as something other than a base, carnal urge. It wasn't. The truth is, sometimes I can be a pathetic hump donkey, and this was one of those times.

After a ton of alcohol, enough for me to stop caring that she'd been passed around faster than the collection plate in a storefront church, we went back to her hotel room to fuck. We start out with some simple foreplay, I start fingering her clit, reach inside to rub on her g-spot, and I feel something weird.

It's not cottony like a tampon, it's kinda slippery. I think maybe it's an IUD, so I wrap my finger around it to pull it out and make a joke . . . and it's a condom.

A yellow, used condom was wrapped around my finger.

I was in such shock, and so drunk, it took me more than a few seconds to register what was going on. The normal, instantaneous logic chain broke down, and I had to revert to deliberate steps:

> Step 1: That is a condom on your finger.
> Step 2: It came out of her vagina.
> Step 3: Since it came out of her vagina, it must be a used condom.
> Step 4: Someone used that condom in her vagina.
> Step 5: That someone wasn't you.
> Step 6: That is someone else's used condom.
> Step 7: YOUR FINGER IS TOUCHING SOMEONE ELSE'S USED CONDOM.

After staring at it for ten seconds and letting my brain work through the logic, I frantically wave my hand back and forth until it flings off onto the ground.

Tucker "WHAT THE FUCK!!!!"
Whore "Eew. Sorry."

I stare at her in disgust, expecting some sort of apology or explanation of her whoreishness, or something that would explain this abomination. She had this contemplative drunken pause, like she was really considering the options.

Whore "Just put it in my ass."

At that moment in my life—young, drunk, horny and hard, with a naked girl who wanted to fuck right in front of me—I could not argue with that logic.

Tucker "Uhhh . . . OK."

It's not sloppy seconds if it's a different hole, right?

Sometimes I disgust even myself.

BAMBI

I definitely hooked up with a lot of girls in Cancun. But not as many as I could have.

This one girl who was an education major at an SEC school (you make up your jokes with that set-up, you don't need me to spoon feed it) left some club with me and was impatient to get back to her hotel room, so we took a cab instead of waiting for the bus. We were both really drunk, but that didn't stop her from trying to make out with me in the cab. Which was fine, until she burped in my face, then got that look of panic that means only one thing:

Girl "Pull over, pull over!!"

I repeated it in Spanish so the driver would understand. It was unnecessary. The language of drunken whore-panic is international. He whipped the car over, and she opened the door to puke outside the cab. But, in her haste, she threw it open so hard, it swung back and hit her in the face, splashing a bunch of the vomit back onto her. I should have helped her, but I couldn't because I was laughing too hard.

Girl "BLAAAAAAHHHHHH!! STOP LAUGHING!!! BLAAAAAAAAAAA HHHHHHHH!!"

I couldn't stop laughing the entire way back to the hotel. I mean—picture that scene in your mind. What option did I have but to laugh at her? Well, I guess I could've consoled her and helped her wipe the vomit off of her face and dress . . . actually no, I couldn't have done that. Someone who cared about her could have. All I could do was cry from laughter.

We finally got back to the hotel, and I helped her out of the cab. Watching her walk into the hotel was almost as funny as the cab door smashing her in the face. It was like watching Bambi learning to walk, if Bambi were a high-functioning alcoholic.

We got back to her room, and it was evident that this girl was in no condition to do anything other than pass out. I walked her to her room and laid her on the bed to make sure she didn't drown in her own vomit (like the other guy):

Tucker "OK, you lie here on your stomach, here's the trash can. If you need anything, call the front desk."
Girl "Are you leaving?"
Tucker "Honey, there's no need for me to stay, we can't fuck."
Girl "YOU DON'T WANT TO FUCK ME!??!?!"
Tucker "You are so drunk, I'm kinda shocked that you're even still alive."
Girl "WHY WON'T YOU FUUUUCK MEEEEEE??!?!?"

Then she started crying.

There she lay, puke in her hair and on her dress, missing a shoe, with tears streaking the vomit stains on her face, crying because some random guy won't shove his penis into her drunk, almost lifeless body. This is a girl people now trust to teach their children. Hate to be the one to tell my Confederate flag-sporting friends, but if this is the type of girl educating your kids, it doesn't look like the South will be rising again anytime soon.

Sweet Caroline

This was one of those things that I'm not sure I would have believed was even possible before I went to Cancun. Simply because I didn't believe people got this drunk until I saw it:

This one bar in Cancun had what I guess you'd call Mexican Karaoke: the bar would give people a microphone and they'd sing along with the songs that were on the PA. There wasn't a screen with the lyrics flashing that you could read, so if you didn't know the words, it just became a drunken scream fest. Which could be fun times also.

Anyway, this one dude had come down to Cancun with his girlfriend (always a bad idea), and they broke up in the middle of the week. He took it harder than she did, presumably because she cheated on him first, and this was his first night out without her. He got the microphone, and requested the song "Sweet Caroline." I guess his ex's name was Caroline . . . so you can guess where this is going: express train to Awesome Town.

He was staggering around the stage singing the song—I'm pretty sure he was crying, but I was in the back of the bar and couldn't quite see—when all of the sudden he fell off the stage and crashed into a bar table. It wasn't that far of a fall, only like three feet or something, and even though the table broke and glass shattered everywhere, he jumped up quickly and got right back on stage to continue singing the song.

Then we saw it: He'd cut himself, right above the eye. BAD. It was shooting blood everywhere, like a UFC fighter who'd just taken a sharp elbow, all down his face and shirt, even dripping onto the stage.

Of course people see this and try to rush up there to help him. What does he do? HE PICKS UP THE MIC STAND, AND STARTS WILDLY SWINGING IT BACK AND FORTH LIKE A WEAPON TO FEND THEM OFF, screaming at the top of his lungs, over the song:

"NO! GET BACK!! I HAVE TO FINISH THE SONG!! I LOVE HER!!!"

This went on for at least a minute, him using the mic stand as a weapon against people trying to help him, as blood and tears poured down his face. Eventually the Mexican bouncers tackled him, and assisted him in his moment of physical and emotional trauma by throwing him out on the street. I would've helped him, but he wasn't with my travel company. Plus, I think he was a Notre Dame kid, so fuck'em. What? It's not like I left him unattended on a temporary tower during a windy day or something. (That's a Notre Dame joke. If you want to know how awful that school is, Google the name Declan Sullivan.)

Eat Your Heart Out Jason Bourne

Mexico is a lawless place. I don't care what the UN says, or what the State Department travel advisories tell you. The fact is that Mexico, as a whole, is a narco-state run by powerful regional cartels, with a hollow and largely irrelevant central government that is nothing more than window-dressing to appease the international community. Freedom is for those who can afford it, law is for sale, and what is fair is determined by who is most powerful. That's the reality of Mexico. Cancun, Playa, Cabo, Puerto Vallarta—they are all much better than the interior of Mexico, but that is only because their survival depends on a steady flow of tourists with money to burn. To protect that, the government does a good job maintaining the appearance of western-style law and order through the direct threat of massive military intervention. Underneath it all, those places are not much different from the rest of Mexico.

I would explain this to every group of kids that came in every week. I'd emphasize to them that as long as they stayed in the normal places where tourists were meant to go, they were safer than a lot of places in America (e.g. Detroit), but if they went off the island, or fucked with the wrong people, they could disappear, and there was nothing I could do about it. Every kid followed my advice and had a good time. Except one.

I really can't remember much about this reject Bubba Sparxxx. He was from a small school in Georgia, he had a thick southern accent, and he was possibly the most ridiculous wanna-be hustler on earth. He brought drugs *with him* to Mexico to sell, and SOLD OUT ON HIS FIRST DAY THERE! How do I know this? Because at the pool party on the second day, he asked me where he could get more.

Which brings us to that night. I think it was the Tuesday night party, because it was the smaller club, but all I remember was watching him being dragged by several large Mexican bouncers to the back of the club. If you're being dragged to the front of the club, it only means that they're throwing you out, no big deal. But if you're getting dragged to the back—that's bad. That means you're about to get face-fucked by a pipe wrench.

I followed them, trying to plead his case. Normally the Mexicans would at least pretend to listen to me when something like this would happen, but whatever he'd done was so bad, they were paying me no mind at all. The kid managed to wiggle his way free and sprint down the hallway toward freedom, but waiting at the end were some more bouncers. The dude was caught between two groups of very pissed-off Mexicans, like the cheese in a violent and punitive quesadilla. They were advancing on him, so he did what any normal piece of southern-fried white trash would do: he grabbed the handle of a nearby push broom and started swinging it at them wildly, trying to keep them at bay. Clearly this wasn't going to work for long, as they were advancing on two fronts. Then he recognized where he was and saw what was next to him . . . I saw the recognition in his eyes before I realized what he was going to do:

He swung the push broom above his head as hard as he could, slamming it into the sprinklers above him. Then he grabbed the fire extinguisher off the wall, ripped the pin, and started charging at the Mexicans, blasting them with fine, white power. Just as he did that, the sprinklers caught and EXPLODED water. You know what happens when one sprinkler goes off? Well, in this club it meant that they ALL went off.

It caused complete bedlam, like what would happen on Twitter if Justin Bieber admitted he was gay.

The sprinklers doused everyone with water, all the fire alarms immediately went off, the klaxon horns blasted, the emergency lights went on, and the entire club—all 500+ drunks—went into a complete panic. The bouncers and the manager freaked out and started running in all directions, as reject Bubba Sparxxx slipped past them and into the night, as cool as his airbrushed blacklight t-shirt.

I actually stood there frozen for a second—drenched in Mexican water, breathing in nasty white CO_2 dust, 130-decibel horns blaring in my ear—because I couldn't stop thinking to myself:

That kid's a fucking idiot, and there's no doubt he will spend the majority of his adult life in a federal prison . . . but that was the most awesome thing I've ever seen in my life.

The Final Straw

At this point, you may be thinking that Cancun sounds like an amazing drunken party paradise. Who wouldn't think that getting fucked-in-half drunk every night and screwing random college girls was a cool job, right? It was . . . for about two weeks.

Then reality starts catching up to you, especially if you're like me and cannot understand the concept of moderation. The human body is not made to withstand dumping poison into it every day. Nor is it built to endure constant sleep deprivation, or deal with deafening club music pumping through it for 12 hours a day. And as much as I like having sex, at some point—even with condoms—all the contagious retroviruses and germs you catch from physical contact begin to overwhelm your immune system.

And the FOOD! Don't even get me started on eating Mexican food. It's awful. Not only is it Mexico, it's Mexican people cooking for retarded American tourists. In the Venn diagram of food, this is where "bad" intersects with "doesn't care about quality" and "foreign sanitation standards" to create truly appalling meals. Even drinking 3000 calories of alcohol a day I lost weight, because I just couldn't eat the slop they served.

After about six weeks, I was coming to the end of my party rope. As much as I loved getting paid vacation, I was getting tired of it. I hated the bullshit of law school, and Cancun was the opposite of that—but this place had its own suite of bullshit that was really starting to bore the fuck out of me as well. It sounds ridiculous to say I was tired of getting paid to party and fuck, but I kinda was.

Then this happened. This incident was the final straw that made me go back home.

Like I said, by this point my liver was made of iron. I would wake up, drink 10–15 beers at the afternoon beach party, take a nap and then drink another 15–25 drinks at night, and still couldn't really get drunk. My body became supremely efficient at processing the poison I was dumping into it.

Well, this particular week there was some sorority there that loved me. They were all kinda mediocre looking, from some Big Ten degree factory,

I honestly can't remember which one. I want to say it was Purdue, but I really don't know. Nice enough girls, and they were super impressed with me, so I liked them.

Anyway, one night we were in some club, and I tried to explain to them how being in Cancun had affected me:

Tucker "You don't understand, I can't get drunk anymore."
SororityGirl "Oh come on, every guy says this."
Tucker "I don't think you understand who you're talking to."

They kept talking all sorts of nonsense and trying to call me out. I got fed up with their hopeless whore logic, and became determined to drink these bitches into a coma.

Tucker "OK, let's do a drinking contest. But it would be unfair for me to take you on without a handicap. So I'll do this: I'll out drink each of you . . . *collectively.* There are six of you. Each of you do one shot, and I'll do SIX."

They looked at me like I told them I have phone sex with dolphins. They really couldn't comprehend this contest; I guess critical thinking night wasn't an event on their rush calendar. I eventually just stopped using words, and lined up two groups of six shots.

Tucker "See—one for each of you, and six for me."

They stared at me in complete and utter disbelief (though, being that they were from the Big Ten, they would have spelled it "udder").

SororityGirl "You can't do that. You'll die."
Tucker "Is that supposed to scare me? If I must face death to get drunk. I willingly accept the challenge."
SororityGirl "Uh . . . OK. Let's do it."

Those first shots are my last clear, unambiguous memory from the night. You know the saying, "Don't write checks with your mouth that your ass can't cash"? Well, that night my mouth was Bernie Madoff and my ass was his Ponzi scheme.

My next memory is intense, awful pain. I'm not even sure I would have qualified as alive in some states. I've woken up from major surgery that was more pleasant than that morning. My entire body ached; my head felt like it'd been stomped by a rhino, I was so dehydrated that I couldn't blink my eyes, and my arms and legs wouldn't work. I would wager that—*when I woke up*—it was one of the ten drunkest moments of my life.

Even worse, I have no fucking clue where I am. This is not my hotel room. This is not a hotel room I even recognize. I begin to realize that there is a girl lying next to me on the bed, shaking me, saying something. She is not happy. She is also not skinny. Or attractive. She may not even be human.

Still struggling to come out of my haze, I also notice that this isn't one of the girls I drank with last night. Though judging by her size, she may have eaten them.

AngryFatty "Tucker."
Tucker "Arrrrr whhhhaaaaa aaaaaayyyy."
AngryFatty "Tucker, wake up."
Tucker "Neeeeeeeeed rrrrrrrrrrrr fuuuuuuuuuuuck."
AngryFatty "Tucker! TUCKER, WAKE UP!"
Tucker "Jesus, alright! I'm awake! What?"

She glares at me with the type of look you give your dog when it shits on the rug.

AngryFatty "Tucker . . . why is there a condom in my ass?"

No matter how much hangover pain you are in, that sentence will make you laugh.

In fact, I was laughing so hard, I rolled out of the bed, fell onto the floor and hurt myself even more. I pulled on the first piece of clothing I could find, and just walked out. I mean, what else could I do in that situation? Investigate?

Out on the sidewalk, I realized that I didn't have anything on my feet. Then, when I saw people gawking at me, I looked down at what I wearing. It was not mine. There I was, barefoot, in dark pink hot pants walking down the street. Everyone was laughing at me. I tried to get on a bus back to my hotel, but I didn't have any money. The MEXICAN bus driver gave me a look of contempt, closed the doors right in my face, and pulled away. I had found the floor of working class Mexican decency, and was now in the basement below it.

Two days later, I left. Cancun beat me, like it eventually beats everyone.

The Consequences

There is no doubt that Cancun changed my life, but the effects of my trip to Cancun reverberated far beyond me.

Before 2004, there was no class attendance requirement at top tier law schools. Law school administrators assumed if you'd made it that far, you were probably a dedicated, anxious nerd just like them. They figured you would WANT to do all the pointless, bullshit stuff assigned to you—without them watching over you—just to prove to your classmates, who you were constantly in competition with, that you were strong enough and smart enough to hack it.

Well, directly because of me and my trip to Cancun, the American Bar Association changed their attendance rules for ALL law schools. Below is ABA Accreditation Standard 304, adopted in August 2004, two years after I put up my website detailing many of my law school antics, where I talked openly about never going to class and living in Cancun during my 2L year (emphasis mine):

1. At any time after the fifth week of a course (or halfway through a summer session course), **a student who has been determined by the instructor to have attended fewer than 80 percent of the class sessions** in any course **will be required to drop the course** from his or her registration upon the instructor's so indicating to the Academic Services Office.

2. An instructor may also impose stricter attendance standards or other sanctions for nonattendance, including lowering of a grade, provided that students are informed at the start of the course of the instructor's attendance rules and possible sanctions.

3. **The instructor** (referred to in paragraph 1) **should take attendance with such regularity as is needed to insure reasonable accuracy in determining a student's attendance record**.

Obviously I was not involved in the discussions that led to the adoption of this rule, but I can tell you that at least two people—people who claim to have been privy to these discussions—have emailed me and told me that this rule was not only passed in direct response to the stories about not going to class I'd posted on TuckerMax.com, but that the rule is known colloquially in the ABA as "The Tucker Max Rule."

I have accomplished many things in my life, and I am prouder of all those things than this—but being responsible for "The Tucker Max Rule" is one of my favorite signature moments. Brady has his gun law, Megan got her pedophile law, and Amber got her alert, and now I have mine.

Postscript [Only for Law Students and Potential Law Students]:

The best part is that I didn't even have to pay the consequences for my little stunt, but ALL future law students do. You're welcome. The funny thing is, I wasn't at all the first to figure out that law school class was bullshit—everyone who's attended law school knows that. Law students are being punished by the ABA not because of what I did, but because I *told the world the truth* about law school.

I'm not apologizing. I don't even feel bad for you law students. The fact is, for 95% of the people who attend, going to law school is a mistake. When I was going, I was just like you are now. I thought I wanted to be a lawyer, but had no idea what it actually meant to be a lawyer. All I knew was that people spoke reverently of lawyers, that everyone said that being a lawyer meant you were a success, that it paid really well, etc. Like all idiotic college kids, I wanted status without having to do much to get it. Law school seemed the easiest route. Sound familiar?

What I didn't know then, that I do now is that easy status and success comes with a very high price: your soul.

If you're in law school, learn from my mistake and quit. Right now, before it's too late and you are too much in debt. Go live your life, do something enjoyable. It'll never happen if you're working as a lawyer. NEVER.

And if you're in college and thinking about going to law school, don't. Kids email me all the time asking for law school advice. It's always the same:

Do you want to waste three years of your life debating stupid and utterly irrelevant minutia? If so, get your JD.

Do you want to get a degree that forces you to spend your life sitting in a drab office, churning out tedious paperwork for a shitty, condescending boss who you'll hate (and then eventually become)? If so, get your JD.

Are you a boring, facile, socially retarded whore, who is desperate for the illusion of money and success, regardless of the cost to your life and the lives of those you love? If so, get your JD.

Do you want to be the type of person who doesn't create anything, doesn't make value for others, who can't be proud of his job, but just fucks other people over? If so, get your JD.

If not, go do something productive with your life, something that adds value to the world, and that does NOT include law school.

DRUGS ARE BAD, MMMKAY?

Occurred, July 2002

About a year after graduating, I went to DC to visit SlingBlade and Hate. Apparently, we didn't ruin enough people's lives in law school, so we decided to attend a party thrown by two girls we went to school with. We weren't "technically" invited, but we just assumed they didn't have our phone numbers and went anyway.

The party was a typical collection of DC young professional shitbags. Whoever said that Washington, DC was "Hollywood for ugly people" is fucking brilliant, because that perfectly describes not only the city, but this party too. Everyone wanted to tell you how important they were, who they worked for, what their SAT score was (seriously, I heard two people talking about that—they were at least 26 years old). It was a giant dick-measuring contest for people who had no other use for their dicks because they all looked like they'd been face-raped by a low-speed drum sander. Name-dropping is hard enough to stomach when you don't give a fuck about the names being dropped. It's even harder when they're dropping out of the mouths of people whose gender you might as well guess with a coin flip.

SlingBlade, Hate, and I fought back in the only way we knew how: We got combatively drunk and mocked everyone.

This story has two different accounts, SlingBlade's and mine. This first section is an email SlingBlade sent out to all of our law school friends a few days later, and after is my account of what happened to me after the party:

SlingBlade's Account

"We arrive at the party that Megan and Chelsea are throwing. Hate proceeds to kick everything off right by waltzing up to Megan's neighbor, who is 50 and has brought two teenage children along, and asking him why he isn't getting his kids drunk. Tucker engages a marginally attractive special-ed teacher. She claims that her autistic students can read her mind. Tucker claims she is an idiot. She decides to nickname him "Big Yellow" for some reason. He threatens to skullfuck her. She calls him a date rapist. Tucker tells her not to leave the party alone.

I decide I will keep score at this party. It's early, but Tucker is in the lead:

Score, Round 1
Hate: -1
Tucker: 5
SlingBlade: 0

Megan and Chelsea give me the tour of their new place. It's boring and I'm not drunk enough. Halfway through a rambling and pointlessly sentimental story about some cheap bric-a-brac they think is precious, I just walk off and go downstairs to get beer.

Tucker is speaking to a girl who looks like Death itself. She is an emaciated wreck. Tucker flashes me a thumbs up and informs me she has a "ridiculous body," which is Tuckerspeak for "I know she's ugly, but I don't care because she's a slut." Tucker continues speaking to her for two hours, for which he is docked points at a compounding rate.

I have lost contact with Hate, who has descended into the basement, but I am able to piece together from the surviving refugees that he is in rare form. People are fleeing up the stairs like the radon detector went off.

I hear bellowing as I head down the steps. Hate is posing for pictures with random people, pulling his shirt down and rubbing his nipples. He takes a camera from someone and then uses an entire roll of film taking pictures of himself. No less than three people profess to me their fear of him. The gauntlet has been thrown down.

Then I lose a pull-up contest to Megan. A girl. Moving on.

Score, Round 2
Hate: 20
SlingBlade: -10
Tucker: -15

Tucker is still talking to Skeletor. Hate is nowhere to be found. I walk into the kitchen, see a girl writing something down and ask her if she's writing down directions to the gym.

SlingBlade has arrived.

I attempt to convince an Asian girl who told me I was offensive that I was black and that she shouldn't be insulting one of her "comrades in the struggle." I tell her about how The Man framed me, and that the drifter was already dead when I got there. She flees.

I start talking trash to Megan's female friend from work. I forget most of it, but a large portion had to do with my preference for little girls and her poor personal hygiene. The clincher was when she told me she had a Great Dane. I told her when I see a girl walking a large dog, I just assume she's having sex with it. She was so mortified she left the party, only an hour after she got there.

I decide to walk up to random girls with a pen in my hand and ask them what their street address is. We have no takers.

Then I start speaking to the third roommate, a UNC grad. It goes like this:

Her "How do you like this painting of the UNC quad?"
Me "Oh, that's stellar. Wait a minute—shouldn't there be a dead pros-

titute in the street here. And shouldn't there be an indigent man on this bench. [Gives her a look of pity] Oh, sorry—'indigent' means 'homeless.'"
Her "You're obnoxious. I don't know why I'm talking to you."
Me "Because I'm the best looking guy at this party and you're still operating under the illusion that you have a shot with me."
Her "Oh really. Guess what—I know your type. You hit on every girl you see and have no standards whatsoever."
Me "You're right. And that's why I'm talking to you."

The conversation ended quickly after that. I proceed to the main party area where the mockeries that pass as girls are and start screaming as loud as I can across the room to Chelsea:

"CHELSEA WHERE ARE THE GOOD LOOKING GIRLS YOU PROMISED ME?? THESE GIRLS SUCK. [Girls give me dirty looks] YES YOU!! DO YOU HAVE AN EYE PROBLEM? ARE YOU TRYING TO EYEFUCK ME!!! DON'T YOU DARE JUDGE ME!!!"

A group of girls is taking pictures. One of them takes a pic with me. Unfortunately she is fat, which I not-so-politely inform her of. I believe I pointed to her stomach and said, "Yeah, they're called sit-ups." I then informed the girl with the camera that I would "need my pics blown-up poster size and framed. But in oak, not mahogany. Mahogany disagrees with my complexion."

Score, Round 3
SlingBlade: 30
Hate: 20
Tucker: -26

I am ready to declare victory. Unbeknownst to me Hate is putting on a little dog and pony show of his own in the living room. I go in there and observe that the only fifteen feet of empty space in the entire house are in a direct circle around Hate. He is sitting on the bottom of the stairs gesticulating wildly and alternately yelling personal insults and laudatory sexual comments at everyone within earshot. A girl walks up to me and introduces herself. After discovering I know Hate, she informs me he is shady. Displaying an exquisite sense of timing, at that exact moment Hate yells across the room to her what a great ass she has.

Another girl asks me what is wrong with Hate. And a third. I tell them that he is angry at them for not being better looking. A guy talks shit about Hate within my earshot. I offer to thump his skull. Guy apologizes. Hate continues undeterred. Little nuggets of wisdom he drops include:

"Hey, Heeeeeyyyyyy, (waves hand) oh fuck it, people with the . . . lawyers and who doesn't want to be that; but HEEEEEEYYYYYY, hi . . . I'M TALKING HERE. That's an ass, likes it in the pooper awwwww yeah."

Some guy has the autistic psychic teacher on his lap. Hate sees this and comes over and begins pounding on his shoulders, and shouting at the top of his lungs:

"YEEEEEEEEAAAAAAAAAAHHHHHHHHHHHH!"

He then awkwardly tries to tackle the seated guy, almost knocking him out of his chair. When this doesn't work, he begins shouting:

"THAT'S OKAY, YOU GO HOME WITH HER. YEAH THAT'S COOL. GO HOME WITH HER! NO PROBLEM!!"

He then proceeds to sit next to them, continuously giving them the evil eye. The guy finally has enough of this, and leaves, realizing that the girl is not attractive enough to fight an angry Hate over. Hate then makes his move, and begins dancing with the autistic psychic teacher. Well, he begins grinding his crotch on her.

And on the desk.

And on a lamp.

It's like the strip scene in *American Pie,* except with a real-life girl who is not nearly as attractive as Shannon Elizabeth, and is not laughing. He then grabs a table and proceeds to wobble-dee shake it and drop it like it's hot. It breaks. Chelsea is staring in absolute disbelief. She says to me, "Hate is out of control. Something needs to be done. He is breaking my apartment!"

I assume by "something needs to be done" that she wants me to go instigate, so that's what I did. Hate is now grabbing the girl's ass, and grinding with her. She is so scared, she goes to Tucker for help.

Chelsea "Tucker, you have GOT to do something about Hate. He broke my Pottery Barn table!"
Tucker "I don't understand why people say alcohol is a depressant. That's not really how it works for us."

Tucker tells Hate that he really needs to "step it up a notch" and takes Skeletor into the other room. They start "dancing." Tucker is basically trying to have sex with her as she gyrates to the music. He loses ten points for dancing with Skeletor, and another ten for dancing at all.

Score, Round 4
Hate: 40
SlingBlade: 30
Tucker: -46

Tucker's friend shows up with a delightful little Japanese girl who sounds like a Chihuahua on amphetamines. She is a 2. Hate is smitten. She is retarded drunk. Cupid has spoken.

Somehow I'm stuck talking to a hideous girl. She tells me that she never looks good in pictures. I try to be helpful, "You know what it means when someone says you don't look good in a picture? If you said 'it means you're ugly' you're the big winner. What have you won? A lifetime of loneliness and Star Trek conventions. Welcome to the club."

I end up talking to her cute friend about my favorite subject—myself. For an hour. She's in love. I realize my work is done so I stop speaking to her and walk away mid-sentence.

Somehow Hate pissed off the annoying Japanese girl, who lets him know she isn't going to be sleeping with him by angrily spitting at him like a camel. At this point Megan and Chelsea demand that I escort Hate off the premises. Hate thinks that "leaving" means he should go lie down in Megan's bed and berate me for screwing him out of a hook up. I find Tucker, who has apparently had sex with Skeletor already, and we drag Hate into a cab.

Hate completely loses his shit. Here is a verbatim transcript of the 20-minute cab ride home:

Hate "Jimminy Christmas ASSHOLES. Call 1–800-821–33 . . . something. They'll give us a free cab. GODDAMIT IM NOT PAYING FOR THIS FUCKING CAB MOTHERFUCKERS. I was going to hook up fucking SlingBlade you asshole. Goddamit why did you screw me. Jesus H Christ Jimminy Christmas Dammit. SlingBlade call our girls, where are the girls goddamit."
SlingBlade "I don't know any girls to booty call."
Tucker "You can have a go at the one I just fucked if you want, but we have to go back to the party and get her. I bet she'd be down."
Hate "JESUS CHRIST TUCKER WHAT THE FUCK IS . . . OKAY FUCKING FINE ITS TIME TO GET WHORES. Cabbie we need some whores." [Hate grabs the seat in front of him, in which the cab driver is seated, and begins shaking the hell out of it]
Cabbie "HEY! WHAT IS GO ON?!?"
Hate "What the fuck God? What the fuck? All I want is to hook up is that too much to ask. Instead I have these motherfuckers who fucked me. Goddamit. TAKE US TO GET SOME WHORES ASSHOLE" [Hate leans in close to the cabbie's ear] "do dooo doo dooo do do, doo doo. STEP ON IT ASSHOLE, STEP ON IT SHOW US WHAT YOU GOT."
Cabbie "We are near airport, cops everywhere."
Hate "GODDAMNED PUSSY IS THAT ALL YOU GOT YOU ASSHOLE,

STEP ON IT, PUT IT ON THE GODDAM FLOOR. WHAT THE FLYING FUCK."

I wrestle him back into his seat, so our very patient immigrant cab driver will refrain from shooting Hate in the face with pepper spray.

Hate "Well SlingBlade which one is it going to be?"
SlingBlade "Excuse Me?"
Hate "WHICH ONE IS IT GOING TO BE ASSHOLE?"
SlingBlade "Which one what?
Hate "Are we going to go get food, or are we going to go get food and then beat the shit out of three or four people?"
SlingBlade "Umm, neither. You're going home to pass out."

There is then ten seconds of complete silence, followed by Hate speaking in a low crazy guy voice:

Hate "Go fuck yourself SlingBlade . . . LET ME OUT RIGHT HERE GODDAMN IT!!"

We are in the middle of an interstate at this point and Hate is trying to pry the door handle off because the cabbie has kiddie locked the back doors at my request.

Hate "GODDAMN IT JESUS H MOTHERFUCKER WHAT THE GODDAMN FUCK LET ME THE FUCK OUT SO I CAN FUCK WHORES AND THEN EAT AND BEAT THE SHIT OUT OF PEOPLE. YOU'RE FIRST SLINGBLADE. LET ME THE FUCK OUT. JIMMINEY FUCKING CHRISTMAS WHAT THE FLYING FUCK GODDAMN IT. I WILL FUCKING FUCK ALL OF YOU. HONESTLY LET ME THE FUCK Out you assho—"

Hate passes out midsentence.

We drag him inside and throw him on his bed. The last thing I hear before drifting off to sleep is Hate through the floor yelling about me and my Zionist plot to destroy him.

Final Score
Hate: 145
SlingBlade: 30
Tucker: -50

Mission Accomplished."

Tucker's Account

Unfortunately for me, the night did not stop once we got home, because of something SlingBlade was fortunate enough to have missed while attending to Hate and firebombing the self-esteem of the various female party-goers:

After Skeletor and I finished our post-dancing quickie, I got really hungry, so we went looking for food. As is typically the case when it comes to 20-something career-first women with under-developed nurturing instincts, Megan and Chelsea's fridge had nothing but condiments and alcohol. Skeletor tells me that her friend brought brownies, so we go find him.

I don't remember the dude's name, but I do remember that he was the exact type of person your parents warned you not to take candy from. He was straight out of a D.A.R.E. lesson. Fortunately he had the brownies on him, because there was no way I was hopping into his windowless panel van to "barter" for them. It was already bad enough that I would have to take the brownies directly from his hand. I was afraid if I touched him, I'd be greasy for the rest of my life.

Greaser "Now, you know these are pot brownies, right?"

I have never taken any drugs in my life. No pot, no coke, no heroin, no meth, no X, nothing. Just a lot of the drink. I have nothing against drugs per se, a bunch of my friends casually do various drugs, and like any rational person I think marijuana should be legalized. But still, I don't do them. It's not my thing, and I wasn't about to start now . . . except I was SO hungry.

Tucker "How strong are these? I never really had pot brownies before." Greaser "This is my first time making them, but I don't think they're very strong. I usually smoke up, but I wanted to try them, and they're barely affecting me. You should be fine."

I tentatively took a bite, and I gotta be honest, it was a pretty good brownie. Maybe a bit tough, like he'd baked sand into it or something, but still delicious. I ate another, and then a third.

I don't know if it was the pot, the sugar coma, the post-sex coma, or just the placebo effect, but before I knew it, I was slouched on the sofa feeling totally relaxed. I found myself really into Pink Floyd. Up until that point in my life, I hated their music; I'd have rather listened to a small child being sexually abused, but now I really understood them. One of the girls who threw the party told me she was really pissed off at how SlingBlade and Hate had acted, but was pleased that I'd been so calm and mellow. She was happy I'd come, and I was welcome any time. In law school, this girl once described me as "worse than Satan." It was surreal. Later that night, as I drifted off to sleep on SlingBlade's couch, I finally understood why people liked pot.

Four hours later, around 5am, the honeymoon was over. I was shocked into consciousness by a paralyzing need to shit worse than I ever had to in my life, even worse than the time I drank tap water in Mexico. But this wasn't diarrhea shit coming—this was going to be one of those times you pass a brown baby out of your colon. The pain shooting from my lower abdomen was so awful, my first instinct was to kill myself to make it stop.

I got up to go to the bathroom, but I couldn't walk. The cramps were so intense, I had to slowly lower myself to the ground, and then army-crawl, arm over arm, to the bathroom. I got my pants off as I crawled, pulled myself up onto the toilet seat and let loose. The turd felt like it came out sideways. It was worse than a spinal tap. I would say it felt like I was shitting out my organs, but they're slippery, they'd come out much easier than this boulder of excrement.

I began by swearing to any God that would listen to me, that I would commit my life to his service if he would only make the pain stop. This prayer changed in to a simple request for the sweet release of death, and ended on an angry note, highlighted by me cursing the entire concept of a higher being, and screaming at the ceiling, challenging God to a fist-fight. I think that's when I passed out.

I only know this because I remember waking up, still sitting on the toilet, and being unable to stand up because my legs were asleep. I fell to my hands and knees in front of the toilet, wiped what detritus I could from my ass, and somehow slinked into the hallway and passed back out on the floor. My pants were out of reach, so I just lay there.

I assume I passed out again, because my next memory is at about 8am. That's when SlingBlade woke me up. By kicking me in the ribs.

SlingBlade "What are you doing? Where are your pants?"
Tucker "Pain . . . brownies . . . shitting . . ."
SlingBlade "Get out of the way, I have to piss."

Such a good friend. I think I shit about three more times before I was able to recover some semblance of normalcy.

This was the summer of 2002. If you read *I Hope They Serve Beer In Hell,* you may remember that my appendix incident happened about six months later, in January of 2003. I have come to find out that the two incidents are almost certainly related:

Apparently, the dude who'd "never made pot brownies before" put actual pieces of marijuana plant in the brownies. It seemed like a logical way to make pot brownies to me when he explained it to me. Mark that down as the one moment in my life where I really, really wished I had done more drugs in high school: I have since been told that pot brownies are made by soaking seeds in oil or something, and then ONLY using the oil to make the brownies. Putting actual parts of the plant in the brownies is a disastrously bad idea. Why? Well, pot is made from marijuana. Otherwise known as hemp. Which is one of the best natural fibers you can use to make . . . ROPE.

I never put the two things together until one of my friends, who's a doctor, read this story:

Doctor "Tucker, your appendix didn't actually rupture, did it? It abscessed right?"
Tucker "Yeah, why?"
Doctor "Well, it's impossible to know for sure, but I would bet that pot brownie is what caused your appendix to abscess. You see, a full rupture is when the appendix tears or explodes. No one is really sure what causes that, but it's probably not from anything ingested. But small, slight tears in the appendix that become infected and then abscess—what yours was—are almost always caused by the patient eating something very rough on the colon. Like hemp fiber."
Tucker "But it was six months later."
Doctor "Abscesses, especially if they are small, take time to really get infected and create enough pus for you to feel it. Plus, didn't you start feeling it in October, you just ignored it, right?"
Tucker "Yeah."
Doctor "That's three months. Timing is right. I bet that's what caused the abscess. And of course, you ignoring it and trying to wait it out like an idiot made it 100x worse."

Motherfucker. I had to get fucking APPENDIX SURGERY because of that shit.

Time to update the final score from the night:

Hate: 145
SlingBlade: 30
Tucker: -5000
Doofus pothead: He's off the scoreboard. He failed at life.

SEXTING WITH TUCKER MAX

Occurred, various 2009–2011

In the movie based on my first book, we wrote a scene where one of Tucker's friends tries to call him from jail after getting arrested. I thought it would be funny if the actor used my real phone number, so on set I had him replace the fake number with the "555" prefix you normally hear in movie phone numbers with my real phone number. In the real movie.

I guess it was funny . . . if you think thousands of random people calling and texting your phone every single fucking day for the rest of your life is funny. Who would've predicted so many people would call me if I put my real phone number in a movie? Well, pretty much everyone except me. It got so bad, I just said fuck it, gave in, and even secretly put it on the cover of my last book as well. Go look at the cover, you'll see it if you have half a brain.

[And yes, if you're one of the people who called, that really is my phone number, and no, I'm not going to return your call or come party with you and your friends, so you can stop leaving voicemails about that.]

Even though this outcome was totally predictable to everyone but me, one thing happened that no one anticipated:

Girls would sext me.

A LOT of them.

I don't know how many girls in America are into sexting, but I would guess that a large portion of them have tried to get me to respond to them at some point in the past two years. At first, all these girls annoyed the fuck out of me. Sexting is fucking stupid; it's only appropriate for repressed teenagers or attention-starved cockteases, not for grown adults who have *actual* sex with other adults. Look, either come over and actually fuck or stop bothering me.

Then it dawned on me: Instead of letting all these faux-whores annoy me, I should flip it on them and do what I always do when dealing with idiots: ruthlessly fuck with them.

I started responding to the sexters, and quickly realized I was in a unique position. These girls were already into me, so I didn't have to waste any time warming them up. They knew I was an asshole, so I didn't have to indulge any of their stupid bullshit, and yet they were STILL coming to me to sext? It was like the perfect storm of fucking-with-idiots comedy.

These are some of the funniest exchanges I had with these girls, divided into categories.

[Editing Note: For the sake of brevity and your sanity, I've edited these exchanges down to only the funny parts. No one wants to read the boring parts of sexting; that's like listening to fantasy football stories. I also removed some of the most obnoxious misspellings, emoticons and abbreviations, (e.g., fbgm, brb, <3, smh) to make everything more readable to educated adults who speak English.]

Absurd

If I happen to respond to a girl's attempt at sexting with me, most of the time it's because I'm bored. In those cases more than any other, my responses are engineered solely to entertain myself. Her sexual gratification is so far down my list of priorities, that just typing those words out makes me laugh. At all times, my first, second, and third goal is to see how long I can get a girl to play along with the most ridiculous shit I can think up.

Absurd #1: Everything is Better with Bacon

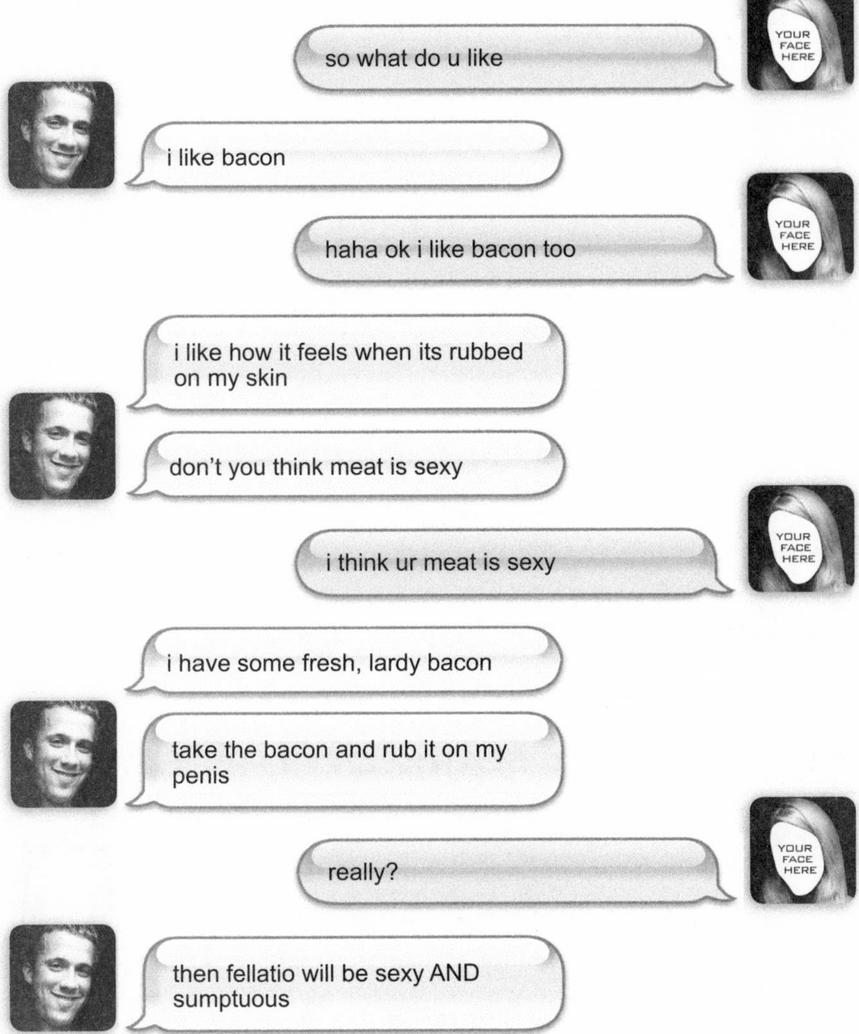
YOUR FACE HERE
so what do u like
i like bacon
YOUR FACE HERE
haha ok i like bacon too
i like how it feels when its rubbed on my skin
don't you think meat is sexy
YOUR FACE HERE
i think ur meat is sexy
i have some fresh, lardy bacon
take the bacon and rub it on my penis
YOUR FACE HERE
really?
then fellatio will be sexy AND sumptuous

how about i just swallow

i like how cum tastes

cum can't taste better than bacon

i dont really like bacon that much

YOU REVOLTING WHORE!

its just bacon

I bet you cut the genitals off baby giraffes for fun

Youre dead to me

wtf

I guess that's OK, I like fucking girls that dont move much

Absurd #2: Mark of the Beast

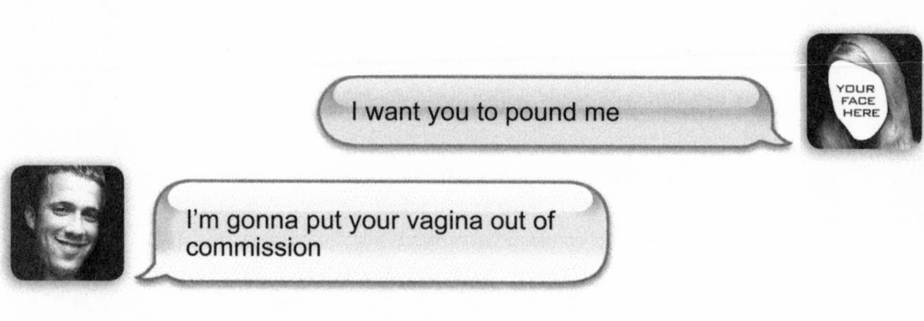

thats what i like to hear
hurt it
YOUR FACE HERE
Im going to tear your pussy a new asshole
YOUR FACE HERE
fuck me so hard
you're going to be my bitch
YOUR FACE HERE
ill be ur bitch
Bark bitch, bark like a dog
YOUR FACE HERE
arf arf
That's terrible. No bone for you until you bark louder
ARF! ARF! ARF! ARF!
YOUR FACE HERE
i pull your pants off your boner is amazing
Its the greatest boner you've ever seen in your life
YOUR FACE HERE
i luv it

Give it a round of applause

clap clap

my boner deserves a standing ovation

standing CLAP CLAP CLAP CLAP CLAP CLAP CLAP CLAP CLAP

I push you down. Youre making too much noise

I kneel in front of you and start to lick your thighs

I stand on the end of bed, naked, body glistening with sweat, grabbing my nuts in one hand and fist-pumping with other, screaming at the top of my lungs

lol

RRRRRRAAAAAAAAAARRRRRRRR!!!!!!!!!!!!!!!!!!!!!!

AAAAAAAAAAAAAAAHHHHHHHHH-HHHHHHHH!!!!!!!!!!!!!!!!!!!!!!

what r u doin?

Sometimes a nigga just gotta hold his nuts and flex

uh,,,ok

You clearly aren't into my masculine display. I go into the bathroom and don't come back.

no come back i like it

You follow me in there. I'm pissing in your sink and pointing at myself in the mirror

lol thats kinda sexy

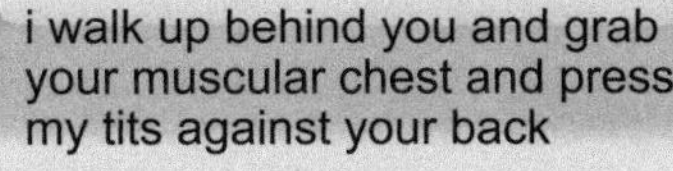

i walk up behind you and grab your muscular chest and press my tits against your back

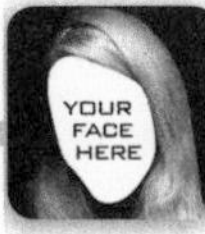

I'm thirsty. Get me a beer

beer?

GET ME A BEER RIGHT NOW, OR I WILL POOP ON SOMETHING YOU CARE ABOUT!

ok ok I get you a beer

I have to drop a deuce. Youre out of toilet paper

No, i have some

I already used it all up. Get me some wheat bread.

not white, its unhealthy

bread?

for wiping

ugh,,,ok

I just decide to walk around unwiped

I grab you by your tits and push you down on the sofa and put my tongue in your ear

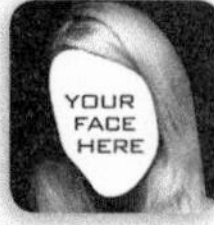

i grab your penis and put it in me its so big and hard

I gently whisper “I want to fuck you in your shitpussy.”

turn me over and do it

I flip you over and start peeing on you

what are you doing?!?

Letting all the other men know you have an owner

Absurd #3: Racist Fucker

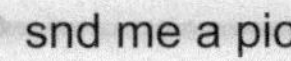

snd me a pic

ok hold on

here you go

wtf
ur not black

i knew you were racist

i hate racist scum like you
oppressing my people

ur white

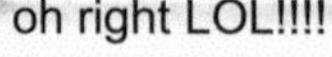

oh right LOL!!!!

there sure is egg on my face!!

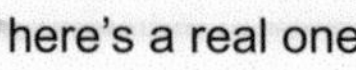

here's a real one

Absurd #4: Imagine All the Potty Mouth

I had to wipe four times. That's so hot, you're turned on

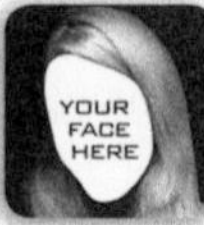

umm . . . too much information

I punch you in the face

why???

I won't tell you. You have enough information apparently

this is not sexting, this is stupid

This is how I sext. how do you?

You talk about the things you want to happen, like the things you are imagining with us

I imagine a world where there's no countries, it isn't hard to do

Sexual stuff!!

Nothing to kill or die for, And no religion too!

YOUR FACE HERE

Wtf?

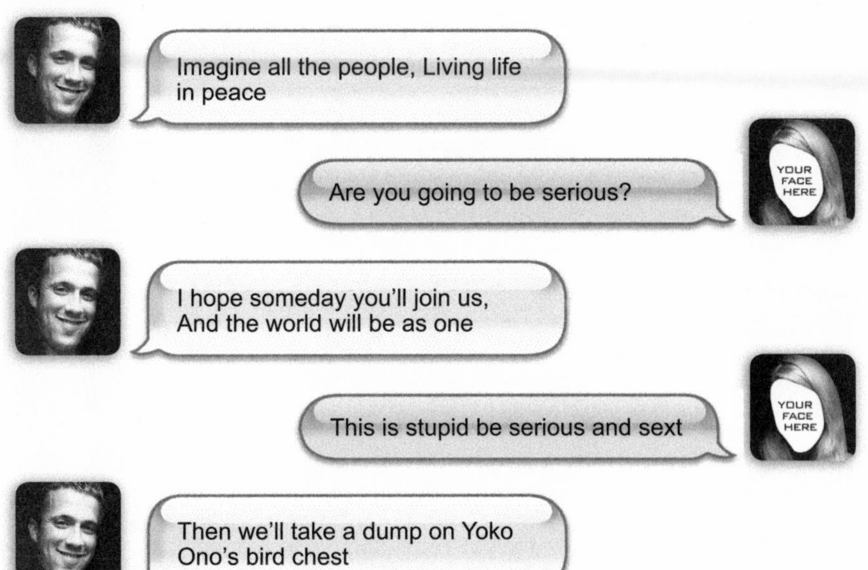

Absurd #5: OMG I Have to Pee

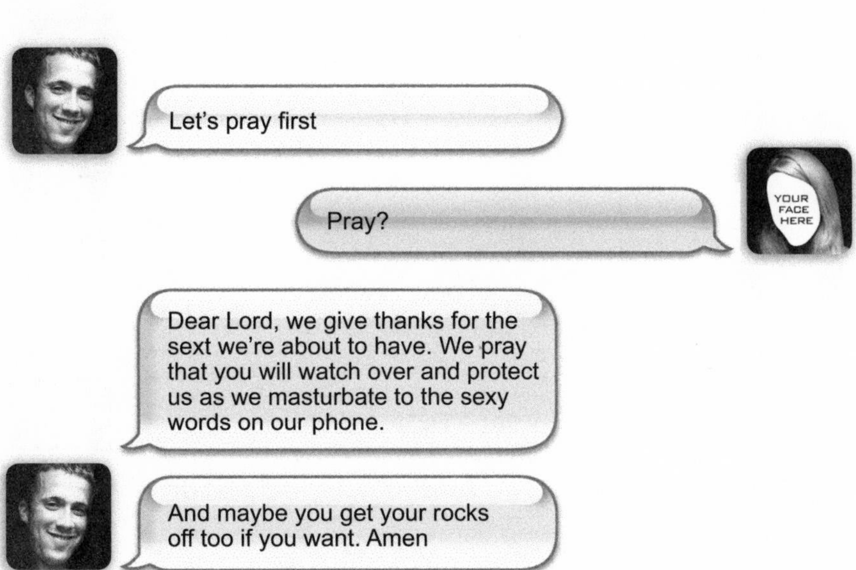

rotfl

i'm praying you make me cum

don't mock my god!!

he is vengeful!! you're going to get more wrath!

ok ok ok

I roll you over and put a condom on you im horny

I don't need condoms

condoms needed esp for u lol

I rub you on the belly. I'm gonna put a baby in there!

whatttt noooooooo!

Fine. Do you have condoms?

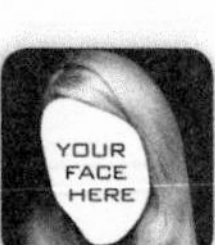

I take it out and roll it over your penis

Are these left over from your ex?

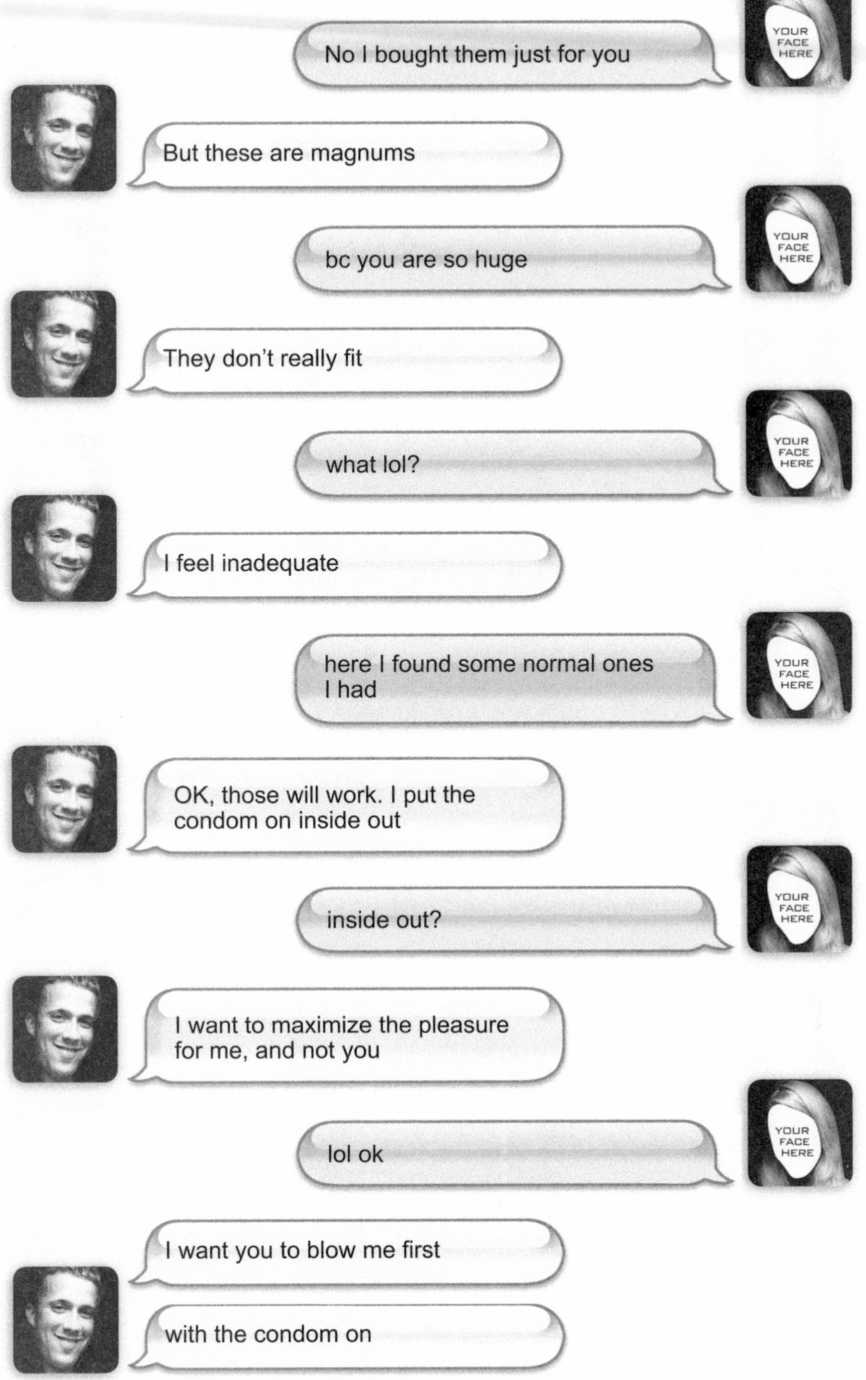
YOUR FACE HERE
No I bought them just for you
But these are magnums
YOUR FACE HERE
bc you are so huge
They don't really fit
YOUR FACE HERE
what lol?
I feel inadequate
YOUR FACE HERE
here I found some normal ones I had
OK, those will work. I put the condom on inside out
YOUR FACE HERE
inside out?
I want to maximize the pleasure for me, and not you
YOUR FACE HERE
lol ok
I want you to blow me first
with the condom on

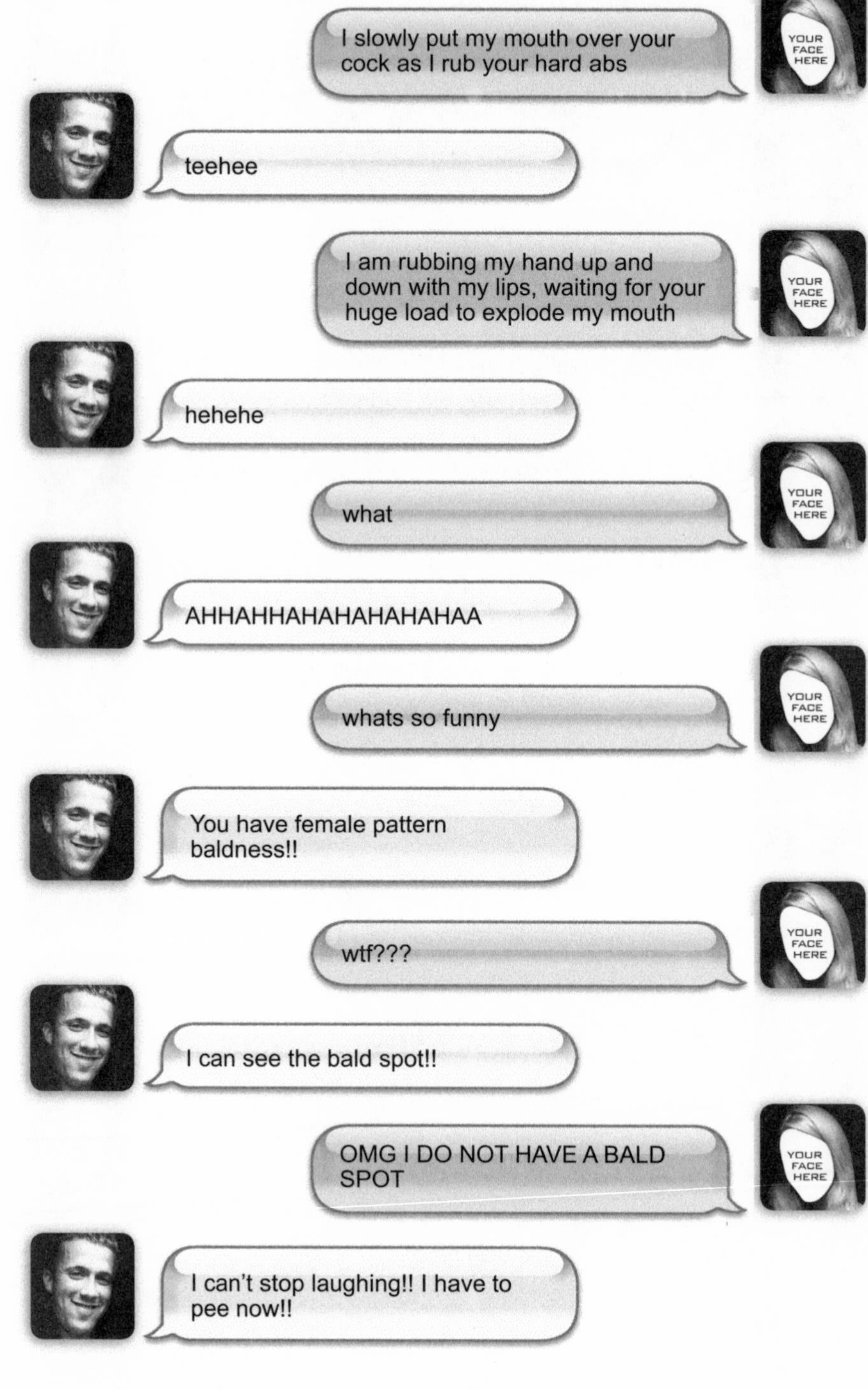
I slowly put my mouth over your cock as I rub your hard abs
YOUR FACE HERE
teehee
I am rubbing my hand up and down with my lips, waiting for your huge load to explode my mouth
YOUR FACE HERE
hehehe
what
YOUR FACE HERE
AHHAHHAHAHAHAHAHAA
whats so funny
YOUR FACE HERE
You have female pattern baldness!!
wtf???
YOUR FACE HERE
I can see the bald spot!!
OMG I DO NOT HAVE A BALD SPOT
YOUR FACE HERE
I can't stop laughing!! I have to pee now!!

Absurd #6: Metasext

Fine with me I can just put my dick in a garbage can and stir it around a little bit and it would essentially be the same thing

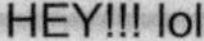

HEY!!! lol

Be serious, I really want to sext with you

me too!

I gently push my tongue onto your clit, and vigorously flick it back and forth.

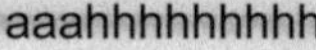

aaahhhhhhhh

you are so good go harder

I tease your pussy with my finger, ready to push it in and hit your g-spot.

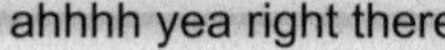

ahhhh yea right there

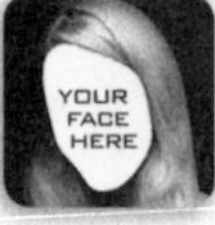

faster i like it fast

I stop and look into your eyes for full effect—ARE YOU TEXTING RIGHT NOW!??!?!?!

What? no!

I mean,,,what?

So turned off. I can't believe youd do that i was trying so hard to eat your pussy good

i liked it what are you talking about?

Worst.Sexter.Ever

Why Halloween Is Awesome

People always ask me what I think is the best night of the year to party. The usual suspects can be easily dismissed. New Year's Eve is amateur hour at its worst. St. Patty's Day can be fun, but any day that celebrates a bunch of drunken, wife-beating bog-people has a built in ceiling (for a fun St. Patty's day trick, go up to hammered people dressed in green and say, "Thank you for your service." Have fun watching them try to explain that they aren't in the military, they're just drunk idiots).

There are other nights that have their pros and cons, but if you're like me and go out to have fun—with getting laid and emotional escapism as a secondary goal subordinated to the primary goal of entertaining yourself—then you know there is only one real choice: Halloween.

Halloween revolves around delicious candy, excessive alcohol, and horny women dressed as sluts. This also describes my vision of Heaven.

That being said, I have a special place in my heart for Halloween for one reason: I get to make fun of people's costumes. The great thing about Halloween costumes is that they're a window into the hearts and souls of the people who wear them. Well guess what—most people are delusional idiots. There is no greater canvas on which to paint a masterpiece of caustic, Tucker Max-type humor than the immense plaid ass of a fatty who thinks she can pull off a Naughty Schoolgirl outfit.

Over the years, I've had some great Halloweens. The absolute very best is told in the "The DC Halloween Party and the Worst Girl I Ever Fucked" story in my last book, *Assholes Finish First.* These are the rest:

Halloween 2002, Part 1

In 2002, TheRoommate and I went on a Halloween pub crawl. For my costume, I wrapped a red ribbon around my shirt, topped it off with a red bow on my shoulder, and put a card on the ribbon that said, "From: God, To: Women."

Get it? God's gift to women (this was 2002, when that was still a fairly original idea).

TheRoommate wouldn't tell me what his costume was going to be until about an hour before we left. He walked out of his room sporting a Carmen Miranda/Chiquita Banana Lady costume and in a pathetic Hispanic accent asked, "Do you want a banana?" I was laughing so hard, I almost had a seizure.

TheRoommate "Help me zip up the back, I can't reach it."

Instantly, I stopped laughing. There is nothing funny about touching another man's back hair.

The pub crawl was a typically awesome Chicago bar event: tons of girls, everyone drunk, everyone having fun, no bullshit or assholes. Except, of course, for me.

One girl came as Punky Brewster (for teenage readers: she was a television character from a creepy 80's sitcom premised upon an old man living with a very young girl; lots of clips on YouTube).

Tucker "How good is your costume? Have you had breast reduction surgery?"
Punky "Can't you tell? Look at them."
Tucker "I said 'breast reduction,' not 'breast elimination.'"
Punky "Come on."

Tucker "That's all the Punky Brewster jokes I have. Unless you want me to put you in an abandoned refrigerator."
Punky "You need more game to get me."
Tucker "Well, when you get bigger tits, I'll break out the bigger game."

She was not pleased. Whatever—what kind of Punky fan doesn't remember the "hide-and-go-seek gone wrong" episode, anyway? Apparently the flat-chested kind.

I eventually came across a girl in a princess costume who looked way too uppity for my taste. You know that saying, "no matter how hot she is, someone somewhere is sick of her shit?" Yeah, well this was the type of girl that had a lot of someones in a lot of somewheres. I decided to try my most sophisticated, suave approach:

I walked up to her, pressed my hand on my ass, then put it up to her face.

Tucker "What's that smell like to you?"

Her face crinkled into complete shock.

Tucker "I think it smells like pineapple, but my friend says it smells like wet dog."

Her expression morphed into disgust and contempt.

Tucker "What? You don't like dogs?"

She walked off.

Tucker "Oh, so I guess you're not [air quotes] 'into farts'?"

At some point, I went to the bathroom, and the guy next to me at the urinals was dressed as Julius Caesar. When he was done, he shook off for what seemed like forever.

Tucker "Better get that checked."
Julius "No man, I'm just afraid of dribbling on my toga."
Tucker "I don't know . . . I bet you have prostate cancer."
Julius "DUDE—WHAT THE FUCK?!?"

I thought for a second I was going to have to fight a guy in a bed sheet, when, right at that moment, another guy—who didn't seem to have a costume on—stumbled into the bathroom, drunk as hell. He saw us standing there, facing each other with our dicks in our hands, and stared at us with the kind of confused look I've only ever seen on a dog and a guido. He quickly snapped out of it, and his face lit up in a smile as he turned around to show us his back. A piece of bread was taped to his ass.

Guy "HEY LOOK—I'M ON A ROLL! GET IT!?!"

My outfit was not much more creative. It was basically just a device to get women to come up and ask me, "What makes you God's gift to women?" Which is pretty much the perfect costume for me since it's a great set-up for jokes. Some of my responses:

- "I love romantic comedies and listening to rambling, disjointed rationalizations."

- "I'm a convicted sex offender."

- "I don't know. What do you think? Tell me your thoughts, feelings, and opinions. I love to listen."

- "I have 20 million dollars and terminal cancer."

- "I won't judge you for the things you are going to do later and not tell your girlfriends about."

- "Bend over and I'll show you. Though some girls think 13 inches is too big."

• "I'm a plastic surgeon and I can fix everything that's wrong with you."

Sadly, most of the girls that approached me weren't cute. That's OK though, I devised the perfect solution: After I made myself laugh with my response, I just stopped talking to them.

Happily, I was able to meet a few cute girls who also thought my responses were funny and were into me. This is good. The problem is, this is Halloween: THE prime hookup night of the year. There are willing targets everywhere, but unless I know for sure that my penis is going to be inside a girl's vagina THAT night, I'm not going to waste even two seconds listening to how she wants to cure pediatric cancer or help rescue cats from blenders or whatever specific whore prattle she's spouting to avoid facing her obvious and crippling emotional issues.

I quickly figured an easy way to feel girls out. Each one I talked to, I would ask her what her costume was, even if it was patently obvious. Then, no matter what she said, I gave my interpretation:

Tucker "What are you?"
Girl "I'm an angel."
Tucker "I think you're a *slutty* angel."

Tucker "What are you?"
Girl "I'm a sexy nurse."
Tucker "I think you're a *slutty* nurse."

Tucker "What are you?"
Girl "I'm a tree."
Tucker "I think you're a *slutty* tree."

Not very subtle, but very effective. I'm sure there were some girls that would have been more than willing to hook up, but seemed a bit ambivalent, so I moved on. Rolling the dice is for craps, not Halloween night.

Tucker "What are you?"
Bee "I'm a bumblebee, obviously."
Tucker "Yes, but are you a *slutty* bumblebee?"
Bee "I'm not a slutty one . . . at least not yet."
Tucker "Well how much sugar and vodka will it take to transform you into a slutty bumblebee?"
Bee "Good question. How about we get some and see?"

We talked and hung out for a while. She was definitely very cute and she seemed nice enough. Okay, maybe "nice" isn't exactly right. Perhaps "willing" is the proper adjective to use here, but whatever—point is, she was down to fuck. After an hour or so of aggressive drinking, she did a shot of something and staggered a bit.

Bee "Well, I think we found how much alcohol it takes to turn me into a slut."
Tucker "Sweet! It's time for you to see my penis."

We stumbled back to my place and sloppily hooked up. I immediately understood why this girl was dressed in a costume that allowed her to hide her midsection. Her face, arms and legs were totally normal, the same as any girl—but her torso was huge. It was ridiculous and made no sense, like someone had glued four broomsticks on a keg. How does that even work, physiologically? Mr. Potato Head is more proportional than this girl.

Whatever, we're both naked and horny, and I've fucked way worse. No turning back now. When you try to jump a lake of fire you don't take your foot off the gas once you've hit the ramp. Plus, I was so drunk, I figured I would either pass out halfway or not remember it the next day. Win-win.

For some reason I woke up early the next morning, still drunk and groggy, and noticed the girl wasn't next to me. There was some noise or something in the living room, but I just assumed she was going to piss or was leaving, so I went back to sleep. My head was killing me, and I wasn't excited by the prospect of fully waking up and dealing with the worst hangover since Jesus woke up on Easter.

When I did finally rise from the dead, KegTorso was gone. I went to breakfast with my roommate and the girl he hooked up with. When it came time to pay, I realized I had no cash in my wallet, even though there should have been $40. What the fuck?

I was desperately poor at this point in my life, and like all poor people, I was acutely aware of precisely how much money I had at any given moment, down to the penny. The event last night was open bar, so I know exactly what I spent on drinks. Plus, I walked home and we didn't stop for food—there was no way for me to have spent that $40. I checked everything at my place—it was gone.

Then I remembered the girl rifling around my apartment that morning.

Holy shit! KegTorso stole $40 out of my wallet!!!

I was kinda in shock. I'm not sure what happened. Maybe she thought I underperformed, and this was her way of paying me back. Maybe she wanted to buy 40 things on the McDonald's dollar menu. Who knows, maybe she just needed the cash. But couldn't she have gotten that much by just taking her torso to the Liquor Barn and getting her deposit back?

HALLOWEEN 2002, PART 2

After the previous night, I was dragging ass all day, which was fine because it was a Sunday and not much was happening. By late afternoon I'd decided to just nurse some beers and call it a night. That was when I got a call from my friend "Jerry."

Tucker "Yo."
Jerry "RRRRRAAAWWWWWWFFFFFMMMMMMGGGGGGAAAAA!!!! Dude!"
Tucker "What the fuck?"
Jerry "HAHAHAHAA RRRRAAAAWMMMGMGGAAAAGGGG!!! Sluts!"

It took me a second to translate from Drunken Retard into English, but finally I got the gist: he was telling me to come to his place because there were hot girls and a full keg. I was reticent, but I decided to go—technically, this was still Halloween weekend, which meant there were still drunk girls in slutty outfits looking to fuck. What man in his twenties says no to that? Not Tucker Max.

I arrived at his apartment, which was this really cool 4-bedroom in Wrigleyville. He was technically right; there were a ton of girls there. They outnumbered the guys like 3 to 1. But he neglected to mention anything ABOUT the girls, like for instance, what species they belonged to.

I've been writing professionally now for several years and I have never struggled with the description of a scene the way I have with this one. I don't think even William Faulkner could find the words to accurately describe the quality of the girls at Jerry's party. It was a menagerie of the abysmal. I wanted to put strychnine in the feedbags of every horse-faced she-pony there. Had I the proper munitions, I would have set off a bomb in that apartment whose explosion you could have seen from space, to save the human race from the potential that these things could ever breed. The only thing that prevented me from committing felony assault on Jerry was the fact that there was a full keg of good beer there.

Let me give you a brief rundown of the girls:

In one room, there were three girls—none looked over 19—dancing wildly to a boy-band song as the flowing velvet and satin of their Renaissance Faire costumes twirled into a kaleidoscope of blubbery foulness. Each girl had at least one major deformity. One was so short and squat she looked like a bowling ball on top of an exercise ball. Another had eyes so far apart they were on different sides of her face; all she had to do was move them independently and I'd have bought car insurance from her. The third girl had the worst teeth I've ever seen, like she had a mouth full of antlers.

Down the hall in another room I found three blondes who, from 25 feet away, were potential Hooters calendar girls. From five feet, they looked like used-up day shift strippers. The cutest one (or should I say, the least used-up) was into me, but she was a good ten years past her prime, and I was far too sober to pretend it wouldn't be like fucking a mayonnaise jar.

The room where the keg was stashed was no better. I met a girl who was four months pregnant, a girl who had a scar on her face that made her look like Tony Montana, and another girl who'd recently undergone breast reduction surgery to alleviate the chronic back pain that is often associated with being a big fat pig.

Most of these girls weren't even wearing Halloween costumes any more. Unless you consider adipose tissue a disguise. The apartment was like a Salvador Dali painting set inside an M.C. Escher print, all come to life. Really, it was that surreal. I've run out of adjectives.

At this point there was nothing else to do besides camp out around the keg and start drinking. And drinking. After an hour of focused aggression toward my bottomless Solo cup of beer, I finally came up for air and saw a girl wearing a Halloween mask so horrifying I jumped from fright.

Then I realized she wasn't wearing a mask at all. That was just her face. It looked like it had caught on fire and someone beat it out with a rake. Apparently my reaction was not an uncommon one, because when she saw me jump back—LITERALLY jump back—as she walked in the door, she said, "Did I scare you? It's OK, I get that reaction a lot."

To her credit, she was actually cool. This girl understood that when you look like you came straight out of George Lucas' imagination, you better have something else to offer— deep thoughts, deep pockets, or deep throats. Plus, she had a great dominatrix costume on, which made her tits look good, so there was something else to look at while I talked to her. Her roommate was there too, and it was actually him that uttered the words that would change the night.

Guy "Yeah, it's interesting living with a dominatrix."
Tucker "I'm sorry . . . what did you just say?"
Guy "She's a dominatrix. That's her job."
Tucker "That's not a costume?? Your actual JOB is to be a dominatrix??"
Dominatrix "Yep."

I spent the next hour peppering her with questions. I learned several things:

1. She makes $200 an hour beating men up. She doesn't even have to take her clothes off, much less fuck them.

2. Her client list includes several rich and famous people, including (according to her) a MAJOR Chicago politician and a fairly well known actor. The Chicago politician enjoys having clothespins stuck to his balls and the actor prefers slave/mistress role-playing.

3. She got into the dominatrix business after making out with a woman who was doing it professionally. This was while she was traveling around with her heroin-addicted boyfriend, who was a roadie for Skid Row.

4. She has two kids to support by herself, and that's why she does it (Who had the stomach to fuck her??? Oh right . . . a heroin addict).

5. The fact that she is so ugly HELPS her in her job. Some guys like getting hurt by ugly women. I guess it makes it more humiliating?

My mind was spinning with the possibilities. What would be the funniest thing to do here?

Tucker "OK, you beat people up for money? Prove it. I want to see you kick someone's ass."

Much to my shock, she agreed to do it. But we couldn't find anyone to volunteer to be her subject.

Tucker "None of you pussies will get your ass kicked by the sea donkey dominatrix? Come on!"
Dominatrix "Hey tough guy, why don't you do it?"

Well, I guess I walked right into that. Thank you, full keg of beer.

Tucker "Fine bitch, I'm in. But don't hit me in the nuts, or tie anything to my penis or any stupid shit like that. You can hurt me, but don't do anything to me that won't fully heal, or I will beat YOUR ass."

I could see the switch flip behind her eyes as she went into Dominatrix mode. In an instant she transformed from a gelatinous heap of burn-scarred flesh to She-Ra Harpy Goddess of Pain. She disappeared into the kitchen and came back with a spatula, a wooden spoon, a carving knife, some grill tongs—basically anything long and hard. She meticulously laid out her implements, and then grabbed me by the hair.

Dominatrix "YOU ARE A PIECE OF SHIT, YOU LITTLE FUCKING TURD!! I OWN YOU, I OWN EVERYTHING ABOUT YOU, YOU FILTHY GARBAGE!!! NOW GET ON YOUR KNEES RIGHT NOW!!!"

I started laughing hysterically, for two reasons:

1. How do people get off on this shit? I can't imagine anything less erotic than violence.

2. I immediately realized how to take this up a level. Think about it—here's this woman who perceives herself to be powerful because she gets paid to beat up important men who have weird psychological fetishes. What's the best way to fuck with her? Make *her* feel powerless, which fucks with her identity. And when you mess with the ideas people hold about themselves, well, that always leads to funny.

Tucker "People PAY YOU for this? I'd demand a refund."

She kinda tried to kick the back of my knees to force me down, and I just laughed more at her. I wasn't even really resisting much or being a dick about it, but I wasn't about to follow instructions. Her inability to control me frustrated her, so she took a wooden spoon and started whipping me on the back with it. It stung for a second, but not bad enough to even wipe the smile off my face. She started really wailing on me with it, and I was still laughing . . . then it broke. In half, on my back.

Tucker "AHHAHAHAHAHHAH—YOU BROKE THE SPOON!!! And it didn't even hurt! Who thinks this is painful? I've had slight breezes hurt more than this. Get someone else over here who can do it right."

Bitch got PISSED. She went back into the kitchen, found one of those 500ft commercial rolls of Saran Wrap, and wrapped what seemed like half of it over my mouth and around my head, barely leaving enough room for me to breathe. Then she started taking off my clothes. This didn't bother me until she got down to my pants. I didn't have any boxers on. She didn't care. She stripped me down to my skintight Patagonia

Capilene long underwear (it was October in Chicago, I was cold, fuck off). Then she bound my hands to a chair with the other half of the Saran Wrap, tied a bandana over my eyes tight enough that I started to see those little starbursts, and went to work.

I'll be honest: She kinda beat the crap out of me. She was beating me with the type of anger usually reserved for people who owe money to Tony Soprano. She went to work on my ass with the spatula and two different wooden kitchen spoons. She bit my nipples. She left welts on my ass and back, and some of them even bled a little bit. She even tried to go at my nuts with the tongs (I stopped that shit real quick by kicking her in the chest). She cycled through everything she brought out from the kitchen. It was definitely painful, but at the same time it was pretty funny, just because she was sweating she was working so hard. Except I still don't understand why this turns people on, but whatever, if they like it, more power to them.

I took the bandana off when she was finished, and looked around the room. She was exhausted to the point that she was dripping in sweat, like she'd just worked out. Perusing the eyes of all the girls watching was weird—I did not perceive this as sexual, but it was real clear that a lot of the girls were REAL turned on. That day-shift stripper I was almost drunk enough to be attracted to was particularly into it, and she looked much prettier and more innocent than I remembered from an hour before. So I persuaded her to go next. The dominatrix tied her up the same way, stripped her down to her bra, and went at her. She was much more erotic and sensual with her. It was actually kinda hot.

In the middle of all this, one of the guys who lived in the apartment but had been out all night, "Brian," came home and walked in on the scene. He later described it in an email as such:

"I come into the apartment to find [Jerry] passed out face first on the computer desk and everyone else crowded into the area over by the kitchen table. There was a girl blindfolded, almost naked, bending over a chair getting spanked in the ass with a wooden spoon by some girl in a red hooker costume who is lifting it up to show everyone her shaved box. I WAS FUCKING SHOCKED."

At this point, two of us were essentially naked, the endorphins of sexual assault were coursing through our veins, and the people watching us were like chimps rubbing their genitals together. Everyone was shit-housed. The place was delicately teetering on the precipice of a hot, disgusting orgy of uglies.

That's when someone suggested we all go into the sauna (this apartment is so sweet; it is two stories, has four bedrooms, two decks, a hot tub, AND a sauna).

It was like the beginning of one of those "artsy" pornos where the director pays lip service to the craft of filmmaking or some shit by employing a thinly veiled attempt at plot. We're all preparing to get into the sauna, stripping off unnecessary clothes, making small talk, even though we all know what the subtext is: whether we're going to have a nauseating fuckfest.

As we wait for the sauna to heat and steam up enough, the dominatrix takes Jerry, who had passed out on a desk about two hours prior, upstairs to his bedroom. The sauna is upstairs too, so after we get beer we all head up, except I hear some noises coming from Jerry's room. His room is built like a loft with a space above his door that you can look over. I drag a three-foot speaker over, climb on top of it, and peer into his room. My eyes met this scene:

Jerry, shoes still on, jeans around his ankles, standing behind the dominatrix, who was bent over the bed. He was not fucking her; he was jackhammering her so hard and fast, he was moving like one of those things that mixes paint at Home Depot.

Unable to contain myself, I start giggling like a schoolgirl. Jerry looks up, sweat dripping off his face, sees me, and his eyes go wide:

"Hey! HEY!!!!"

It was NOT a yell of surprise. It was a yell of anguish that said, "Oh God, everyone will know I've done this."

His screaming sent me into convulsive spasms of laughter, which caused me fall off the speaker and crash into a cheap coffee table, smashing it into pieces. I just left the mess and ran into the sauna, still laughing and bleeding. Now we know who else would fuck this sea donkey dominatrix in addition to a heroin addict.

There were five other people in the sauna—Brian and four girls—all in towels. The good thing is that everyone thought the story was as funny as I did. The bad thing is that you don't want to watch (nearly) naked ugly people laughing spastically. Horrifying.

Then the dominatrix walked in. She was completely naked except for her black knee-high leather hooker boots. To this day I have never seen anything so violently repulsive, yet so oddly erotic. Remember how great I said her tits looked in that costume? Yeah, well pancake batter holds a nice shape too . . . in the ladle. But when you pour it out onto the griddle? Flapjacks. She walked her naked body, complete with shaved box full of Jerry-semen, right over to Brian and sat on his lap.

This was a tense moment. Mostly because everyone was worried we were going to have watch an ugly girl fuck. The dominatrix, being attuned to this tension, made a point of cutting it—by immediately playing with Brian's junk and then putting his penis in her mouth. If that's not a sign to get the fuck out of a sauna, and the apartment I don't know what is.

The fallout from that party came down for weeks. At first Jerry tried to deny that he slept with the dominatrix. Sorry buddy, I saw it, and it was so traumatic I broke your coffee table. Then he changed his story and claimed he was raped. That's a pretty strange claim—it's not often you personally witness a "victim" absolutely CRUSHING a piece of ass from behind.

For Brian, the guy who walked in on the girl getting turned out by the dominatrix, well, I'll let him describe what that party did to him:

"It affected me in ways that I never thought possible. Last night I got stoned and was going over the events in my head and I came to the conclusion that I need to get my act together quick. I guess that sometimes it takes a freshly fucked hideous dominatrix trying to blow you in your sauna to make you think, 'What the fuck am I doing with my life?'"

Halloween 2003

My ex-girlfriend Bunny and I dated for about year, from like end of 2003 to mid-2004. We had a dysfunctional relationship, didn't work as a couple, and probably shouldn't even have dated at all. The good news is that all the bad shit was a result of dating; since we've broken up, we've become best friends.

The first time she really saw me in action was a month or so after we started dating. We went to a Halloween party in Chicago that some friends of mine were having. I don't really remember much of that night because I was incredibly fucked up; I was probably drunk enough to play tag with myself. Also, there wasn't any one big event that made me take notice; it was just a pretty typical fun night out. The next day, I vaguely remember thinking I had a good time and said some funny stuff, but that nothing really "story worthy" happened.

When I said that to her the next day, Bunny almost shit. She had a very different take on my actions that night. Bunny doesn't drink much, so she was stone sober all night and remembered everything. I asked her to sit down and write out what I did that was funny, because if it was really as good as she said, I wanted to email it to my friends. This is the email she wrote back:

"Honey, I thought you might have exaggerated a little in your stories, but seeing you drunk last night at the party . . . I've never seen anything like that. By the end of the night, when people would see you coming they would audibly gasp and then go the other way. I think a dozen people at least left the party because of you. I have never laughed so hard. Here are some of the things I can remember:

- At the party, you introduced me to your friends, who were very nice. A lot of other people would come up to you and say what's up or slap five, and you'd nod and say what's up. Then you'd turn to me and say, "I don't have any fucking idea who that guy is."

- You reduced Sarah [a female friend of mine and Bunny's] to tears in front of everyone, because you said she is nuts. I think your exact quote was, "Look at yourself—you can't even hold your drink straight. Everyone around here seems to have no problem keeping the contents of their cup IN their cup. You on the other hand seem to have an inability to hold a glass level. You are obviously insane." This was what made her cry. I apologized to her later for you.

- You must have asked 100 different people if they thought they were better than you. No matter what their answer was, you yelled at them, "YOU'RE NOT BETTER'N ME!"

- You and Brian made fun of a lot of people together. One I remember: You tried to make an Asian guy apologize for WW2. He said he was Vietnamese. You told him to apologize for the Vietnam War. He said he was born in 1980, five years after Vietnam ended. You told him to apologize for using sweatshop labor to flood the US market with cheap imports and taking American jobs. He said his dad was American. Then you called him a "dust child" and he got really mad. What does that mean?

- This one girl was dressed as a Wonder Bra. You went up to her and said, "You know why they call it a Wonder Bra? Because when she takes it off, you wonder where her tits went. Fucking BULLSHIT!"

- You found a bag of ice, and you carried it around the party yelling out, "I'm so hot, I'm gonna melt all this iiiiiiiccccceee! Look at the ice melting . . . because I'm so hot."

- You complimented a girl on her costume and said she did a really good job with it, and she thanked you. Then you said, "I assume you were intending to come as a piece of shit, right?" I apologized to her for you.

- She got mad and tried to make fun of you. Then you said something very mean. You said you wouldn't fuck her with Rosie O'Donnell's dick. I tried to find her to apologize, but I didn't see her at the party after that.

- A girl was telling me about her boyfriend, and you interrupted, "Does this story involve penetration? If not, just shut the fuck up, no one cares."

- We met a very nice man who was an African-American and a homosexual. You called him a "blaggot." He thought it was funny.

- You tried to convince a guy who was dressed as a break dancer to follow you around holding his boom box over your head, playing various theme songs to your life. You told him you'd pay him to do it three nights a week. Then you had a long discussion about what songs worked with what events. Most of your song choices were bad.

- One girl dressed as a Franzia box of wine. It was a funny costume. You spun her around and then yelled out that her costume was all wrong, the nutritional label should say the box contained at least 100 pounds of fat. I apologized to her for you.

- I think you may have caused a divorce. I didn't hear what you said, but Brian told me later that you asked the girl where the sign in sheet for her vagina was. They got into a huge argument and then left the party. I think the subject of the argument was whether or not the girl wanted to have sex with you.

- Some girl told me that you called her a stupid gutterslut. I told her you meant it in the most respectful way possible.

- One girl who was kinda fat came dressed as a lady bug. You told her she looked like a fire hydrant. Then you asked her how many dogs had pissed on her. I apologized to her later.

- You convinced your friend's girlfriend to let me lick her breasts in front of everyone. I have never seen a guy more happy with you. I think he was the only guy at the party who liked you. I liked you then too. Her tits were awesome.

- Then you made fun of her because she wasn't drinking. She was pregnant. You said she should drink anyway, because "some birth defect children are entertaining, like that Baby Ruth guy in *The Goonies.* He's HILARIOUS."

- We discussed children. I said I would love any baby I had, even if it was retarded. You said you wouldn't love a retarded baby, that you'd poke it in the brain with a needle and throw it down a hill, like the Spartans did. It was very mean.

- I went to the bathroom, and when I came back you said, "Bunny, we've made a lot of progress. She narrowed it down to 7 guys that could've gotten her pregnant." Thankfully they thought you were hilarious.

- This one girl was dressed as a dinosaur, and was obnoxiously roaring at people, asking them to guess what kind of dinosaur she was. It was annoying. You said she was a fupapotamus. Everyone laughed, and she got very upset at you, and tried to respond. You said that if she had any more emotions to convey, she should bake them into some chocolate cookies because she'd already eaten all the desserts and other people were hungry too. I saw her crying in the bathroom later and apologized to her for you, even though she deserved it.

- This one guy was telling you some story about his job, and you blurted out, "No one cares that you had to work doubles at the dirt factory to make ends meet. Get to the fucking point buddy."

- You almost got in a fight with a guy who was supposed to be the Publishers Clearing House Prize Patrol. He walked out on the deck, and you yell out, "GET YOUR FUCKING BALLOONS OUT OF MY PARTY, THIS IS MY PARTY AND YOU DON'T BRING BALLOONS WITHOUT MY PERMISSION." He acted like a dick to you, so you continued, "WELL, here's ANOTHER person who thinks he's BETTER'N me." I think he threw something at you or pushed you or something juvenile like that. I thought you might fight him, but you got in his face and yelled, "I REALLY ENJOY BEN & JERRY'S ICE CREAM!" It made no sense. He was confused too, and just went back inside.

- You looked over the side of the deck onto the people smoking down below, and started laughing to yourself. Then you tried to stand on the wall of their deck and piss all over them. You said something about cancer not being the only risk of smoking. I told you not to do it because it would be very mean, but you said, "If the thought of something makes me giggle for longer than 15 seconds, then I do it."

- The deck is also three stories up and I told you that if you fell you'd die, but you said, "Relax. Things always work out for me because I do whatever I want without worrying about the consequences."

- Thankfully, you were too drunk to climb the wall, and after many failed attempts, you got frustrated and just peed on your bag of ice.

- Then you spotted a bullhorn on a table. When you saw it, your eyes lit up like an 8-year-old on Christmas morning. You kept saying, "Here I am Sap, straight outta your nightmares" and tried to pick it up. While holding a 1.75 of vodka in your right hand and the peed-on bag of ice in your left, you somehow managed to sling the bullhorn over your shoulder. Instead of trying to turn it on with your free left hand, you tried to manipulate the dial with the right hand, which was holding the bag of ice (that you peed on) and vodka. Brian said you looked like a tard trying to tie his own shoelaces. You mumbled something about how it didn't work.

- Then someone who I presume was a resident of the apartment came over very quickly and disarmed you of the bullhorn and ran off with it before you could really resist. You looked so deflated. It was sad.

- After that, Sarah, Serena, and Rachel wanted to leave with me and you for the fivesome. They were kind of reticent to go with you though because they were afraid you were going to make fun of them. I think you could have come with us if you'd been nice to them for one minute, but I don't think you were even listening to me. You were too depressed about the bullhorn.

I'm sure I'm forgetting other things. There was so much, it was hard to keep track of it."

And yes, you're reading that email correctly—I turned down an orgy with me and four girls, because I was depressed about losing a bullhorn. That's the problem with alcohol; the bad decisions it causes you to make don't always lead to fun.

Halloween 2006

I was living in NYC at the time, but for Halloween this year I was back in Chicago. I hadn't really given much thought to my costume at all, and after rushing around last minute and not being able to find any costume at all that didn't suck, I decided to do the obvious thing: Go as Tucker Max.

In my narcissistic line of thought, this seemed brilliant. I had a famous website, it was about 10 months after *I Hope They Serve Beer In Hell* had come out and made the best seller list, and of course, since I knew who I was, everyone else should too. Plus, I wouldn't even have to get a costume—I'm always in costume. What a great idea!

In my mind, I saw the night going like this:

Girl "Did you come as Tucker Max?"
Tucker "Yep."
Girl "I love him!! He's so cool, I bet his poop tastes like candy!!"
Tucker "Well you can find out if you want—I'm the REAL Tucker Max!"
Girl "OH MY GAWD!!!! BATHE ME IN YOUR SPLOOGE THEN SHIT IN MY MOUTH!!"

It didn't work out like that. There were three problems:

1. Going out on Halloween wearing a grey t-shirt and jeans doesn't say, "I'm someone famous going as myself." It says, "I'm not wearing a costume."

2. I wasn't anywhere near as famous as I thought. The most common response I got when asked about my costume was, "Who the fuck is Tucker Max?"

3. Going as yourself—even IF you're *actually* famous—is still really fucking stupid and lame.

Here's the thing: I could've lived with all of those problems, because for the most part, I don't give a fuck. But the truly bad part about having such a lame costume was that I couldn't really even participate in the best part of Halloween—making fun of other people's stupid costumes—because they had a trump card to play: "Where's your costume?"

I figured out a way around it. Any girl that would point that out, I would re-direct with such ridiculous, nonsensical shit, she'd lose focus on my costume. Some examples:

A girl in a brightly colored dress with a unibrow painted on her face:

Tucker "What'd you come as, an Armenian?"
Girl "NO! What about you, what did you come as? Nothing?"
Tucker "Don't you worry about me. Who are YOU supposed to be?"
Girl "I'm Frieda Kahlo."
Tucker "Who's that?"
Girl "She's only one of the greatest painters ever!"
Tucker "Oh hell, I don't pay attention to all that artsy crap. I only like vaginas and violence."

From a sexy witch:

Girl "I don't get what your costume is."
Tucker "I'm a magician."
Girl "You aren't really dressed up as one."
Tucker "Well, I only have one magic trick. I drink 15 beers and talk about myself a lot."
Girl "That's not magic!"
Tucker "Then how else do I wake up next to girls I don't remember meeting?"

This girl looked like a slut, so I thought she was not in costume like me. Turns out she came as Christina Aguilera. It went downhill from there:

Christina "What is your costume?"
Tucker "How can you not like my costume?"
Christina "You don't have a costume."
Tucker "Yes I do, you just haven't figured out what it is."
Christina "What are you, a frat guy? A normal dude? A bad dresser?"
Tucker "Do you want to have sex?"
Christina "No!"
Tucker "Then I'm not telling you what my costume is."

This girl was hot, and had an awesome anime costume on that showed her tits off:

Tucker "Come over here and tell me about your sexy outfit."
Girl "You can't hit on me, you don't even have a costume on. That's lame."
Tucker "Well now . . . I'd call you a cunt, but I don't think you have the warmth or the depth."
Girl "You can't just say the c-word to me! You need to apologize!"
Tucker "OK, I'm sorry that you're such a cunt."

She went BALLISTIC. It was awesome. I'm truly unsure how I didn't get kicked out of the bar for that one.

That kind of shit is funny for a while, but it doesn't help with the end goal of Halloween: hooking up. D-Rock was with me, and we decided to try being nice. It didn't last long. This one girl was dressed as a monkey (NOT a slutty monkey, much to my disappointment), and kept asking everyone what their favorite animal was.

Monkey "What about you? What's your favorite animal?"
Tucker "The hooker."
Monkey "That's not an animal!"
Tucker "I'm not talking about fancy expensive escorts, I'm talking about the street hookers you see on 'COPS', the ones sucking dick for crack, those."
Monkey "What are you talking about? Those are people!"
DRock "Have you ever watched 'COPS'?"
Monkey "That's ridiculous! What's your favorite ANIMAL."
Tucker "Fine, fine. Then I guess . . . retards would have to be my favorite."
Monkey "RETARDS?!?"
Tucker "Oh Christ, you aren't going to claim they're not animals either, are you!!"

She found my jokes unfunny and offensive. In fact, she threw a fit, which was made funnier by the fact that one of her friends (who was laughing) came as a Catholic priest with a cabbage patch doll tied face-first to his crotch.

D-Rock was aghast at her hypocrisy. It's very difficult to argue with D-Rock—he's ridiculously smart, tenacious, and takes joy in crushing the half-baked mush that most people consider "thoughts." Her efforts to defend her position were made more difficult by the fact that she was an idiot.

D-Rock "Hold on—so it's not OK to make fun of retards, but your friend can mock the throat rape of a child?"
Monkey "That's different!"
D-Rock "How? Don't get me wrong—that is a brilliantly funny costume your friend has—but making light of the traumatic sexual misconduct of hundreds of Catholic priests upon thousands of innocent and defenseless children is at LEAST as offensive as implying that mentally handicapped are animals."
Monkey "How can you say that about mentally handicapped people?"
D-Rock "You mean, aside from the fact that ALL human beings ARE animals? Well, the fact is, most of the mentally handicapped have IQs that are commensurate with dogs, dolphins and chimps. I'm not making a joke about it; that's just a fact. Just like your friend's costume is joking about pedophilia—also a fact. Both jokes are predicated on the same idea—transgression of the obvious but unspeakable, and you are a hypocrite for liking one and not the other."
Monkey "No, it's different!"
D-Rock "Enlighten us how."

The crazy thing is, he was piss-wasted when he said this. Dude's ridiculous.

She tried to stammer through some preposterous whore logic, but D-Rock methodically shredded her. They went on like this for five minutes, and though it started out funny, it quickly became time to invoke the slaughter rule. I tried to help.

Tucker "Look, there's got to be some middle ground here: we can all agree that it's funny to sexually abuse retarded children, right?"

Even her friends laughed at that. She did not. If it hadn't been held together by her skull, I'm pretty sure her brain would've exploded. For a second I thought she was going to cry.

Tucker "Now now, don't cry—it'll be OK. My penis will solve all your problems."
Monkey "Fuck you and [to D-Rock] fuck you and fuck your terrible jokes!! I hope you die!"
Tucker "I must be reading you all wrong—are you saying that you *don't* want to hook up?"
D-Rock "Tucker, the only way she's gonna give you any pussy is if you adopt her cat."
Monkey "You are the most disgusting and vile thing I've ever met! I wouldn't touch you with a ten-foot pole!!"
Tucker "It's a shame that you don't feel the same way about carbs."

The fat joke lost her friends. Hit too close to home, I guess. Gluten addiction—the silent cock-blocker.

The best costume in the bar was this girl in a zombie outfit. The way she did it was amazingly elaborate and convincing, and she was pretty cute too.

Tucker "That's a great outfit."
Zombie "Thanks, I worked on it for a while."
Tucker "Do you think Jesus was the original zombie?"
Zombie "Jesus, like Jesus Christ?"
Tucker "No, Jesus my gardener. Of course Jesus Christ. You know, with the rising from the dead and what not."
Zombie "OH MY GOD YES! What a great idea!"

I was just trying to make a funny joke so she'd have sex with me, but she went nuts about all the similarities between Jesus and zombies, going on and on about Max Brooks books and *Shaun of the Dead* and basically giving me a tour of modern zombie scholarship, and where she thought

Jesus could fit into it. She really knew her shit. This was 2006, when the zombie craze was still kinda new and cultish, and at that point, I'd never met anyone so obsessed with the subject. I'm sure if I were a zombie nerd too, I'd have been in love. Unfortunately, I don't give a fuck about mystical creatures that don't exist, whether they are made up by religious fanatics or by sci-fi nerds. And I was too drunk to pretend otherwise.

Tucker "Look, I don't really care about the undead. I really only care about what your vagina feels like. You ready to get out of here?"
Zombie "What . . . no."
Tucker "PRAISE HIM!"

D-Rock and I drank a bunch more and acted like stupid jackasses to different groups of girls with varying success, until this one girl who was dressed as some sort of slutty pirate bumped into me. She was kinda cute, so I handed her my camera.

Tucker "Will you take a picture of me? Just me?"
Pirate "Are you kidding?"
Tucker "I don't joke about these things."

She thought this was hilarious. Game on. She and her friends were really cute, and started talking to me and D-Rock. Slutty Pirate was into me, and we were all having a good time—except for one girl. She was dressed as Velma from "Scooby-Doo", and was that one girl in the group of friends who is angry and rageful to the world, and expresses it through bitchiness to guys who try to talk to her friends. Even though she wasn't a traditional cock-block, just an angry bitch, girls like her can be as poisonous as an intentional cock-blocker. I start off by deflecting and parrying with her for a while as I hit on the slutty pirate.

Velma "Are you trying to flirt with my friends?"
Tucker "Of course I'm flirting with your friends. How else can I find a girl to have some crazy, hanging-from-the-chandelier-type sex with me?"
Pirate "Do you even have a chandelier? If not that's just false advertising and setting me up for disappointment."

Tucker "Well . . . no, actually I don't. And no one has ever pointed that out before. But I do have a pull-up bar. We can tie some string around my wine glasses, throw'em over, and I'll fuck you as you hang from that."

Pirate seemed into it, but Velma came back at me even harder.

Velma "What a ghetto chandelier. Not much of a baller, are you? Is that why you didn't wear a costume, you couldn't afford it?"

This was the line in the sand moment. With girls like Velma—the ones who have a confrontational, challenging approach to guys—you can't hesitate or back off. They set ego ambushes for men, and then emasculate them at the first sign of weakness. Not a problem for me, I could easily verbally destroy this girl. But I'm trying to seal the deal with her friend, so I can't be too mean, or I'll lose that hook-up.

Tucker "You know, the real Velma had a reason to be angry: She was a closeted lesbian who lived in a van with a dirty stoner, a talking dog, a closet homosexual, and his fag hag. What's your reason?"
Velma "I'm not angry."
Tucker "Oh please. You've been pissed off since we got here. What is it about your life that's making you so angry? Don't like your job? College jeans not fitting any more? Mom being overly passive-aggressive? Got played by a guy and can't get over it?"

The look in her eyes and her friends' reaction gave it away.

Tucker "That's it! You got played!"
Velma "No! No I didn't!"
Tucker "What happened, tell us. Come on, we're guys, we'll give you the perspective you aren't seeing."

Her friends filled us in as she pretended to pout, but of course she loved the attention and interrupted them to make sure every fucking detail was precisely correct. I don't remember the specifics of the story—like all girls, they endlessly elaborated on meaningless bullshit and made a two-minute story into a thirty-minute epic poem—but from what I recall, Velma really liked this guy she was casually seeing, but when he found out she was sleeping with other guys, he said mean things and there was a bunch of drama and the cow jumped over the fucking moon.

They could have summed up her problems with one sentence: Velma is a batshit crazy whore who is unwilling to accept the consequences of her actions, and instead decided to lash out at other people so she wouldn't have to face the reality of her broken and dysfunctional emotional life. I never understand why women think drama and bullshit are attractive to guys. They're not. I'm going to be real clear about this, ladies, so pay attention: Prince Charming doesn't come to rescue cunty lunatics.

Tucker "Everything that dude did seems reasonable. I don't see what the problem here is."
Velma "We weren't even officially dating! He should accept me exactly how I am and not care how many other guys I may be sleeping with or what else I do!"
Tucker "You don't see how someone could think you were being slutty, and be turned off by that?"
Velma "No!"
Tucker "Look, I'm not trying to judge you about it. I'm slutty sometimes too. And personally, I like sluts; they're the most fun. But if you're going to act like a slut, you should be ready for some guys to call you a slut."
Velma "I'm not a slut!"
Tucker "You're *not* a slut? Really? If you told your dad how many dicks have been in your mouth, what would he say?"

Obliterated. Verbal headshot, through the scope and out the brain, Carlos Hathcock style.

I wish I had video of her facial expression. You know that episode of "The Simpsons" where Ralph starts "dating" Lisa and tries to hold her hand, and she screams out in front of everyone, "I'M NOT YOUR GIRLFRIEND!" Then Bart plays the tape of it back and points out precisely where you can see Ralph's heart break? Her expression was like that: rage, contempt, anger, and deep sadness, all rolled into one. Not only did this exchange crush Velma to the point where she basically stopped talking, but her friends thought our little exchange was hilarious and essentially chose US over HER.

We spent the rest of the night drinking with them. The slutty pirate—who had no issue owning her sluttiness—led the mutiny and let me know pretty quickly that we were going to fuck.

Tucker "I have to warn you though; I like to take things fast physically, but slow emotionally."
Pirate "How fast and slow?"
Tucker "Well, for example, I'll fuck you in the bar bathroom right now, but won't tell you my middle name until at least our third date."
Pirate "So we're definitely going on dates?"
Tucker "Please . . . don't make me lie to you so I can sleep with you."
Pirate "Hey now—I never said I *wanted* to go on a date. I'm just making sure you aren't one of those guys who's gonna drag me to some shitty restaurant just because you feel guilty that we had sex."
Tucker "AHHAHAHAHHAH—oh, honey. We're going to get along great, don't you worry."

High on my victory, I must have ordered eight rounds of shots for me and all the girls, even Velma. And of course I gave toasts every time, each one more ridiculous than the last. This is the only one I remember:

Tucker "Every man dies . . . but not every man truly drinks!!"
Pirate " We still have a ghetto chandelier to fuck from. You aren't going to get too drunk to fuck, are you?
Tucker "Don't you worry about me—I don't get drunk, I get awesome."

Silly, overconfident Tucker.

Slutty Pirate and I stumbled out at about 3am, and since Chicago is a 5am bar town, D-Rock wanted to stay out. I just gave him my credit card.

Pirate "You're leaving your credit card with him?"
Tucker "I have to. He only has cash on him, and he's gonna spend it all on alcohol. If I don't leave him with something, he'll end up taking an ambulance home."

Now, I knew Slutty Pirate was slutty when I met her—that's one of the things I liked about her—but I was not prepared for what her actual vagina would feel like. She was so loose, when I got inside of her my penis was confused. I had been intent on fucking the hell out of her, but once I actually started, all I wanted to do was find a vaginal wall to rub against to create some friction. You can't start a fire by jabbing a stick in the air, no matter how fast you do it.

I don't remember finishing or what happened to solve the issue. We were both so drunk, I'm pretty sure I was just happy to be alive. I drank so much that night, it took five weeks off my life.

At some point, I wake up about ten seconds away from puking violently. I try to spring out of bed, but the girl is sound asleep on top of me. Doesn't matter, puke's coming, so I just keep going and she gets flung out of the bed with me, crashing to the floor. I'm not sure about this, but I think I stepped on her chest in my scramble to get to the porcelain. At the very least, she grunted like I had.

Thankfully, it was a pretty short and sweet puke. It all came out in a few hurls and was done, and I got back to bed and passed out immediately. Thinking about it as I sit here writing this, I honestly think I just left the girl lying on the floor when I came back to my room and crawled into my bed. It would make sense—who thinks about that shit when they're totally hammered and just puked up two gallons of alcohol and stomach acid?

All I wanted was to sleep for about three days, but of course, at 8am my phone rang several times.

“Mr. Max, this is Visa Fraud Protection, we’re calling about some suspicious activity on your card.”

When you wake up at 8am with your credit card company calling you because they think it’s impossible to drink as much as was charged to your card . . . you begin to understand what makes Halloween so awesome.

Fat Girls Cross Tucker, Hilarity Ensues

Some people have a misconception that I hate fat girls. That's just not true. I don't care about fat people one way or the other. If someone wants to go through their life with Oreo crumb dandruff and TV remotes lodged in the rolls between their FUPA and their gunt, that's their decision. So what if they're unable to climb a flight of stairs without risking massive coronary failure? As long as I'm not on the same staircase and their behavior doesn't affect me, how could I have *any* emotion about it, much less *hate* them for it? I can't and I don't.

What I DO hate are people whose annoying bullshit negatively impacts my life. You can be fat or skinny, tall or short, stupid or smart, man or woman—it doesn't matter. But if you, by your actions towards me, make my life more aggravating or difficult, then you get a negative reaction from me. Two of my favorite examples:

The Fat and the Furious

Occurred, January 2010

I was in NYC for a weekend and went to dinner with a girl I've known for a long time, "Laura." She's a cool girl, the type who has tons of friends from all different social groups and loves mixing them. Sometimes it works great and people who'd otherwise never meet make new connections;

other times, it explodes in her face, like a bukkake of anger and resentment. This was one of those.

The dinner itself was pretty basic, nothing memorable, until we were all finishing our entrees. Out of nowhere, this fat Asian girl—with a face so wide I thought she was Pokémon for a second—comes running up to the table screaming like Godzilla just stomped on her village. Apparently she knew one of the people at the table and got excited by the serendipity. Then, like she owned the fucking restaurant, took a chair from another table and wedged herself into ours. And I literally mean wedged: if the fit had been any tighter, she'd have squished her slanty eyes round. I lean in to the guy next to me (who was cool):

Tucker "Who the fuck is this fatty?"
Guy "No idea. I wouldn't call her fat though. I think 'bovine' is a better description."

Not content with just being fat and pushy, she was also talking at the most obnoxious volume possible to her friend, like there wasn't anyone else at the table. A waiter walked by—not our waiter, just a random waiter—and she SNAPPED HER FINGERS AT HIM to get his attention and give him a drink order.

I don't know about you, but I've had a lot of shitty jobs in my life, and many of them have been in the food service industry. Very little pisses me off like someone being a bitch to a waiter. Especially a fat bitch. Again, to the guy next to me:

Tucker "What the fuck is going on? Is this a joke? Seriously, maybe a high maintenance hot girl is tolerable, but what purpose does a high maintenance fat girl serve? She's like a human speed bump."
Guy "No . . . speed bumps serve a purpose."

Then she does something I've never seen before in my life: She reaches over to another girl's plate, picks up a carrot, and starts eating it. Not the girl she knew, mind you—the girl on the other side of her.

FatBitch "Are you going to finish that?" (she asks this as she chomps the food in her fat fucking mouth)
Random "Uh . . . well . . . uh . . . no, I guess not."
FatBitch "Cool, thanks."

But once wasn't enough—she started doing it to everybody else's plates! Examining them like some kind of leftovers buffet, then reaching over, picking things up off them, and eating them.

I am totally serious. Granted, these were the dinner scraps left on people's plates after they had finished, but still—she was eating table scraps. It was surreal. She was eating parsley, zucchini rinds, everything. I couldn't believe it.

Our waiter came back to the table with her fruity drink, just in time to see her reach across the table, grab a carrot off someone's plate and pop it in her mouth. His eyes got wide with shock, and he looked at the rest of the table, wondering—like all of us—what the fuck was going on. We had no answers for him.

Humans don't do this. DOGS DON'T EVEN DO THIS! You know who does this? Stockyard hogs. Fine, bitch. You wanna act like a pig, I'm gonna take you to slaughter:

Tucker "What are you doing?"
FatBitch "What?"
Tucker "That's what I'm asking you—what THE FUCK are you *doing*?"
FatBitch "I'm sitting here talking to my friend."
Tucker "Is this like a joke or something? This has to be a set-up. You're eating food off of other peoples plates!"
FatBitch [getting annoyed] "So?"
Tucker "So you think it's cool to be an annoying cunt and then SCAVENGE SCRAPS LIKE A FUCKING ANIMAL!!"

She gets visibly red, and spews her retort across the table, sending food shrapnel everywhere:

FatBitch "Fuck off!"

Laura was giving me desperate, pleading eyes. But it was too late for that. I'd gone into a full-on berserker's rage:

Tucker "Why are you rooting around in our leftovers like a fat cow? Is it that hard to fill your four stomachs? Or is that just how they roll in the barnyard you were fattened up in?"
FatBitch "I'm not fat!"
Tucker "Are you kidding? Your back fat could have its own bra! Look at yourself—you look like a Hefty bag filled with vegetable soup!"

That last comment got repressed snickers from the dude next to me and Laura. FatBitch can't really even respond, she's so flustered at this point, so she just stammers at me for a second.

Tucker "Sorry you'll have to repeat that, all I heard was, 'MOOOO-OOOOOO.'"

Her friend decides to chime in.

FatFriend "That's not funny! I hate assholes like you, with your degrading bullshit about fitting into societal standards!"
Tucker "Fit into societal standards?? I bet she couldn't even fit onto a veterinarian scale."

This enrages her, and she heaves her massive torso up, presumably so her internal organs aren't crushed by her back breasts, and yells:

FatBitch "You can't say that to me! I'm a person!"
Tucker "Do you know your eyes disappear when you get angry?"
FatBitch "That's because I'm Asian!"

Of course she didn't mean for that to be funny, but I absolutely lost it. The magnitude and timing of that bit of unintentional comedy was so fucking perfect, I almost puked from laughing.

This was too much for FatBitch. She picked up a piece of bread—the only thing left at the table she hadn't stuffed into her fat face—and threw it at me. SHE THREW BREAD AT ME. I'd fucked her up so badly, she could no longer speak, and had to resort to physical violence. It hit my water glass, but didn't even knock it over.

Tucker "With arms that size, you should throw a lot harder."

She screamed at the top of her lungs:

FatBitch "FUCK YOU, ASSHOLE!"

The whole restaurant stopped and stared at us. She stormed off, her friend leaving with her. Unwilling to give her the last word, I yelled the first thing that came to my mind:

Tucker "All right, all right—you can have the last ice cream sandwich!"

TRUE FRIENDSHIP

Occurred, September 2007

One night in Chicago, I was out with a friend of mine. This girl he was really into, but hadn't yet sealed the deal with, was coming out to meet us, and she was bringing her roommate. He asked me to play wingman for him, and I'd agreed because I owed him a big favor.

Friend "I need you to distract her enough that I can separate them. Can you do that for me?"
Tucker "Come on dude. Who are you talking to?"
Friend "It's not quite that simple. The roommate is super clingy with my

girl, and really insecure. You might have to hook up with her, or at least pretend to want to, to get them separated."
Tucker "You're saying this like it's a problem."
Friend "I have to warn you . . . she's, uh . . . not skinny. She's got a really cute face, and she's a cool girl. And I'll pay your bar tab."
Tucker "You'll pay my tab? Exactly how fat is she?"
Friend "Well . . . she's from Milwaukee. And she went to Wisconsin for undergrad. And she's lived in Chicago for three years now."
Tucker "You'd better be kidding."

Almost at that exact moment, they walk in together. His girl is good looking, with a great body. The girl I am supposed to run interference on could be the picture next to the definition of "Chicago Girl." Really cute face, upper body a bit thick but with the sweater she has on, it's passable, but her ass . . . oh my. From the waist down, you'd think she was a starting guard on the Bears. Her legs were basically just telephone poles. No ankles, no knees, just a hinged log of fat.

Tucker "I hate your fucking guts."
Friend "YOU OWE ME! YOU HAVE TO STAY! I'M PAYING YOUR TAB!"
Tucker "You'd better have a high limit on that card. I'm going to drink myself into a coma."

Like I said, I'm not always mean to fat girls. It's more about reacting to how someone is as a person, not just blindly attacking someone based on some physical attribute. The nice ones get normal treatment, the bitches get thrown in the trunk. And though I had to at least be nice enough to this girl to occupy her attention for the night, she actually turned out to be a cool person. Terribly insecure and a bit dumb, but fun and nice, so I was able to at least have a conversation with her. And she was a drinker, so we both got fucking plowed, which helped.

As we got drunker, she mistook my persistent and engaged conversation for attraction. Like most insecure girls, because she thought I was into her, that made her more into me. And she LOVED my sarcastic, asshole sense of humor, which of course, was like catnip to me. Without an audience,

I can be pretty average, but put me in front of a bar and someone who thinks I'm funny and gives positive feedback, and I'll dance like a minstrel.

I was making all sorts of jokes about all the various people in the bar, constantly cracking her up and enjoying her as my audience. I started in on this other fat girl who was chowing on a plate of nachos. I was dropping pretty basic fat girl jokes, shit like, "I wonder if she's going to unhinge her jaw when the entree comes," or, "That girl looks like the monsters you have to fight in HALO." She feigned dismay as she laughed:

Fatty "You're so mean!"
Tucker "Not mean, just honest."
Fatty "You should be nicer!"
Tucker "Whatever, fatties don't have feelings. They're not like real people."
Fatty "Yes they do! Do you think I'm fat?"
Tucker "Do *you* think you're fat?"
Fatty "I mean, I know I need to lose some weight. But I'm not fat. I don't think I'm like her . . . am I?" [pointing to the cow with the nacho plate]
Tucker "No, you are not as fat as her."

She got a look of happiness and contentment.

Tucker "Hold on—because you're not *the fattest* girl in the bar, you're OK with how fat you are? That sounds like Fatty Logic to me."
Fatty "No it's not! I'm not fat . . . am I? I'm not!"
Tucker "I don't know . . . here's one indicator: When you fly Southwest, how many seats do you have to buy?"
Fatty "SHUT UP! ONLY ONE!"
Tucker "OK, so you aren't morbidly obese. That's good. I guess."

We talked about her weight for a while, and though it was obvious she knew she was overweight, she kept trying to avoid facing the issue by re-directing the conversation to non-sequiturs.

Fatty "Well, what about who I am, like, as a person? Doesn't that count at all?"

Tucker "Of course it does. It's very important. In fact, I'm sure you have a lot of inner beauty . . . it's just hard to see under lots of blubber."
Fatty "I don't have blubber! I'm in shape!"
Tucker "Well . . . round *is* a shape . . . but it's not a GOOD shape for a woman."
Fatty "I'm not round! I go to the gym every day!"
Tucker "Do you do anything there?"
Fatty "YES!"

This morphed into a conversation about weight, BMI, societal perceptions of women, female body issues, etc., etc. I kept playfully teasing her, she kept taking the bait, and then we moved into the issue of guys, and how they interact with her.

Fatty "I don't understand, lots of guys will fuck me, but they never want to like, hang out with me at bars and take me out and stuff."
Tucker "They probably can't afford to take you to a meal."
Fatty "Shut up! I don't eat that much! Seriously though, why don't more guys want to take me out? I'm a nice girl. I'm fun."
Tucker "You're kidding right?"
Fatty "No. You don't think I'm fun?"
Tucker "That has nothing to do with it. Have you ever heard the saying 'Mopeds are like fat girls; they're both fun to ride until your friends see you'?"
Fatty "That's terrible!"
Tucker "It's also true. I can't be the first person who's told you this."
Fatty "I'm not fat! I maybe need to lose a few pounds . . . Seriously, you don't think I'm FAT do you? I'm only like . . . 165 pounds!"

This girl was fun and sweet and nice, and I really did like her as a person. But she was still a delusional fatty, and she was still engaging in some of the most desperate, validation-seeking behavior I've seen in a person. She knew she was fat, she knew I knew she knew she was fat. She just wanted to hear the opposite from me so she wouldn't have to feel bad in the morning about housing two Char dogs with everything and an 18-pack of Miller Lite the night before. This left me really with only one choice: playfully ignore the intent of all her questions and then openly fuck with her until she cracked.

Tucker "Just because it says '165 lbs,' on your driver's license does not make it true. I am 185, and I'd bet the bar tab that you're within 10 pounds of me. You're 165 if your thighs are hollow."
Fatty "I'll get on a scale right now!"
Tucker "Even if you are, you're like 5'6". I guarantee your BMI is past the 'Obese', and has moved into the 'Can Only Leave The House With A Crane'."
Fatty "I'm not 5'6", I'm 5'9"! And just because I'm a little overweight doesn't mean I'm fat!"
Tucker "AHHAHHAHAHAHAHAA! A 'little' overweight? I'm not blond, my hair is just yellow! I'm not a drinker, I just pound alcohol! Do words have meaning to you??"
Fatty "I'm not that fat!"
Tucker "I'll say this: I've played sports my whole life, I'm still in great shape, but if we were fucking, I wouldn't let you get on top because I'd fear for my internal organs."

That pretty much crushed her. She almost started crying. I had to quickly backpedal, because even though my buddy was close to closing his deal, he is a slow closer, and it looked like we were all going back to their place. I wasn't about to put all this grenade work in, only to lose it at the last minute and have the thing explode all over me, like some fucking amateur.

I tell her I was joking (I was, but only a little), and we get back on good footing. We all go back to their place, get some beers—I make sure it's light beer, because I'm trying to help here—and talk about other things. As soon as my friend and his girl go into their room, she brings the conversation back to her weight. She even goes so far as to ask me for diet advice.

Tucker "You can't go on a diet. Diets don't work. You have to change your lifestyle. But staying a healthy weight is not hard, you just have to make your health the starting point of eating decisions, and eat the types of things humans are meant to eat, and avoid the things we aren't."

Fatty "OK, like what?"

Tucker "Well, let's start with the easiest. You know what processed sugar is, things like high fructose corn syrup?"

Fatty "Yes."

Tucker "Stop eating it."

Fatty "It's not that simple."

Tucker "Yes, it is."

Fatty "But candy is so delicious!"

Tucker "Are you just baiting me into jokes now? Look, if you cut processed sugars out of your diet, and changed nothing else, you'd lose 10 pounds in three months. And if you stop eating white carbs altogether—things like rice, potatoes, bread, etc.—you'll lose 20. You could easily be 30 pounds less, changing really only those things, and not even working out more."

Fatty "But I love bread and potato chips!"

Tucker "Yeah, I can tell."

Fatty "Fuck you!"

From there, I spent an hour explaining eating and nutrition to her. I explained how all the common ideas behind diet and nutrition are wrong and perpetuated by a corporate machine that only cares about profit, I went over things like why humans shouldn't eat grains and processed sugars, why organ meats and certain fats are good for you, how certain types of exercise can be counterproductive, how to use controlled fasting to lose weight, gave her a basic introduction to the ideas of Weston Price and described paleo eating, etc. I'm not sure of the precise things I said to her—I was "grenade fucking" drunk and don't really remember, plus I'm constantly learning more about this. I can't remember where my informational state was at that point in my life.

I do remember that it was turning her on. I don't know if it was because she was impressed by my fancy smart talking, or because I was talking about food, or maybe I just smelled like bacon. But for whatever reason, she was very turned on by the end of my little instructional session.

Yes, I'll tell the truth: We fucked.

I blame alcohol and testosterone.

The next morning, my buddy collected me and we left. He tried to tease me about it:

Tucker "Fuck you, this is your fault!"
Friend "HAHHAHHAHAHAA! I never said you had to actually fuck her!"
Tucker "You took so long to close your fucking deal, I got too drunk to resist. You owe me asshole. You owe me. BIG. Like her."
Friend "It couldn't be that bad."
Tucker "Dude, I woke up afterwards to her eating a bag of Doritos in bed, watching 'Gilmore Girls'."
Friend "HAHAHHAHAHAHAHHAHAAHHHAHHAHA."
Tucker "She had the audacity to claim that she was going to start losing weight, but she wanted to finish the junk food she'd bought already. She said she didn't want to waste anything."
Friend "HAHAHHAHAHAHAHHAHAAHHHAHHAHA."
Tucker "The worst part is she didn't even offer me any."

The Deadliest Vacation

Occurred, January 2011

[**WARNING:** If you are one of the few people in America who have never seen the TV show "The Deadliest Catch", this story will make about 80% less sense to you, and you might want to skip it. The show is easy to explain—it's a reality show about Bering Sea crab fishermen—but that explanation does no justice to the characters and situations the show reveals. You should watch a few episodes not only to help you understand this story, but also because it's awesome. If you're one of those fucking people who've never even HEARD of "Deadliest Catch" because you don't own a TV, I'm not sure how to relate to you, and I'm not sure why you're reading this book.]

Part 1: The Invitation

Because my real email address is in my books and on my website (and has been there for almost ten years now), I get a lot of email. Every possible type of email you can imagine getting, I've gotten, as well as a bunch you'd never even think of. I thought I'd seen everything that can come over email. Then on November 5th, 2010, I got something I never could have expected:

From: Mike Fourtner <[redacted]@hotmail.com>
To: Tucker Max <tuckermax@gmail.com>
Subject: Deadliest Catch

Tucker,

Don't know if you watch much TV or not, but in your Beer in Hell book, you referenced American Chopper, so I know you watch a little bit of Discovery Channel.

My name is Mike Fourtner and I work on Crab Fishing boat out in the Bering Sea in Alaska. I work on a boat called the Time Bandit, one of the boats featured on Discovery Channels TV show Deadliest Catch. Just wanted to let you know that we are in the middle of Filming Season 7 of Deadliest Catch right now and your Beer in Hell book was quite the topic of conversation this season. A friend of mine, a girl of course, gave it to me to read. Lets just say that at 2 am while I'm in the captains chair driving the boat to our next set of crab pots, I would start laughing out loud and very hard!! A few times Andy or Johnathan, our captains, would get up to see what the commotion was and I had tears in my eyes as I was trying to explain what I just read!!!

We've all come to the conclusion that you are basically a very highly educated Alaskan Crab Fisherman at heart . . . . . . the only difference between you and us is the degree you hold . . . . . and the smarts to never have done what we do for a living!!

Not sure if you're into fishing or not, but if you ever come to Alaska we'll take you out for a day on the Time Bandit to catch some halibut or salmon. Bring the friends and we'll supply the Alaskan hotties. If we get enough of them, we might have a full set of teeth between all of them! Call if you ever want a trip on the Time Bandit . . . . .360-[redacted] Thanks for the laughs!!

Mike

I almost fucking shit myself in excitement. "Deadliest Catch" is, after "The Wire", my most favorite TV show ever. I've been watching this show for six years, and I've seen these incredibly tough guys battle ridiculous temperatures and 40-foot waves and all that shit to haul in the delicious crab that I love to eat so much. I'd be really excited if they were fans of my book, but fuck that—they're inviting me to fish with them? And not just any boat—this is the *Time Bandit*! That's the coolest boat on the show! Are you kidding? That's like Michael Jordan asking me if I want to play some pick-up basketball with him.

The first thing I do, before I get too excited, is make sure it's real. This is the internet after all.

> From: Tucker Max <tuckermax@gmail.com>
> To: Mike Fourtner <[redacted]@hotmail.com>
> Subject: Deadliest Catch
>
> OK, is this a serious email? Because I am a HUGE Deadliest Catch fan, but I don't want to get my hopes up in case this is a spoof. If it's real, I'm 100% in. If not, FUCK YOU, this was meaner than any shit I've ever said to any fat girl.

We went back and forth on email, and I gave him my number. Almost immediately, a 907 area code came up. That's Alaska. If this is a spoof, they went all out.

Tucker "Hello."
Mike "Hey! This is Mike Fourtner, from the *Time Bandit.* Is this Tucker?"

It was him. Unquestionably. That was the cheery, perpetually happy voice of Mike Fourtner, the *Time Bandit* deckhand I'd been watching on TV for years. I talked to him for a while, and then he told me to hold on, someone else wanted to talk to me. A gravelly voice I immediately recognized, but could barely understand, came on.

Johnathan "Hey, is that that fucker who wrote that book?"
Tucker "It's that fucker."
Johnathan "That shit was pretty funny. You coming fishing, fucker?"

For the entirety of this story, all quotes from Johnathan Hillstrand are approximate. It's hard to understand what he's saying, either on the phone or in person, because he sounds pretty much exactly like the Hamburglar. RUBBLE RUBBLE RUBBLE!

I ended up talking to both of them for like 30 minutes, and they were cool as fuck; exactly like they are on the show. We talked about the logistics of me coming up, and by the end of the conversation, not only had they invited me up in January for opilio crab season, they told me to bring friends. I immediately forwarded the email to Nils, then called him.

Tucker "This is real. I just talked to them on the phone; it's their voices. You can't fake 30 years of whiskey and cigarettes."
Nils "This is crazy! Who gets invited to go FISHING IN THE BERING SEA DURING CRAB SEASON???"

I ended up taking Nils, Bunny, and Drew Curtis (who went to high school with me and started Fark.com). I was tasked with figuring out all the logistical details for the trip up to Dutch Harbor. So I did what I always do when I have to do anything that isn't writing, fucking, or fighting—I made my assistant do it.

He spent an entire day figuring everything out, but came to an impasse. Apparently, there is only ONE company that flies from Anchorage to Dutch Harbor. And EVERY single seat on every flight was booked. For the ENTIRE month of January. Ian looked at boats; apparently it takes four days to get there. He even looked at chartering a plane, but it cost some excessive amount that I wouldn't have paid to drink with Jesus himself (and don't say anything about him not drinking—the ONLY thing he drinks in the Bible is wine; you know that guy had to be awesome to drink with).

Here I was, having gotten the invitation of a lifetime to go crab fishing with some of the only people on earth who I admire, and there was no fucking way to even get to where they were. I was crestfallen. I didn't know what to do, so I called Fourtner for ideas.

Mike "Every seat is booked? Makes sense; all the processing plants are flying their people in, plus all the Discovery crews, and they only run two planes a day. Shit—I just remembered: I haven't even gotten my flight in here yet for opies. I live in Seattle, I just come up here for king and opie seasons. Lemme talk to Andy and John, we'll figure something out."

Mike called me back the next day with a plan that blew me away: They were going to charter a plane from Anchorage, and we could ride on it. They'd meet us in Anchorage, we'd all get on the charter and fly to the *Time Bandit,* then ride on the boat with them to Dutch Harbor.

Tucker "We get to ride on the *Time Bandit*? Like out to sea and shit?"
Mike "Yeah. There's a ton that goes on that you don't see on the show. You see, we dock the boat in King Cove between king crab and opilio crab season, not in Dutch Harbor. It's about a day's ride or so. Wait till we ride the charter plane from Anchorage to King Cove. There's no airport at King Cove, it's just a gravel runway. There aren't even any buildings there—the one that was there blew down during a storm, and they never rebuilt it."
Tucker "Is this a joke?"
Mike "Oh no. Look it up on Google Maps. If you're really lucky, we'll have to buzz the runway the first time and scare off the bears. That's happened before."

I got off the phone and immediately typed "King Cove Airport" into Google Maps. Holy shit. He was right—there really wasn't anything there but a gravel strip and some utility sheds.

What the fuck have I gotten myself into?

I talked to Fourtner and Johnathan Hillstrand at least every other day for the next week or so as we sorted out all the details and travel arrangements. It was fucking incredible what these guys were doing for us. Granted, they had to charter the plane anyway, but they were going out of their way to help us get there, and aside from some phone conversations, they didn't even know me. What amazing people.

I had to do something to pay them back. Since we got to Anchorage on January 6th and left on the charter on January 7th, I figured I had to take them out that night and do it up right. I got in contact with a radio guy in the Anchorage area (who was friends with Johnathan), and in return for doing a bunch of radio stuff, he helped me set up a party at a bar, got a limo for us, everything.

Johnathan "There gonna be girls there?"
Tucker "Who the fuck are you talking to? I'll make sure the sturdiest whores in Alaska come out."
Johnathan "There better be. We're going out to sea, there's nothing but ugly for a month."
Tucker "I also got us a $500 bar tab at Chilkoots."
Johnathan "500!?!?! That's not nearly enough. We'll go through that in an hour."
Tucker "An hour?"
Johnathan "Oh yeah. Shots are $7 a piece up here."
Tucker "So?"
Johnathan "40 or 50 over the course of the night, it adds up."
Tucker "50 shots at $7 a piece is only $350, dumbass."
Johnathan "No you stupid fuck, 40 or 50 per person. There's ten of us, add in beer too. We've had 5 grand tabs before."
Tucker "50 SHOTS PER PERSON?!?"
Johnathan "Oh yeah. On a heavy night, we'll go through a bottle of Crown apiece. Sometimes more."
Tucker "Dude—that's insane!"
Johnathan "You sound like my fucking doctor."

Part 2: The Anchorage Party and the $200 Bear Mace Special

The day finally comes. We all arrive in Anchorage on various flights. I'm the last one to the hotel, and by the time I show up, everyone is already in the hotel bar drinking with the *Time Bandit* crew. Fourtner hands me a beer:

Fourtner "You all have no idea what you're in for, do you?"
Tucker "Have you ever thought that you're the one who should be worried?"
Fourtner "Yeah, yeah. Be ready—we're going to get you as drunk as 15 Indians tonight."

Almost immediately, Johnathan orders up a round of shots and hands one to me.

Johnathan "Here you go, pretend you're a man." It's Crown Royal, obviously. And Crown Royal is whiskey. And I fucking hate whiskey, for good reason.
Tucker "I'm allergic to whiskey."
Johnathan "Jesus Christ. Alright, get Little Lord Hayfever over here a vodka shot."
Fourtner "And some Benadryl too."

OK, OK. I can play that game too. Johnathan says something about what the set-up at the bar is, and how he hates big crowds or some bullshit.

Johnathan "So, is there like a VIP at this thing for us, or what?"
Tucker "A VIP!?! No one can touch the fancy crab boat captain!!"
Johnathan "I don't mean it like that!"
Tucker "I don't think this DIVE BAR in ANCHORAGE, ALASKA has a VIP room, but we can stop and get some velvet ropes for you if you want. We'll have the crew rope off a four-foot area around you and carry it around as you walk, so no matter where you go, you'll have your own VIP right there with you."
Nils "And Fourtner can stand there with a clip board, so when people come up to talk to you, he'll check and see if they're on the list. If not, they can't even speak to you."
Tucker "But it'll be empty. It'll just be an obviously blank sheet, but he'll check it for every person who comes up to talk to Johnathan or get a

picture or anything; 'What's your name? Lemme check. Nope, not on the list.'"

Nils "No, it'll be blank, except for two names; Moses and Rae Carruth's dead baby."

Tucker "And we can have someone who does nothing but yell out the rules for getting into the VIP, like 'Do you love chain-smoking, Crown-Royal-pounding, crab-eating captains? Is the sea your mistress and the bar your slut wife? Then step into the VIP. He has only two rules: no drama and no pants.'"

Johnathan "YOU CAN'T FUCK WITH ME LIKE THIS! I'M A CRAB BOAT CAPTAIN GODDAMNIT!!!"

We gave as good as we got for another hour or so, and once everyone warmed to each other, we started trading stories. Fourtner tells one about when he got tired of crab fishing, and decided to try something else for a while, so he got a job delivering mail. He hated it, and decided to quit and go back to fishing the day he found himself chasing a dog down the street, spraying its ass with mace as it ran away. Somehow the combination of alcohol and bravado leads Johnathan to bet me I can't get someone at the bar later that night to take bear spray in the ass.

Tucker "Are you kidding? Done."

Nils "Seriously though—can we go seal clubbing tonight?"

Fourtner "Probably."

Nils "Sweet! Do you think I could club a baby seal to death using another dead baby seal?"

Before we can go to the party at the bar where the tab and fans are, we have to go to the local radio station to do an interview. Damn near twenty of us take the limo and once there, they take me and Johnathan up to the booth for the interview.

It was a pretty standard interview; I showed up way too drunk, they begged me not to curse because of the FCC, I did anyway, etc. (you can see the whole interview on **www.tuckermax.com/kfat**). At the end, I had to get one more joke in at the drive-time DJ's expense:

Tucker "Hold on—you're a black guy from Mississippi, you can read AND you have a job? You must be the star of the state. They must have a statue of you down there."

That's not even a line I would write about, except for the reaction that Johnathan gave. He went out of the booth and said:

Johnathan "Did you hear what he just said on the air? He's fucking crazy!!"
Tucker "Hold on—you work on a crab boat in the Bering Sea, and you think I'M crazy?"
After that, it was on. We get to the bar and it is packed with people; I have no idea how many were there. I spent at least two hours doing nothing but taking pictures, signing shit, and doing shots with random people, progressively getting drunker and drunker. That's all fine and dandy, but I still had a bet to win. The bar had a DJ with a microphone, and he kept yammering all sorts of gibberish. I got hold of it and got to the important tasks at hand:

Tucker "Does anyone want to have their ass sprayed with bear mace?"

Shockingly, no one responded. This is Alaska; the unofficial state motto is, "someone here is ready to do anything for money":

Tucker "OK, for $100. Who will do it for $100?"

No one.

Tucker "Fine, $200. Who will take bear spray in the ass for $200?"

No takers.

Tucker "Jesus Fucking Christ, $200 is what America paid for Alaska! Someone here HAS to be willing to get bear spray in their ass for that price."

Finally, some random guy agreed.

Guy "$200 cash?"

I show him the money.

Guy "OK, I'll do it. I'm in the Army, I breathe CS gas all the time. How much worse can this be?"

Everyone cheers and gets ready to watch. Then I think about something I had not considered.

Tucker "OK . . . does anyone have any bear mace?"

Like an idiot, I'd left that part out of my calculations. Thankfully, we were in a place where bear attacks actually happen, and someone produced a canister of bear mace.

Tucker "We have the bear mace! Everyone, to the deck!!!"

Bear mace is just a very strong form of the same pepper spray you can buy for your key chain. But it's called "bear mace" for a reason: It is strong enough to *stop a bear.* Keep that in mind as I describe this next scene to you.

I don't know how many followed me outside, but there had to have been at least 150 people packed onto the deck. I pulled the dude aside and explained the rules to him. Completely arbitrary rules that I made up on the spot.

Tucker "OK, here's what you have to do: drop your pants and bend over. I'll spray the bear mace on your asshole, you get the money, and you're golden. Sound good?"
Guy "I have to drop my pants?"
Tucker "Of course, dumbass. I'm not spraying your clothes for $200. I can do that for free. The bear mace has to go onto your bare asshole."

He agrees. Right there, in 10-degree weather, this guy completely drops his pants, bends over right in front of me and spreads his ass cheeks. [This is the part of the story where I don't make a gay joke, and you make all the obvious ones for me. Well, I have two things to say: 1. Who do you think you are?, and 2. What gives you the right?]

I bend down and get about two feet from his butt—close enough to smell his poorly-wiped ass—all but stick the bear mace nozzle into his bunghole, and let loose. The guy took about a half-second of spray, then jumped in the air and turned around to face me. Since I am an asshole, I did the only thing that made sense: I kept hosing him down. In his crotch. And his chest. And face. Until the canister was empty. And then for some reason, I threw it over the fence, like I was trying to dispose of the evidence of a crime or something (and yes, there is video of this as well: **www.tuckermax.com/mace**).

Predictably, as soon as the bear mace hit the air, it cleared the area. The entire deck went from packed to empty in less than five seconds. Instead of running like everyone else, I did the smart thing, and immediately rubbed my itching eyes—with the very hand I used to spray the bear mace. Awesome. Great job, you fucking moron.

The next 30 minutes is something of a blur, probably because I couldn't see out of my swollen, capsaicin-filled eyes. Bunny said that I looked like I had the worst case of conjunctivitis ever, so she took me to the bathroom to wash out my eyes with clean water. At the time, I remember thinking, "Damn, if rubbing my eye with my finger did that, I wonder how fucked up the other guy is?"

I found out immediately:

The bar bathroom was small. It had two sinks, a mirror, one toilet and one long piss trough. There was a mop sink in the floor behind the door, with a nozzle about waist high. In the mop sink, completely and utterly naked, stood the bear mace guy with his entire penis and ballsack jammed up against the nozzle, sloshing arctic cold Alaskan water all over the bathroom, like when you put your thumb over a hose and crank the spigot wide open. I wasn't sure what to say, then I remembered something.

Tucker "You forgot your $200."

He slowly turned around to face me. I'm not sure he really even recognized me. His eyes were so red, I would say he was crying, but that's not accurate—it's more like his soul was pouring out of his ocular sockets. There was so much snot coming out of his nose, it looked like brain matter. You ever see video of people who get pulled out of collapsed buildings after earthquakes? He looked like one of those people. He was in so much pain and agony that shock had overtaken his senses and his body had port-holed and shut down all but the most basic survival systems. He looked like a living war crime.

He slowly turned around and maneuvered his ass so the water nozzle basically wedged in his butt. I reached the wad of bills out to him. As the freezing cold water shot through his ass crack and sprayed over the bathroom counter, he pitifully reached his hand out and took the money. Realizing he didn't have any pockets to stash his winnings, he just stared at me, then turned back around and put his balls back on the cold water.

I hope that this will be the only time in my life I gave a wad of cash to a naked man.

I took my iPhone out for a picture. Then I stopped. I just couldn't. This dude was in so much pain, he wasn't even human anymore. I had sprayed bear mace over every inch of his genitals—don't you think I'd caused enough suffering? I didn't ALSO need to get a picture of him to extend the suffering beyond that night and that bar. And yes, it is funny when I read that sentence out loud to myself.

After that, I somehow got roped into a conversation with a bunch of Alaskan natives. I said something about Eskimos or whatever, and then got a long elaborate lecture about all the different types of Alaskan natives. Apparently, there are *big* differences between Eskimos, Inlanders, Aleuts, etc.

Tucker "I don't understand—firewater is still firewater, even if it's cold. You're telling me there are different types of mud people?"

They didn't think this was as funny as I did. They kept trying to explain the differences to me, but it made no sense. Also, I was very drunk and didn't give a shit.

I have to say one thing about Anchorage though: There were WAY more hot girls than I anticipated. Well, there were at that bar on that night anyway. I was super impressed. My penis counted at least five girls it wanted to see the inside of.

So what happens? OF COURSE, some girl outside my penis's starting five ends up back in the limo with me. How? I don't know. Apparently, she was an aggressive bitch to the other girls, and I didn't notice. I blame alcohol. So does my penis. It refused to stay up with her when we tried to fuck in the limo. And then again when we got back to the hotel, though I'm not blaming alcohol for that one.

Girl "What's wrong?"

Tucker "I don't know."
Girl "What the fuck? You can't fuck me because you drank too much?"
Tucker "No, I don't think it's alcohol. I've drunk way more than this and still fucked without a problem; the only explanation is you. You're just not attractive enough to get my drunk dick excited."

I was kinda kidding, but not really. I planned to just go to sleep for a few hours, then wake up and fuck her later, no big deal. But she wouldn't stop annoying me and complaining. I told her to shut up and go to sleep. She decided she didn't want to. I laid her options out: comply or leave. She seemed to think there were other options for her, even though I distinctly listed only two. So I solved that problem: I took all of her shit and threw it out in the hallway. Clothes, purse, shoes, everything.

Tucker "You can be an annoying bitch if you want, but not around me."

Nils, Bunny and Drew were walking down the hallway as this happened, and watched her pick up her stuff and run off.

Drew "At least he didn't make her leave through the window. He's growing up."
Nils "Judging by her face, he should have."
Bunny "NILS! BE NICE TO THE WHORES!"

I posted this Tweet, then went to bed:

I shot bear mace into someones asshole, at a bar, for $200. Alaska is fucked up. There is no law here. This is beyond Thunderdome.

7 Jan via web ☆ Favorite Retweet Reply

Retweeted by IanClaudius and 100+ others

For some ungodly reason, Bunny, Nils, and I got up early the next day for breakfast. The only two people awake were Fourtner and Andy Hillstrand, Johnathan's brother and the other captain of the *Time Bandit.* Andy hadn't been out with us the night before, so instead of being hung over, he was fresh as the morning dew. And even though I'd watched the show for six seasons and seen every episode and knew that Andy was a funny dude, I wasn't prepared for exactly how fucking hilarious he was in person. We spent about 90 minutes listening to him tell some of the greatest stories I've ever heard. Highlights:

- What it was like growing up with four brothers in Alaska:

"We weren't poor, but this was Alaska, so there wasn't much up there. All we had to play with was sand and rocks basically. So we'd put a bunch of sand and rocks into tube socks and hit each other with them. We called'em 'Wammy socks'. Or, when those broke, we'd just have rock fights with trash can lids as shields."

"My dad gave all of us Swiss Army knifes once. It was our prized possession. Then Neal and my other brother popped a bunch of his buoys with it, and he took each one from us, and broke the blades off, and gave it back. Ever seen a Swiss Army Knife without anything sharp on it? Pretty useless."

"That's actually how our boat got its name. Our dad used to say 'I got these five retarded little midgets, I might as well just call the boat the *Time Bandit.*' It's based on that movie. And the fact that he thought my brothers and I were all retarded midgets."

- On his brother Neal Hillstrand, who is also on the show (but you don't see as much of him as you do Andy and Johnathan):

"Neal's nickname growing up was 'Neal the eel'. It was because Mom would always find eels in his pockets when she'd wash his britches. She finally asked him why the hell he had eels in his pants—it was because he was eating them. He'd spend days away from home, just hanging out on the beach, cooking eels he'd catch."

• On his father's parenting techniques:

"Our dad owned a few fishing boats and a cannery. He was tough on us too. He made us work on his boats pretty much from as early as I can remember. He laid it down for us, 'You're going to work, and if you don't like it, go upstairs and suck on your mommy's tit.' I was like, 'Dad, I'm six years old.'"

"Dad had a little anger problem too. He basically hired and fired pretty much everyone in Homer, Alaska several times, including us. One time Johnathan and I fucked up something real bad, and he got real pissed, 'You're fired, and you're out of the family. Change your fucking name!!' I had to move into an abandoned shed out back with Johnathan for six months. We had a fucking blast back there though."

"We have the *Time Bandit* now, but he was such a fucker, we not only had to buy it from him at market price, he wanted to lend us the money but charge us more interest over what I could get a loan from the bank for. I told him to fuck off and took the loan from the bank."

"Even though we bought the boat from him, he'd still get pissed at us every day, and still try to fire us, 'I'm taking the boat back!' I was like, 'We bought it from you fucker, you can't!'"

"Let's see, what were some of his other words of wisdom? He used to say things like, 'I gave you every means in life to kill yourselves and you've all failed.' Or he would constantly tell us that 'You're all mistakes.' He said he wanted daughters because they were cheaper to raise."

• On dealing with the Alaskan natives:

"The old time fisherman used to shoot every seal and sea lion they saw. Hated them, because they fucked with the lines. But we can't really hunt most of these animals anymore; they're protected now. But if you really want, you can probably get ahold of a dead seal or something, you just have to get it from a native. The natives, they can kill pretty much anything they want. They'll trade you a seal pelt for a bottle of whiskey still to this day."

"Yeah, some of the natives are kinda messed up. I've seen them rape their buddies. I'm not kidding. They'll get that drunk. One time we were walking back from the bar in Homer, and we saw something moving under the dock. I thought it was a sea lion or something, and we got closer, turns out it was an Eskimo. He was kicking his buddy to see if he was awake, and he wasn't, so then he just stuck his dick in his ass. He was raping his buddy, right there under the dock!!"

PART 3: *THE TIME BANDIT*

After breakfast, we got all packed up and went to the airport for our charter flight. Despite the gallons of poison I poured into my stomach the night before, I was feeling great. The rest of the crew, not so much. For example, Eddie was still so hung over, he puked in the parking lot:

Yes, that one picture is Eddie picking up the eggs that came out with his puke. Sophisticated, these crabbers.

One of the really cool things about flying a charter was that we didn't have to go through security or any shit like that. As we sat in the plane and waited for everything to get loaded and the pilots to start it up, I noticed that the crew was visibly anxious and worried.

Tucker "What are you guys afraid of? It's just a charter plane."
Fourtner "Man, these things make me nervous. I don't want to die in a plane."
Tucker "Fuck that. Plane death is way better than dying by falling into the Bering Sea. If we smash into a mountain, that's it, it's over in a second. If you fall into the Bering Sea, you have two minutes to consider how stupid you are as you freeze to death."

They weren't convinced.

As we approached the island, we banked multiple times, then headed down through the clouds for what seemed like forever. Finally we broke through, 30 yards above the ocean, and about 100 yards from a huge mountain to our left. It seemed close enough to touch.

As we flew around the island to make our final approach, Bunny's eyes were wide as saucers. I looked back at her, and she said in the most pitiful voice I've ever heard, "Where are we going to land? There's nothing here!"

Fourtner had mentioned in an email earlier that the place we were flying, King Cove, was a pretty desolate place. But that doesn't really do it justice. Here are some pictures:

We eventually did find the airport, and landed. On the GRAVEL runway. We came to a stop near the only thing at the airport, a parked truck all by itself. It was the one Fourtner asked the locals to bring out for us. Complete with keys in the ignition.

Tucker "They just left it there with the keys in the ignition?"
Fourtner "Yeah man. There's nothing to worry about, you can't steal it. There's five miles of road on this entire island."

King Cove is where the *Time Bandit* is docked between fishing seasons. It's extremely small. It was half dock, half town. As far as I could tell, pretty much all of the buildings in Cold Bay (the name of the town) were made of corrugated metal sheeting, including the grocery store. The store had a surprisingly wide variety of food considering it was on the ass end of the world. You had to pay dearly for it, however. For example, bags of Doritos were "on sale" for $3.50, marked down from $7 each. Apparently the threat of bears is very real in King Cove. In fact, a bear actually ATE someone in Cold Bay in the '90s. Like, ATE him, in broad daylight. It's on Wikipedia, so it must be true.

Then we got our first glimpse of the *Time Bandit.* I'm not sure what I expected, but the boat itself is both smaller than I thought it would be, and much more imposing. It's smaller because it's only like 115 feet long, which isn't that big for a commercial fishing vessel. But it's more imposing because you see all the equipment up close, and you realize even more than before that it is no fucking joke. You touch the massively heavy crab pots, your foot slips on the deck—everything becomes real. This wasn't a TV show anymore. This was real iron and steel, and it was slimy and wet and icy. In 30-foot seas and 50-mph winds, every single thing on the deck of this boat could kill me.

The inside was seriously cramped. If you've seen the show, you know what the boat looks like, but man, it is really tiny on the inside, almost like a submarine. I mean, I was not prepared for the fact that basically, there isn't enough room in the galley for everyone on the boat to be in there at once.

We all got onto the boat, stowed our stuff away, and then watched the crew get everything settled and situated for the 24-hour ride to Dutch Harbor. The guys were running up and down the mast, climbing over the pots, tying things down, checking the crane, all kinds of shit. I watched them and explored the boat and took everything in—the cabins, the galley, the engine room, the steam room, the storage tanks, etc.—I watched everyone get squared away, and I re-asked myself the same question that everyone asks when they watch the show:

"Could I do this job?"

Here I was, on the fucking boat, with the guys who actually do it, watching them go through everything—and I have to say, at that moment in time, I was starting to think that maybe the show overstated and overdramatized crab fishing. Maybe it wasn't so hard. I mean, I still respect the hell out of these guys—but given some time to get used to things, I was pretty confident I could do it.

By the time we pulled off, Neal Hillstrand—the third Hillstrand brother on the boat who gets way less camera time than Johnathan or Andy because he curses so much, but is fucking hilarious as you'll come to see—had cooked up a fantastic dinner. I was shocked that such a huge spread could come out of such a small kitchen, but man, it was not only abundant, but delicious too. I ate a bunch of food. Drew wasn't eating as much.

Tucker "What's wrong dude, you don't like it?"
Drew "No. Just worried about getting seasick."
Tucker "You won't get seasick."
Bunny "Me too. I'm not going to eat."
Tucker "Oh my God, what pussies. Bunny, you better not be a pukey mess and embarrass me!"

We left King Cove at 5pm, and expected to get into Dutch Harbor at about 5pm the next day. It got dark fast and we sat around and watched movies and hung out for a while. Maybe an hour into the trip, we hit some choppy seas. Nothing horrible; like five-foot seas. But it was very noticeable to me, and the room was moving a lot.

On the show, the fishermen are always loud and obnoxious and hard-living. And that characterization is true. But they are also understated in how they deal with people they don't know. They don't tell you what to do, because they aren't that type of men. That's why they're fishermen— because they don't like taking orders from people. But they will tell you what you *should* be doing, even though it's in subtle, understated terms. As the seas rose, Bunny didn't feel well. And I wasn't feeling the best either.

Neal "Maybe you guys should lie down."
Scottie "Lying down helps you get over seasickness."
Tucker "Nah, I'll be fine. How bad can it be?"

Nils and Bunny took their advice and lay down. I didn't, because clearly I know more about the sea than people who have fished their whole lives.

As time went on, I got worse and worse. But I tried to ignore it. Some people learn by watching others. Some learn by making mistakes. I learn by getting my ass handed to me. Feeling really sick, I decided I needed fresh air, so I went out on deck.

At 7pm, the dark, empty deck of a crab boat is a strange place. It's pitch black and there's no land, no life, nothing whatsoever. It's complete, barren, unforgiving void. It's just plain disturbing. The water frothing beneath the sides of the boat is literally black. Dying that way—by falling in and freezing—must be horrific.

I didn't have much time to ponder this, because almost as soon as I got out there, I realized I had to puke. I went to the rail, and booted all over the side. As I recovered from my vomiting, I was still leaning on the rail. The boat hit a wave, nothing big, but big enough that I lurched a little, and found myself having to hang on to not fall over. Then I realized something:

I am leaning over the side of a crab boat that is moving pretty quickly through the Bering Sea. It's completely pitch black out. The water is 34 degrees. I am alone out on this deck.

Umm . . . does anyone even KNOW I'm out here?

Even though I was no longer in any immediate danger, I threw myself back from the rail like it was a pissed-off rattlesnake, then scrambled inside the cabin, and upstairs to the wheelhouse. Andy was at the helm, and Drew was talking to him. Apparently, I did not look good.

Drew "Jesus."

Andy "You OK man?"
Tucker "No. I just puked."
Drew "I didn't hear anything."
Tucker "I was out on deck. I was there for about 15 seconds before I realized that maybe I shouldn't be out there by myself. If I fell overboard, you'd never know, would you?"
Andy "You wouldn't believe how long it takes greenhorns to figure that one out. If you fell off the deck without us knowing, you might as well just swim to the bottom so you can die faster because there's no way in hell we'd know you were gone in the first place."

I had little time to think about how close I came to potentially dying, because I had to puke again.

Tucker "Andy do you have a garbage can over there or something?"
Andy "Just open the window and hurl right out."

I sat in the other captain's chair, opened the window, and let loose a stream of vomit like I hadn't done in years. This was an old-school, body-getting-revenge-for-too-much-drinking type of vomit. I am not sure how long I held my head out the window, or how much I puked, but it felt like forever. I looked at the clock, wondering how much longer we had left on the trip. Judging by how much pain I'd been in, it had to be like 2am or something.

It was 8pm. Only three hours into the 24-hour trip. FUCK.

At some point, Neal replaced Andy on wheel watch. Drew was up and as chipper as could be, talking and hanging out. Drew is a great guy, but goddamnit if I didn't want to punch him right in his smiling fucking face. There is nothing worse than being vomitously ill and having to be around someone who is happy.

Drew "How's it going?"
Tucker "Wonderful. Have you been sick yet?"
Drew "Not yet. I feel fine. I'm surprised as hell too, I figured I'd be death on wheels the entire way."

I promptly popped the window open, stuck my head out and puked again.

Neal "Tucker's barkin' at the seals."
Drew "Pretty sure he's scared em all off."
Tucker "Oh shit. I puked right on the *Time Bandit* logo."

I hadn't noticed it before, but I had hit the skull and crossbones logo dead in the face. It looked like the logo had booted.

I eventually stopped puking. Mainly because I had nothing left in my body. I went downstairs and lay down as the waves violently crashed over the galley portholes. Bunny was worried we'd sink. I'd have accepted death if it made the puking stop. I had to hold on to the bunk sides to stay put, but eventually I fell asleep.

I don't know how long I was asleep, but I do know what woke me up: a crash of glass, a LOUD horn blowing in my ear, and someone screaming about getting on the survival suits. I jumped up to find a broken coffee pot on the floor and Johnathan laughing his ass off at me.

Johnathan "Did you break that, you fucker??"

He was obviously kidding—the coffee pot broke because we hit a rogue wave that knocked it off the counter—but I was so dehydrated, sick, and confused that I honestly thought for a second I was in trouble. Then we hit another wave, and I had to puke again. Fast.

I ran into the bathroom and puked right in the toilet. It was one of those awful vomits that are nothing but bile. I heard some scrambling outside, and in between vomits, looked up to find Scottie Hillstrand (Johnathan's son), filming me vomiting in the toilet. Thanks guys, that's awesome.

I couldn't sleep anymore. It was around 7am, and still pitch dark outside, so I went up to the wheelhouse. Andy was back at the helm, and Drew and Fourtner were up there too.

Drew "Tucker, I've heard of people looking green with sickness before, but this is was the first time I've ever actually seen it in person."
Tucker "Fuck off. Have you puked?"
Drew "Nope. I feel great. How many times for you now?"
Tucker "Five. I think. I want to die."
Andy "You're lucky we left yesterday. There's a storm behind us, if we'd have left today, we'd have 15- to 20-foot seas the entire way."

The waves hit the boat in groups of seven. The first one wasn't too bad, the second one was worse, the third progressively worse, and so on. By the time the seventh wave hit the boat, the *Time Bandit* was literally 90 degrees different from lowest to highest pitch. At the low side, the window next to me was almost even with the sea. At highest pitch, the window was like 60 feet above the sea.

Tucker "So let me get this straight. You guys are out on the deck crab fishing in waves like this?"
Andy "This is nothing. It gets a lot worse than this."
Fourtner "Oh man. I'd pay good money if our whole season was like this. Man that would be great, wouldn't it Andy?"

He sounded almost wistful. About waves that seemed like fucking tsunamis to me.

Tucker "What are these, like 40-foot waves?"
Andy "No no no. They're probably 10–15 footers. Maybe a 20 every once in a while."
Tucker "Oh fuck off!! Are you kidding? This isn't bad? What's bad? How much worse before you stop fishing?"
Andy "Oh probably 40-foot seas things start to get pretty dicey. At 50-foot seas, I pull'em in."
Tucker "50-FOOT SEAS!!! Three times higher than these? How high is that? That's like over the flag pole!"
Andy "Yep. That's what people don't understand who watch the show—it's not the fishing that's hard. It's doing it on a pitching deck in 40-foot seas that's hard. The cameras are bolted to the deck, so they pitch and roll with the boat. You see the guys slip and slide, but you don't see the boat move. They have to do it that way, or the viewers get seasick watching the deck go all over the screen, but people don't understand the degree of difficulty that the pitching deck provides."
Tucker "No fucking shit. This is ridiculous. Andy, you know that job you never offered me, as a crewman? I'm turning it down."
Andy "Ha. Really sorry to hear that man."
Tucker "No fucking way could I do this. You know, watching this on TV

you think, 'Oh sure I could do that if I had to.' Absolutely fucking not. I could not do this."
Fourtner "Hey Tucker. Would you rather be seasick for 24 hours or bang a fat chick?"
Tucker "I'd rather fuck a whale. Literally. An actual honest-to-God whale."
Andy "We've got those out here too."

The flag on the front of the boat, which had been new when we left King Cove, had started to shred. I'd heard Fourtner make reference to winds that would cause the flag to shred but I thought it was some kind of figure of speech or something. The flag was actually shredding itself in the wind.

Drew "How fast are the winds going out there?"
Andy "Hey Fourtner, lean out there and find out how fast the wind is blowing."

Fourtner stepped outside with a wind gauge (with just shorts and t-shirt on). He stepped back in, a puzzled look on his face as he examined the meter.

Andy "How fast is it blowing out there?"
Fourtner "I don't know."
Andy "Didn't you just take a reading?"
Fourtner "Yeah. It broke."

The plastic fan on the top of the meter that measured wind speed was broken. Two of the fan blades had blown off. The meter said "67.3mph," which was the last measurement before the wind, which was apparently moving much faster than that, had shredded it.

Something you may not understand about this conversation—Andy and Fourtner weren't being dramatic or fucking with us or bragging or anything like that. The way they talked about these conditions—which seemed like something out of *The Perfect Storm* to me—was totally matter-of-fact. This was nothing to them, because they really do work in conditions WAY worse than this. I'd seen it on TV, so I knew that, but

I'd never felt it—and *feeling it changes everything.* You can watch all the porn on the internet, but until you stick your dick in a pussy, you can't really understand why everyone on earth is obsessed with sex.

At that very moment, I felt ill again. I popped open the window and puked my brains out. Right into the wind. Ever heard the phrase pissing into the wind? Well, I mouth-pissed into the wind.

Tucker "BLEEEEAAAAARGHHH AAAAAAAAAAHHHH FUCK ME ITS ALL OVER THE PLACE."

Everyone collapsed into hysterical laughter. Apparently, looking at vomit all over my jacket and face was HILARIOUS. Thanks guys, you can all go die. There are many, many people on Earth who would have paid good money to watch me get my comeuppance in this manner.

Andy "Hey Tucker next time you need to puke, do it out the starboard side of the boat."
Tucker "What's starboard?"
Fourtner "Jesus Christ."
Andy "The side where the wind isn't blowing directly into. The opposite side of where you just puked."
Tucker "OK, right. Good idea."

About an hour later, I needed to puke again. I tried to cross to the other side of the boat but it was pitching so hard I made it about halfway across before I was literally thrown back to the port side.

Tucker "Is there a garbage can over there?"
Drew "Yeah lemme get it."
Andy "Nah don't waste a perfectly good garbage bag. Open that door behind you where Fourtner was and puke out the back."

I opened the door, leaned out, and then the boat pitched hard. I fell back in the cabin. Nils was in the room as well by then, and both he and Drew started to head over to help.

Andy "Just wait. He'll be fine. But if he falls out, then go over there—fast."

I eventually got to the door, leaned waaaaay out on the deck, and hurled with all my might. Into the wind, again. Except this time, because I was doing it through a door, half of it blew back into the cabin.

Tucker "BLEEEEAAAAARGHHH AAAAAAAAAAHHHH FUUUUUUUU UUUCK GOD FUCKING DAMMIT."

I gave one last huge hurl, slammed the door shut, and held onto the doorknob for stability. Not only was I covered in puke but I was drenched head to toe in sweat, rain, and seawater spray. I looked like a drowned rat, staring down at the floor at his puke blowback in resigned horror. Fourtner was choking he was laughing so hard.

Tucker "Andy, I am so sorry about this."
Andy "No worries man. You're not the first to do that; you won't be the last. Plus that was entertaining."
Tucker "I wasn't even this bad the first time I got drunk."

I collapsed into the other chair, exhausted, wet, covered in vomit, and tired as hell. My complexion was a distinct shade of green. This inspired Captain Jonathan, who decided that now would be the perfect time to blast me with a full can of silly string. PSSSSSSHHHHT. I didn't even twitch. I just sat there.

Jonathan "OK Tucker, give us your ATM card and PIN number or we're staying right here out at sea."
Tucker "Jonathan, if I thought for even a minute that would actually get me on land, I'd fucking give you everything I owned right now."

You don't think of fishermen as environmentalists. But really they are. If anyone would care about the environment, it's the people who deal with it every day and make their living directly from it. Two exchanges we had as we crept into the dock really brought this point home.

We passed another shipping vessel, something that looked way different from the crab boats. Fourtner said they were net draggers. He called them "drag fags."

Fourtner "They deploy these massive fishing nets that have wheels on the bottom and roll along the bottom. I hate those things. Those guys absolutely obliterate the sea floor. They just destroy every goddamn thing in their path."
Drew "So environmentalists aren't wrong about those ships then?"
Fourtner "Nope. They're terrible."
Drew "How come they don't regulate them more tightly then?"
Andy "Because they feed 66% of the world's population with drag fishing like that. That, and they've got real good lobbyists."
Drew "On the show I see you guys having to measure the size of crabs to see if they're big enough, and you also toss back all the females. They don't regulate the by-catch at all on the draggers?"
Andy "No point. It all comes up dead."
Fourtner "Fucking drag fags."

Of course, they aren't always environmentally conscious. Later on, we were taking pictures of some ducks.

Jonathan "Those ducks out there, they're endangered."
Drew "Really? Why's that?"
Jonathan "Because they're delicious."
Neal "Taste like tenderloin."

Tucker "How do you know what they taste like?"
Neal "They weren't always protected."

PART 4: DUTCH HARBOR

I could probably write a 20,000-word article just about Dutch Harbor, and the city of Unalaska that surrounds it. It's one of the most contradictory and compelling places I've ever been. It's both completely modern and really old at the same time, but in weird ways. For example, it was an important base during World War II (it was the only place in America other than Pearl Harbor that the Japanese bombed). The island is covered in all sorts of abandoned, overgrown pillboxes and bunkers. Many of them sit next to huge logistical cranes used to load massive freighters. It's the largest fishery port in the United States; the island is basically nothing but boats, warehouses, and processing buildings. But only about 4,000 people live there year-round (the population more than doubles during certain fishing seasons, due to all the people who fly in to work at the processors). There are only seven miles of paved road on the whole island, but there are at least a thousand vehicles there. The airfield is so small they have to close the road that runs next to it when planes take off, so they don't clip passing cars. There are only two bars, but they're always packed. The island is incredibly naturally beautiful and filled with all sorts of endangered and protected animals that all but interact with you. We would eat breakfast every day next to an inlet where otters were diving for shellfish and dozens of eagles would perch not even ten feet from the windows.

The beauty is surrounded by depressing, industrialized blight and decay; nothing is what it initially seems. When we landed, everyone was so stoked to see an eagle. I snapped like twenty pictures the first day. I eventually stopped. There are fucking eagles everywhere. There are so many eagles on the island, they outnumbered all other birds. Not only that, they're disgusting, vile creatures. They basically live out of the dumpsters. Johnathan said he was so tired of looking at them, he hated eagles now. He called them trash birds, and joked that he tries to hit them with his truck. To me, this picture perfectly symbolizes Dutch Harbor:

I know I kinda expected that Dutch Harbor would be this raucous, drunk brawl of violent fishermen, but it wasn't at all like that. It was a pretty chill week, actually. We spent six days and nights in Dutch Harbor, and a lot of that time was spent exploring the island, or taking pictures or just hanging out and relaxing. Part of the reason for this is that the nature of crab fishing has changed dramatically with the implementation of seasonal quotas over the last decade. They've effectively cut the crab fleet from 250 boats to 80 boats. That's a lot fewer drunk fishermen. Also, Dutch Harbor authorities made a conscious effort to eliminate that sort of behavior. They even closed the legendary bar on the island, The Elbo Room. Johnathan said he knew of at least 10–12 killings that happened at the bar, and that he was glad it was closed, "Eventually, you get tired of picking the glass out of your skull from people hitting you in the head with beer bottles."

But even though Dutch Harbor wasn't like the old days any more, we did drink. A lot. And there were some pretty funny stories.

Nils & Keith

The second night on the island, we were in the hotel bar. Pretty much everyone you know from the show was there too: the *Time Bandit* crew, the Harris Brothers, Eddie the Samoan, Keith and his brother, Sig, and the *Northwestern* crew, you get the idea. Here's the thing about them: Everyone is pretty much exactly like they are on TV, which makes it pretty much the opposite of all other reality TV. All the personality traits and conflicts and foibles you see—they are all real.

Except for one person: Keith, the captain of the *Wizard.*

It's not that Keith was fake or anything like that. The thing about Keith you don't realize from the show, because you rarely see the captains or the crews in the same room together, is that he REALLY stands out from the rest of the fishermen. For example, everyone in the bar either drinks beer in bottles, or whiskey, or both. Keith drinks red wine. And wears a turtleneck. And has a huge '70s mustache. And just has a way about him that is very different. If I hadn't seen the show, I'd think he was the general manager of a chain restaurant. Something about him was just . . . off.

I couldn't pin it down until one night it was pretty close to last call and Nils, Drew, Bunny, and I walked out of the hotel bar. Keith was in the lobby talking to Fourtner, who was waiting to give Captain Andy a ride back to the *Time Bandit.* We said hi to Fourtner, and Keith walked past us and right up to Nils. I'm going to transcribe the dialogue as I heard it, and let you make your own judgments:

Keith "Hey there. How tall are you? Are you taller than Fourtner? I think you are."
Nils "Sure am. I'm 6'5"."
Keith "Mmm, I like you tall boys. Especially when you throw back those shoulders and stand tall like that."
Nils "Uh . . . yeah."
Keith "You guys can really push stuff around, tall guys are always so big and strong."

Nils "Nice to meet you."

I couldn't believe what I just heard. Fourtner's eyes went wide, like methhead, anime wide. Drew got visibly nervous. I just kept walking.

Tucker "Did that just happen? I have the worst gaydar in the world . . . but did what I think happened, just happen?"
Nils "Oh yes. I grew up in the Bay Area, stuff like that used to happen to me all the time."

Look, I'm not making any accusations or saying anything. Keith is married with kids. I'm just telling you what happened. That exchange is verbatim, and you can take whatever you want from it.

But of course, I'm an asshole, so I didn't let it end there. The next night, we were in the same bar, all drinking and talking and having fun, like always. I decided to take it up a notch, so I called over the waitress.

Tucker "We'd like to send Keith a glass of red wine, what's his favorite?"
Waitress "Oh, Liberty School cabernet." She didn't even pause. She knew it immediately.
Tucker "Awesome. Put it on our tab, and tell Keith it's from 'the tallest guy in the room.'"
Waitress "The tallest guy in the room?"
Tucker "He'll understand."

About thirty minutes later, the waitress returned to our table. With a Coors Light for Nils, from Captain Keith.

Johnathan "Jesus Christ."
Tucker "Dude, you're so in."
Nils "I don't want to be in!"

The funny part about this whole charade was that when we would tell other boat captains and crews about it, they steadfastly *refused* to believe it, even when Fourtner would back us up. Most of them can't stand that floating pedophile— some, like Johnathan, openly loathe Keith—but not one of them was biting at our story. It was kind of heartwarming, in that charming, old school, hyper-masculine kind of way. Sure, Keith is a total fag, but it's not like he's a gay or something!

Johnathan and the Horses

Johnathan Hillstrand seems like this hardcore badass who'd just as soon fight you as look at you. And that's true. But make no mistake, he's a total softie to the people he cares about. When he was at my house in Austin for the Super Bowl this year, I swear to God he spent more time watching the Puppy Bowl than the Super Bowl (I have two TVs in my living room). He'll probably get pissed I'm going to tell this story, but I have to:

We were sitting in the bar drinking, and even though it was only 4pm, the sun was starting to go down. Johnathan pipes up all of the sudden:

Johnathan "Hey! Who wants to go see wild horses?"
Bunny "I do!"
Nils "What is this, a fucking Rolling Stones song?"
Tucker "Wild horses? This is an island. In the north Pacific. With no trees. There are no wild horses here."
Johnathan "Like hell there aren't. Come on, let's get some carrots and apples and head over."

Like I said earlier, Dutch Harbor had a fairly substantial military base on it during World War II. The US Military at the time decided to use horses instead of using all gasoline powered vehicles on the island, probably because logistically fuel would have been in short supply but horses had plenty to eat, because a thick covering of natural grasses blankets most of Dutch Harbor. After the war, the military closed up shop on Dutch Harbor, and I guess transporting the horses back was either too costly or otherwise unnecessary, so they were released into the wild. You would think it'd be too cold, and they'd die. You'd be wrong. The herd still exists to this day. And Johnathan knew where they liked to hang out.

This was clearly not the first time he'd gone to feed the horses, because Johnathan went into a long explanation about the herd, what they liked to eat, where they hung out, their social patterns, everything. Johnathan pulled up about 20 feet from them and stopped. He held an apple out the window and waved it around. I asked him which one was Sarah Jessica Parker. The horses immediately recognized what Johnathan was waving and came over to see us. We got out of the truck and fed the horses carrots and apples, which they greedily munched down.

Drew "Horses are really smart. You don't have to worry about them biting you, they just want the food."
Tucker "You sure about that? I've been bitten by a horse before."
Drew "I dunno, all the ones I've been around have never bitten me."

And at that exact moment, one of them bit the ever-living shit out of Johnathan's hand.

Johnathan "OW FUCK GODDAMN IT!"
Tucker "See? Horses are fucking dicks!"
Johnathan "I had to pull like hell to get my hand out. That fucker wasn't going to let go!"

Of course, we mocked him about this:

Bunny "Can you imagine having to go back to the boat later without a finger and having to explain that? 'Been at sea over 30 years, lost a finger to a horse.'"
Drew "I feel bad for the next folks to come out here and feed them. Now they like the taste of human flesh. They're gonna find a pile of human skeletons, picked clean."

Neal Hillstrand

One of the grave crimes against humanity perpetrated on the fans of "The Deadliest Catch" is the systematic editing-out of footage of Neal

Hillstrand from ever making the show. After spending a week with the crew of the *Time Bandit,* I think I am qualified to say that not only is Neal Hillstrand the funniest Hillstrand, he's the funniest fisherman on the Bering Sea.

There is so much to tell you about him, I'm not sure where to start. He divorced his last wife because she hit him in the head with a shovel. When he was a kid, he had bad teeth, so his grandmother pulled them out. With pliers and whiskey. His dad wouldn't let him have a real gun as a kid, so he taped real bullets onto the end of his pellet gun, and shot things with that (the pellet hit the primer and discharged the bullet). These are just the things off the top of my head.

Part of the reason he gets edited out of the show is his fault: You ever heard the term "cursing like a drunken sailor?" Neal Hillstrand IS a drunken sailor. Pretty much every piece of footage that the Discovery Channel has of him, he is cursing to such an extent that you couldn't even bleep the curses, because it would just be a steady stream, like when the emergency signal comes on your TV.

Plus, part of the problem is that the dude drops these vaguely philosophical and always hilarious quotes, but they are hard to understand unless you either know him or they are put into the proper context. For example, after watching Keith hit on Nils, Neal blurted out,"I need some mustard for my hotdog and right now I'm at the same picnic." Or one time, these people were talking about horse racing, and during a lull in the conversation, Neal said, "Horses don't like black people." Or, after cutting the hell out of one of the knuckles on his left hand working in the engine room, he told us he wasn't upset because, "Who needs a finger when you've got a penis?"

But not everything he says is out of the Fisherman's Yogi Berra manual. Here are some of the funny things he said that don't require such context:

Neal "What do a nine-volt battery and a woman's ass have in common? You're going to eventually put your tongue on both."

Neal "The Alaska state motto is, 'When you leave here you're ugly again.'"
Drew "I think I saw one hot girl at that strip club."
Neal "Yeah, I think Alaska has a hot girl behind every tree."
Tucker "What? This is tundra up here. I haven't seen a tree yet."
Neal "Alaska has no trees."

Tucker "I think that dude's retarded."
Neal "If not, he had no excuse."

Neal "I knew it wouldn't go well with my first wife."
Bunny "Then why'd you marry her?"
Neal "She was thin."

- My favorite Neal story happened on our next-to-last night there. These four girls came into the bar who would have been ugly as hell anywhere else on earth, but in Dutch Harbor looked OK. They were WAY out of place though—these were not crabbers, they were not natives, and they weren't the typical processor workers (who tend to be Filipino). Neal explained that they were Coast Guard Observers. I am still not sure what the fuck they're supposed to do, but from what I can tell, Coast Guard Observers are naive and stupid and fuck a lot of crab fishermen.

The funny part is that these girls recognized me, and came up to talk. They were all fans, and one of them told me that she was afraid to try anal sex because of my first book. I told her I didn't give a shit about her problems. Since they were the only attractive and single girls on the island, I guess they thought this meant they got to fuck me. No chance. I said I'd fuck a whale, not some annoying fat bitch who won't shut the fuck up. I think I made a bottom dragger joke or something, and then ignored them. Of course, Neal the Eel was all into them. I told them that he was experienced with anal, and he did the rest, scooping them right up.

The next morning, we went over to the *Time Bandit.* When Andy got into the captain's chair, he got this weird look on his face and then erupted in a rage.

Andy "Oh goddamnit! Who fucked in my fucking captain's chair?"
Tucker "Neal. No doubt!"
Andy "NEAL! Come clean this fucking chair, it smells like anal sex up here!"
Tucker "I'm pretty sure he fucked her in the ass. She was looking for anal last night."
Drew "It actually smells like shitty pussy, I think."
Andy "They do this all the time. All those fucking girls want to get fucked in the captain's chair. I need to fucking Saran Wrap this thing at night."

Fourtner, Elliott, and D-Girls

Then there's Mike Fourtner. Mike's one of the few non-captains on the show who gets a lot of camera time. That's because he is just a real upbeat, positive, and gregarious guy on camera, which is pretty much exactly what he's like in real life.

Even more than that, he's a great guy. For example: One night at the hotel bar pretty much the entire *Time Bandit* crew was there with us getting shitty drunk. When it came time to go, I picked up the tab, and I noticed something immediately wrong with the bill.

Tucker "What the fuck is this? Call the waitress over; she obviously made a mistake. There's a Shirley Temple on the bill."

Fourtner raised his hand sheepishly, "Uh, yeah, that's right. That's mine."

I was so confused.

Tucker "Are you fucking kidding me?"
Fourtner "I'm driving tonight."
Tucker "We can walk to the next bar!! There's only seven miles of roads on the whole island!!!"
Fourtner "Yeah, but still. I'm the driver."

Tucker "OK fine, but when you're the DD you drink water or something, not Shirley fucking Temples!"
Fourtner "What can I say? I like the taste."

I made him pose for this picture:

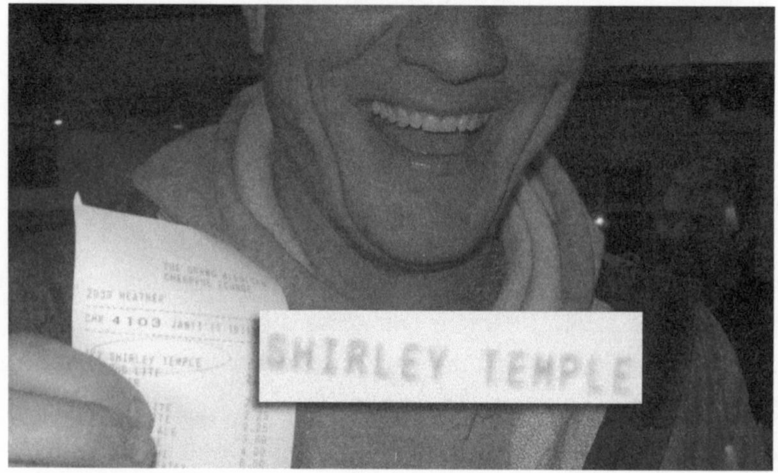

So he may be a fucking dork, but still legitimately one of the nicest guys I've ever met. The type of dude you'd want to marry your sister or something. Which makes the next story that much funnier:

If you watched Season 7, you know all about Elliott, the captain of the *Ramblin' Rose.* He's a young guy, 27 or so, and his was one of the new boats. Like all young guys who are getting their first shot at something, his insecurity manifested itself in over-cockiness and stupid arrogance. Andy, trying to be politic, said, "He has a lot of enthusiasm." Whatever. I'm not even criticizing him—we've all been like that in our lives at some point, me especially—but the fact is, he looked a little bit like a douche on the show because he's a LOT like a douche in real life.

One night, Elliott was at a table with some of the Discovery Channel production assistants, some of his crew and assorted others—one of them being a *Time Bandit* crewmember, Travis. I don't know exactly what happened, but apparently Elliott was being a complete douche to one of the Discovery Channel girls, rubbing all up on her and grabbing her tits and shit, and she got pissed. Travis told him to stop because he was making everyone else at the table uncomfortable. Elliott responded to this reasonable and calm request by actively trying to pick a fight with Travis. It was clear what was going on: Elliott was pissed at this girl for fucking him in private but dissing him in public, and instead of getting pissed at her, he directed his anger at Travis.

He's worked on the Bering Sea for years, so there is no doubt Elliott is tough, but he's not a big dude. Travis is a big, freakishly strong dude. I fear no man, but I'll say this: if I ever had a conflict with Travis, I'd do everything in my power to solve it peacefully. Travis was totally calm the whole time, but Elliott was either too drunk or too angry or too stupid to back down. This was not going to be a good situation. Impressively, Travis wasn't taking the bait. Elliot continued to push. Finally, Travis stood up, threw his hands up in the air in exasperation, and yelled across the bar:

Travis "WHY ME!? WHY?? WHY . . . ME!?"

Howls of laughter from the bar. About half the bar had been paying some sort of attention to the events in the corner by this point. Elliot yelled something angrily and pointed his finger at Travis. Travis rolled his eyes.

Travis "FOR THE LOVE OF GOD, WILL SOMEONE PLEASE COME AND SHUT THIS MOTHERFUCKER UP!?"

Fourtner "I'll handle this."

Fourtner is a big guy, bigger than Travis, big enough to pass for an NFL linebacker, and at least a foot taller than Elliott. If Fourtner told me to leave a bar, I'd leave the fucking state. Fourtner strode across the room and pushed Elliott out the door. Angry words were exchanged in the hallway for a couple minutes. Nothing worse than that happened however, and things basically went back to normal.

Elliott eventually came back in, he talked to the girl for a second, then she stormed out and Elliott followed. Bunny followed them out to see what was up. She returned 30 seconds later.

Bunny "It's relationship drama. I went out there and I heard him say 'you fuck me, and then you treat me like that?' He was almost crying."

I would make fun of Elliott getting punked by a soulless Hollywood D-girl, but I've been there too. Being tough enough to fish the Bering Sea and dealing with LA girls are NOT the same thing, brother.

The Egg Ambush

Our last day on Dutch Harbor rolled around, and we got up early, had breakfast with the otters and eagles and sea lions for the last time, and then got our bags and got ready to leave. We had a 3pm flight out of Dutch Harbor, but before we departed, there was one more mission for us.

The whole week Johnathan had been telling us about his plan to get revenge on another boat. You see, one of the new boats on the show this year, the *Seabrook* crew, had snuck onto the *Time Bandit* and painted a red lightning bolt—which I guess is their logo—on the *Time Bandit* crane. This pissed everyone off, but Johnathan especially. He told us his plan to get them back basically EVERY SINGLE DAY since we met up with him in Anchorage. Here it is, translated from Bering Sea Hamburglar to English:

"We're going to get everyone in town onto the *Time Bandit,* and ride by and throw every goddamn thing we have at them. Eggs, paintballs, fireworks—we're going to dump it all on them and ruin their fucking lives. You don't ever fuck with the *Time Bandit*! You want a fight, we'll give you a fight! You bring a knife, we bring a fucking Howitzer!"

Seriously, we must have heard this speech like ten times. It was motivational at first. Then it was annoying. So I started making fun of him.

Tucker "What if the eggs block out the sun?"
Johnathan "THEN WE FISH IN THE SHADE!!!"

Anyway, the night before, Johnathan was emphatic that we get to the *Time Bandit* no later than 11am, so we could all be there and take part in the ambush. No argument from me.

That morning, we were a bit late, so we didn't get in a cab until right at 11am. This shouldn't have been a big deal—there's only seven miles of road on the island; it doesn't take more than ten minutes to drive anywhere.

Cab driver "Where to?"

We immediately realized something: We don't know the actual name of any of the docks. How the hell would we give the taxi driver instructions? Even though Dutch Harbor isn't a big place, one of the few things it does have—aside from thousands of bald eagles that eat trash—is a lot of docks. It's basically all docks and processors, so you can't just say, "Take me to the docks." There are ten different sets of docks, all over the island.

Tucker "Do you know where the *Time Bandit* is docked right now?"
Cab Driver "The what?"
Tucker "The *Time Bandit*."
Cab Drvier "Never heard of it. Is that a crab boat?"
Tucker "Uh . . . really? You don't know the *Time Bandit*?"
Cab Driver "Nope."

I guess if you live in Dutch Harbor, the last thing you want to do is watch a TV show about crab fishing.

Tucker "OK . . . uh . . . do you know the *Northwestern*? It's docked next to them."
Cab Diver "Oh sure, I know where that boat is."

We went past the airport and down the docks to where the boat had been all week. We saw the *Northwestern . . .* and then a huge empty space where the *Time Bandit* had been all week.

Tucker "God damn it! We missed it! We fucking missed it! They already fucking left. I fucking knew we were late. FUCK!!!!!"

I was PISSED. Not only was the ambush going to be fun, but to be completely honest, I kinda wanted to be on the actual show, and this was pretty much my only chance. God knows I wasn't ever going to actually *work* on a fucking crab boat, especially not after the 24-hour pukefest on the way in.

Drew "Let's keep looking. Maybe they just moved the boat again."
Tucker "They've already left! Fuck! We're fucked. This sucks. Let's just go to the airport. Fuck it. We lost."
Drew "Drive a bit further down the dock."

Thank God Drew was there. I would have given up. He had the taxi driver go around for ten more minutes as I pouted and cursed under my breath . . . and then as luck would have it, Drew was right: There was the *Time Bandit,* docked, but hidden behind a random building.

We got onto the *Time Bandit,* happy as pigs in shit. But Andy was the only one there.

Tucker "Where is everyone?"
Andy "Buying eggs."
Tucker "Still?"

Andy "You've never seen Johnathan when he gets obsessed with something. He can go overboard. Here they come."

We went down to the deck. Johnathan burst out of the truck, hands raised triumphantly.

Johnathan "We spent 500 fucking dollars! We bought every fucking egg on the island!! Two thousand eggs!! We're going to ruin their lives!!"

That's when I took this picture. If you look in the middle, you see the egg that Johnathan threw at me in mid-air:

The *Seabrook* knew there was going to be some kind of retaliation; they're not stupid, plus the Discovery crew had to make sure they were on the boat when it happened so they could get it on film. I don't know if they knew ahead of time exactly what was going to happen or when, but I do know they weren't prepared for the biblical shitstorm of eggs that was about to rain down on them. It was so epic, Discovery Channel scrambled the helicopter to film it! I had done some serious shit in my life, but never anything cool enough that a helicopter had to record it.

This was not a half-assed assault. We distributed people all across the boat, with enough egg ammunition in each place. We'd thought out not only the initial ambush, but how to counter the possible counter-ambush. There were two paintball guns on the boat. Scotty was perched up in the crow's nest with one, and Justin had one next to Cameron on top of the crab pots. Their job was to shoot anyone on the other boat who tried to throw anything back at the *Time Bandit.*

At 11:30am, with camera crew ready on both boats, we left the dock. We slowly passed by the *Ramblin' Rose,* which was docked next to the *Seabrook.* The crewmembers who were on deck literally dropped what they were doing and stared in disbelief at the thousands of eggs we had laid out all over the boat.

Andy "Leave the *Ramblin' Rose* alone. They're not the enemy today!"

As we approached the boat, the crew of the *Seabrook* was busy readying the ship to head out to the fishing grounds. We all crouched down and hid behind whatever was available. Andy slowed the *Time Bandit* to a snail's pace. I can throw an egg pretty far, but Andy, being the expert captain that he was, pulled up alongside the *Seabrook* at a distance of under five feet. At this distance, a little girl could hurl an entire carton on deck.

Four crewmembers who were on deck stopped what they were doing to look at us, confused as to why our boat was so close.

Crew member "Hey! What in the hell is all this?"

Andy's voice came over the *Time Bandit*'s loudspeaker:

Andy "FIRE!"

And our eggs blotted out the sun.

That poor guy who was standing out on deck got it the worst. I think every single one of us took a shot at him. He took one egg right to the temple, and went down like a bag of shit. The rest of the *Seabrook* crew ran for cover in the front of their boat, where they were protected for the most part.

Andy "Target the windows! Aim for the wheelhouse windows!!"

Hundreds of eggs smashed into the wheelhouse windows. We covered every window in no time. One of the production crew cameramen on the *Seabrook* side was up there as well, on the outside, filming from their vantage point. I hit him at least twice, and I wasn't the only one who managed to do it. We hit everything. Every last square inch of the ship was covered in egg.

It took until about this point for the *Seabrook* to start throwing eggs back at us. A bunch of their crew came running out from the front and hurled eggs at us. I think that they were waiting behind cover until we ran out of eggs so they could return fire—not a bad plan—but we just weren't running out of eggs. There's no way they could have foreseen this, either. I mean seriously—who brings two thousand eggs to an egg fight?

The *Time Bandit* does, that's who.

As our wheelhouse passed theirs, I dumped three entire 18-egg crates on their wheelhouse. It was awesome. Andy floored it and we sped away. A huge cheer went up on deck. I am not exaggerating in the slightest: the *Seabrook* was yellow. Bright yellow. Barely any red visible anywhere.

We tied up back at the pier and went down into the stateroom to watch the footage from the four cameras on our boat. They caught absolutely everything. It was even better on video.

Tucker "There's nothing more satisfying that an undeniable, overwhelming, total victory."

The Epilogue

Pretty much every "reality" show on TV is bullshit. Reality TV and the people on it are more unreal than most scripted series at this point. If they aren't literally scripted like "The Hills" or "The Amazing Race" then at the very least they're completely controlled by the producers to achieve the drama and results they want, like "Survivor" or "Jersey Shore." I don't even think I need to mention what a joke reality "stars" are; that's become cliché.

Before going to Alaska, I knew "The Deadliest Catch" was different. But now that I've been there, now that I've hung out with these guys, now that I've thrown up on their boat and gotten hammered with them and lived in their world, I can tell you with authority that they are no bullshit. Not in any way.

That's the thing about these guys—they were pulling crab out of the sea and ass out of the bars before the cameras came and they'll be doing both well after the cameras leave. These guys aren't in this for any other reason than because it's what they do. THAT is what makes the show so good—it IS real. You can't pretend to fish crab. These guys pull 1,000-pound metal cages out of the ocean in 40-foot seas for three straight days without sleep. And it's HARDER in real life than you can imagine from watching it on TV.

Andy said it best, "Man, the show is cool and all, but it hasn't changed much really. Crab fishermen have always been the craziest, the toughest, the loudest, the best. We were rock stars long before "Deadliest Catch." I could have run a cannery, or fished for halibut or captained an oil tanker or anything like that. That's why I became a crab fisherman in the first place: We make the most money because what we do is the hardest and most dangerous fishing job there is. That's why we do it."

[Note: The best way to see all this for yourself is to look at the pictures on my website (**www.tuckermax.com/deadliestvacation**). And you can see me and everyone else on the "The Deadliest Catch" Season 7, in the episode called "Sea Change."]

DEDICATION

I want to dedicate this story—something I've never done before—to Justin Tennison, a member of the *Time Bandit* crew who hung out with us all week, and passed away a month after we left. He was a truly great guy who went before his time, and that sucks. RIP, Justin.

Sexting with Tucker Max: Mean

This may come as a shock to some of you, but I have a slightly volatile personality. I don't suffer fools well. And when I'm in a bad mood, I suffer stupid whores looking to sext even worse. It's not like I want to sext when I'm in a *good* mood. You really think it's going to be sunshine and kittens when I'm pissed off? The girls who persistently annoy me to sext with them find out.

Mean #1: Stupid Is as Stupid Types

people like you make me understand why domestic violence occurs

gtfo ur gunna fuck me

hello

4 realz?

Mean #2: This Blowjob Blows

are u thinkin bout fucking me

Im gonna fuck you til your pussy grunts.

Imma make it say UGGGGNNNNN like Master P

lol

thats what i like to hear

i like it hard

Im want to blast out your teeth with my love cannon

lol

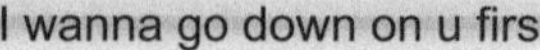

I wanna go down on u first

My penis is about to become a huge part of your mouth's life

I immediately take your whole cock in my mouth

My head goes up and down on your dick, flicking my tongue over it, savoring every inch

Why can't you keep your teeth off my dick? I've never sucked dick, but it can't be that hard

Im giving you a perfect blowjob

no teeth perfect

I've eaten popsicles before, and I managed to keep my teeth off those

im not using teeth

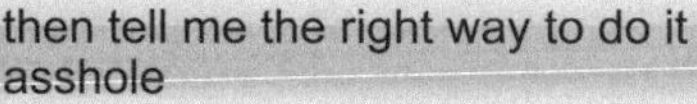

then tell me the right way to do it asshole

This blowjob sucks. Where did you learn to give head? The Paris Hilton sex tape?

are you criticizing my sexting blowjobn??? this doesnt make sense!!!

I'm going to have to talk to your family about this.

my family?

Your uncle told me you gave good head thats why I agreed to sext with you

WHAT IS GOING ON???

Look, your dog has his penis out

at least you turn someone on

THIS IS NOT APPROPRIATE

Mean #3: Hookt on Phon-icks

youre so dumb, I'd have to think of a different girl to finish

smh

wtf

SPELL OUT WORDS PROPERLY YOU FUCKING MOUTHBREATHER

y do u care abt grammer and capitalization

?

Capitalization is the difference between helping your Uncle Jack off a horse and helping your uncle jack off a horse

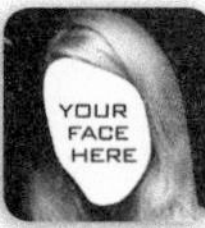

i dont get it

Wow. You're not even smart enough to realize how dumb you are.

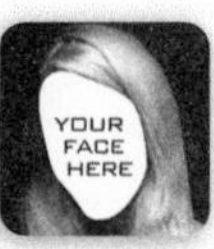

lol

You've done something amazing. George Orwell would like a word with you

whos that? some friend of urs?
does he wanna sext or sumthin?

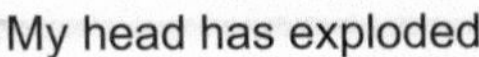

I don't know whether to masturbate
or cry for the future

Mean #4: Whore OnStar

This girl was supposed to drive from her town about two hours away to fuck me here in Austin, and this exchange starts about the time she was supposed to be getting on the road. This didn't begin as sexting, but this dumb bitch drove me so nuts AND KEPT INSISTING that we sext, I lost it on her and tried to say the most offensive shit I could think of, to see if I could get her so upset she wouldn't even come over. It was impossible—like trying to rattle a 911 operator:

What ase you doing?

Happy Hour got to me and i
wanna fCuk right now!

How are you going to drive two
hours drunk?

i'm trying to sobes up now So i
can cum

not my fualt i like didn't eat
anything today to look good for u

what a moron. Don't come. You're clearly too immature to fuck me.

that's hard to do, but you did it

I'm not immature, I just didn't think a few drinks owuld do this to me. im sorry im gunna leave soon

on my way :)

you'll let me in right?

You are a fucking moron. Or still drunk

Why are you being so mean?

Can I come now? Or are you like so mad at me?

You might as well try. I can't think any less of you than I do right now. It has to get better for you

What does that mean? Lol.

Like 3o away. lol, you probably think I'm dumb don't you?

Dumb seems smart compared to you

No I'm not! lol hahah i cna prove you wrong, but you'll think i'm dumb bc of my drawl lol

Maybe I can sing for you too! I sing country! lol!

i wont be talking much though, my mouth will be doing something else lol

You've disgusted me so much I doubt I'll even get hard.

Well . . . idk. Take something. Or get drunk. lol.

Almost in Austin, whats the exact address?

Jesus Christ. It's because of women like you that in no language on earth does the phrase 'smart as a woman' appear.

Just because I'm dumb don't mean I can't have sex you know lol. I look extra hot for you

The hottest thing you could do right now would be to die in a firey wreck

lol your makin me laugh. I hope you don't mean that.

Take your steering wheel and yank it violently into the next concrete embankment you see. -That'll get me hard

What's an embankment?

You have to be kidding. Only dogs and retards are this stupid.

haha lol

Seriously whats the addy?

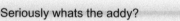

See that river? Aim your car for it.

quit lol! I called me grandparents and got the addy off the paper I left in my house. be there soon. are we just staying in for the night?

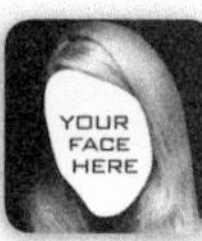

I do want you to do unforgiving things to me

OK, I'll throw you off my balconey

Lol thats a little too far, just up against the wall for me :) I love being fucked like that

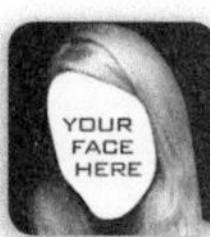

im going to make you blow a homeless guy

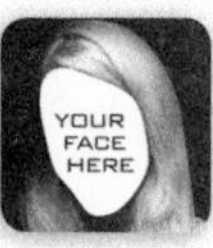

lol no thanks only u :)

and you have to fuck a dog. And a camel. to prove your love

A camel? lol

I'm not a slut u know

can I stick a Mason jar up your ass?

hey I drink beer outta those! My asshole is tight, youll like fucking it.

Are you dead yet?

im about to be, textin and drivin.

turn your radio to full blast, that should complete the moron trifecta

Where is your place exactly, I can't find no numbers

i think im close

let's talk dirty more

I'm going to piss on you

Fine you can do that. But I'll squirt on your face while you eat me out. And you'll drown lol!

im gonna piss in your pussy

your gonne give me a huge load in my pussy

with your huge cock inside me

the only thing im putting in you is my maglite. right in your skull

lol stop!

fuck me Tucker i want to be tied up and you pin my legs behind your head and cum in my pussy

I want to bind your wrists so hard they turn gangrenous and fall off

I want you to flip me over and be the first guy to ever do anal with me

With a broom! That's so hot

lol nooo! I want to lick the sweat dripping down your balls

I'm going to give you a bunch of pain killers. Then drop you off at the homeless shelter

How many times have you woken up in a dumpster? Tomorrow will be +1

stop bashing me! lol

I bet your pussy smells like the dumpster behind an Olive Garden

But your pussy has more food in it

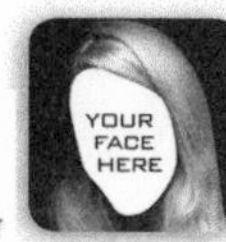

That's a turn off . . .

How much food DO you have in your pussy?

None??? sushi, lol. like in your book lol

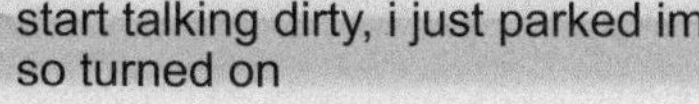

start talking dirty, i just parked im so turned on

I want to fuck you in a public park. Hard. So long and hard you pass out!

thats more like it ,thats so hot, i want you so deep inside me I can't even remember my name

And after you pass out, I'll leave you there, and let a bunch of dudes jack off on you, like a bukkake video. When you wake up, you'll have so much dry cum on you you'll think you've been baked into a pie

okay tucker, please stop, that is making me ill.

Fine, no gang rape, but when you wake up, you need to pick up all the dog shit people leave behind in the park. Some people are so inconsiderate of others.

Tucker! That's not sexting!!

And then I want you to eat it. Thats dirty, right?

You need to be civil with me.

That's not good sexting

Tucker! Stop it! Talk about eating my pussy!

Porridge is just shitty oatmeal

What? lol

I parked on [redacted]. thats close right? Or should I park somewhere else

Park in the least safe place you can find. Anywhere on Martin Luther King Blvd works

Where is that?

Mean #5: Post "Coital"

[this one picks up after I'd already told her I'd "cum" in sexting]

now i want you to do something amazing to me

whats the coolest sexual trick you know?

My favorite trick is acting like the girl isn't there, and get my nut as fast as possible

I just did that trick

thats not a sexual trick!

Oh . . . OK well, I know how to make the girl disappear after I fuck her. Thats a trick right?

no!!! thats not what I mean!!

i mean like licking my clit in a cool way

or fucking me some way where it like, involves a trick

u know, like, sex tricks lol

Tucker?

hello?

Please don't interrupt me while I'm ignoring you

what?

your responding

no im not

yes you are!

u just responded!

what are you talking about, im ignoring you so youll leave

????????

whats going on

i dont want you to go

now I have to pay attention to my life again

Mean #6: That's (Beef) Curtains

You reach down and rip my panties off. You want my pussy so bad you are rock hard

I tease you and make you stare at it for a minute

I'm confused. It kinda looks like a cheeseburger turned sideways.

a cheeseburger?

lol. be serious! Now you go down on me

OK, I'll eat you out. I move slowly down to your pussy

im so hot now, I want to just push your face right into my pussy, but ur too strong

I'm having trouble here. I can't really eat you out with this gas mask on

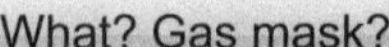

What? Gas mask?

I don't know what's been in your pussy

lol quit!

Have you been tested?

YES!

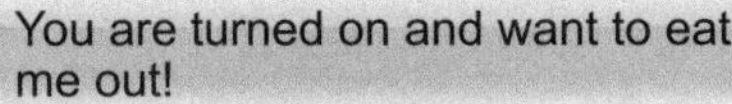

You are turned on and want to eat me out!

OK, I'm so turned on, I take the gas mask off, say a prayer, and lick your pussy

Oh yeah, lick it hard, bite me on the clit

I'm having trouble again

?

I spread open your labia in search of the clit. It looks like I am opening a burnt grilled cheese sandwich.

omg im gonna puke

ur ruining it

you're ruining it! Puking is for AFTER sex!

FUCK OFF UR FUCKING DISGUSTING

whatever, im hungry anyway

When I put my face on your pussy, it plugs my nose and I can't breathe properly.

just lick my clit like you said

OK, but your pussy is so fat, I can't really find your clit

I DO NOT HAVE A FAT PUSSY!

Mean #7: Nail in the Coffin

You slowly drag your tongue down my thigh

Hey, there's a sign on your crotch!

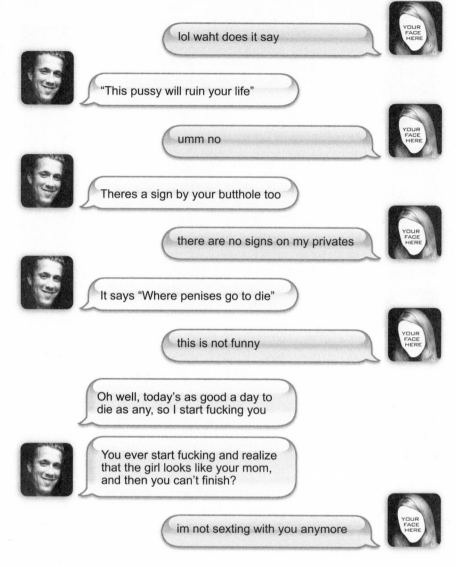

lol waht does it say

"This pussy will ruin your life"

umm no

Theres a sign by your butthole too

there are no signs on my privates

It says "Where penises go to die"

this is not funny

Oh well, today's as good a day to die as any, so I start fucking you

You ever start fucking and realize that the girl looks like your mom, and then you can't finish?

im not sexting with you anymore

Mean #8: Abortion > Dead Baby Jokes

I rub your belly and softly whisper in your ear . . . "Im gunna put a baby in there"

Noooo

why not? well make beautiful abortions together . . .

don't joke about that

ok no jokes about babies.

except this one

you know whats harder than nailing a dead baby to a tree? nailing it to a dead puppy

stop seriously dead baby jokes r not funny

have you ever tried to nail a dead baby to a dead puppy? its hard!

omg im gunna vom

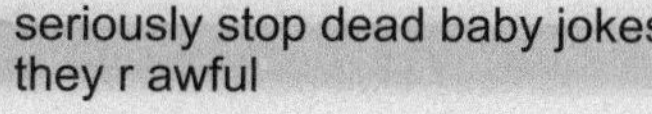

seriously stop dead baby jokes they r awful

no they are awesome

not to me I had an abortion

Hold on—its not ok for me to make a dead baby JOKE, but its ok for you to make an ACTUAL DEAD BABY????

FUCK OFF AND DIE!!

is that what you said to your baby after the abortion?

hello?

mommy are you there? it's me, your dead baby

why didnt you love me?

The Fight Stories

Some people who read my books ask me how I don't get into fights. It's not normal people who ask this question—it's almost always guidos or meatheads who can't comprehend any social interaction that isn't highlighted by a direct threat of violence. But still, the question is there, quite a bit.

I always laugh when this comes up, because the underlying assumption is that since I haven't *written a story* about getting into a fight, that I must not ever get into fights. Listen up parents, this is the kind of reasoning that develops when you have kids before you're ready and you send them to a bad directional state school: Just because I don't write about something, doesn't mean it doesn't happen. Lack of inclusion does not imply exclusion. I've never written a story where I mention feeding my dog, but she eats twice a day.

Here's the problem with writing stories about fights: There is no way to do it that isn't lame. What do most fight stories sound like? "I kicked his teeth out and cracked his skull with a hammer! I'M FUCKING AWESOME RAAAAWWWWRRRR!!!"

Come on, no one wants to read that shit, and for the most part, most of my fight stories are just as stupid and unfunny as everyone else's.

I have two exceptions:

The TMZ Debacle

Occurred, March 2011

South-by-Southwest (SXSW) is an annual conference in Austin, TX that hosts most of the big players in tech, internet, and music. It's a pretty good conference, as conferences go, but that's only measuring it on the scale of conferences. That's like rating individual Vietnamese public toilets against each other. Even the cleanest and best is still a hole in the ground filled with festering excrement.

One of the big reasons so many people go to SXSW is not the conference—it's the parties. In tech circles, SXSW is famous for its great parties. But here's the thing you have to keep in mind—they are great *to tech nerds.* For these Asperger's geeks, any event that serves alcohol and has attractive women in attendance BY CHOICE is *legendary.* For me, walking into any one of the SXSW parties is like a recipe for University of Chicago PTSD. These are basically the exact same people I went to college with—really smart and good at their jobs, but totally unable to drink, party, or be socially daring—and graduated a year early to get away from. Here's all you need to know about SXSW parties: Most of the people at them wear backpacks.

One night during SXSW, I was hanging out with some of my Austin friends, plus Drew Curtis, who was friends with the founders of some new start-up, so we went to their party. All the nerds at the party were super excited because Ashton Kutcher and Demi Moore were supposed to show up there. This party sucked the same way all SXSW parties sucked, but it was even more annoying for a different reason: Popchips.

Popchips was co-sponsoring the party with Drew's start-up buddies. Besides putting their name on all the fliers and signage, they also hired three girls to pass out bags of Popchips to everyone at the party. Two problems:

1. Popchips are not only fucking disgusting, they are beneath me. Poor Irishmen eat potatoes because they can't afford anything else. Fuck that. I eat meat.

2. The Popchip whores would not leave me alone. This was not a huge party, maybe 100 people there, so pretty much every two minutes they'd walk by and aggressively demand I take some Popchips. I might not have been annoyed if 1) the girls were attractive (they weren't) or 2) Popchips were made of charred meat (instead of "natural potato ingredients" which is what it says on the label).

Eventually it got to be too much. I can handle the boredom of hanging out with nerds, and I can manage incessant Popchip peddlers, but not together. Together they formed a Voltron of frustration and mischief that got me looking for ways to amuse myself. I noticed that the bar had a massive ceiling fan, with huge fan blades that looked sharp as hell. I wondered how sharp they really were. Never one to shy away from the scientific method, I decided to experiment. I grabbed a bag of Popchips and threw it into the ceiling fan. The spinning fan blade whipped the bag across the bar. Perhaps these Popchips could be useful after all.

I grabbed like ten more bags, and started throwing them into the ceiling fan one after the other. Sadly, they did not slice open like I had hoped. The fan blades either weren't sharp enough or the fan wasn't going fast enough; I don't know. What I DO know is that with proper loft you can get the fan to fling the full bags of Popchips all across the bar and directly into people's faces. Which is pretty awesome, and more than enough to keep me entertained.

As we were all laughing at this, I felt something brush my arm. It was a tiny little Asian dude in a red baby tee that had "SECURITY" across the front. Isn't it so cute when parents let their kids stay up late and mingle with adults? He started squeaking at me:

Security "Alright buddy, let's go, you're outta here."
Tucker "Maybe . . . but not for you. You aren't doing anything to me."
Security "What? I'm throwing you out. You have to leave, let's go."
Tucker "No. *You're gonna need more people.*"

He got this confused look on his face, like never in his life had he considered someone NOT recognizing and bending to his baseless and preposterous authority. As if nothing more than a t-shirt made him so powerful that he forgot people could be bigger than him, and that a threat without anything to back it up doesn't mean anything.

Then it clicked, his eyes went from confused to wide and afraid, and he ran off. Don't pull your gun unless you're prepared to use it! This is going to be even more fun than throwing potatoes around the bar!

This was not planned at all—it was just a reaction to his tone and manner. If he had been cool, I probably would have just left. But he was such a pompous little shitbird, I refused to comply. No chance. The day I let a tiny steamed dumpling in a baby tee push me around, I'll just turn in my balls and go write for *Maxim.*

A few minutes later, this tall string bean in a red security shirt that was a little better-sized came up (with the Asian dude hiding behind him), and tried the same thing on me. Except he said I had to leave "right now."

Tucker [dripping with mocking sarcasm] "*Right now*? So I can't stay, and leave later? Well . . . that changes EVERYTHING! I just didn't understand the first guy."

It was hard choking back the laughter. He didn't know what to do—and he wasn't about to enforce his implied threat with ACTUAL violence either—so he kinda stood there for a second staring at Short Round like a confused dog, and then walked off. The only thing I needed now was a mirror to hold up so they could see the "SECURITY" on their shirt, and laugh along with me!

Then this tiny little dude—the smallest yet, but without a red baby tee—came running over, face crimson with anger, screaming at me.

Owner "You have to leave!!!"
Tucker "What for?"
Owner "For throwing ice!!!"

That pissed me off, a lot. I stuck my finger right in his face as I defended my honor:

Tucker "I did NOT throw ice, I threw POPCHIPS!"
Owner "Well then get out!! I own the whole building!"
Tucker [mocking] "Oh no! He owns the building!"
Owner "I'm calling the cops!"
Tucker "Call them."
Owner "You're going to jail!!!!"
Tucker "Yeah, OK. Let me know when they get here."

Dude went ballistic. He pulled his phone out, flipped it open, put it to his face and started talking.

Owner "911, I need the cops here ASAP!"

Here was this tiny little man making a tiny little call into his enormous cell phone . . . but he didn't dial. He didn't hit the 'send' button. He didn't do anything that would even approximate making a real phone call. It took me a second to realize, because I kinda couldn't believe it—he was PRETENDING to call the cops. Like a parent would do to a child. I turned to everyone I was with:

Tucker "Did he even hit send?"
Girl "No."

At that point, everyone was openly laughing at him and his ridiculous charade. I thought he was going to pop a blood vessel in his face he got so angry. Poor guy—it was like high school all over again for him. And here he thought owning a bar would make him cool.

I was actually hoping the cops would show up—I was going to try to get them to arrest the bar owner. I think I might have been able to do it. First of all, one of the girls with me was an ER nurse and knew most of the Austin cops. Second, this dude was clearly an insecure idiot, and if I could just think of the right way to frame the incident to the cops, I might be able to get the cops to arrest him. I knew I would have to leave, of course, but if I could get the cops to arrest the owner of a bar I was thrown out of, it would be worth all the trouble.

But of course he didn't call the cops, even after I called him out, because he knew what I knew: the cops aren't coming, especially not on one of the busiest nights of the year, when real crimes are happening. Plus, they don't write tickets for narcissistic injury. Sorry buddy, I can't go to jail just because I made you feel small inside.

Instead, he finally did something smart—he went to the club across the street, and got three REAL bouncers from there. These were big muscular dudes. I thought to myself, *OK, that's enough guys,* so when they came over, I just left. Walked right out. That was it.

On a scale of one to "getting out of a DUI in Harlem", this story didn't even register on my "should I write about this?" scale. Funny to me in the moment, absolutely, but it didn't even cross my mind that I'd write about it.

Then, the next day, TMZ emailed me asking for a comment about "getting kicked out of a SXSW party and calling some girl a greasy guido."

What? I couldn't believe it. After all the ridiculous shit I've done in my life, THIS is what TMZ wants to do a story on? Come on Harvey Levin, where were you guys when I was doing all that awesome shit?

I gave them my number and talked to them. The guy writing the story was really cool—the exact opposite of that long-haired surfer douche on the TV show—and much to his credit, basically got all the facts of the story right when it ran:

Tucker Max: It Took 5 Bouncers to Boot Me from Party

"I Hope They Serve Beer in Hell" author **Tucker Max** was tossed out of a party at the South by Southwest film festival Sunday night, TMZ has learned -- and it took FIVE bouncers to do the job.

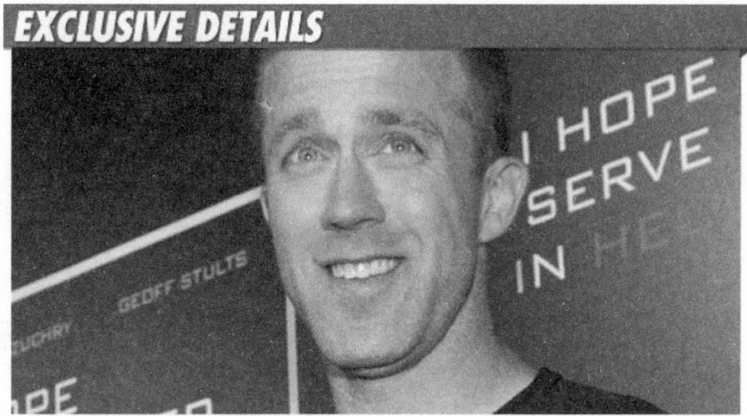

Tucker tells TMZ, "I had been invited to this boring and annoying SXSW party ... I decided to amuse myself by throwing bags of Popchips into the ceiling fan, trying to get them to explode over all of us. Juvenile? Yes. Hilarious when you're drunk? Absolutely."

But security at the Hangar Lounge in Austin, TX wasn't laughing -- and according to Tucker, the two in-house bouncers weren't man enough to kick him out ... so they had to recruit three additional hired guns from across the street.

Potato chips in a ceiling fan? Lots of alcohol? Pissed off security guards? Sounds like awesome material for a new book.

Tucker Gets into Fight, Hilarity Ensues

Occurred, July 2010

I casually mentioned that I liked to drink a specific type of sweet tea vodka in my last book (Deep Eddy, which is the fucking best). The guy who owned the company, Clayton, found out and invited me to hang out with him on his boat. He told me to bring some girls and we'd spend the day water-skiing, drinking and hanging out on Lake Austin.

[Here's the best part: He asked ME to bring the Deep Eddy to HIS boat. I had to BUY Deep Eddy for the dude who OWNS the company. WTF??]

We ended up having a great time, and when it got dark, we moved the party to Clayton's lake house, with its sweet two-story dock, beer pong table, stereo, grill, etc.

The guy who introduced me to Clayton, Taylor, came by. He was on a boat with a bunch of other people I didn't know—two guys and three girls. One of the girls was with Taylor, and the other two were married to the two guys. The girls were pretty cute, but all three of them were bitchy.

Normally, bitchy girls don't fly with me, but I wasn't fucking any of them, and I had my own girls, so whatever. It was the guys though that really rubbed me the wrong way. Almost immediately, I hated the guys, "Euro-Trash" and "DipShit." Aside from the fact that they were born on different continents, they were mirror images of each other: spoiled trust fund kids who have been handed everything in life, soft as chewed bubble gum, and filled with the type of arrogance that comes from entitlement rather than hard work. You can't help it if your parents were rich and ignored you, but you still get to decide how you act in the world, especially as an adult. These two apparently decided they were going to suck in every way possible.

Just take the boat they were in for example. DipShit owned it. His daddy had bought it for him, and he told everyone it cost $200k (Taylor says it really cost $150k). He bought a nice boat, then put in $25k worth of stereo equipment, a fog machine, lasers, and a champagne bucket and a stripper pole. It was like he opened the douchebag catalog and bought every cliché, and then put them in a boat.

Normally, I just ride these types of idiots like rented mules until they leave or cry. But this time was different—I wasn't at a bar, I was at someone's home. Clayton is about as different from me as one could be: into meditation, Buddhism, pacifism, etc. Super nice guy and fun to hang out with, but not the type of guy who tolerates my special kind of social aggression. And since this was Clayton's house, and I was his guest and liked him, out of respect, I tried my best to just let everything go.

It was hard. Aside from all the obvious problems with that type of insecure trust fund brats (the douchey boat, constant name-dropping, always comparing prices, being condescending to people, etc.), these two were also just general fucktards. It started when we were upstairs playing beer pong. DipShit kept spilling his beer all over the floor, basically on purpose. I calmly told him, "Hey man, Clayton is being really nice letting us come here, don't be a douchebag and disrespect his house like that." After that, he actually poured more out just to spite me—but in a passive-aggressive way over in the corner, not in my face at all. It took every ounce of self-control not to directly confront him.

I could have eventually let that pass if there hadn't been any other provocation. The turning point occurred when the pizza guy came. Clayton's dock is way, way down the hill from the road, and on the phone Clayton told the pizza guy we'd tip him more if he brought the pizzas all the way down to the dock. So the dude walked like 200+ yards, much of it in the dark on stairs, down to the dock. It was a very cool thing to do, and Clayton went to tip him, but ran out of cash paying for the pizza.

Well, DipShit had bragged earlier about how awesome and expensive his boat was—you know, the one that his DAD BOUGHT FOR HIM. I'd been the good boy all night long, but I just couldn't resist this opportunity to call him out in front of everyone:

Tucker "Hey trust fund, why don't you help Clayton and give the pizza guy a good tip?"
DipShit "Fuck that."
Tucker "You just got done bragging about all your money, show us how rich you are."
DipShit "I have a $200,000 boat, I could tip him anything I want, but fuck that, I'm not tipping shit!"

Then he dramatically walked out, like this was a movie or something.

I tipped the pizza guy all the cash I had and apologized to him for that scene. I was flabbergasted. I knew this dude sucked, but I had a hard time believing ANYONE sucked that much in real life. He was like a parody of a trust fund brat.

The next hour or so was weird. I'd called DipShit out in front of everyone, he'd punked himself, and everyone including his friends knew it. But nothing really happened because he was too much of a coward to say anything else, and I was trying to let it go so I wouldn't fuck up Clayton's party. Eventually everything settled into some sort of quasi-normal party pattern, with everyone drinking and playing beer pong. The two trust fund brats pretty quickly retreated to their boat downstairs—but not before they ate a bunch of pizza.

What I hadn't realized right away was that I'd unintentionally drawn a clear line in the sand between DipShit and me. It's comical now to think about the juvenile way the fight started, but this is really what happened:

Clayton asked me to go downstairs and turn on the stereo inside his boat so we could hear music upstairs while we played beer pong. I did. Then, like two minutes later, the music went off. I went downstairs to check it out, and the A/V cord was unplugged. Weird. I put it back in, the music started, and we were all good. Then two minutes later, it went off again.

OK, that wasn't an accident. You see, Clayton's boat was docked right next to DipShit's boat, where those two were sitting (along with Taylor, who'd gone down there a few minutes earlier). It was obvious that one of them had unplugged the stereo. Mind you, they didn't SAY anything to me about the music. And they didn't SAY anything to me about unplugging it. They just sat there staring at their twats.

Nothing pisses me off like passive-aggressiveness. If you have something to say, fucking say it, and deal with the consequences. If you won't say it to a person's face, then shut the fuck up and move on. Pretty simple.

I was still hanging onto the last thread of non-confrontation in my body at this point, but I wasn't *not* going to say something. So I walked over to their boat. Taylor was looking at me, while the two pussies sitting next to him were looking away. In the heat of the moment, this was the least confrontational thing I could think to say:

Tucker "Taylor, you're my friend and you know me. You tell these two fucking pussies not to touch that fucking stereo again, or they're going to deal with me."

DipShit finally decided to pretend he was a man.

DipShit "What the fuck are you going to do?"
Tucker "Why don't you come up here on the dock and I'll show you what I'm going to do, you fucking BITCH."

That's the best the Tucker Max School of Conflict Resolution has to offer, I guess.

Well, apparently those two had just enough alcohol in them, and had blown each other up with just enough drunk courage, that they decided to come off the boat onto to the dock at me, and push me. Then—

See, this is why I hate writing about fights. There's almost no way to talk about this incident without sounding lame. I either come off like some wanna-be tough guy, or I go out of my way the other direction, and make it sound like I got my ass kicked, or what happened was an accident. Whatever. Here's exactly what happened, with as little editorializing as possible:

EuroTrash pushed me, I pushed him back, and Taylor—trying to be a peacemaker—got in between us. Then DipShit got in my face and put his hands on me, and I pushed him away, and Taylor got between me and him. Then EuroTrash came back at me and pushed me again.

I took a short step back with my right foot, which helped me load my right arm, and immediately threw a tight right cross. It was a serious angry punch, and I landed it perfectly. In a flash, the space between my first and second knuckle on my hand connected perfectly with the lower left side of his chin. In MMA/boxing, it's called "the button" because when you hit it clean, the dude goes out—and that is precisely what EuroTrash did. His head whipped around, his body followed him, he stumbled, crashed into a pole, bounced off Clayton's boat, and crumpled onto a heap onto the dock.

I hit that motherfucker so hard I changed his DNA. Knocked out.

Look: I'm not trying to claim I'm some tough guy. I know real tough guys—guys in the military, MMA fighters, guys who work on oil rigs and crab boats—and I'm *not* one of them. None of this should be taken as me bragging about how I'm some awesome fighter. Please. There are a LOT of guys out there who can kick my ass . . . but those doughy trust fund cum-sniffers are not among them.

At that point the girls came downstairs from the upper deck, and all hell broke loose. It was like a baby had stepped on a cat: screaming, hollering, pushing, crying, hair-pulling, more pushing, everything. I don't really remember the specifics of what was said, because I never listen to what spews from the mouths of histrionic whores, but there is one thing I distinctly remember:

DipShit comes up behind EuroTrash, takes one look at his buddy crumpled in a heap of failure, gets pissed, and takes a step towards me.

Bad call. When someone takes a first pitch fastball and deposits it 450 feet away over the centerfield fence, the last thing you should do is throw him that same pitch in his next at-bat. I cocked my right arm again, more than ready for him, and he looked into my eyes.

I've never seen a more raw, honest expression of fear in my life. He wanted no part of me. He took several steps back and let Taylor get in between us, then of course acted tough again. Good choice, DipShit.

Seeing that my job there was done, I calmly walked back upstairs, leaving the mess for the whores to clean up. As I walked up the stairs, I could hear the girls I had come with arguing with the whores who'd come with DipShit:

Whore1 "Who does Tucker Max think he is??"
Whore2 "What's wrong with him?"
Girl "What's wrong with your friend?"
Whore1 "He thinks just because he wrote some book, he can do anything he wants."
Girl "Your friend started this acting like a douchebag."
Whore2 "Welcome to Austin, bitch!" [she really said that, and this one makes no sense for them to say—their friend was the one who got KTFO. Again, there is no accounting for what stupid whores say]

And that's when it got REALLY spooky. When I got upstairs, there was only one person still up there: EuroTrash's wife. She was just sitting there, sipping her beer. I stared at her for a second, fully expecting the worst of the whore wrath yet.

EuroWife "What happened?"
Tucker "Your husband pushed me, so I hit him in the fucking mouth, that's what!"
EuroWife "Why are you yelling?"

She was right; I had raised my voice a little. And she had responded in a perfectly calm way—in fact, it was fucking spooky. Complete and utter calm. No expression on her face, no emotion in her voice. Not even disguised anger. It was as if she was asking me where the bathroom was.

I kinda stopped and stepped back to take stock of the situation. Either this girl is about to stab me and has the greatest poker face since Phil Ivey . . . or she is feeling absolutely nothing right now.

Tucker "Uh . . . sorry . . . I didn't mean to raise my voice. But yeah, your husband got his face punched. By me. I think he's hurt."
EuroWife "OK."

Even though I'd hit her husband so hard his arms and legs had stopped working and all he saw was an Indian with an extra horse beckoning him into the woods . . . she had no emotional reaction to it. Nothing.

Wow. This girl is a psychopath. It was like talking to Dexter. Thank God I fought her pansy ass husband and not her. She'd kill me without even blinking.

That was pretty much it for the night. After that they got in their boat and took off (and then took EuroTrash to the ER). Clayton was not too happy with me, so my girls and I left. Another night ruined (read: made awesome) by Tucker Max.

But the story doesn't end there. A few weeks later, I get this email:

"Tucker,

As you might have already heard from Taylor, the injury on my foot was severe enough to result in a fracture-dislocation on my midfoot, requiring surgical repair. I had surgery on my foot on July 9th, and am instructed not engage in travel or flying for the next 8 weeks. This caused me to miss an important business meeting in Washington DC, and my wife and I had to cancel our European holiday.

Attached are the receipts from the charges in incurred when I went in for surgery at Texas Orthopedics. There were a few charges that preceeded [sic] these, like the boot and x-rays/CT scans, but this was by far the largest. In all fairness, it does take two to tango, so I am asking you to consider paying for half of the attached out-of-pocket expenses.

I look forward to hearing from you.

EuroTrash"

He even sent me the receipts, and the X-ray of the screw in his foot:

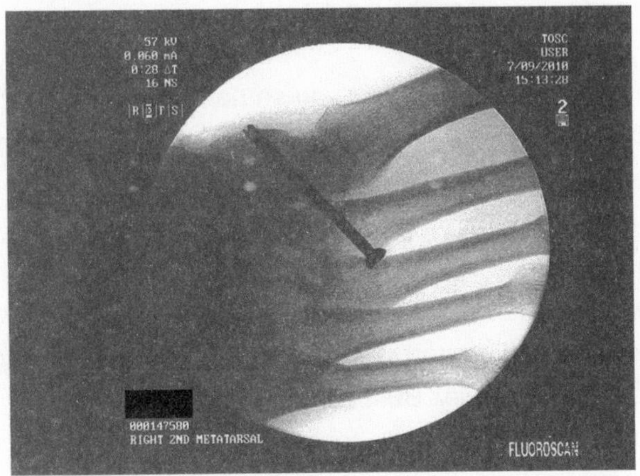

TEXAS ORTHOPEDICS UL
4700 SETON CENTER PKWY STE 200
AUSTIN, TX. 78759-4107
512-439-1000

Merchant ID: 8085993783
Term ID: 00079200000800916393500

Phone Order

VISA Entry Method: Manual

Total: $ 902.85

07/20/10 11:47:05
Inv #: 000033 Appr Code: 054712
Apprvd: Online
AVS Code:
CVV2 Code: MATCH M

Customer Copy

THANK YOU!

TERMINAL I.D.:

MERCHANT #:

VISA

SALE

TOTAL $1462.52

I almost fired off a quick email telling him to lick my ass, but thought better of it. Instead, I took a few days, contemplated the best approach, and then fired off this missive:

"EuroTrash,

This is a long email, so if you don't want to read it, I understand. Here's the executive summary:

- I'm not paying for shit.

This is the overlong explanation of why. Excuse my lack of brevity, but I'm a writer by trade. You know how we are.

1. Are you really saying that I hit you so hard in the FACE, that I broke your FOOT!?! Dude, if you wanna suck my dick, just come out and say it. No reason to be coy.

2. I have no idea if the incident that we were involved in actually caused you to break your foot. You could easily have kicked your dog in frustration over getting embarrassed in front of your wife and friends, and broke your foot that way. But I assume you have some way of proving this, as you don't seem to be foolish enough to just make something like this up. So let's discuss the primary reason I'm not paying for anything:

3. What happened was—in both legal and moral terms—your fault. I am not sure how much you understand about the American legal system, so I'll try to explain why. But please bear with me—even though I have a JD from a top American law school, I am no expert. I spent most of law school drinking and partying and not in class (which ironically is why I am now a rich and famous writer, funny how life works). But I was awake enough to absorb the legal concepts of "assault" and "proximate cause," and I'll be happy to explain them to you in the context of what happened between you and me:

Assault, generally speaking, occurs when one person commits, or threatens to commit, an act of violence against another. So when you decided to launch yourself off the boat at me and violently shove me, that was assault. From there, the events as I remember them were: me pushing you away from me, DipShit pushing me, me pushing DipShit away, you pushing me again, and then of course, me blasting you in the face.

That is not two people having a "tango." That is you and DipShit committing assault, and me defending myself. One of the key things to remember is that I only threw one punch at you (actually you probably don't remember that, as your brain was bouncing around your skull after the first punch and didn't register anything for awhile, but you can ask anyone, they remember). Your multiple assaults on me threatened my safety, and my single right cross made you a non-threat, so I didn't throw another punch. Had I continued to hit you as you staggered around the dock like a mortally wounded deer, any punches after the first would have been assault on my part. But I didn't do that. I just went upstairs and finished my game of beer pong.

This brings us to "proximate cause." It's kinda intricate, so I'll quote Wikipedia for the precise definition:

"In the law, a proximate cause is an event sufficiently related to a legally recognizable injury to be held not just the actual physical and temporal cause, but also the legal cause of a given injury. This actual cause is the first phase of proximate cause, and that means "but for" the action, the result would not have happened. To get to the level of proximate cause, our analysis must move one step higher. The act causing injury must have been the but-for cause plus the end result has to be fairly foreseeable to the actor at the time she acted. Proximate cause adds this element of reasonable foreseeability to the but-for test to determine whether it would be fair to hold an actor responsible for the full consequences of the resulting harm."

Confusing I know, but what it basically means is that even though my fist slamming into your jaw was the "actual" cause of your broken foot, your assaults on me were the "proximate" cause. You pushing me twice was the triggering event for everything that happened afterwards, and what happened (me punching you in the mouth) was the predictable result of your actions (being a douchebag, pushing me, etc). In the plainest English possible, you are shit out of luck.

That covers the legal issues, which basically cover any sort of money issue. Yet, even if I were not legally obliged to pay you, if I felt morally responsible, I would still cough up the money.

But I don't feel the least bit of compunction. You got what you deserved. I don't know where you come from or what kind of life you've led, but where I come from, when you shove someone, that means you want to fight. I tried—very poorly, I admit—not to get into a physical altercation with anyone that night, and I take no pride in knocking out a clearly over-matched, lithe little European dude. I also genuinely regret the fact that it wasn't DipShit I punched in face—as he had also assaulted me and more importantly, deserved to be hit much more than you did. But unfortunately, you were the one who pushed me twice. So you were the one who got his jaw jacked.

And you are going to have to be the one to pay for it. Physically and financially.

Regards,

Tucker Max"

Never got a response. I guess two ass whippings were enough.

Meet My Friend Hate

Occurred, Various 1998–2011

Everyone thinks SlingBlade is my funniest friend, and that's understandable: He's a bottomless font of hilarious one-liners that just barely covers a reservoir of anger fueled by a lifetime of rejection in the face of a heartbreakingly childlike desire to be loved. I know—hilarious, right? Here's the thing: when I was actually in law school SlingBlade wasn't the guy who entertained me the most. That was my roommate, Hate.

The Backstory

The most important thing to understand about Hate—and I can't emphasize this fact enough—is that he's a legitimately good guy. He's such a good guy, that to know him is to like him. Take law school for instance: if you ever meet anyone I went to law school with, and they tell you I wasn't cool or hilarious in law school—they're lying (probably because they're jealous that my life is awesome and their lives suck). BUT, if they tell you that pretty much everyone at Duke besides my friends hated me—that IS the truth. Even though Hate bore the stain of living with me and being one of my best friends, he was still so popular that he got elected Social Chair during our 2L year anyway (which is basically just a popularity contest).

In most ways, Hate is everything you'd want in a son or a husband or a friend. He's honest almost to the point of absurdity. He once returned $5 in extra change TO A WENDY'S, like some sort of modern-day Abe Lincoln. No shit, he got home, discovered the mistake, got back in the car and drove to the restaurant. FORTY MINUTES LATER! The Wendy's people were so confused, they didn't know what to do. They almost wouldn't accept the money, like they were worried they were being set up or something. I don't blame them—who does that?! Hate does.

His moral rectitude and conscientiousness doesn't stop at shitty fast food, either. I've never seen a guy treat women better than he does. He is the complete opposite of me in every way— all about respect and chivalry and all that stupid shit to the point of almost being a doormat. This girl once told me, "When law school started, we all thought Hate was going to be the dick and you were going to be the nice guy. Then we got to know you guys more, and we realized it was the opposite."

Of course, that begs the question: Why did everyone think Hate was going to be a dick?

If you didn't know him, like these girls didn't when we started law school, you'd say he looks pissed off all the time too. And you'd be right. He does look pissed off all the time, because deep down, he IS pissed off. Yes, SlingBlade is angry too, but he at least understands his issues and the fact that he is impotent to change them. The difference is that Hate used to be completely and totally unaware of his anger problem. Because he unconsciously holds his anger in, he was legitimately convinced that he was a chill, relaxed, normal guy. Don't get me wrong, he was . . . sort of, but not really. If you know anyone who holds in negative emotions, you know that even if they can hold the rage down for awhile, it's never a viable long-term solution. It's GOING to come out.

Hate's suppressed anger issues begin with his height. He's short. Hate will tell you he's 5'6", but even Earl Boykins would be like, "C'mon, son." He's 5'4" on a good hair day. Making jokes about getting on rides at Six Flags and telling him to get on his tippy-toes because, "life happens up here" hits real close to home. He's not soft, though. He is a strong, athletic guy, built like an iron bowling ball. Picture an Angry Bird, or Gimli from *The Lord of The Rings.* Now picture him on a stepstool, trying to reach a glass in the cupboard above the stove. That's Hate.

Most short guys are defined by their height, and as a result, have a Napoleonic Complex. Because short kids usually had a rough go of things when they were young, they're hypersensitive to disrespect or perceived slights in adulthood. Typically, they express their anger in an outwardly focused, confrontational manner and start fights with anyone over anything, because they are compensating for their smaller stature.

That isn't Hate at all. He is the opposite of that. Hate was raised by good parents who taught him to follow the rules and always do the "right thing." Like a good little boy, he listened to them. And it was the worst thing he could've done.

The rules your parents teach you to live by are very different than the rules the world actually runs by. Most of the conventional wisdom is not only wrong, it's a lie told to us by people who want to control us. It doesn't help *us,* it helps them. Pretty much everything we're told as children (and adults, really) by the established power structures in our lives are made-up fairytales used to reinforce that control: Santa Claus (be good or no toys), the Easter Bunny (obey or no candy), the tooth fairy (give us your body or no money), fat-free frozen dinners, religion, and metering lights on the highway—the list goes on. It makes sense if you think about it; the only way you can truly control people is to lie to them.

Here's the thing: learning that the world is not what you were taught is usually just part of becoming an adult. The people who blindly follow the rules are getting fucked, and the people who don't can get away with theft and murder (and I mean this literally, e.g. Ray Lewis and Goldman Sachs). At some point, we all figure this out. Sometimes it's explicit, other times it's just a feeling in our gut.

How we react to this realization defines our lives. I reacted by accepting it as a reality, then getting pissed off and resolving, no matter what the consequences, never to be one of the sheep. SlingBlade cracks a bunch of jokes, then buries his depression in video games. Hate took the path most people take: He pretended this wasn't the case. He wanted to believe in the inherent fairness and equality of the system. He wanted to believe everything his parents and teachers told him. He was sincerely good so Santa would bring him presents. He took his vitamins and said his prayers because Hulk Hogan told him to. He didn't just buy into the bullshit; he went all-in. It was like he would tell himself, "No matter how bad things get, if I just keep doing the right things, being the good guy that I am supposed to be, then eventually things will work out."

The problem is, they never did. The older Hate got, the *less* things went his way. He kept doing the "right" thing, checking off all the boxes and doing everything you are "supposed" to do to be a success, and he kept getting fucked. All the while, the guy doing the *wrong* thing (me, for example) kept getting what he wanted. Sisyphus led a less futile existence than Hate: at least Sisyphus got in a workout. All Hate got was Bitterness and Resentment high-fiving each other over as they Eiffel Towered his exhausted psyche. THAT is why he was so mad deep down—because he believed in the system . . . and the system ran train on him.

Unfortunately, Hate was no Tyler Durden. He could never muster the courage to reject this plight and join any sort of symbolic Fight Club. Instead, he became Hate's Raging Internalized Emotion. The harder he got fucked, the more energy he spent keeping it down. As anyone knows, you can't hold the lid down on a pressure cooker forever. It's eventually going to explode. By the middle of law school, he was so fucking pissed off at the world that any little thing, no matter how trivial, could trigger an explosion of anger.

Once our other roommate Credit and I figured this out—that Hate was a barely-contained ball of seething rage—we did what all twenty-something males would do to their good friend: we spent all of our free time figuring out ways to get the Hate Volcano to erupt for our amusement. The explosions were glorious in their magnitude and hilarity.

This story is about those explosions, and how Credit and I made them happen.

The Pizza Incident

Generally, Hate is a non-violent person. He is polite and solicitous, and saves all his aggression for the rugby pitch—or whatever you call the field where they play that 19th-century game of hot-potato smear-the-queer. I don't know how many actual fights Hate has gotten into in his life, but I'd be willing to bet 100% of them involved coming to the defense of other people. The first time I ever saw it happen, it seemed like a relatively minor incident. In retrospect, I should have seen it for what it was: a harbinger of how Hate's anger would impact our lives for years to come.

We were all out one night in Durham, and we'd gotten good and drunk on cheap beer. When the bar closed, we decided to go across the street to get a slice. This pizza place was a replica of every late night pizza joint in America: long glass counter, petrified slices under warmer lamps, greasy garlic knots and vaguely Middle Eastern employees with hard-to-place accents.

Brownhole and I make some stupid smartass remarks—they weren't funny enough that I even remember them—while Hate quietly examined each slice of pizza, looking for the perfect combination of freshness, cheesiness, and topping distribution. Even when he was drunk, Hate still cared about getting good value. Brownhole and I just paid and walked outside to talk to everyone else who was on the street.

We're talking and eating, when I see one of the girls' eyes go wide. She starts pointing into the pizza place and I turn to look. There, through the glass, I see a scene straight out of *Do The Right Thing:*

One of the guys working behind the counter is waving around a huge knife and trying to climb over the counter to get at Hate. The only thing stopping him is the other counter guy. Hate is screaming at the top of his lungs, also trying to get over the counter. The only thing stopping *him* is genetics—poor little guy.

It takes me a second to react because, seriously, WTF??? I was just in there 30 seconds ago, joking with everyone. Everyone was happy. Now some dude was trying to stab him??? Once it registers that this dude really is WAVING A KNIFE at my friend, I drop my slice and rush inside.

Hate "OH I'M THE ASSHOLE? I'M THE ASSHOLE!!! FUCK YOU, YOU'RE THE FUCKING ASSHOLE!"
PizzaGuy "YOU FUCK, I KILL YOU!! YOU WANT SLICE? I GIVE YOU SLICE! I SLICE YOUR FUCKING EAR OFF!!!!"

Brownhole and I pull him out of the restaurant not one second too soon—just as the guy with the knife got around his hairy, unibrowed co-worker and emerged from behind the counter. This was not a joke. This motherfucker had murder in his eyes.

It took a minute to settle everything down, and once we did, we got the hell out of there. The American Bar Association frowns on being involved in involuntary manslaughter cases. Of course everyone was still kinda weirded out. The guys in the group didn't really care, per se, but c'mon: How the fuck do you go from ordering pizza to a knife fight in under 30 seconds? This isn't a Mexican bordertown.

The best part is, I'd been an asshole to the girls all night but by the time we got back to our place they'd completely forgotten about it because they were so upset with Hate. Never mind that for 99.9% of the night, he'd been this great guy buying them drinks and listening to their pointless whore prattle.

Girl "Hate, why were you acting like that?"
Tucker [just fucking with him] "I know, I really can't believe you'd do that, Hate."
Hate "IT WAS YOUR FAULT TUCKER!! That guy called you an asshole after you left—WHICH YOU WERE—and I was defending you!! That's what caused the whole thing!"

To this day, I honestly have no fucking clue what I said that started this. Why the fuck would I remember a passing remark to some terrorist sleeper cell pizza guys? Fuck'em if they can't take a joke, right?

Girl [sincere] "Hate, you shouldn't blame other people for your outbursts."
Tucker [still fucking with him] "Yeah, Hate. Violence and anger are so uncool."
Hate "OH WHAT THE FUCK!!!"

The Italian Restaurant

This is probably not the *best* Hate story from law school, but it is my personal favorite:

Credit was dating this one girl in law school, "Rachel." Both she and Credit are Jewish, so it was a match made in haggling, self-loathing heaven. One night she and a bunch of her female friends from their temple or Hillel or whatever decided to throw a dinner party at the one nice Italian restaurant in Durham. She told Credit to bring his male friends. He doesn't have any friends, so he brought me and Hate.

This was one of those dinner parties young girls have and pretend to enjoy, in order to show each other how sophisticated they are. Translation: it was really fucking boring. Plus, all these girls were in the same social circle, so all they did was gossip and talk about girls who weren't there. Since they were Jewish, I was at least hoping to hear details of their Zionist plots against Palestinians or stories about how they have their horns and tails cut off at birth, but no dice.

Normally, mixing me with alcohol and boredom is a recipe for disaster. The only known antidote is the possibility of immediate sexual contact. Fortunately for everyone not interested in hearing the harsh truth about the state of Israel, there was a pretty cute Jewish girl next to me at the table. And once she realized I was a naughty goyim she could secretly have forbidden sex with, I had my entertainment for the evening. As usual, Rachel was a bitch to Credit and he fawned over her, because they're a typical Jewish couple.

Hate was seated between me and this quiet, mousey girl. When Rachel introduced her to Hate, she perked up right away—Hate is not Jewish at all, but his last name is VERY Jewish-sounding. She talked to him for a few minutes, thinking she'd found a nice Jewish lawyer-to-be. And then he told her he didn't go to any temple because he was Protestant, and she had no use for him. This one was looking for a husband; non-Jews needed not apply.

Credit had sold Hate on coming to this thing by promising Rachel would sit him next to a cute girl who would be shorter than him and would be into him. He rushed home from rugby practice and quickly showered, all so this snotty little J.A.P. could immediately brush him off, just because he wasn't a Christ-killer. And he still had to pay for his lousy meal.

Compounding all of this for Hate was the fact that he was really hungry. This restaurant was supposed to be one of the best in Durham. If you know anything about restaurants, you know that small towns like Durham in southern states like North Carolina are lucky if any of the "nice" restaurants are better than Macaroni Grill. This place wasn't. Not only that, but they had awful service too. Everything took forever to get there. Hate is never late, ever, and because he'd just come from rugby practice and rushed to get to dinner on time, he hadn't eaten anything for several hours.

When the bread came, like ten minutes after we'd been seated, the waiter put it across the table from Hate. He asked Rachel to pass the bread, so she did what anyone would do, she took a roll and passed it from person to person. By the time it got to Hate, all the bread was gone. Remember that scene from *Office Space* when they're celebrating a birthday and everyone gets a piece of cake but Milton? Yeah, it was like that. There was nothing left in the basket but a pack of saltines. Which Hate ripped open and ate like we'd just picked him up off a lifeboat. He even dipped them into the butter. As buttery crumbs spilled from his mouth, the mousey girl shot him the most repulsed look I've ever seen. It was like she was watching the fine dining equivalent of "Two Girls, One Cup".

Ten minutes go by and still, no one has come to refill the breadbasket. Hate is frustrated. Finally the waiter comes by to take our drink order.

Hate "Can we get more bread please?"
Waiter "Of course."

Five minutes go by. Nothing. Hate is peeved. The waiter brings our drinks.

Hate "Did you get the bread?"
Waiter "Oh sorry!"

Ten excruciatingly grain-free minutes go by. Hate is getting visibly annoyed. The waiter comes to take our dinner order.

Hate "Do you have the bread?"
Waiter "Oh my God! I'll get that as soon as I take your order! So sorry."

The girl who had suggested the restaurant tells everyone that she has to leave, because she had plans to eat somewhere else. This girl also went to law school with us, and was possibly Hate's least favorite person in the school. Normally, her leaving would have made Hate happy, but 1. She suggested the spot that was sucking on every level, 2. She was now going off to eat, while he had to keep waiting for his food, and 3. She had taken the last two rolls right before the basket had gotten to Hate, and both were sitting there, with the only the soft middles eaten out.

On this point, I am fully behind Hate. What kind of greedy, selfish, entitled bitch takes not just two, but THE LAST TWO rolls from the roll basket when it's clear not everyone has gotten one, and then just eats the center out of both?? I could tell you what kind, but I'm tired of getting emails from the Anti-Defamation League.

This was a turning point in the night. Hate passed all his preliminary stages of anger, and sat ready to blow. He was so hungry, he'd eaten all the ice out of his vodka soda. But he's so polite that he wouldn't make a big deal out of it, or go get some bread himself. He just sat there, steaming at the indignity of being ignored and dismissed. The waiter comes by with our second round of drinks.

Hate "I asked for more bread, it never came."
Waiter "Oh sorry . . . we just ran out."

At that point, we'd been in the restaurant about an hour. Hate was trying to hold it together, but he addressed the waiter in a voice that was equal parts desperation and frustration, and just a bit too loud for the situation.

Hate "Well, can I get an appetizer or something?? I'm starving!"
Waiter "Your entrees will be out in no time. If I order an app now, it'll just come out with them."

He let out a huge sigh and threw his hands up in the air, then sat there, staring off at nothing and muttering to himself, with his jaws locked in angry tension, like two tectonic plates on the verge of slippage. He reacted like a Celtics fan does when Kobe Bryant gets a bailout call—they want to get pissed at the unfairness of it, but they can't muster anything but resigned exasperation, because they knew it was coming. The girls, of course, were aghast at his embarrassing display. Every good Jewish girl knows that the appropriate response in this situation is excessive eye-rolling and withering passive-aggressiveness. Credit and me? We started giggling, hoping against hope to see the Hate Volcano blow.

Five minutes have passed since the waiter said the food will be "out in no time." Hate's nostrils are now flared like the bulging magma vents of Mount Kilhuea. Credit and I are periodically checking him for signs of seismic activity.

Ten more minutes pass. Hate has completely abandoned any pretense of socialization, retreating into his cocoon of rage. Credit and I are now flicking our eyes back and forth between our conversations and Hate so much, we look like we're watching the Chinese National Ping-Pong Championships.

Fifteen minutes pass. Hate has firmly grasped his knife and fork, and has begun staring a hole through his plate. It's becoming hard for me to contain my excitement. Christmas is so close!

Twenty minutes. Hate is white-knuckling his utensils. The veins on his head throb and pulsate. In a disaster movie, this would be the part where Morgan Freeman comes on to tell us a comet is headed for earth, and it can't be stopped.

At some point between the twenty and twenty-five minute mark, it happens:

With his knife and fork still in his hands, Hate violently gorilla slams both fists down into the table. All the plates on the table jump up, the glasses clink and fall over, and he yells at the top of his lungs:

"CRIMINY!"

The mousey girl next to him yelps in surprise, and a look of true primal fear fills her face. For a second, I think she was honestly scared for her life. All the other girls sat wide-eyed and speechless, like they'd just seen a shooting. Credit and I, too, were speechless. But we couldn't talk because we were laughing. And I could NOT stop. I'm sitting here at my computer, over ten years later, still laughing my ass off as I fucking write this.

I mean . . . who says "criminy"??? What's next, "fiddlesticks"??? "Jiminy Cricket"???

Here's the thing: After he'd hammer-fisted the table so hard it almost broke, it's not like he started laughing. Hate wasn't doing this to be funny. He was VERY serious. He sat there, just as angry as before his outburst, hands still death-clutching his utensils, staring a hole into his plate, waiting for the food, like a guy who takes his role as the king at Medieval Times a *little* too seriously.

No one said a fucking word until the food came—which of course happened only one minute after Hate's explosion. The only sounds were the girls picking up the glasses that fell over, Credit and me cackling like uncontrollable hyenas, and Rachel trying to shush us. I don't think anyone talked as they ate, nor do I remember a thing about the food, and still this was probably the most enjoyable meal of my life.

The Italy Trip

The summer between our first and second year, Credit and Hate went to Italy to do a summer session at a law school there. The first thing they did when they got back was tell me all about it. It was awesome—not because of the sights or even anything they did, but because Credit basically spent the entire time getting under Hate's skin in the most subtle and ingenious ways.

Credit tells the story of the bus tickets:

Credit "So no one checks your tickets on the buses in Rome; they are run on the honor system. But every once in a while, a cop will get on and check everyone's ticket, and if you don't have it, you have to pay a huge fine. We would buy our tickets most of the time, but one night we were out drinking and we'd both lost our tickets, and you can only buy them during the day. And it was far from our place, like six miles or something. I'm not walking that, no chance. You can go ahead and fine me or whatever, but there is no way I'm walking six miles. Hate on the other hand . . . well, you know Hate. Breaking the law—ANY LAW—is a black and white issue to him. So he watched me get on the bus, and then started the long, SIX MILE walk home. While drunk, at 1am. It takes two hours

for him to walk home. Two hours! Can you imagine? And it started raining. He was soaking wet when he got home."
Tucker "But was there a cop checking tickets on the bus?"
Credit "Of course not! They're Italian, they're not working late night weekends."

No response from Hate as Credit told this story. Just suppressed anger. Then, as if he had spent the entire time crafting his defense, he finally pipes up:

Hate "Credit, did you tell Tucker about the place we had to stay? Because of you??"

Credit can do nothing but laugh.

Hate "OK, so I organized everything for this trip. I arranged the travel, I got us registered at the school, I did EVERYTHING. The only thing I asked Credit to do was find us a place to stay in Rome. That's it. ONE THING. That's the ONLY thing he had to do."
Credit [still laughing his ass off] "Hate, it *was* a place wasn't it? And we *stayed* there, didn't we?"
Hate "Ooohhhh—you want to play that game? Tucker, listen to this place. It looks like Section 8 housing. Building had to be 200 years old. We had a communal shower/toilet area we had to share with a bunch of other people. The entire room wasn't even as big as one of our bedrooms here. You could stand in the middle and almost touch both walls with your arms outstretched. There was no desk or anything. We slept on cots. Cots. Actual cots, that may in fact have been left over from the American occupation during WWII. And of course, no air-conditioning. Which in the summer in Rome was awful. I would wake up every morning drenched in sweat."
Credit "Hate, it wasn't *that* bad."
Hate "Oh no, in fact, it was worse. At first I just sucked it up and dealt with it, because I assumed that this was the only place we could get. This is Rome, it's hard to find temporary places, OK fine, at least we're in Rome.

Then we get invited to a student thing at the apartment of another girl in our program, who goes to Georgetown Law School. Her place was amazing. Huge, totally furnished, everything; better than our place here. Well, at the very least this girl must be rich or something, so I assume her daddy paid for this or something, and we could never have afforded this anyway."

Hate's anger is starting to hit a crescendo, and Credit is laughing so hard, he's almost crying.

Hate "NO!! She is paying LESS THAN WE ARE. And get this—she got the place through the service the school has for the summer students. CREDIT COULD HAVE DONE THIS!!"
Credit "Max, you don't understand how awesome it was—he was screaming at me in this apartment, with all these law students around who didn't know him at all. They were all nervous and freaked out."

From the second they'd come back from Italy, Credit had repeatedly busted Hate's balls about this "two inches on the cot," or something. I wanted to see how this tied in, and what better time to ask than right as Hate was reaching the brink?

Tucker "But what's the deal with the smaller cot or whatever?"
Hate "Oh, that's just the icing on this cake of bullshit."
Credit "OK, when we got to our place for the first time, since it was so shitty, I let Hate pick the cot he wanted, and I took the other one. Well, after a few days, Hate started to suspect that my cot was larger than his cot."
Tucker "We're talking about cots? Like, these are just two pieces of fabric tied between sticks?"
Credit "Oh yeah. No doubt. It was impossible for these to be more shitty. So anyway, Hate starts obsessing over the cots, every day he's talking about the cots, and how maybe I got the larger cot, and on and on. So one day we bought a tape measure and measured them—"

Credit is laughing too hard to even continue, and Hate can't contain himself.

Hate "HIS COT WAS TWO INCHES WIDER THAN MINE!!"
Credit "Hate, I let you pick the cot you wanted!"
Hate "It doesn't matter—YOU GOT THE LARGER COT!! EVEN AFTER YOU FUCKED EVERYTHING UP!!"

Credit sums up his most faux-serious voice, and still laughing, says:

Credit "Hate . . . let's not live in the past."

Hate exploded with indignant fury, cursing and storming around the apartment for at least another hour.

The Apartment

Those vignettes above were all from the first year of law school. Second year was when Hate, Credit, and I moved in together. Now with closer proximity to Hate, Credit and I devised dozens of little things to fuck with him. For example:

1. Chores: We'd conspire to adjust the chores so that he always had to do everything. For example, if it was Credit's turn to take out the trash, we'd both claim it was Hate's. His pure astonishment and righteous indignation at the thought of having to take out the trash TWICE in a week was a bouquet of hilarious.

Hate "Credit, take the trash out."
Credit "I think it's your turn, Hate."
Hate "It is not, it's yours, I took it out Monday."
Credit "I took it out Tuesday."
Tucker "Yep, he did. You're up Hate."
Hate "There was no trash on Tuesday!!"
Credit "I seem to remember taking trash out."
Hate "FUCK BOTH OF YOU! THIS IS THE SAME TRASH FROM

YESTERDAY! I EVEN REMEMBER THE CANDY BAR WRAPPERS HERE! NOW TAKE IT OUT!"
Credit "I ate a Snickers this morning."
Tucker "I think I saw Credit take the trash out."
Hate "WHAT THE FUCK?!??!"

2. Food: We'd always eat his food and then lie about it. You see, the three of us were at that stage in our lives just past the free-for-all of college food allocation, but not quite into the responsibility of adult food budgeting. Because we each bought our own food, but stored it together, Hate devised a complex system to divide the refrigerator and pantry up into sections for each of us. It makes sense he would do this—think of the attributes that go into making the type of person who would create a fastidious and explicit system for fair and equitable storage of food. Credit and I paid lip service to following his rules . . . but it was only so we could break them in the most subtle and infuriating ways.

Like eating his peanut butter. We'd CONSTANTLY eat his peanut butter, making sure to leave just enough so that the next time he went to make a sandwich, there was only enough to thinly cover his bread (he liked it thick). He'd get pissed off and rant and rave, but we'd always be in the clear—because we'd eat enough of our own peanut butter that it looked like we were only using our own. Hate, being too good of a person, couldn't conceive of someone eating double the proper amount of peanut butter just to fuck with him, so instead he blamed himself.

Sometimes we'd use his peanut butter completely up, and replace it—except with low-fat peanut butter. You haven't lived until you've seen a grown man flip his shit when he goes to make a PB & J and finds low-fat Jif in his cupboard. One time we switched it up and replaced the bread of his we ate with potato bread instead of whole grain wheat.

Hate "Max, what the hell is this??"
Tucker "Bread."
Hate "THIS IS POTATO BREAD!!"
Tucker "So?"

Hate "WHY WOULD YOU BUY THIS??"
Tucker "I replaced your bread, just like I said. Plus, I only ate about ten slices of your last loaf, and I bought you a whole new one. So . . . you owe me a few slices out of there."
Hate "WHAT THE FUCK IS POTATO BREAD?"

3. The TV: We had two TVs in our living room, one little one and one big one. So anytime there were two things on TV, we would vote on what got the big TV and sound, and what got the little TV and mute. Credit and I made it a routine to outvote Hate. I cannot tell you how many times we'd force ourselves to sit there with some awful movie on the big TV, and baseball would be on the small TV, just so we could listen to Hate bitch and moan.

Hate "Are you two fucking serious? Why is "Dawson's Creek" on?"
Tucker "I like Pacey. He's just so comforting."
Credit "Yeah Hate, plus James Van Der Beek looks like Tucker."
Hate "THIS SHOW IS FUCKING AWFUL! THE FUCKING PIRATES ARE ON, AND YOU TWO FUCKING SKIRTS WANT TO WATCH DAWSONS FUCKING CREEK! FUCK!!!"
Tucker "Hate, we voted fair and square."
Hate "THIS IS BULLSHIT!!!"

4. The Debates: One of the things Hate, Credit, and I shared was our passion for pointless debates about stupid shit. Didn't matter whether it was who was the hottest Golden Girl (Blanche), what sport was the hardest (no resolution, but sports not involving physical violence need not apply), or which girl I brought home was the most fucked up (all of them), we were always debating nonsensical shit.

Movies were usually the biggest debate topic though. We would argue endlessly about movies. Here's the thing with these debates: while Credit and I just engaged in them as purely fun intellectual exercises, Hate took them VERY seriously. If you tried to argue a point that he didn't like or agree with, it could quickly become intense and personal. For whatever reason, his identity was in many ways tied up with his position on movies, so he'd defend them vigorously. To counteract that over-seriousness, Credit and I would start the most ridiculous debates.

One weekend a Sean Connery movie was on, which started a debate that quickly became intense, because Sean Connery is Hate's favorite actor:

Credit "Hate, best Sean Connery movie—*Untouchables*?"
Hate "What? No chance! What about *Indiana Jones*? *The Name of The Rose*? *Goldfinger*? There are so many better ones. Costner ruins that movie."
Credit "But Credit, that's the role he won an Oscar for."
Hate "An Oscar?!? Jesus Christ!! Martin Scorsese hasn't even won an Oscar, fuck the Oscars!" [Note: this was like 2000 or so, before *The Departed*]

I was in the bathroom taking a dump. Thanks to the layout of our place and the fact that I usually shit with the door open, I could hear the debate begin. I couldn't hear all the details, but I didn't need to. Credit and I are like Peyton Manning and Marvin Harrison when it comes to inciting Hate's rage. I yell out from the bathroom:

Tucker "Hate, what about *Medicine Man*?"

I don't know if you've seen *Medicine Man,* but it's fucking terrible. Arguably the worst Connery movie ever, and easily one of the worst major studio releases of that year. Everything you can imagine is wrong with the movie; for fuck's sake Lorraine Bracco is supposed to be his sexy sidekick! So yeah, a complete disaster of a movie. Hate immediately bellows back from the other room.

Hate "*MEDICINE MAN*?!?"
Tucker "Yeah, you know the movie about him being in the jungle and curing cancer and shit!"
Hate "MAX, SHUT THE FUCK UP!!"
Tucker "Did you even see *Medicine Man*?"

He walks closer to the bathroom and, without actually coming into view of the open shitter door, yells even louder:

Hate "Of course I've seen it, 'I DISCOVERED THE CURE TO THE PLAGUE OF THE 20TH CENTURY AND NOW I'VE LOST IT'—oh Christ, Max shut the fuck up!"

Credit and Hate went back to a more serious discussion.

I finally finish pooping and come out into the living room. Hate is standing in the middle of the room, about five feet from me. In the calmest but most condescending voice I can muster, I look at Hate and say:

Tucker "Hate, I guess you didn't hear me from the bathroom: What about *Medicine Man*?"

His face twisted into a knot of sneering rage. He bunched his fist up, cocked it back, and took a step towards me. He immediately got hold of himself, but it was clear as day what had just happened:

For the very briefest split second, Hate was going to take a swing at me. Because of *Medicine Man.*

Far from getting upset, Credit and I broke down laughing. Hate tried to deny it at first, but Credit had seen it too—Hate's emotions over Sean Connery had gotten so out of hand, he was going to throw a punch at his friend and roommate.

The Airbag

During the same week Credit and Hate got back to Durham from Italy, we all had to run some errands to get ready for the first semester of our 2L year. The last one took us by the law school. A friend of ours was out front, looking like he was waiting for a ride. He didn't see us, so Hate lightly tapped the horn to get his attention.

Oh, we got his attention . . . because the horn wouldn't stop honking.

AAAAAAAAAAAAARRRRRRRRRRRRRRRRRRRRRRRRRRNNNNNNN

Credit "Hate, what are you doing?!?"
Hate "IT WON'T STOP!!"

AAAAAAAAAAAAARRRRRRRRRRRRRRRRRRRRRRRRRRNNNNNNN

Hate hits it a bunch more times, trying to get the horn to unstick. No dice. Mind you, we are right in the middle of Duke's campus, and Hate can't stop because the car is in motion, in a street, with cars behind us and in front of us. But this fucking horn won't stop honking.

AAAAAAAAAAAAARRRRRRRRRRRRRRRRRRRRRRRRRRNNNNNNN

Tucker "HATE! WHAT THE FUCK!!"
Hate "IT WON'T FUCKING STOP!!!"

Hate starts pounding on the front of his steering wheel, trying to get it to stop. Nope.

AAAAAAAAAAAAARRRRRRRRRRRRRRRRRRRRRRRRRRNNNNNNN

We are still driving, and every single person is staring at us. Immigrants don't lay on their horns this much during regional ethnic parades. Go out to your car right now and lay on the horn for ten seconds. It'll drive you nuts. Now picture us driving around campus with a horn going off like that . . . *except it doesn't stop* . . . and there is a red-faced bowling ball of anger behind the wheel thrashing back and forth, screaming into a dashboard.

AAAAAAAAAAAAARRRRRRRRRRRRRRRRRRRRRRRRRRNNNNNNN

We turn a corner, and standing there is a group of at least 50 freshman undergrads doing a campus tour. Every single one is staring at our car in confusion. Credit and I were laughing our asses off before, but the combination of Hate's anxiety over this horn going off, and the genuinely quizzical expressions of these kids as to why some asshole in an old Nissan Pathfinder would honk like this is too much to handle. I have to grab my dick and pinch it off to stop from pissing myself with laughter.

AAAAAAAAAAAAARRRRRRRRRRRRRRRRRRRRRRRRNNNNNNN

Hate is now completely freaking out. He's stopped sparring with the steering wheel, and instead has turned to violently ripping the entire cover off the front of it while simultaneously trying to keep control of the car. This doesn't work well; the car drifts and jumps a curb before Hate can pull it back onto the road. The freshmen's heads have followed us from the corner all the way down the street, like watching a streaker break out of the middle of a funeral procession.

AAAAAAAAAAAAARRRRRRRRRRRRRRRRRRRRRRRRNNNNNNN

Hate finally gets the entire front cover off the steering wheel and mashes primally on the internal mechanics until the horn stops.

Credit and I have tears rolling down our faces. Hate is totally frazzled,not laughing at all. It takes a long time for all of us to compose ourselves. When we get back to our apartment, I notice something:

Tucker "Hate . . . where the fuck is your airbag?"

Hate drove an old 1994 Nissan Pathfinder. This was before the airbags were built into the steering column, and instead were basically just slapped onto the front of the steering wheel. I used to have a lot of dirtbag thief friends in high school, so I had a sneaking suspicion about what happened.

Hate "What do you mean?"

Tucker "Dude, look at all that empty space between the steering wheel cover and the steering column. And see how it says "Airbag" on the cover? There is supposed to be an airbag here. But it's not here. That's probably why your horn got stuck."
Hate "Why would my airbag be missing?"
Tucker "Well, it probably got stolen dude. You can sell those things to shady parts dealers for a lot of money. Did your car get broken into recently?"

Hate kinda looked at the constituent parts for a while, confused. The wheels turned in his head, and it hit him.

Hate "Oh . . ." [he got a look of painful and pitiful resignation on his face] ". . . my cousin drove the car this summer when I was in Italy."

Credit and I broke down in laughter again. That was all he needed to say.

Hate's cousin couldn't be more opposite of him—a liar, a thief, a con, everything. The absolute archetype of the prodigal son. Pretty much any time anything is fucked up in Hate's home life, you need look no further than his cousin to find the explanation.

Tucker "Dude . . . your cousin stole your airbag . . . dude!!"
Credit "Wow."

This was fucked up though. This wasn't like taking $20 out of his wallet. This was quite literally putting his life in danger.

Tucker "Are you going to do anything? Confront him?"
Hate "No. He'll just deny it and act all offended and that I even suggested it was him."
Tucker "What are you going to do then?"

Hate sat there for a minute and ran through his options, one by one, until he settled on the most depressingly obvious choice.

Hate "Drive around without an airbag I guess."

Another brick in Hate's wall of anger . . .

THE JIMMY JOHN'S INCIDENT

While there was no shortage of little things Credit and I would do to piss Hate off, nothing we ever dreamed up could have had the impact on his repressed, psychotic rage like the events of November of our 3L year.

In law school, everyone interns between their 2L and 3L year at the firms they presumably want to work. After you spend your summer there, you go back to law school for your last year, and then some time in the fall the firm tells you if you have a permanent job offer after you've graduated. If you do, then your 3L year is even more of a joke than law school normally is—why worry about anything if you already have a job, right?

Once we all got back to school from our 2L summer associateships, the months went by and the formal offers started rolling in. PWJ and El Bingeroso got theirs before they left their firms for the summer, Jojo, GoldenBoy, Credit, JonBenet, Brownhole, and SlingBlade all got theirs in September or October. That left Hate and me.

Hate was already nervous because other people at his firm got their offers much earlier. Then Halloween passed and he still didn't have an offer. He was all but catatonically freaked out. Whispers started about his offer. Credit used his peanut butter one day by accident and Hate screamed at him for an hour and broke a lamp. The whispers became louder.

Then he got the letter. He excitedly tore it open to find . . . no job offer from his firm.

This is awful for a ton of reasons. It means you now have to take class seriously. It means you have no job security. It means you now have to go through the interview process again during 3L year. Which is the mark of Cain both at school (almost no summers from Top Ten law schools don't get offers) and within law firms (what 3L is interviewing again at a top law firm without an offer from his 2L summer firm?). That is just disastrous. Ultimately, it means you've done something really wrong.

Hate did not handle this well. Coming back from our summer jobs, Hate was probably the most excited of the entire group. He'd landed a spot working in the best firm in Philly, and finally, he thought, all the dues-paying and bullshit he'd put up with in his life was paying off. He was going to graduate with a prestigious job, make $125k/year to start, and live in Philadelphia—a great sports town with lots of short girls who would be impressed with a guy who had a job and didn't hit them. Now, all that shit was gone and he was fucked. Again.

Credit and I steered clear of him for at least a week. He had this seething, Boy-Named-Sue anger that permeated everything he did. He was like a coiled spring, and though we loved provoking his anger into fits of rage, Credit and I were not stupid enough to do it when he might direct it at us personally.

[In fact, no one really gave him much shit, because they were too busy shitting on me. If you read *IHTSBIH,* you know that story about my 2L summer when I worked at Fenwick & West, and how my firm summarily fired me *during the summer* because I was such a drunken disaster. Not only that, because my email about the incident leaked out beyond my circle of friends, and pretty much everyone in the legal world knew about it. So like Hate, I came back to Duke for my 3L year without a job, but unlike him I also returned as the laughing stock of the entire legal world.]

About a week after he got the bad news, Hate's Raging Internalized Emotion reached new and dizzying heights during an episode that has gone down in law school legend and come to be known as "The Jimmy John's Incident."

By 3L year, we'd graduated from two TVs in the living room—one big and crappy, one small and crappy—to DirecTV in all three of the apartment's bedrooms. Why? Three words: NFL Sunday Ticket. Credit was a Jets fan, I'm a Redskins fan, and Hate is a Steelers fan. We *needed* every game on. And because there were some Sundays where all three teams were playing at the same time, we not only needed three TVs, we needed three receivers too. On Sunday morning like clockwork, we'd bring the TVs out of Credit and Hate's rooms and put them in the living room, so all of us could watch the games together, like in a sports bar.

Hate had gotten his letter on Monday. It was now Sunday, and for the first time all week, something was going to go right for him: The Steelers were playing, and they were favored, and the Steelers don't let their fans down. For those three hours, Hate could forget about all his problems and enjoy some football.

He woke up early, set all the TVs up, got all the games on the right channels, and instead of cooking, he decided to treat himself to a delicious and relaxing take-out meal while he watched his team win. He asked us if we wanted anything, then left. Twenty minutes later he came back with his favorite fast food item—a Jimmy John's Turkey Club Sandwich, complete with sour cream and onion potato chips and an ice-cold Coke to wash it all down.

He'd timed it perfectly, and arrived at the apartment right as all the idiot TV talking heads were finishing up their "analysis." He sat down on the sofa, placed his bag on the coffee table, and almost like a Japanese tea ceremony, set about placing all of his items in perfect harmony. First he took the Coke out, opened it with a crisp release of CO_2, took a sip, put the cap back on (he likes to keep it as carbonated as possible, weird I know) and placed it to the side. Then he took his chips out, opened the bag, popped one in his mouth, and placed the bag to the other side. Finally, he took the sandwich out, unrolled the paper, laid the hoagie out in front of him, and opened it. Hate likes to put his chips on his hoagie and eat them that way, to give it a crunchier texture. He started placing the chips when all of the sudden:

Hate "OH WHAT THE FUCK!! MOTHERFUCKER THAT FUCKING SHIT!!!!"

This was a serious anger eruption, at least 30 seconds of uncontrollable, unintelligible cursing. Credit, his girlfriend Rachel, and I were also in the living room watching TV, and we all kinda jumped at the vitriol in his tone. We didn't say anything as he went on and on; it was that intense. Finally, we understood the problem:

Hate "I TOLD THAT MOTHERFUCKER TO NOT PUT FUCKING MAYONNAISE ON THE FUCKING SANDWICH AND NOW LOOK AT THIS!!!"

Clear as day, slathered all over one side of his hoagie, was the yellowish white goop. Hate DESPISES mayonnaise. If mayonnaise were a racial minority, Hate would have gone to jail for hate crimes against it years ago. Before we could even really do anything, Hate shot up from the sofa, paused for a second looking for something to strike, but finding no target for his anger, took both his hands, grabbed the coffee table, and flipped it into the air as he released a primal scream.

"FFFFFFFFFFUUUUUUUUUUUUUUUUUCCCCCCCCCCCCCCCCKKKKKKKKKKKK!!"

This was a straight up Incredible Hulk move. Coke bottle, chips, sandwich—everything goes flying. Here was Hate, so angry about the fact that a condiment he didn't request was on his sandwich, that he FLIPPED OVER A COFFEE TABLE.

And as you might expect, Credit and I completely lost it. To this day, whenever I laugh really hard at something, I compare it to how hard I laughed in that moment, at that incident, because for my life, that is the gold standard of laughter.

As Hate stood there fuming, his lunch spread across the living room, Rachel did not laugh. She was not as accustomed to Hate's ridiculous outbursts. Instead of laughing or instigating him, she thought the best thing to do was try to help.

Rachel "Oh my God . . . Hate, are you OK?"

Like any good girlfriend, she immediately got up and started cleaning, asking Hate if he was OK. She put the coffee table back upright and even reassembled his lunch—which was essentially unharmed because the Coke had the lid on, the chips mostly stayed in the bag and the sandwich stayed in its wrapper.

Rachel "Hate, I like mayonnaise, I'll eat this, lemme go get you another sandwich without it."
Hate "No no." He was forcing back his rage in the face of her genuine concern, "I'll just eat it."
Rachel "Hate seriously, I can go get you another sandwich, it's fine."
Hate "No."

He wanted to really let loose and go on a patented Hate rage storm, but he couldn't, not with her there. Here was this nice girl trying to put everything back together for him, and because he was such a nice guy, all he could do was swallow the rage in the face of her sincere concern. In fact, he was kind of ashamed by it.

Of course, Credit and I were still laughing too hard to even speak. Oh God, what I wouldn't give to have a video of the next 30 minutes with Hate trying to make the best of this awful situation. He took a chip and did his best to scrape off all the mayonnaise, but you know as well as I do—getting mayonnaise off bread is the culinary equivalent of a rape shower. Scrub all you want, it doesn't change what happened here.

With every squishy, slightly mayonnaise-flavored bite, Hate's face contorted with indignant contempt and furious anger. It was like watching someone literally eat shit and die. Every chew was another reminder of how unfair life was, how he was always on the receiving end of the fucking, how he always got the short end of the stick. It was the perfect metaphor for his life—every bite was a reminder that he couldn't win.

By the end of the sandwich, Credit and I were fucking exhausted. Credit even had the hiccups. Who knew that one pot-smoking sandwich-monkey could bring one man so close to complete collapse?

The Leftovers

When we were moving out of our place at the end of law school, it was a pretty chaotic scene. We were all moving to separate cities, so we had to divide up our stuff and figure out who owed what to whom before anyone left. I was leaving first because I wanted to get down to Florida early for some reason—I'm sure it involved having sex with some spirit-crushing skank—so I was basically sticking Hate and Credit with all the bullshit tasks that come with moving out of an apartment, like the fucking dick that I am.

About an hour before I left, Hate and I were running down all the stuff that had to be done and issues that had to be resolved.

Hate "What about my bucket, Max? Are you going to replace that?"

Earlier that year, my car had been stolen from the apartment complex. For some random reason, I had a bucket in my car when it happened, and when the police found my car, it had been completely emptied of everything in it, bucket included.

Hate "And you still owe like $300 for rent and bills. How are you going to pay that?"
Tucker "Well, all the furniture in the living room is mine, and my mattress is here. How about I leave that, and you can sell it, and keep all the money."
Hate "What? Sell the furniture??"

Tucker "Hate, this is some pretty nice stuff, I mean, you can probably get more than $300 for it."

Hate erupted at this suggestion—for obvious reasons—and went into a diatribe:

Hate "Jesus Christ, Max, this is fucking ridiculous. We still have to pay this month's rent, we still have to rent this place out for the summer to cover our lease, we have to clean everything to get the deposit back, WHICH I PUT DOWN, we also have to—"

I'll spare you the details. It was basically a ten-minute monologue about all the ways I have failed him as a roommate and let him down as a friend over the past few months, and everything else generally on his mind. I think that's what he said; I wasn't really paying attention. He ended with this:

Hate "AND I'M STILL MISSING A BUCKET! That is a lot of shit to get done! What the hell are we going to do, Max?"

He was seriously upset; the veins in his neck were pulsating, there were tiny flecks of spittle around his mouth and his lips were pursed into a tight circle. This demanded a serious response from me. I looked him in the eyes, and in the most concerned voice I could muster, I responded:

Tucker "Hate . . . let's just hope for the best."

Even Hate laughed at that. And I left.

I received approximately 20 pissed off emails from Hate over the next week, but I think my favorite was from Credit. It was about how, when they finally sold the sofa—for like $50—they found what I had been doing for the TWO YEARS we lived in that apartment:

Stuffing every single piece of junk mail I'd received behind that sofa.

Because of the way the sofa was positioned in the living room you couldn't see behind it, so when they moved the sofa, approximately 100 pounds of direct mail spilled out. It was an avalanche of my bullshit literally dumping itself right at Hate's feet, one last fuck you from life before he left law school.

Credit said when Hate saw the mess, he didn't yell, he didn't scream, he didn't violently lash out at the sofa or the wall. He didn't say or do *anything.* He just stood there for a second staring at the massive pile of mail and catalogs, then shuffled out of the apartment and went for a walk by the lake.

Credit said it took three huge garbage bags to haul away all that trash, but it was worth it for that reaction from Hate. I'd finally broken Hate, and I wasn't even there to see it.

TUCKER RUINS A WINE TASTING

Occurred, October 2002

I let a female friend of mine sucker me into going to a young professional wine tasting event with a bunch of her co-workers. Though I love wine, I hate formal wine tastings because of the type of people who tend to go to them. They attract the worst kind of pseudo-intellectual, the type of person who knows nothing, thinks they know everything, and looks down on everyone else who doesn't share their stupid pretensions. Fuck all of those people. As soon as I got there I realized this event would be like that, so I tried to escape, but my friend saw me.

Friend "Tucker! So happy you're here! Thank you so much for coming. I owe you big."
Tucker "Yeah, wine's not the only thing you're gonna swish and spit tonight."

So there I am, irritated as an unwiped asshole because I am surrounded by the type of people I loathe most: uppity, idiotic, pompous douche-nozzles pontificating on shit they don't actually understand, because they think it makes them look cool in front of people they don't actually like.

So what do I do? Shut up and deal with a few hours of discomfort in a mature, adult manner? Stand quietly by myself in the corner until it was all over? Pretend I was enjoying myself so as not to cause discomfort to anyone else?

FUCK THAT, AND FUCK THESE SHITBIRDS!

The only way I could endure this tsunami of suck is to do what I always do in these types of situations—entertain myself at the expense of the posers I hate by shattering their illusions and destroying everything they stand for:

7:15pm: I strut into the foyer. I am surrounded by people who think they're better'n me. I decide to bust out my best redneck voice, and belt out, "Put tha women n' chittlins' to bed, Imma gettin' loaded tonight!" Their eyes go wide. They're not sure how serious I am. They will learn.

7:18: We get our tickets. It's $25 apiece. Still in overly loud redneck voice, "TWANTY FIVE DOLLERS! Exactly how much wine is we gettin' hur?" The woman doesn't know I'm a fucking asshole, so she's nice, "Well, it's a tasting event. We encourage people to try many different kinds." I smile, "So ike'an drank as much of tha wine as I want?" She is hesitant, "Well, yes . . . I guess so." I bellow out, "SOUNDS LIKE A WAGER TO ME!!!"

7:22: I walk to the first table. A French vineyard featuring a beaujolais. I stare at the bottle, and ask them, in my best redneck accent, "How yew say that'n wurd?"

7:23: After six failed attempts at the pronunciation, they begin to suspect I am mispronouncing it on purpose. I think the realization came when I said, "So that'n thur is it like dijonnaise?"

7:24: They just pour me some. I gulp it down. "Hey Francois, tell Pierre he makes sum damn fine grape juice!"

7:27: The next table is a vineyard pouring a chardonnay and a cabernet. They politely ask what varietal I would prefer. "I ain't sure, cause I like both colors of wine, red AND white."

7:34: I get the cab. It's actually really good. "Reminds me'a this'n wine I dun got last year. My cuzin made it in'iz tub. I got drunker'n fire on it."

7:44: The next table has a truly great white. "I LIKE IT!" The vintner enjoys my excitement, and asks my thoughts on the bouquet, "Do you get the floral notes, especially the lily?" I am confused, "Lily? You mean that thar's flower juice!?!"

7:50: I consider buying it. The exchange we have didn't really lead to that outcome:

Redneck Tucker "Yew got a box'a thisin ik'an buy? I bet disin comes in a fancy box, don't it?"
Wine Guy "No, only normal bottle."
RedneckTucker "You ain't got nuttin bigger, like a jug?"
Wine Guy "Do you mean a magnum?"
Redneck Tucker "Nah, I ain't black."

8:10: A new table. This wine sucks. I don't hide my disdain, "What am I 'posed to do with this'n stuff? Kill termites with it?"

8:12: I look at the price, "$90 a bottle?? I pay $6 a gallon for wine 'round the corner!" The table scowls at me, "So where's the Boone's Farm table? They know hawta price wine." The vintner gets saucy with me, "They don't have a table, just a couple of folding chairs and a cooler outside." I stare at him seriously, "You thank yur better'n Boone's Farm? Them's fighten wurds, buddy."

8:20: The next table has pinot noir, "Hey guys, let's drank some shots of this'n Pie-Not-Know-Ear stuff."

8:30: I have run out of wine vendors to harass. I start in on random groups of pretentious douchers, "So what flavor's yer favorite?" They look at me like I'm Sarah Palin's retarded Republican baby.

8:40: Another group of women, "Which flavor gets yew closer ta anal?" Didn't go over well.

I thought my little act was hilarious. No one else really agreed. With all the wine snobs and the cute girls annoyed with me, I stopped wasting time on jokes, and just staggered back to the booths with good wine, and greedily poured anything I could grab down my throat. People were staring and whispering. Crowds would open wide swaths in my path wherever I walked. Judging by the general reaction to me, one might have thought that a leper was tossing stray body parts around the room.

Once I reached the fucked-in-half drunk stage, I found the only person who I had yet to either insult or piss off. She was a stunning black woman named Stacy, who looked, to me at least, very similar to Vanessa Williams. Of course, I was blitzed, so in reality she could just as easily have looked like Ricky Williams. Who knows, they all look the same to me (women, I mean, not black people). I ambled over to where she was standing, in front of a booth that had a white zinfandel:

Tucker "Isn't this wine supposed to be over in the 'Assorted Hooch' section of the event?"

She giggled. Game on.

Tucker "Oh, so you think you're better'n me? You want a straw and some ice for your fancy looking pink juice?"

She thought I was hilarious. Finally an audience!

We started talking, and somehow the topic of my employment came up. This was in 2002, like a month after I started writing full time and had just put my site up, so the truthful answer to, "So, what do you do?" would have been something like, "Not a fucking thing."

Tucker "I am a connoisseur of opportunity."
Stacy "Well, if you're looking for a job, I might have a houseboy opportunity available."
Tucker "Houseboy? What does that entail? Is it part of my job to have sex with your undressed body?"

Stacy "Well, being that I am a lesbian and live with my girlfriend, I don't think so."
Tucker "You're a lesbian? Well Stacy, there's a quick way to catch my interest."

I asked if her girlfriend was as attractive as her. Stacy told me she was the "femme" in the relationship, and that I wouldn't find her live-in girlfriend nearly as alluring. She even went so far as to say that her mate vaguely resembled Pete Rose. I asked if her girlfriend was a switch-hitter like Pete, and the conversation just went downhill from there. I had endless questions for her—I mean honestly, can you imagine this couple? Being a little tipsy herself, Stacy answered all of them, some with astonishing candidness:

Tucker "Why'd you go lesbian to begin with?"
Stacy "I don't know. It was kind of an accident at first, but then I realized I liked it."
Tucker "Are you a lesbian because you hate men or because you like women?"
Stacy "I definitely don't hate men. I just like women a lot."

Tucker "What's with the butch/femme thing?"
Stacy "Hot girls are too much maintenance, and butch girls are better in bed."
Tucker "So that means you're high maintenance and you suck in bed?"
Stacy "Hehehehhehe. You're funny."
Tucker "You should see me naked."

Tucker "Who does the housework?"
Stacy "We allegedly split, but she does most of it. I work more than her."

Tucker "Could your girlfriend beat me up?
Stacy "Maybe. She's built."

Tucker "Do you two ever watch porn to get in the mood? And if so, what kind?"

Stacy "No, we really don't watch much porn. Sometimes 'Red Shoe Diaries', but usually only if we're high."

Tucker "When you and your girlfriend hook up, is it like the lesbian hookups in porn movies? I mean, if I want to get a mental picture of you and your girlfriend, could I use lesbian porn as a template?"
Stacy "Yeah, I guess. I haven't seen a lot of lesbian porn, but I can't imagine it's much different. Maybe different music. She likes Indigo Girls a lot."

Tucker "Do you two use a dildo?"
Stacy "Of course. How else am I supposed to get dick?"
Tucker "Do you want me to hit that softball? Well, I guess your girlfriend is probably a better softball player than me."
Stacy "She did play in college."
Tucker "Of course she did!"

Tucker "So what is the dildo situation, i.e., who is the fucker and who is the fuckee?"
Stacy "It all depends on our mood, but normally I'm the one getting fucked."
Tucker "Strap-on or hand-held?
Stacy "Both."
Tucker "At once!"
Stacy [coy shrug]
Tucker "Stacy, you are a naughty little monkey! And I mean that in the non-racist way."

Tucker "So what type of dildos? Like, different colors and types? Different sizes and textures?"
Stacy "Yeah, I have a lot. My favorite is the one made of Pyrex."
Tucker "She fucks you with a measuring cup?"
Stacy "No, it's shatter-proof glass."
Tucker "I know, I won the chemistry award in my high school. So what about anal penetration?
Stacy "Of course, but only with the smaller ones. And I need to be drunk."
Tucker "Alright, but here's the big question, at least for me: Is your girlfriend with the dildo better than a guy with a penis?

Stacy “Oh yes, definitely. Dildos are the shit. The dildo lasts forever, does exactly what it’s told, can change sizes, is disease free, won’t get me pregnant, and my girlfriend’s only concern is making sure I cum. Can you show me a penis that does all that?”

Tucker “I now have a new a goal in life.”
Tucker “Do you and your girlfriend ever include guys?”
Stacy “No. She’s not the ‘include a guy’ type.”
Tucker “What type is she?”
Stacy “More of the ‘shot and a beer after the game’ type.”
Tucker “So you’re dating a guy without a penis?”
Stacy “Sometimes I feel that way.”
Tucker “Do you date the ‘include a guy’ type?”
Stacy “I have before.”
Tucker “So, is this lesbian thing permanent, or are you just a tourist?”
Stacy “I don’t know. Maybe. I just kind of go with what feels right.”
Tucker “You want to hook up with me don’t you?”
Stacy “You have to start at cabana boy, and work up from there.”
Tucker “Just get me the coconut oil, and I’ll get started.”

Honestly, I don’t think I’ve ever been more attracted to a woman than I was to Stacy at that point. I’m not exactly sure why. It might have been her rare synergistic combination of startling physical beauty and sagacious wit. Perhaps it was because she had just discussed anal sex and lesbian threesomes with me. Maybe it was the three gallons of wine I had in my system. Probably a magical combination of all of the above.

In one of the greatest coups of my life, Stacy wrote down her number (her cell phone, not her home phone), and told me to call her, that she thought I was hilarious and would love to hang out with me.

And in perhaps one of the biggest disappointments of my life, at some point later that night, I lost Stacy’s number. I couldn’t leave my apartment for like three days after I realized what I had done; I was that upset.

But then I got drunk again and moved on.

THE EX-GIRLFRIEND THREESOME FALLOUT

Occurred, Summer 2009

The last story in *Assholes Finish First* is called "Good Game, Great Game, and No Game," and was about one of the most unusual, ridiculous nights of my life. To get the full effect, you kinda have to read the story, but basically the only two ex-girlfriends from the last five years of my life (Alexa and HotNurse) randomly met each other at a party, became fast friends, and decided—with neither input nor permission from me—that we were all going to have a threesome.

And we did. And it was really fucking awesome. And they left the next morning without any drama, any bullshit, nothing. It was one of those rare moments in life where everything worked out and something amazing happened.

That night and that threesome were perfect. When you reach that kind of perfection, you can't try to hold on to it. Any sort of perfection is fleeting, and if you try to hold on to it, if you try to control the uncontrollable, you destroy it. Better to relish the moment, then let go of it and move on. I basked in the glow of my awesomeness for a day or two, bragged to my buddies, took down all the notes so I could write a little story about it, and that was it.

Two days later, I got a text from HotNurse.

HotNurse "Alexa and I are at a club. It kinda sucks. See you after?"
Tucker "Just you, sure."

HotNurse "Can both of us come?"

I thought temptation might come. I was prepared. Be strong. Don't be an idiot:

Tucker "I can't stand her."
HotNurse "I know. But she's fun. And it'll be even better than last time :)"

FUCK. Intellectually, I know that there is really only one way for this to end: disaster. I should say no. The smart move is to say no. I want to say no.

But HOW do I do that? In the moment, how do I say no to two really hot girls asking to come over and have a threesome with you? I even tried to say no a few times, but it was a pitiful effort and HotNurse plowed right through it. She knew, and I knew—I couldn't say no.

They came back over, we fucked all night again, and it was almost as awesome the second time. But the next morning, I started to see the cracks in the dam:

Alexa "Come on, take us to breakfast! I want pancakes!!"
Tucker "Shut the fuck up. This was a perfect night. If we don't end it now, it'll turn into a shit storm. Go home, both of you."

That was a Friday night. On Saturday night, I already had plans with a different girl, so when HotNurse started texting me about her and Alexa coming back over, I basically just put her off by telling her I was at a business dinner and couldn't deal with it. That didn't work, so I silenced my phone and ignored her texts.

The other girl and I ended up back at my place. Then, about 2:30am, I hear this ridiculously loud, obnoxious banging on my door.

Girl "What is that?"
Tucker "Oh God . . . I hope it's the cops."

Girl "You *hope* it's the cops?? Why?"
Tucker "Because there's only one other option, and it's way worse."

Then, almost as if they heard me, I hear a severely drunken Alexa and HotNurse start yelling.

"TUUUUUUUUUUUCCCCCCCCCCCCKKKKKKKKKKKKKKEEEEE RRRRRRRR!!!"

Fuck. I picked up my phone and looked at it for the first time in three hours. There were probably 30 texts and 10 missed calls. All from HotNurse. All the while, there is constant banging and kicking of my door, and drunken whore screaming.

Girl "Who is that? Are you going to answer it?"
Tucker "I don't even know how to explain this. Just ignore them and they'll get tired and go away."
Girl "Ignore them? They're going to kick the door down!"
Tucker "Let's hope not."

As I lay in bed with this random girl, I tried to pretend like it was no big deal. Watching my phone light up with calls and texts, listening to two drunken girls try to kick in my door so they could have *another* threesome with me—one I'd already turned down—I paused and thought about the decisions I'd made in my life that led me to this moment. I couldn't help but think about the famous exchange in *No Country For Old Men:*

Anton Chigurh "If the rule you followed led you to this, of what use was the rule?"
Carson Wells "I don't know what you're talking about."
Anton Chigurh "I'm talking about your life. In which now everything can be seen at once."

Between the shouting and the pounding and the kicking, I chuckled to myself, thinking about the philosophical implications of it all. After a minute, the girl interrupted my train of thought:

Girl "They sound crazy! What should we do?"
Tucker "Be very quiet, so they don't know I'm in here."
Girl "Should I worry?"
Tucker "Just for my soul."

I felt like Anne Frank hiding from the Nazis. I am not joking or exaggerating when I say they pounded on my door and yelled at the top of their lungs for at least 30 minutes. It got so bad, not one, but TWO of my neighbors came out in the hallway and screamed at them to shut the fuck up. The second one had to threaten to call the cops before they left.

Here's the thing: My apartment building in LA is not an open one; you have to have a key to even get in the building. They not only came over to my place after I told them I wasn't home and then stopped responding to their texts, but they then BROKE INTO my building to get to my apartment door. And then, made so much noise, for such a long time, that TWO DIFFERENT neighbors had to threaten them to get them to leave.

HotNurse had to come over Monday, and I asked her about what happened, and why my neighbors complained to me (I knew the answer, but as far as she knew at the time, I wasn't in my apartment that night). She was clearly embarrassed and didn't really have a response other than "I was drunk."

So, that should have been the end of it, right? I mean, after that ridiculous debacle, with every last shred of the facade of sanity fully stripped away, no one in their right mind would submit themselves to any threesome that was so clearly and preposterous dysfunctional, right?

It's like you don't know me at all!

You ever been in Vegas with a gambler who's on an incredible run and up a huge amount, then takes a bad beat and loses half of his run on one hand? EVERYONE knows what's going to happen next, it's as reliable as the Law of Thermodynamics: He's gonna start chasing his losses trying to get it back, refusing or unable to walk away from the table, until the whole thing blows up in his face. If he walks away from the table, he's still up huge. But he can't. He's a gambler.

Four days later, just like that degenerate gambler who needs to walk away from the table but can't, I went double or nothing. Alexa and HotNurse came over again, and we had another threesome. And the inevitable happened.

It's funny when you see an ex again after you haven't seen her for a long time. You're so far removed time-wise from the trauma of the break-up that you kinda look at her with a clean slate. At first you see all the obvious positive qualities and remember why you liked her so much and, for a second, you almost wonder why you broke up. Then the rest of her comes out, and you remember why you broke up: "Oh yeah, she's a crazy fucking bitch."

I don't remember the exact sequence of events or the igniting incident, but I do remember the next morning that Alexa did something that reminded me of exactly who she was, and why I'd cut her out of my life, and it triggered me. I flipped shit on her. Went ballistic. Yelling, screaming, cursing, and breaking shit that ended with me throwing her out of my apartment.

HotNurse "I've never seen you that angry. What happened?"
Tucker "I had a flashback to dating her."

A good thing gone too far becomes bad, and going back to the well one more time with the three of us took something wonderful, and ruined it. I knew it would happen, it was inevitable, but I couldn't help it: I'm a slave to my dick.

After that, I chided myself for letting Alexa find ANOTHER way back into my life, and I made it real clear to HotNurse that not only would be no more threesomes, I didn't want to physically see Alexa in my presence again. Ever.

When these threesomes went down, HotNurse and I were in the "broken up, but not really, and maybe getting back together" stage of our relationship. There was a time when I thought we might get back together, but not after this whole debacle. Had it been any other woman than Alexa involved, we might have weathered it and, who knows, even built off it.

Probably not though. I think this set of events was almost certainly a symptom of larger problems, and not the cause of them. People will ignore a lot of reality in order to maintain their fantasies. Shit, I could ignore a marching band going through my living room if I was fucking one girl while another ate my ass out. HotNurse and I eventually broke up, and went our separate ways.

Epilogue

This all concluded in July 2009. I immediately started intense promotion for the *IHTSBIH* movie and was really busy. HotNurse kept hanging out with Alexa, our lives went in different directions, and we didn't talk for a while.

In September 2009, HotNurse met a guy—also famous—and started dating him soon after that. As I write this, HotNurse is married to that guy (I've never met him, but we have friends in common who all speak very highly of him), she has a beautiful child with him, and she seems legitimately happy.

She is still friends with Alexa, who knows a good thing when she sees it. In fact Alexa not only went to their wedding, SHE WAS IN IT.

You read that right. Alexa was one of HotNurse's *bridesmaids.*

Less than a year after they were eating each other out as I alternately fucked them, Alexa stood behind HotNurse as she got married. To a *different* guy.

I have no idea if he knows. Maybe he had a threesome with them too. I don't know, I don't care, I didn't ask, and it's not really my business. But still—how fucking weird is that? I am kinda blown away by it. Not in a bad way—I'm not mad or upset by it. I'm not sure there's a word for the feelings I had upon learning this. Something between confusion and shock, I guess. With a big dollop of relief plopped on top.

I imagine this is what Seth Macfarlane felt like after he woke up late the morning of 9/11 and missed his American Airlines flight from Boston to LA—huge relief that he wasn't on that flight, but also guilt, because all those other people were.

I don't know. All I'm really sure of is that if I were marrying a girl, and she and her bridesmaid had had a threesome with her very last ex less than a year before . . . I think I would have an issue with that bridesmaid being IN the wedding, along with a few questions about my soon-to-be-wife. But as we all know, I'm not normal in a lot of ways.

I'm gonna end this here because, quite frankly, the next logical step in this story is a whole bunch of self-reflection and soul-searching, and that would ruin the funny parts. HotNurse is happy with her husband; I'm happy; Alexa is still a sociopathic whore—let's quit while we're all ahead.

Stuff like this is the reason people say fact is stranger than fiction. Fiction has to make sense. Reality doesn't have to do shit.

In The Trunk

Occurred, November 2009

Remember all the stupid shit you lusted for as a kid? New Air Jordans, some whore trinket, that new CD—that shit dominated your desires. The whole world would end if you didn't get it. I can remember an entire year of my life where all I wanted on earth was a black Raiders hat (I was an N.W.A. fan, not some wanna-be Raiders fan living in Kentucky, so fuck off).

Then, like every other male, I discovered the ultimate toy to lust after—pussy—and that was pretty much that. I've basically forgotten or stopped caring about all the stuff I used to care about when I was little. Except my desire for one specific thing that not even pussy could drive off:

A loud, obnoxious, bass-heavy stereo system for my car.

Since as long as I can remember, I've wanted four 12's slammin' hard in my trunk. I've wanted to come down the street and bump every motherfucker off the block. I wanted the hoppers and hood rats running for cover, scared of my system because it bangs so hard it might explode their chest. I never cared about my slab drippin' in candy paint, or rolling on 24's, or poppin' trunks, or hittin' switches. That flexin' bullshit is about impressing other people—I don't give a fuck about them. I care about the bass in my trunk banging so hard, it feels like an earthquake.

Yes, I am white. No, I don't go to Tyler Perry movies or listen to Steve Harvey's radio show. No, I've never been a wigger or tried to appropriate urban culture or adopt an identity that wasn't authentic to me. It's not about that. For me, having a system that rattles you to the soul is about the music.

See, I love Southern rap. I grew up on it. I could talk for hours about why rap is America's second great original art form (after jazz). I could write 10,000 words about the crucial artistic and emotional influence The Geto Boys have had on me, and the influence Rap-A-Lot has had on my business career. I can't even name one member of Linkin Park and I doubt I could pick Dave Matthews out of a crowd, but I could make a convincing case that Scarface is not just the most important rapper, but one of the most important American musicians. *Ever.*

Most people don't get Southern rap, even some rap fans. They think it's too slow, or it's too angry, or they criticize the content of the lyrics. Of course, they listen to it on the earbuds that come with their iPods or on the factory system in their Honda Accord . . . please. Southern rap can't just be heard, it has to be *felt.* You gotta go where it's a sticky 95 degrees in the shade, and listen to "Choppin Blades" in a car with all the windows down and the bass hittin' so hard it rattles your brain stem . . . and it all makes sense.

But even though I've owned plenty of cars, and I've had enough money to get a pretty good stereo system for a while, I've held off. Not because I had outgrown it—fuck that. I refused to half-ass my shit. I may have grown up on Southern rap, but liking an art form and internalizing the value system of that art form are two very different things. Growing up I used to watch all these motherfuckers who were the definition of hood rich come to the basketball courts, and it never made sense to me.

I remember one specific dude who was like five years older than me, who always used to ball at the same public courts as me. He was out of school and worked some bullshit dead end job, and the only two things that mattered to him were pick-up ball and his car. It was a 1983 Chevy Monte Carlo (he kept it clean though), and damn, his shit BUMPED. He had a legendary stereo in Lexington; you could hear him five minutes before you saw him.

One day, he showed up to the courts with a "For Sale" sign in the window of his car. Some of the older guys asked him what he wanted for it.

Guy "I'm thanking . . . if'cha wanit wit'da stereo, it be like, bout 8 thou. Wifout da stereo, I take tree thousand, prolly."

He was totally sincere, and the guys nodded in assent at this pricing, which they seemed to find very reasonable.

I was fucking shocked. I was only like 14 or 15 at the time—and don't get me wrong, I lusted after his stereo system—but even to me, this was the height of idiocy. His stereo was worth more than his car? By almost TWO TIMES? And not only that, but I was pretty sure this dude still lived at home with his parents. This was the early 90's in Kentucky, so most of my friends and I lived in houses that cost about $60,000. For the price of JUST his car stereo, he could've had a down payment on a fucking HOUSE. A place to LIVE. Instead, he bought a CAR STEREO?? How fucking stupid is that?

That's why all those people I grew up with are still poor and stuck in Kentucky—it's not ultimately about opportunity or education or anything like that. Yeah, that shit helps, but it's more about the values you have, and how those values guide the choices you make. I swore to myself that I would never be that guy. Hood rich is for people who find out they're gonna be a dad on the set of Maury Povich. That's not who I wanted to be. That day, I made three promises to myself:

1. I was going to have a system at least that good, if not better.

2. I would only put that system in a serious luxury car, something so expensive the stereo cost less than 10% of the cost of the car, and most importantly,

3. I had to be rich enough to pay cash for the car. No loans, no financing, no debt. If I can't cut a check and drive it off the lot, I can't afford to put a system in it.

That day came in the fall of 2009, shortly after I moved to Austin. I did my research, and decided to get a Range Rover. Shopping for a car that costs more than the average annual salary of 90% of the people in this country is a different experience. You aren't treated like a customer, more like a client. There's no hustle, no hard sell, there's not even a discussion of price at all, since their prices are fixed. You can either pay or you can't. The salesman, Patrick, gave my dog some treats and got me a cappuccino as he explained all the dials and gadgets and horsepower and all the other stuff I didn't give a fuck about. It was time to lay my full hand on the table:

Tucker "Look, you don't need to do all this. I don't care about any of that. I barely understand how an internal combustion engine works. All my friends who know shit about cars say Range Rovers are awesome. I'm sold. There is only one thing I care about: Can I put a bumpin' system in here?"

A look of honest confusion filled Patrick's face.

Tucker "You know, like, can the deck and wiring handle a speaker upgrade, or am I going to have to rip it out and put all new shit in? Because that sort of work gets expensive."
Patrick "Why would you want to change the stereo? The factory system on this is the upgraded Harmon Kardon stereo system. It's amazing, it comes with . . ."
Tucker "No no no. I'm not listening to the Beatles, man. I'm talking about putting four 12-inch subwoofers and two 1000-watt amps in the trunk. Banging. Bumping. You ever heard a car driving by, and the bass is so loud, you can feel it? Like that."
Patrick "I . . . uh . . . I don't really know . . . I've worked here for almost a decade, and no one has ever asked that question before."
Tucker "Really?"
Patrick "Tucker . . . this is a Range Rover dealership."
Tucker "You've never had a drug dealer or something come in here to buy a car?"

I was being serious, but he had no idea how to take me. I had my assistant figure it out, and he was pretty sure that the factory wiring on

Range Rovers not only could easily accommodate the system I wanted, but it was made so well and with such tight tolerances, it was actually one of the best vehicles to put that type of system in, because you didn't have to hunt down all the rattling that comes when you bang in a cheap car. [You know what I'm talking about: you pull up next to some dinged-up piece of shit Mercury Cougar and all you hear is big bass beats being swallowed up by what sounds like a bunch of people playing Yahtzee with soup cans full of pennies. None of that shit with a Range Rover.]

I went in the next day, cut a check, drove it off the lot, and took it right to the stereo store.

Tucker "I want the best system I can get, without having to add another battery to the car."

I picked this store because it was in the poor area of town, so I assumed he would get it. Nope. I don't know what it is about the automobile and auto-accessories industries, but these motherfuckers will talk all day about all the stupid shit I didn't care about. Hertz, watts, treble, splitters—DO I LOOK LIKE A FUCKING AUDIO NERD TO YOU?!?!? I JUST WANNA BANG!!

Tucker "Look man—I don't care about this shit. I just want so much bass, I get hearing loss. I want to have to put a defibrillator in my car, because the bass interrupts my normal heart rhythms. I don't want to turn heads—I want to bring the walls down."
Salesman "I think we can do that."
Tucker "Let me be clearer: If I DON'T get a noise pollution ticket in the first three months, I'm coming back here to get my money back."

He thought I was kidding. Without screaming curses into his face, I emphasized that I absolutely was not. Then he looked at me like I was fucking crazy. It was the same look Patrick gave me at the Range Rover dealership. What is it with these people?

He finally quoted me a price on a system. I gave it to my assistant, and he found all the component parts on the internet for about 70% less (I may be rich, but I'm not stupid), so I ordered them and then took them in for the stereo people to install.

It was the longest three hours of my fucking life. I felt like I was waiting for a kid to be born, only better since I actually wanted this thing and I already knew I'd like it before I even played with it.

When they finally called and said it was done, my dog and I basically ran there to pick up the car. The installation guy was trying to explain some bullshit to me, but I ignored him, hopped right into the car, plugged my iPhone in, put on "Break 'em Off" by Paul Wall, and cranked that motherfucker. There's a short intro without bass, then it hits . . .

"Imma break 'em off real bad, Imma show 'em pourin' up deuce ridin' slab . . ."

BOOOOMMMMM

That shit hit so fucking hard, my dog Murph yelped from shock. I high-fived the installation guy, and tore out of the parking lot:

It was time to find a cop.

Ain't it the fucking truth: When you're doing something wrong and don't want the police, they're like roaches. But when you're looking for one because you want to bump him off the block, they're nowhere to be found.

I drove around for three fucking hours looking for a cop. Well, it might have only been 30 minutes, but it felt like three hours. [Actually, I did see a bike cop, but fuck that. I have self-respect.]

Finally I found a cop car sitting at red light, all alone. I pulled right up to him, put all four windows down, turned my stereo up to only about 25% max volume, and stared at him (I can't remember the exact song I had on, I think it was "Knockin' Doorz Down" by Pimp C).

He immediately heard it, looked around, and saw I was the only car at the light. It had to be me who was playing music that loud.

We made eye contact.
His eyes said, "What??"
My eyes said, "WHAT!!"

He cocked his head like a dog when it hears a new noise. Here this cop is, going about his day, when some 34-year-old white guy in a Range Rover with a goofy mutt hanging her head out the back, cranks his music so loud it rattles his handcuffs. He throws his hands up in a sort of "What are you doing?" gesture. I don't move a muscle. I just kept staring through him. Yeah motherfucker, I DO have an eye problem.

Still confused, he rolled his window down, said something I couldn't hear, and turned one hand in a circle, clearly motioning me to reduce the volume. Not taking my eyes off of him, I violently crank my stereo knob so fucking hard I almost take it off. The volume went from "you can hear it a block away" to "registering on the Richter scale." The bass hit my chest so hard I had trouble breathing. And just to rub it in that much more, I start bobbing my head with the music.

He hit the roof. I mean this both figuratively and literally. He got so fucking mad he jumped up in his seat, and I think his head may have hit the roof of his squad car. He immediately hit the lights and siren, so I calmly pulled through the intersection (the light had turned green at some point), and pulled over.

I was giddy! Going over this situation in my mind as I was making the "Noise Pollution" playlist the night before, I'd decided that I wouldn't even turn the music down when the cop came to the window. I pictured this bumpkiny Roscoe P. Coltrane waddling up to my window, watching him try to yell over my music, and then I'd say something smart-ass like, "I'm sorry, can you speak up? Mike Jones is being a little loud."

Yeah, well, my imagination had not accounted for a thick-necked trooper white-knuckling his blackjack and storming at my car with veins bulging from his forehead. Confronted with how muscular and pissed off the real life cop actually was, my excitement ebbed and I turned the stereo all the way down and abandoned all smart-ass remarks. I'm pretty sure if I'd said any of that shit I'd planned on, this story would be about my struggles learning how to eat solid food and walk again.

Cop "WHAT THE FUCK ARE YOU FUCKING DOING!?!"

I can't transcribe the cop's entire lecture. There is only so much room in a book. The cop screamed at me for at least ten minutes. It was like Bobby Knight coaching a team on the And One street ball tour.

Cop "Well? What do you have to say for yourself?"

It was too late to back down. There's no such thing as a lukewarm hell. As calmly and respectfully as I could, I said:

Tucker "Officer, are you going to give me a noise pollution ticket or not?"

You ever dumped someone who didn't see it coming at all? You know the look on their face? That look of complete disbelief mixed with repressed rage, the look that tells you if you don't get the fuck out of there, something is gonna get broken? He got that look.

His face twitched, but he didn't say anything. Then he spun on his heels, abruptly turned, and walked back to his car. For a second, I was legitimately scared. I may have pushed this dude too far. This is a cop, and he has rules he has to obey, and I knew I hadn't done anything that bad—but this is still TEXAS. People have been given the death penalty for less.

He'd been back there for about five minutes when two other cop cars pulled up. Fuck. They talked for a while. One of the new cops came and got my license, registration, insurance, all that stuff. They checked EVERYTHING. He even checked my VIN number to make sure it matched the registration AND insurance. I've been pulled over at least 25 times in my life for various things, and I've NEVER seen that. Judging by how long the one cop was in his car on his computer, my guess is that he ran my name through not just the standard law enforcement databases, but every fucking database on earth—VICAP, INTERPOL, FreeCreditReport.com, everything. They asked for permission to search my car, and of course I gave it to them—this was a brand new car; there was nothing in it. Still, they went over it with everything but a fucking drug-sniffing dog. After they finished, there was another twenty minutes of sitting in my car waiting for them to decide what they could do to me and get away with. Finally, the original cop came up to my window with his violations pad.

Cop "Sign here."

I didn't say shit, I just signed it and handed it back. He ripped it off his pad so hard it tore in half. I think that actually means he's supposed to write up a new one, but he didn't, he just tore the stub off and gave it to me and stormed back to his car. I'm pretty sure protocol says the cop is supposed to explain the various ways to pay the ticket or whatever, but I wasn't about to press my luck. And besides, I had what I wanted.

The (Almost Banned, Now Complete) Miss Vermont Story

Part 1: Introduction

There are certain people whose influences define and shape your life: your parents, your friends, your teachers, the people you fall in love with. I have the same basic list of people as you probably do . . . but since I'm Tucker Max, there's someone else on my list:

The first person who ever sued me because of my stories.

If you've been a fan for a long time, you may have read the old Miss Vermont Story on my website. You may have even been a fan long enough to remember when she sued me in 2003. That means you know the basic facts of what happened . . . but you don't know the *whole* story.

In 2003, I gave my first rough draft of "The Miss Vermont Story" to PWJ to read. He'd met and hung out with MissVermont, so I wanted his feedback on how I portrayed her and the events. Instead of emailing me his notes, he called me. The seriousness in his voice shocked me:

PWJ "Dude, you have to cut a BUNCH of stuff out of here."
Tucker "Why? What did I get wrong?"
PWJ "No no—it's not what you're getting wrong. It looks right to me. But if you print this story as you have it now, she's going to sue you. I met her; I guarantee this will emotionally break her. You make her look like a fucking moron, and you make her mom look psycho."

Tucker "I don't MAKE them look like anything. You met her, you know that's the way she is."
PWJ "Oh dude, I know."
Tucker "I don't understand—truth is an absolute defense to libel. It's all true. End of story."
PWJ "No, that's wrong. Dude, you really should have gone to class more in law school."

PWJ went on to explain that it was much more complicated than that and elaborated on a bunch of shit that I would have learned had I gone to class instead of doing things like fucking excessive numbers of UNC sorority girls and spending entire months in Cancun.

Because this story was going to be the first time I would use the real name of the person I was writing about—*without her permission*—I had to have all my shit straight. I'll spare you the tedious and boring legal explanation, but it boils down to this:

If I was going to use her real name, then everything I wrote not only had to be true—which it was—but it had to be PROVABLE in a court of law. In order to insulate myself from liability for any portions of the story that were potentially defamatory—which is like 650% of the story—there had to be witnesses or some other factual record of the event. Even if something was completely true, if I couldn't prove it in a court of law, then she could not only sue me, she might be able to win. Because most of the events took place in public places and were easily provable, I could still write the story, but if I wanted to stop her from suing me, I was forced to leave out a lot of cool details. This frustrated the shit out of me—if it's the truth, why can't I say it?? But ultimately, I recognized that PWJ's abundance of caution was the right move, and I restrained myself.

Well, in the seven years since I wrote and published that story, two things happened:

1. Despite my precautions, Katy Johnson and her mother sued me anyway.

2. I beat those bitches like rented mules (in technical legal terms: I won the case).

Because of that, I can now do what I couldn't do before: tell the WHOLE story of my relationship with MissVermont, plus, I can update the story with everything that happened *after* she sued me, which has never been told . . . until now.

Part 2: The (Now Complete) Miss Vermont Story

Occurred, June 2001

It all started the summer after I graduated from law school. I moved to Boca Raton, Florida and took a job managing my father's restaurants. Considering that the general intellectual level of South Florida is somewhere just above "functionally retarded," I wasn't really expecting to meet a girl I would like as a person. And boy, was I right. The first few months were nothing more than emotionally uninvolved sex with morally suspect girls.

One day I was at my gym, The Athletic Club of Boca Raton. It is a massive airplane hangar of a building: a gym, health club, spa, lounge, and restaurant rolled into one. For several years it had been the "in" place to work out in Boca, one of the prime meat markets in a town full of butcher shops. It was the type of place where guttural grunts, flexing in tight shiny shirts, and spending hours talking to people on elliptical machines passes for foreplay. Welcome to South Florida.

I usually tried to avoid peak hours and the throngs of scantily clad gold-digging whores positioning themselves for third husbands. Don't mistake me—staring at immense fake breasts spilling out of sports bras is fun for a while, but it gets old quick, especially when those breasts are attached to women whose over-enhanced faces tell a story their vacant personalities do not. They've circled the drain more than a few times, and no manner of plastic surgery or trips to the spa can hide the despair in the eyes left by years of whorish behavior and emotional prostitution.

I was in the free weight section of the gym, and one girl kept catching my eye, more for what she wasn't showing than what she was. She had on a navy blue hat pulled tight over her face, a loose fitting white cotton T-shirt, and green basketball shorts. Not the standard Boca female gym outfit. Staring at her between sets, I realized that she was attractive. And by trying to hide that attractiveness, she became even better-looking. The logo on her shorts said, "Vermont Law," which gave me the perfect in. My law degree would finally show a return.

I approached and asked if she'd attended law school at Vermont. She told me she hadn't, that she went to undergrad there, but that she was attending Stetson for law school. I told her I just graduated from law school at Duke, and the look on her face told me all I needed to know. A few more minutes of playful banter and it would be time to close the deal.

It was about 7:30, and I had nothing to do the rest of the night, so I decided to speed the process up:

Tucker "So, what are you doing tonight?"
MissVermont [She lowered her head slightly and brushed her hair behind her ear, sure signs of attraction] "Nothing."
Tucker "You hungry? Want to get something to eat?"
MissVermont [She looked up at me, her eyes bright, and said in an earnest, non-seductive way] "I'm always hungry."

I swear to God those exact words came out of her mouth. I was so shocked because that is pretty much the last thing you'd ever expect any girl in South Florida to say, right after "I don't mind that you drive a Toyota."

She agreed to meet me at Max's Grille at around 8:30. By the time I got to the restaurant, I had forgotten her name. Great. I got one of the managers to stand by the door with me until she came in. He introduced himself to her, she gave him her name right back, "Hi, I'm Katy Johnson." I'm sneaky.

I'll be honest: She looked amazing. There are pics of her in the book, but they don't do her justice; she really is better looking in person, that night especially. She wore a peach colored dress that might as well have been painted on her nicely shaped body, full breasts taut against the upper lip of the fabric, cleavage everywhere . . . I was excited.

I have charmed my share of women, but I wish I'd recorded what I said that night. The conversation was great; I was hitting all her buttons in exactly the right way. Anyone who has ever played sports knows the feeling of "being in the zone." It's when you have one of those transcendental games, where everything works, when you see the entire court, the game slows down while you keep going at full speed, you're three steps ahead of everyone else, everything you throw up goes in, and when you miss, the rebound comes right back at you. I was having one of those nights.

One of the specific things I remember us talking about was that she was Miss Vermont, twice, and that she hadn't finished in the top ten in either the Miss America or the Miss USA pageant. She had all sorts of endorsement and movie deals set up if she had only finished in the top ten in either, and she was so upset by this failure that now she didn't know what she was going to do with her life. Her life had been so thoroughly dominated by pageants that she had even moved to Vermont and transferred to the University of Vermont during undergrad in order to establish residency there (she wasn't 100% positive that she could win either of the Miss Florida titles). It was painfully clear that Katy was the epitome of a pageant girl. She had defined her life to this point by being judged in that way, and now that it was all over, she was adrift.

There is a saying I have found to be very true: "Tell beautiful women they are smart, and smart women they are beautiful." Seems basic and obvious, but the basics are basics for a reason.

Tucker "I don't know anything about pageants, but I have watched some, and all those girls seem so stupid. You are just as hot as any of them, but unlike them, you're obviously really smart. If the judges don't see that, they're the idiots. Don't let it get you down."

She turned to me, put her hand on my arm, tilted her head, and said "Really?" I just looked at her, with a controlled smirk on my face, and didn't say anything. I've had girls melt on me before, but I'd never actually seen it happen as graphically and completely as it did at that moment.

So let's see . . . pageant girl, spent her whole life being judged on external things, twice on the biggest pageant stage, twice judged as falling short, nothing left to fall back on so she gets depressed and insecure, needs to find some kind of external validation . . . meets a guy who is smart, good looking, into her, socially adept . . . should be obvious where this is going.

After dinner, we went next door to a bar called Gigi's for some cocktails. On the first drink, she said to me, "I can't believe I'm doing this. I never drink this much." This would become the on-going theme in our relationship. Then she got real close to me, moved so I could easily see down her dress, and said:

MissVermont "Tucker . . . do you find me attractive?"

She was searching for even more validation; I smiled, but didn't say anything. Once you've given some, the best thing you can do is withhold the rest. Like a drug dealer. The first one is free, but the second . . . you gotta pay for that one.

She literally put her leg over mine and sort of halfway climbed on top of me, pushing her breasts in my face.

MissVermont "Do you think I'm hot?"
Tucker "What do you think?"
MissVermont "I don't know. That's why I'm asking."
Tucker "Maybe. I'm becoming a fan. There's a lot to like about you. We'll see though."

She took the bait so hard that if we were in the ocean, she would have breached like an orca. The next thing I knew, we were out in the middle of Mizner Park (the outdoor piazza where Max's Grille and Gigi's are located), making out in the middle of the grassy median. It quickly got out of hand; I was pushing her dress up, she was undoing my belt, and we were moving towards passionate and semi-anonymous humping.

I tell her that we have to relax, that we can't do this here. Predictably, she thought I was playing hard to get, and this only made her want me more. In response to me backing off, she desperately intensified her attack on my loins, slipping a hand down my pants, and bringing one of my hands up to her now-exposed left breast.

I tried to figure out a way for us to fuck. My apartment was a no-go; I had just moved in to my new place and didn't have any furniture yet, not even a sofa. She lived with her parents, so that was out. I would have just fucked her right there—it was Tuesday at 12:30, and the park was empty—but I really didn't want to get caught having sex under a gazebo right in front of the restaurant where I worked.

Remembering that she drove, I asked, "Where did you park?" She pointed right behind us, and sitting there on the curb, not twenty yards away, was the solution:

A white Ford Explorer. Without the third-row seat.

I did my best to make it romantic:

Tucker "Have you ever hooked up in your car?"

Hey—that's romantic for me, alright?

She smiled, so I grabbed her arm, and we half-sprinted toward the car.

I've hooked up with enough girls to make an educated comparison, and let me tell you—I have rarely seen anyone so eager and enthusiastic about sex. Our clothes were off, in the back of an SUV where there is not much room to spare, in less than 30 seconds. About a second after that she mounted me, and we fucked like the plane was going down. When we were finished, she curled up next to me, sweaty and exhausted, and said:

MissVermont "You have a lot of experience, don't you?"

The next day, around 11am, I got an exasperated and hysterical voicemail from Katy. She was distraught, nearly crying. It was such frantic gibberish that I couldn't understand anything, so I called her. Apparently, that morning her mother was looking in Katy's car for something, found my boxer-briefs on the floor, which I had, in my post-coital stupor, unwittingly left there.

Now, as I'm sure you know, girls don't generally enter pageants at age 5 because they have some overriding desire to dress like a prostitute and parade themselves in front of creepy old men. They do it because they have evil, overbearing mothers who push them into it in order to live vicariously through their daughters. They don't see their daughters as distinct people they should love and care for; they see them as accessories to their egos, and they measure themselves by what their daughters do. Needless to say, this sort of malignant narcissism is VERY toxic. And though I didn't know it at the time, Katy's mom was one of the worst examples of this type of pageant mom.

For example, Katy was talking about her mom at dinner, and said in the most nonchalant voice ever, like it was a totally reasonable thing, "Yeah,

I'm a terrible cook. When I moved to law school, my mother was afraid I was going to starve. But then I had a pageant coming up, so she hoped I did starve." She didn't understand why I was looking at her in horror after she said that.

So of course, when she found the underwear, Katy's mom completely flipped out and stormed into Katy's room, woke her up, called her a whore and a tramp and all sorts of other awful things as she thrust the boxers in her face. To her credit, Katy kept her cool and told her mother that they were her workout underwear, and that she wore them under her shorts to the gym the day before and just forgot to bring them in the house. Her mom bought the story.

In fact, it was only after her mom bought the story that Katy called me in hysterics. I should have known that a hysterical voicemail AFTER the problem had passed was an awful sign, but I was 25 years old and the worst kind of idiot: I knew nothing, but thought I knew everything.

For our second date, I had her over to my place to cook for her. I forget what I made; I think it was miso-glazed Chilean sea bass with Asian baby vegetable stir-fry and polenta croquette. To make this the right way, you have to do it from scratch, which is a lot of work. I grew up in a restaurant family, I can do all that prep work, but fuck that—it's a serious pain in the ass. Why would I now spend an hour buying the perfect ingredients, two hours prepping them, and then another 30 minutes cooking them just to impress some girl I wasn't all that into, and that I'd already fucked?

Instead, I took the easy way out: I went to my restaurant, picked up all the ingredients already prepped by a Haitian making $8 an hour (who's way better at it than me), and had her arrive at my place as I was in the middle of cooking the whole meal—which was actually little more than heating everything up on the stove. I had done this with girls before, and it's a money move—it spares me from doing any actual work, while the girl sits in the kitchen drinking wine and watching me showcase my cooking talents.

MissVermont was more blown away by me cooking than most girls and—after basically pounding a large glass of wine—came over to me as I was standing at the stove searing the fish, pulled my pants down, and went down on me right there in the kitchen.

The fish burned a little, but whatever. She still ate well.

We saw each other somewhat consistently over the next two weeks. It was a relationship defined very much by sex. She could not get enough of me, especially sexually, and I was a big fan of her always-eager body. According to her, I was introducing her to a whole new world. These are verbatim quotes:

MissVermont "I didn't know what sex was before you."
MissVermont "You're like a disease. A Tucker sex disease."
MissVermont "You infiltrate me and my body craves you. You're an addiction."

Look, I'm not *that* good. She was just inexperienced, and the few guys she'd been with sucked, so she thought I was that good. Like when I play basketball with Asians, I look like Dwayne Wade compared to them.

She claimed she'd only been with two guys before me. I generally abide by the "whatever she admits to, multiply by 3 and add in at least one black guy" rule of counting women's sex partners, but given the facts I observed over the next few weeks, she might have been telling the truth.

For example, she was very schizophrenic about sex. One day, she'd want to fuck every minute of every hour, not caring if we ate or slept. Two days later, she wouldn't come home with me after a date. It was like she couldn't resolve the battle in her consciousness, and vacillated between eager slut and chaste prude.

Most tellingly, she just didn't have sex like she knew what she was doing. There is a difference between an inexperienced girl reacting to her first real sexual encounters and an experienced woman acting inexperienced to manipulate the guy. I've been with both, and she was quite obviously the former. For instance, after a few days of intense sexual activity, Katy was having problems with soreness and was waking up with nausea.

Tucker "Just go to your gynecologist, make sure everything is OK."
Katy "Oh . . . OK, I guess I can do that . . ."
Tucker "What?"
Katy "Well, it's just that . . . I don't have a gynecologist . . ."
Tucker "You don't have one? Why not?"
Katy "I've never been to one."
Tucker "WHAT? YOU'RE 23 YEARS OLD!!!"
Katy "I know . . . it's just . . . my mom wouldn't let me go. She said I don't need to see one until I lose my virginity."
Tucker "Oh my lord."

I emphasized how important it was to have a doctor regularly look inside her ham wallet, and that even if it meant lying to her mom and just paying for it out of her own pocket, she really needed to see a gynecologist. She was hesitant, until I showed her some WebMD articles about STDs and HPV and cervical cancer, and the accompanying pictures. She quickly made an appointment. A few days later she called me and left this voicemail:

MissVermont "Tucker, I just got back from the ob/gyn and we need to talk."

Now tell me—if a girl you'd been sleeping with, who was complaining of nausea, called and left you that message, what would you have done? I freaked out, found the tallest flight of stairs I could, and was busy orchestrating a complicated plan to "accidentally" throw her down them. I finally got her back on the phone. No, she wasn't pregnant, but, and again I am quoting:

MissVermont "Oh no, nothing like that, and I don't have any STDs. My ob/gyn said the soreness is because of you. He said you need to be gentler with my pussy."

I still laugh every time I think about that phone call.

The next time we had sex I was less selfish and much gentler, and I guess it worked well, because she came so violently she almost passed out.

MissVermont "Jesus Christ, you are amazing. Where did you learn to do that?"
Tucker "Home schooling."

It was around this time, after about two or three weeks of fucking, that I saw her website. She had told me earlier what she was doing now that her pageant career was over—going to law school, pageant consultant work, running her charity organizations, and trying to start her career as a cartoonist—but I hadn't really paid much attention. I just assumed she was lip servicing that shit, and would eventually go into real estate or PR, like all washed up beauty queens.

She wasn't bullshitting. She emailed me about something else, and included a link to something she was proud of: her newest cartoon. I clicked on the link . . . and spent the next three hours utterly and completely absorbed in the rabbit hole I'd fallen down. Her actual site has been down for years, but the lawsuit briefs have screen shots of some parts of her site that were up at the time. Here are a few of them:

[To see the rest in full color, go to page 311. And if you're having trouble reading some of them, you can also see the full size versions at **www.tuckermax.com/missvermont**]

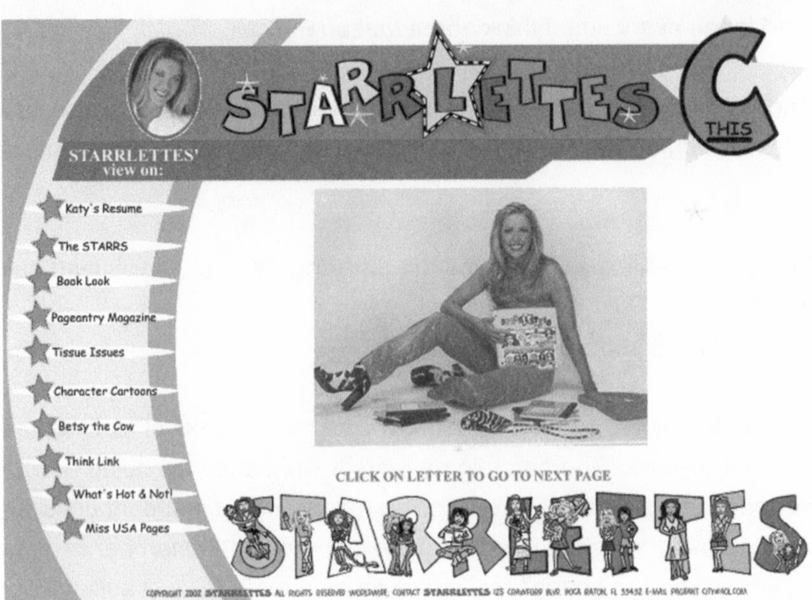
STARRLETTES C THIS
STARRLETTES' view on:
Katy's Resume
The STARRS
Book Look
Pageantry Magazine
Tissue Issues
Character Cartoons
Betsy the Cow
Think Link
What's Hot & Not!
Miss USA Pages
CLICK ON LETTER TO GO TO NEXT PAGE
STARRLETTES

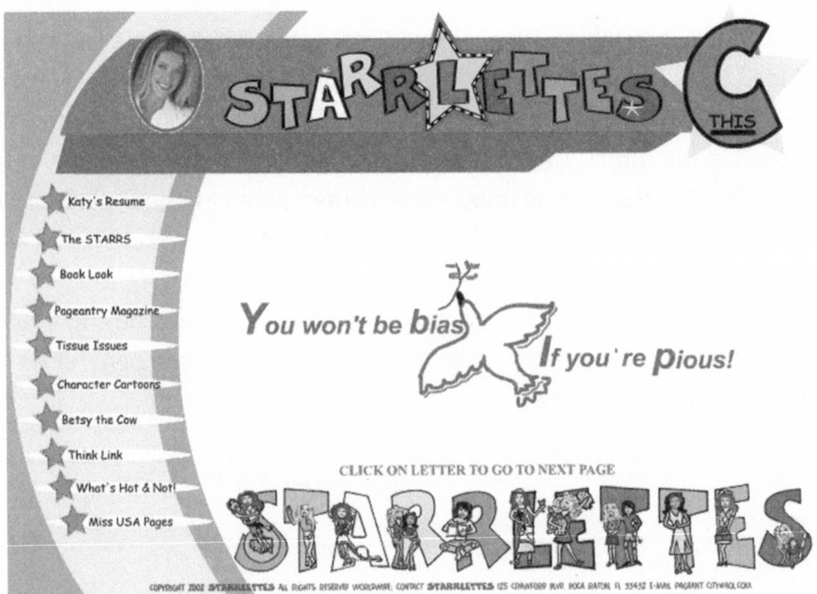
STARRLETTES C THIS
Katy's Resume
The STARRS
Book Look
Pageantry Magazine
Tissue Issues
Character Cartoons
Betsy the Cow
Think Link
What's Hot & Not!
Miss USA Pages
You won't be bias
If you're pious!
CLICK ON LETTER TO GO TO NEXT PAGE
STARRLETTES

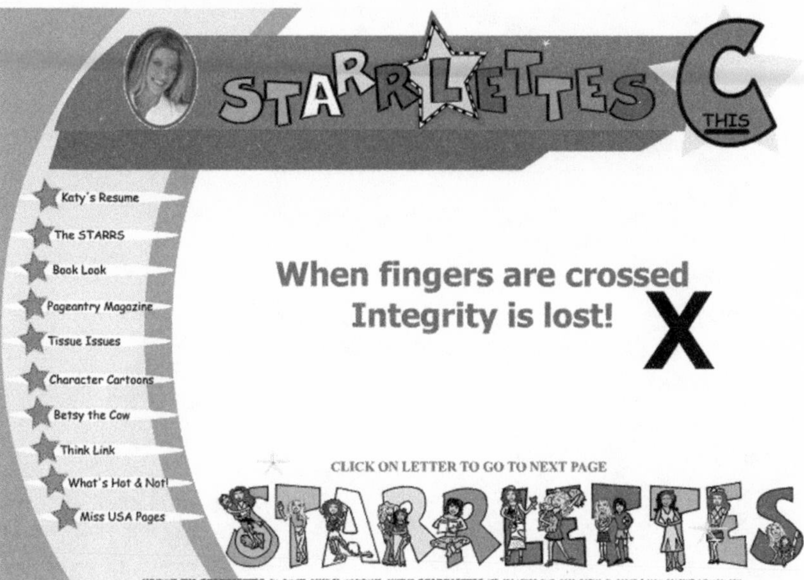
STARRLETTES
THIS
Katy's Resume
The STARRS
Book Look
Pageantry Magazine
Tissue Issues
Character Cartoons
Betsy the Cow
Think Link
What's Hot & Not!
Miss USA Pages
When fingers are crossed
Integrity is lost!
X
CLICK ON LETTER TO GO TO NEXT PAGE
STARRLETTES

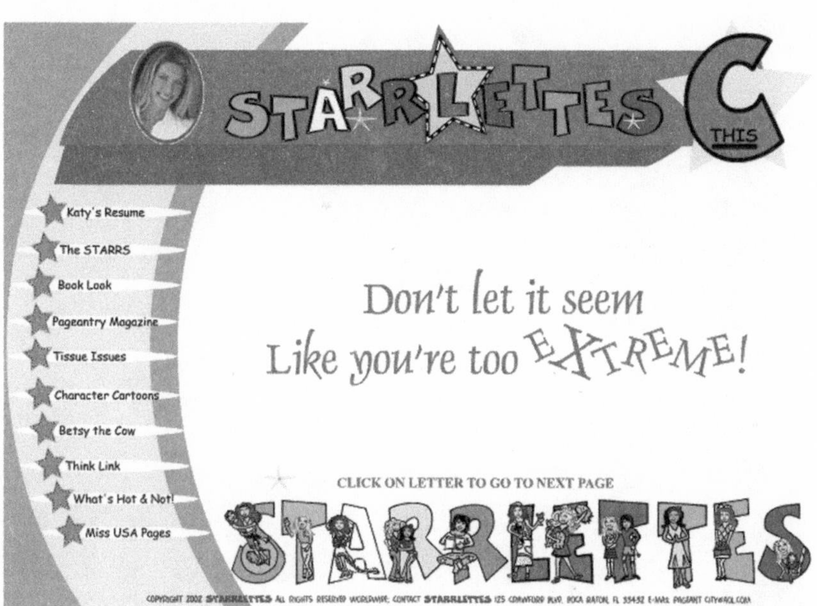
STARRLETTES
THIS
Katy's Resume
The STARRS
Book Look
Pageantry Magazine
Tissue Issues
Character Cartoons
Betsy the Cow
Think Link
What's Hot & Not!
Miss USA Pages
Don't let it seem
Like you're too EXTREME!
CLICK ON LETTER TO GO TO NEXT PAGE
STARRLETTES

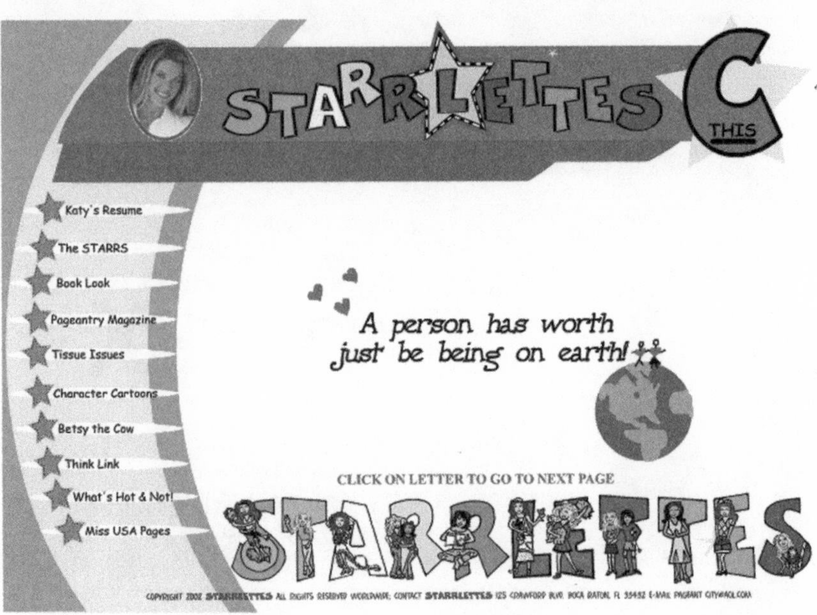
STARRLETTES
C THIS
Katy's Resume
The STARRS
Book Look
Pageantry Magazine
Tissue Issues
Character Cartoons
Betsy the Cow
Think Link
What's Hot & Not!
Miss USA Pages
A person has worth
just be being on earth!
CLICK ON LETTER TO GO TO NEXT PAGE
STARRLETTES

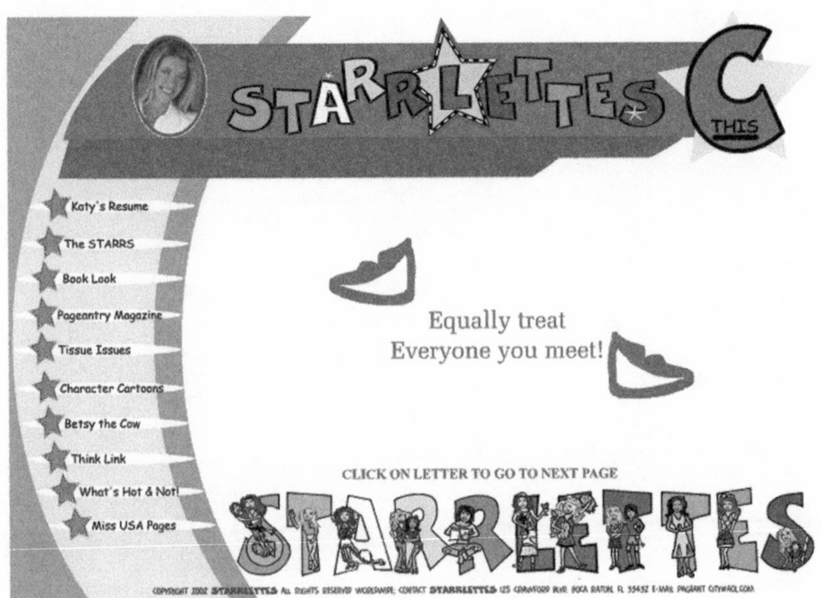
STARRLETTES
C THIS
Katy's Resume
The STARRS
Book Look
Pageantry Magazine
Tissue Issues
Character Cartoons
Betsy the Cow
Think Link
What's Hot & Not!
Miss USA Pages
Equally treat
Everyone you meet!
CLICK ON LETTER TO GO TO NEXT PAGE
STARRLETTES

STARRLETTES
Katy's Resume
The STARRS
Book Look
Pageantry Magazine
Tissue Issues
Character Cartoons
Betsy the Cow
Think Link
What's Hot & Not!
Miss USA Pages
It shows Maturity
To keep your Purity!
CLICK ON LETTER TO GO TO NEXT PAGE
STARRLETTES

STARRLETTES
C
THIS
Katy's Resume
The STARRS
Book Look
Pageantry Magazine
Tissue Issues
Character Cartoons
Betsy the Cow
Think Link
What's Hot & Not!
Miss USA Pages
Dependable love
Comes from above!
CLICK ON LETTER TO GO TO NEXT PAGE
STARRLETTES

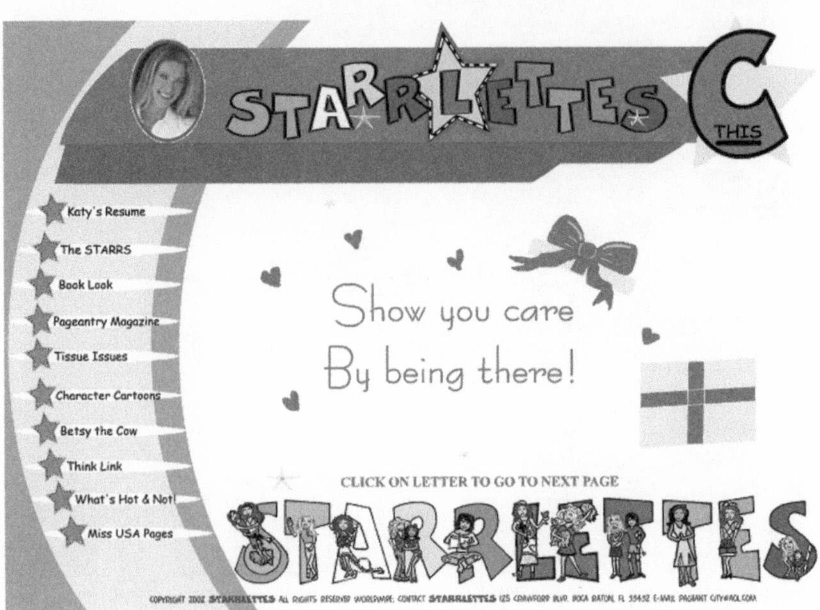
STARRLETTES
C THIS
Katy's Resume
The STARRS
Book Look
Pageantry Magazine
Tissue Issues
Character Cartoons
Betsy the Cow
Think Link
What's Hot & Not!
Miss USA Pages
Show you care
By being there!
CLICK ON LETTER TO GO TO NEXT PAGE
STARRLETTES
COPYRIGHT 2002 STARRLETTES ALL RIGHTS RESERVED WORLDWIDE; CONTACT STARRLETTES 125 CRAWFORD BLVD. BOCA RATON, FL 33432 E-MAIL PAGEANT CITY@AOL.COM

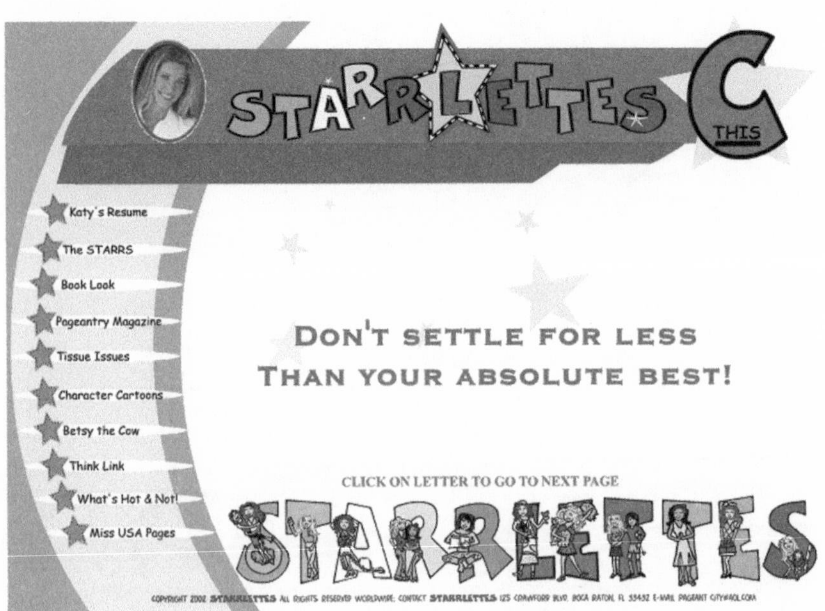
STARRLETTES
C THIS
Katy's Resume
The STARRS
Book Look
Pageantry Magazine
Tissue Issues
Character Cartoons
Betsy the Cow
Think Link
What's Hot & Not!
Miss USA Pages
DON'T SETTLE FOR LESS
THAN YOUR ABSOLUTE BEST!
CLICK ON LETTER TO GO TO NEXT PAGE
STARRLETTES
COPYRIGHT 2002 STARRLETTES ALL RIGHTS RESERVED WORLDWIDE; CONTACT STARRLETTES 125 CRAWFORD BLVD. BOCA RATON, FL 33432 E-MAIL PAGEANT CITY@AOL.COM

Once I recovered from the gales of laughter that rocked my body, I did what any reasonable 25-year-old male would do after seeing these cartoons: I sent the link to all my friends.

GoldenBoy: "This can't be real. This is some elaborate joke Tucker has constructed."

PWJ: "Oh, this is all too real. Tucker doesn't have the artistic talent to put this together on his own. This is the work of a true genius. Or a completely broken nutjob, like most of the girls that would sleep with Tucker."

Hate: "Max, I have to admit, I'm jealous. You've upped the ante for all of us. This is not just a normal crazy pageant girl, but a crazy pageant girl who broadcasts her craziness to the whole world."

SlingBlade: "Hold on. She lists her biggest accomplishments as creating her abstinence and sobriety groups, which are respectively called, "Say Nay Today" and "The Sobriety Society." And this is the same girl who got drunk and fucked you in the back of her car? On the first night you met? I hate women. Look at this shamelessly hypocritical nonsense:

"Life will be better if you live by the letter."
"What should I do? Strive for virtue!"
"Keep pure 'til you're mature"

Two can play at this game:

"If in life you don't succeed, be a whore to meet your needs."
"No ifs, ands, or buts, all women are sluts."
"Why didn't I rate, now I'm just filled with self-hate."
"I made a website that's boring, it helps me rationalize my whoring."
"I'll tell this guy I've only touched two dicks, even though the real number is one-hundred and six!"

This went on for a few weeks, me continuing to see MissVermont, my friends continuing to mock her website and laugh at updates about our "relationship." GoldenBoy's wedding was coming up around that time, and since everyone thought she was so hilarious, I decided to invite her to go with me as my date. My thought process was simple: She's hot and unintentionally entertaining, both for my friends and for me. Plus, my friends want to meet her. GoldenBoy even went so far as to ask for one of the action figures of herself she sold on the site as his wedding gift, but alas, she was out of them.

We decided to drive to the wedding, which was in the Outer Banks of North Carolina. Why drive instead of fly? Two reasons. 1. She couldn't have her mom find out she was going with me (more on that later), and 2. She wanted to have sex in every state along the way. The drive was rather uneventful, except that we forgot to have sex in South Carolina. No big deal, we can do it on the way back to Florida.

GoldenBoy had rented three massive six-bedroom houses on the beach for all of his friends. The pre-party had already started at his house, so when I got there I quickly introduced her to everyone and started drinking. I pretty much ignored MissVermont and let all of GoldenBoy's friends from college hit on at her. Of course, my ignoring her only made her want me more. Insecure women are funny.

Later that night, Hate, BrownHole, JonBenet, Credit, and I were at our house bullshitting and drinking before bed. MissVermont was already asleep. At some point, BrownHole accidentally spilled his glass of water on JonBenet. When sober, JonBenet is a great guy, and everyone loves him. But when he's drunk, he becomes demonic. This particular night, for whatever reason, his friend accidentally spilling water on him was a grievous transgression that he would not accept. Without warning, he shot up, flipped the table over, grabbed the glass out of BrownHole's hands and fired it against the floor, sending broken glass all over the house.

Everyone was quiet for a second—the way people who aren't used to seeing violence are—and then I busted out laughing. I mean, how can you not laugh at a drunk moron spiking a pint glass into the floor? That basically ended the night, and we all went to bed.

My friends got their first indication that MissVermont might be a little "different" the next day at breakfast. PWJ had come in at like 3am (he got so drunk in the airport bar that they wouldn't allow him on his flight) and we were recounting JonBenet's little spat with the glass, when MissVermont broke into the conversation to clear up her confusion as to whether the glass shattered or not:

MissVermont "Did it broke?"

That was what she actually said, out loud. To everyone at the table, in total seriousness. My friends were so shocked, they almost couldn't laugh. It was like a third grader was hanging out with us. They got an even better indication of what she was like when we were talking about what we'd read recently:

PWJ "I actually kinda like the Harry Potter books."
MissVermont "I do too! Don't you just wish they were real?!? I wish I could play Quiddich and meet Hermione and everyone!! It's just so . . . MAGICAL!!!!

She was as excited as a 6-year-old. And just as sincere.

PWJ "Uhhh, I guess . . . so what else do you read? Lots of magazines probably?"
MissVermont "I don't read magazines; I just look at the pictures."

Then she took a magazine out of her purse and flipped through it as we talked. She came to a photo spread of several musicians.

MissVermont "Rock stars are so hot. I'm such a groupie."

PWJ "A groupie? How many have you hooked up with?"
MissVermont "Oh no, I don't sleep with them or anything, but I am such a groupie."
PWJ "I don't think you have a proper understanding of what that word means."

We spent most of the day nursing beers and watching James Bond films. Our favorite was *Goldfinger* because of the scene where Sean Connery is with some girl at the pool, and when some other agent comes along to talk to him, Sean smacks her on the ass, and tells her, ". . . Run along now. Man talk." We all crack up laughing at this flawless execution of '60s sexism, but then JonBenet makes me a bet:

JonBenet "I bet you won't do that to MissVermont this afternoon at the reception."
Tucker "Who are you talking to? Are you calling me out? About disrespecting a whore?"
Credit "I don't know Max, I don't think you have it in you."
Tucker "Fuck both of you."

MissVermont eventually came back to the house (she'd gone for a walk on the beach with Brownhole) and my friends quizzed her about her conversation with BrownHole, laughing the whole time, as MissVermont recounted the wonderful conversation she had with him, and what a good listener he was, etc. Eventually PWJ had enough and let her in on the secret,

PWJ "Katy, BrownHole is trying to hook up with you."
MissVermont "No, he's being so nice."

Isn't blind naiveté charming?

Like the idiots we were, we got caught up in beer and Bond, and before we realized it was 5pm and the ceremony had already started. We threw on our clothes and got there just in time to see GoldenBoy and Golden-

Wife take their vows. Like a bunch of assholes, we walked right in during the ceremony and plopped down in the pews, ignoring the people standing in the back of the church.

Our entrance was made even more distracting by MissVermont's ensemble. She wore a short, skin tight, strapless, cherry red dress. With sequins. And a push-up bra. I heard one wedding guest whisper something about "the girl with the boobs." I beamed with pride.

Not many people realize that "Here Comes the Bride" is taken from a Wagner opera involving a prostitute, but it was appropriate for MissVermont. PWJ had actually made it on time because he was playing guitar in the wedding, and was so distracted by MissVermont's entrance that he forgot the music to "Canon in D" halfway into it. That's how inappropriately she was dressed. Of course I thought it was awesome, but I'm an asshole.

After disrupting the wedding, it was time to ruin the reception. The reception was at a bed & breakfast only accessible via a single dirt road. Most people parked their cars at a gas station and got on the 15-passenger shuttle that took people back and forth. MissVermont and I instead drove her Explorer there, and thus got a nice early start on the drinking. By now you've figured out that MissVermont is an amateur and unaccomplished drinker, about the level of a normal 17-year-old high school girl. She apparently did not realize this about herself, because as soon as we got there, she followed my lead and got a martini.

Tucker "What are you doing? You can't handle your liquor. Be careful."
MissVermont "I'm fine. I can do it. Don't worry."

If there are two words you never, under any circumstances, want to hear from the mouth of a delusional, emotionally-broken cum-dumpster, they are "I'm pregnant." Followed closely by, "Don't worry." They're like a detonation charges on an atomic slut bomb.

Everyone poured into the reception area, and once the crowd was large enough, it was time to settle the bet. I was talking in a group with JonBenet, PWJ, Credit, and Hate. Katy came up and started talking to the group. After about ten minutes, JonBenet and I exchanged glances, I slapped her on the ass, and said: "Run along baby. It's time for Man-Talk."

Miraculously, my friends held it together. She gave a slightly hurt look, an "OK," and walked off. They all immediately broke down laughing. I took my deserving place as King of the Reception! It may have been GoldenBoy's wedding, but I had won the crown! (There is actually video of this incident: **www.tuckermax.com /mantalk**)

For a while. Though it was funny at the time, this one act vaulted Katy from the ranks of the "random whore" into the rarified air of the "unforgettable whore," and set off an unbelievable chain reaction that leads all the way to you reading this story. Here is how:

After such a curt brush off, MissVermont—presumably to make me jealous—started flirting with GoldenBoy's college friends, the same ones that she was talking to the night before. They had no idea she was such a novice drinker, and fed her three cosmopolitans over the next hour or so. I wasn't paying much attention, until she wandered over and slurred out:

MissVermont "Is Man-Talk over?"

Oh great holy Jesus. She was so drunk she sounded like Joe Namath at an open bar. I just shook my head in disbelief, and turned away from her. Three minutes later, I hear a giant crash behind me and turn to find MissVermont wobbling around, staring at a smashed martini glass at her feet.

JonBenet "I guess it did broke."

It was only 7pm. Dinner wasn't until 8:30.

All of GoldenBoy's friends quickly helped her clean up. I grabbed some chunky college girl who PWJ had been hitting on, who had a room at the bed and breakfast, and told her, "You need to look after her. She is already shit faced. Take her to your room and put her to bed." Then I refilled my drink and walked to a separate part of the party. I had to leave because I was so fucking pissed, both at her and at myself.

Additional backstory: When I asked GoldenBoy if I could bring MissVermont to his wedding, he and his fiancée said it was fine with them, but GoldenBoy, having gone to law school with me and knowing me well, solicited a promise:

GoldenBoy "Tucker, *this is my wedding.* You can't bring one of your typical 'girlfriends' and then just start ignoring her in the middle of it because you get bored with her. She is welcome to come, but no scenes, okay?"

I agreed and gave him my solemn promise on this. Now, I know what you're thinking, "Hey, if he can't take a joke, fuck him, right?" Normally, I would agree, but this was a different situation. GoldenBoy is one of my best friends on earth, and I am loyal to my friends, so I was genuinely distressed about this development. Of course, I was the main reason for the impending disaster, but still—I was upset about it.

After about an hour, I went up to check on MissVermont. I found her alone in the room, lying on the girl's bed, barely awake, muttering the same thing over and over:

MissVermont "I never drink . . . I shouldn't have done this . . . I never drink . . . I just wanted Tucker to like me . . . I never drink like this."

Oh man. This was just not going well. By this point, I've started to get pretty shit-housed myself, and I'm upset about breaking my promise to GoldenBoy. So I deal with these "emotions" the only two ways I know how: burying them in alcohol, and lashing out at MissVermont. I snapped this picture of her:

The famous picture of us together at the wedding, taken only an hour or two before the above

We all eventually sit down to dinner, with MissVermont still passed out upstairs. My table is at the back of the reception hall, quite obviously the "boisterous and embarrassing friends" table. Along with me and a vacant spot for MissVermont, there is a motley crew of miscreants, drunks, and assholes: GoldenBoy's high school friend, "TheShepherd," a 6'4" huge Irish Catholic guy who can drink like, well, an Irish Catholic, and has repeatedly been arrested for breaking every type of law related to drinking, including public intoxication, underage consumption, disturbing the peace, bar fighting etc. TheShepherd's sister, PornStar, a hot redhead who had the "fuck me" eyes of a bad porn actress. A couple who were college friends of GoldenWife and already so drunk they were barely able to sit up. Strangely, I was the only one of the law school group there. Total bullshit, those assholes are just as loud and drunk as me!

Or maybe not. In no time at all, the gallons of vodka coursing through my veins combined with PornStar flirting to make me hit on all the Tucker Max Drunk cylinders. I have the table in tears laughing as I'm telling them the standard stories, making fun of my passed-out date, etc. PornStar came to the wedding dateless, and at one point leaned towards me, seductively whispers something in my ear about what she wanted to do with my penis, when all of a sudden, I felt a tap on my shoulder.

MissVermont "Hi."

HOLY DRUNKEN WHORE BATMAN, IT'S MISS VERMONT!

She was putting on her best obsequious, "I'm sorry" puppy dog eyes. It was not working, because 1. I was fed up with her stupid shit, and 2. She was still too drunk to do it right.

Tucker "What are you doing up? Are you OK?"
MissVermont "Yeah. I'm sorry. I never drink."
Tucker "Well who could have guessed? I mean, people often pass out at wedding receptions . . . at 7pm."
MissVermont "Sorry. I felt better, and I wanteded to come see you."

She actually said "wanteded." Not stuttering or anything, she just tacked an extra syllable onto the word.

Tucker "You are either the smartest, most manipulative, most cunning woman I've ever met . . . or you're a complete idiot. I can't figure out which."

Her reappearance actually made the rest of the dinner funny, as PornStar glared hatefully at her, TheShepherd quizzed her about her pageant life for the amusement of the table, and I sat back and watched it all. Needless to say, the fun was short-lived.

The next few hours are somewhat hazy in my memory, but for some reason or another MissVermont and I got into a huge fight. Well, this isn't quite true. I can't remember the details of what we said to each other, but I do know the precise reason we were fighting:

I was still really pissed off that she couldn't handle her liquor and embarrassed me at my friend's wedding, the very wedding that I'd promised would be incident-free. I didn't recognize my complicity in her actions, because I was fucked-in-half drunk. Also, I'm Tucker Max. Nothing is ever my fault, not even the things I do wrong.

This culminated in her seeking solace in PWJ, asking him for a hug, and then whispering in his ear, "God, your heart is beating so fast." Her self-esteem wasn't helped any when PWJ just walked away, shaking his head. In the meantime, I was drowning my sorrows in vodka and PornStar's tits, which were barely covered up by her sundress.

Ironically, GoldenBoy was unaware of the MissVermont theatrics because the rest of the Duke Law crew was putting on such a show that my drama was pushed off stage. One of the older female guests brought a small dog to the wedding, and Credit got the dog drunk. It was wobbling around, its barking all slurred, and the woman freaked out. Hate was dancing with several old women, throwing them around the reception tent like it was an audition for a Gap swing dance commercial, until one of them sprained her ankle. PWJ was hooking up with a college freshman in her room in the bed & breakfast while her father was quizzing GoldenBoy on her whereabouts. But alas for PWJ, this little amorous adventure came to a halt when she stopped kissing him, leaned over, and puked on his foot.

Around 11pm, MissVermont—pissed off that I was paying attention to another girl and ignoring her—came up to the bar and ordered another cosmo.

Tucker "What the fuck do you think you're doing? Haven't you embarrassed me enough today?"
MissVermont "You're a bad person."
Tucker "Well, you're a stupid person. I guess we all have our flaws."

Rather than stay and yell or argue more, I just left. I took the keys to her Explorer and drove back to the beach house, where the post party was going to be. I didn't know this at the time, but MissVermont completely freaked out about this, and PWJ and BrownHole had to convince her not to call the cops and report her vehicle stolen.

I got to the beach house, cracked a beer, and waited. And waited. And waited. Where the fuck was everyone? When people finally started pouring in, I found out why everyone was late: Hate had crashed the van that was supposed to shuttle everyone from the bed & breakfast to their cars. Apparently, the parents had gotten together and picked the person they thought most sober to drive the shuttle van. Somehow—much to the dismay of the Duke Law crowd—they picked Hate.

I guess they didn't know him well enough to know that his brooding scowl is NOT a sign of sobriety. He got behind the wheel, jammed the accelerator, and immediately drove the van into a ditch filled with mud. It got stuck. With the bride, groom, and both sets of parents inside. When they couldn't get it out of the mud (by this time everyone other than MissVermont, who stayed in the van, was coated in mud), they simply walked the mile back to the gas station.

Eventually, everyone got to the house safely, and the real partying started. Thankfully, MissVermont was nowhere to be found. Someone told us that she needed to pass out again, and BrownHole had taken her to the other house to put her to bed. Of course he did. This caused eruptions of laughter.

PWJ started talking to PornStar:

PornStar "So, wasn't the ceremony nice?"
PWJ "I don't know, I was up there feeling nervous, trying to play guitar. I don't remember much."
PornStar "That was you playing guitar?"
PWJ "Yep."
PornStar "God I want to fuck you right now. If my brother wasn't sitting five feet away, I'd totally take you right here."

PWJ almost sprinted the ten feet to me and pulled me out of a conversation:

PWJ "Hey man, we're friends, and you owe me. That girl wants to fuck me." He pointed to PornStar, talking to her brother in the kitchen. "She says she won't fuck with her brother around. Hook me up."

I had already let one friend down that night by causing an incident at his wedding, so I was determined to make up for it by helping my other friend sleep with a girl who I wanted for myself.

Tucker "Consider it done."

I grabbed two bottles of cheap champagne, and thrust one under TheShepherd's nose.

Tucker "You have red hair and you're stupid, so you must be Irish. People say the Irish can drink. I call bullshit. I'm the rockstar of this wedding. Let's see just how tough you fucking micks really are."

I called out a 6'4", 250-pound Irishman who'd been drinking since he was in the womb. I don't really remember anything after that.

I have been told that I was spotted on the porch, singing Irish drinking songs with TheShepherd, making up my own words. There are also reports that we were on the roof. Apparently I tried to tackle a mailbox on the walk back to my house. I only know this because of the huge bruises on my shoulder the next morning, and the destroyed mailbox in the front yard.

PWJ got the better end of this deal. He fucked PornStar in the bathroom, the hot tub, the bedroom, and the backyard. She licked every inch of his body at least once, and, in his own words, "sucked me until there was nothing left in me to get out." You owe me, PWJ.

My next clear memory is waking up in my bed the following day. My head felt like it had been run over by a truck. I was lying with my face over the side of the bed, and there were at least six towels lying on the floor under my face, all soaked with some brown fluid. As I rolled around on the bed trying to regain consciousness and use of my limbs, I realized two things:

1. The room stunk. Bad.

2. There was vomit all over me. And everything else in the room.

I eventually regained enough coordination to walk out of my room, and found Credit and Hate. Upon seeing me, they started laughing.

Tucker "Dude, man . . . did last night happen?"
Hate "Oh yes, Max. You were quite the show."
Credit "You missed the best part. After you came home and passed out, you started throwing up all over the bedroom, and MissVermont was running around the house yelling, 'TUCKER IS DIED! TUCKER IS DIED!!'"
Hate "Does that girl know how to conjugate her verbs?"
Tucker "What did you do?"

Hate "I just told her to roll you on your stomach and leave you alone. You do this all the time, you'd be fine."

MissVermont found me and started yapping at me about something I didn't care about, her feelings or whatever. I just ignored her, took a long, hot shower, packed my shit and crawled into the back of the Explorer and went to sleep. I figured by the end of the 16-hour drive home, I could sleep this awful hangover off. I was rudely awakened a few minutes later:

MissVermont "WHAT ARE YOU DOING? WE HAVE TO DRIVE BACK TO FLORIDA!"
Tucker "That's what you're here for."
MissVermont "I CAN'T DRIVE THE WHOLE WAY!"
Tucker "The longest journey begins with the first step. You can do that."

She huffed and puffed, but I wasn't moving. She eventually gave up and pulled out, and I fell back asleep.

I was jarred awake not even 30 minutes later as we were pulled over by a North Carolina State Trooper, and got a speeding ticket. The violation: going 70 in a 45. MissVermont really wanted to get home, I guess.

I drifted in and out of consciousness over the next ten hours. As we drove into South Carolina, I told her to slow down, that the South Carolina State Police were notorious for their speed traps on interstates. She ignored me, so I went back to sleep. I was awakened 30 minutes later by her hysterical sobbing. She got pulled over—just like I said she would—this time for going 95 in a 65.

Tucker "You can stop crying, it won't get you out of the ticket. South Carolina State Police don't fall for that shit."
MissVermont "SHUT UP!"
Tucker "I told you not to speed."
MissVermont "FUCK YOU! THIS IS ALL YOUR FAULT!"
Tucker "When are we going to fuck? We're almost out of South Carolina."

MissVermont "MY PARENTS ARE GOING TO FIND OUT ABOUT THESE TICKETS!! WHAT AM I GOING TO DO!?!? THEY ARE GOING TO KNOW I WENT TO NORTH CAROLINA."
Tucker "You didn't tell them?"

I didn't know this beforehand, but MissVermont had not been totally honest with her parents about what she was doing that weekend. In fact, she had lied through her teeth. She told her mom she was going to spend the weekend with a pageant friend in Tampa. It probably won't come as shock, but a mother who insists that her 23-year-old daughter live at home and thinks she is still a virgin, isn't going to be cool with her driving to a wedding four states away with a guy.

The rest of the ride home was uncomfortable. Well, it was uncomfortable for MissVermont, not really for me. I slept pretty much the whole way, only driving the last three hours or so. We got back, and she dropped me off at my place and sped off, not really saying a word.

At this point in the story, you may be feeling sorry for MissVermont. Don't get too caught up in your pity. I did not find out about this until about six months later, when Hate and Credit told me, but after she had her little hysterical fit about me dying from vomit, she went upstairs to BrownHole's room, crawled into his bed, and hooked up with him. He swears he didn't sleep with her, but admits that she, and I am quoting, "gave him a terrible blow job." BrownHole is a thief and a liar, but that has the ring of truth—the girl could not suck a dick if there was a tiara on the other side of it.

BrownHole *did* tell me about this: The next day as I was passed out in the back of the Ford Explorer and she was packing to leave, MissVermont left an autographed 8x10 pageant picture in the sunroof of his car. This is just absolutely fucking bizarre, as if she were saying, "Here's some shallow representation of my image for you to remember me sucking your dick by." She called him a couple of times over the next few weeks, sometimes for advice about me, sometimes just to talk. She told him that she got his number from my cell phone "when Tucker wasn't looking." She tried to get BrownHole to fly her up to DC to visit him, but he wouldn't do it (his only goal is to snatch up my leftovers, not to fall in love with them). So before you think the shit only flowed one way in this exchange, remember: Women don't have to be smart to be deceitful and sneaky.

After the wedding, my friends just had a fucking blast riding me about her and everything that happened. SlingBlade picked up right where he left off:

> In honor of the momentously funny events of GoldenBoy's wedding, I've written some new rhymes that MissVermont can use. Tucker, please forward these to her so she can accompany them with her childlike scribblings:
>
> "I'm such a gullible sucker, why did I sleep with Tucker?"
> "To feel better in the end, I tried to hooked up with his friend."
> "I wear tight clothing, because my actions fill me with self-loathing."
> "My comic is called the 'Starrlettes,' though it'd be true to life as the 'Harlots.'"
> "I want to put an end to my life, because you can't turn a ho into a housewife."
> "But I really don't think I'm a ho, just perhaps a bit psycho."

And my personal favorite:

> "There's no Miss USA crown on my head, now I wish I was died."

I hadn't called her during the week after we got back from the wedding, when she called me one day at work. She apologized for her actions at the wedding, and asked if she could see me again, that she had something for me. I told her to come by the restaurant, that I would see her, but only in public. I alerted my staff that a crazy woman was coming, and to be ready to call the cops if something happened.

MissVermont showed up in a skin-tight white tank top, breasts thrust forward in a super Miracle Bra. Her yellow tennis skirt was nicely cut about five inches below her crotch. At first, I wasn't sure if she wanted to stab me or sleep with me. Her demure smile and coy "fuck me" eyes gave away her hand: she wanted to fuck me. She got right next to me, placed her hand on my arm, her breasts slightly brushing against me.

MissVermont "I'm sorry. I brought you something."

She handed me a picture that almost put me into shock. Let me attempt to give a fitting description of this thing:

A silver frame around a 5x7 picture of Katy and me at the wedding reception, me in my suit and her in her red dress, minutes after we arrived, and before our first drink. Across the top of the picture, painted in white sparkle paint, are the words, "Alpha Male." There are little yellow streamers painted down the side. On the back, in silver paint, is this message:

"Tucker,

Thank you so much for taking me to the wedding! You are the best!

Love, Katy."

I was completely befuddled. I had no idea how to react to this. I still don't. Like I said before, this girl was either the shrewdest, most conniving woman on earth, or the stupidest human I'd ever met. I still couldn't figure out which.

So what happened? I'm weak in the face of hot eager pussy, so of course we started seeing each other again, sort of.

Katy tried to say it was just as friends, but it only took about three days before we were fucking again. This continued, in a weird sort of dysfunctional dance, for a few weeks. One thing I can say about her, she did love to learn new things, which may have been one of the reasons she loved hanging out with me.

For example (this is important later in the story), one day I told her I knew how to shoot, and she got all excited about it, so I took her to a gun range to teach her. She had never shot a gun before, so I showed her the basic Weaver Stance and A-frame Stance, how to aim, how to load, how to fire and clear a pistol, etc. She was fascinated, and loved it so much she started going to shoot on her own.

And yes—before you say it—I fully realize how stupid it was to teach an emotionally unstable woman who was obsessed with me how to fire a gun.

One day we were lying in a slightly drunken post-coital embrace, and I said something about how fall was coming and asked when she was going back to law school. She got this sheepish look on her face and told me that, technically, she wasn't going back, at least not this semester. She wasn't on summer break; she had been forced to take an "extended leave of absence."

Tucker "What did you do? Cheat on a test?"
MissVermont "No no, nothing like that?"
Tucker "Get caught fucking one of your professors?"
MissVermont "No! It has to do with my mom."

After a long time, I finally coaxed the whole story out of her, and I have to be honest: It was so incredible and shocking that I almost didn't believe her. I am still not even sure I believe her, but this is basically what she said:

Katy had been having some problems in law school. She wasn't real clear about all the specifics, but it had something to do with getting into a fight with her "chief social rival" at Stetson (her words), and this somehow led to Katy and her mom getting into a huge, knock-down drag out fight.

So instead of dealing with the stress from this in the normal way that a 22-year-old girl would—getting drunk and filling her empty soul with anonymous dick—Katy decided to put some flour in an envelope, seal it up, and mailed it to both her mom and her "rival."

Predictably, this did not go over well. Police got involved, Katy was quickly discovered as the culprit, the Stetson administration freaked out, and Katy got into some serious trouble. I'm still not sure how she didn't go to jail—she was very unclear on the details, saying she got out of most of the trouble by claiming it was just a joke and that her mom and the other girl didn't want to press charges. I know that her mom is VERY well connected politically in the state, and that may have had something to do with it. I still don't even know if I believe this story but the way she told it was very convincing, and the fact is, she didn't go back for her second year of law school at Stetson.*

*[SIDENOTE 1: This event Katy told me about was before 9/11. Remember after 9/11, when envelopes with anthrax started showing up in federal buildings and other places, and postal workers and old people died? And how one of the places that anthrax laced envelopes showed up was at the offices of the *National Enquirer,* which are located in Boca Raton, Florida? Weird. This coincidence has pretty much freaked me the fuck out ever since. And Katy is lucky she pulled that stunt before 9/11, or she'd still be in jail.]

*[SIDENOTE 2: Several years ago, I got an email that was supposedly from the "chief social rival" that described the anthrax incident—except she said Katy slipped the envelope under her door—basically confirming Katy's story to me. Granted, I have no way of verifying who the email was from or if the person was telling the truth, but I tend to believe it for this reason: I got that email when the original version of this story was up on my website . . . which had NO mention of the fake anthrax incident.]

But here's the thing: Whether she's lying or telling the truth almost doesn't matter—this bitch is fucking nuts either way. If she's telling the truth, that means she thought it would be a good idea to make someone think they had been exposed to a fatal chemical warfare agent. And if she was lying, it means she was trying to get some sort of reaction out of me by claiming she'd faked domestic terrorism.

I mean—which one is worse? I can't decide; it's like trying to decide what I want to eat at Arby's. But either way, the bitch is fucking nuts, and I kinda freaked out. I wasn't sure what to do at that point. I wasn't sure she wasn't totally psycho, but then again, she looked really good in tennis skirts, and would come fuck me whenever I wanted.

The perfect situation came up later that week: a manager at Max's Grille called in sick, and I had to work his shift, so I invited MissVermont and two of my female friends to dinner that night. I spent most of the dinner working, but they all sat together and had a great time, with me coming over to the table at various times to inject the special Tucker magic that always makes social situations so much more fun and interesting.

After MissVermont got a little drunk—I guess she actually *finished* her second drink this time—she decided to be naughty. She comes over to where I'm standing, pulls me off the floor, into the men's bathroom and into a stall, where she proceeds to pull down my pants and start sucking my dick.

As much as I was trying to ignore it, there seemed to be an increase in traffic in the bathroom. Whatever, I'm getting blown by MissVermont in the bathroom; everyone else can wait to take a dump. She finished up and we happily go back to our various places in the restaurant. [On a side note: I got in A LOT of trouble for that. A couple of the waiters told the general manager, who told my dad, and well, though my dad thought it was funny, he still got mad at me.]

Even though she was probably not going to last a long time with me anyway, that night ended up sealing MissVermont's doom. While giving me head in the bathroom earned her some cool points, she lost them all and then some during the conversation she had with my two married female friends:

MissVermont "I hope I look like you when I'm your age."

MissVermont was 23. My two friends were 25 and 27, respectively, and both were—and still are—MUCH hotter than Katy. Beyond that, I might be a lot of things, but loyal is possibly the biggest one. These two women are two of my best friends in the world, and to piss them off is the quickest way to get on my bad side. My friend's quote summed it all up, "Who the fuck does she think she is? And HELLO—she's not looking great herself. I guess pageants make your face a little leathery." Her reaction after I told her about the anthrax thing? "Oh my god, Tucker, she is a complete disaster in every way. You can't see her. You can't even fuck her anymore. What if she goes psycho on you?"

Considering what she'd already done, it was impossible even for me to argue with that logic. I will fuck nutjobs sometimes—I am a man after all—but even I have my limit. I started ignoring MissVermont more and more, started regularly fucking another girl, and was preparing to go to a wedding in Las Vegas, which made it easier to cut MissVermont out of my life. After a few days of this, I thought she had finally gotten the picture and moved on with her life too. At least I hoped she had moved on.

The day came for my Vegas trip, and as I left my apartment to go to the airport, I saw something under my windshield. At first, I thought it was a leaflet for a local band or church, but as I approached the car, I realized it was MUCH too big for that. I unfolded it, saw what it was, and almost shit a brick:

Yes, that is a gun target. A gun target that she shot up, and then placed on the windshield of my car. WHAT THE FUCK??

Oh, but it gets better. I turned it over to find this message:

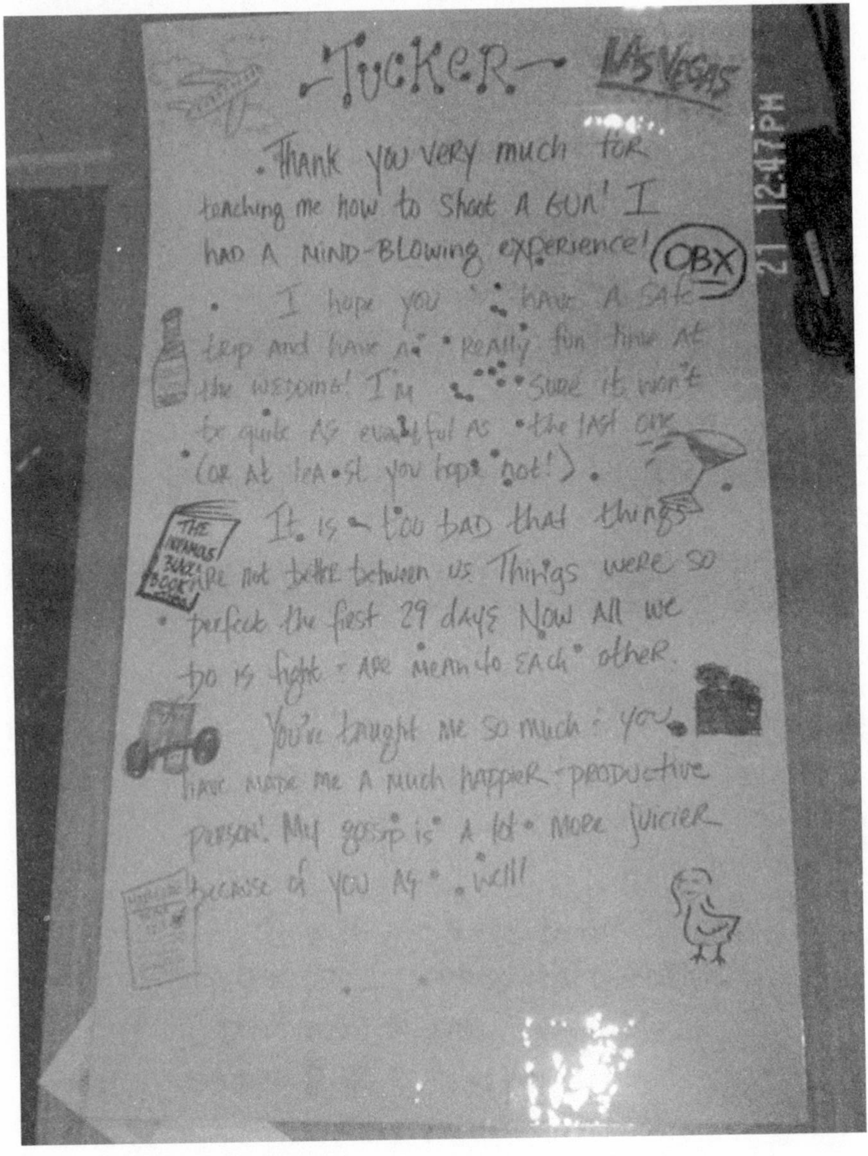

Tucker → Las Vegas

Thank you very much for teaching me how to shoot a gun! I had a mind-blowing experience! OBX

I hope you have a safe trip and have a really fun time at the wedding! I'm sure it won't be quite as eventful as the last one (or at least you hope not!).

It is too bad that things are not better between us. Things were so perfect the first 29 days. Now all we do is fight & are mean to each other.

You've taught me so much & you have made me a much happier & productive person! My gossip is a lot more juicier because of you as well!

The pictures she drew around the text are really quite amazing, especially once you know the backstory with each. It's like a collage of all the high points of our relationship, as seen through MissVermont's eyes:

This I guess is her telling me where I'm going that weekend. Thanks, because my destination wasn't on my ticket or anything.

This is a bottle of beer. Presumably because she drank a lot with me. I'm not at all sure why she decided to put the "XXX" on the side. That's usually reserved for either designating porn or whiskey. I'll give her the benefit of the doubt and just chalk that up to inexperience with the drink.

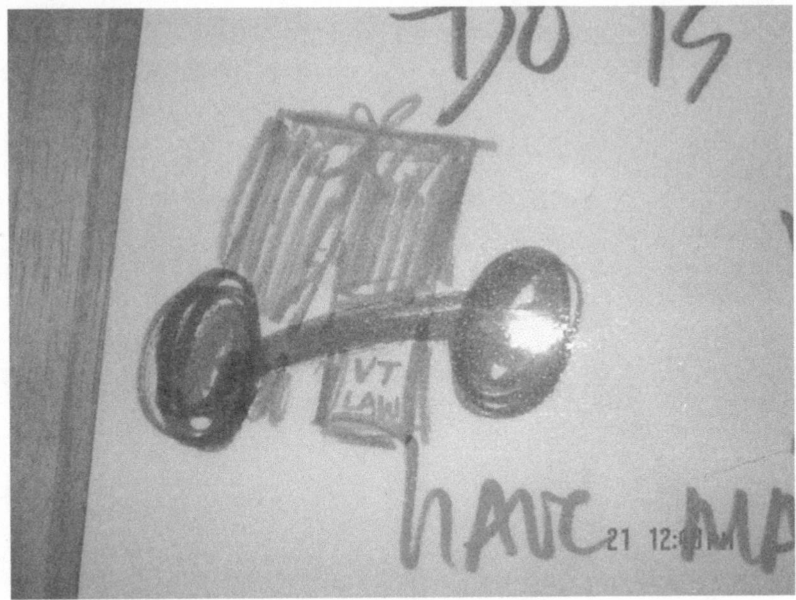

This is her way, I guess, of alluding to how and where we met.

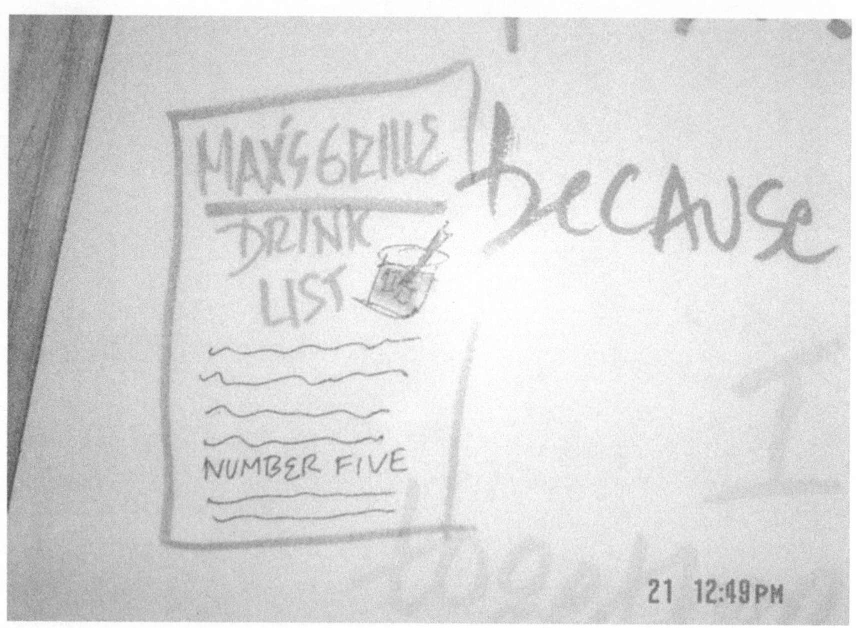

This is a specific reference to drink #5 on the Max's Grille Specialty Drink Menu, that at the time was called a "Sex in the Park."

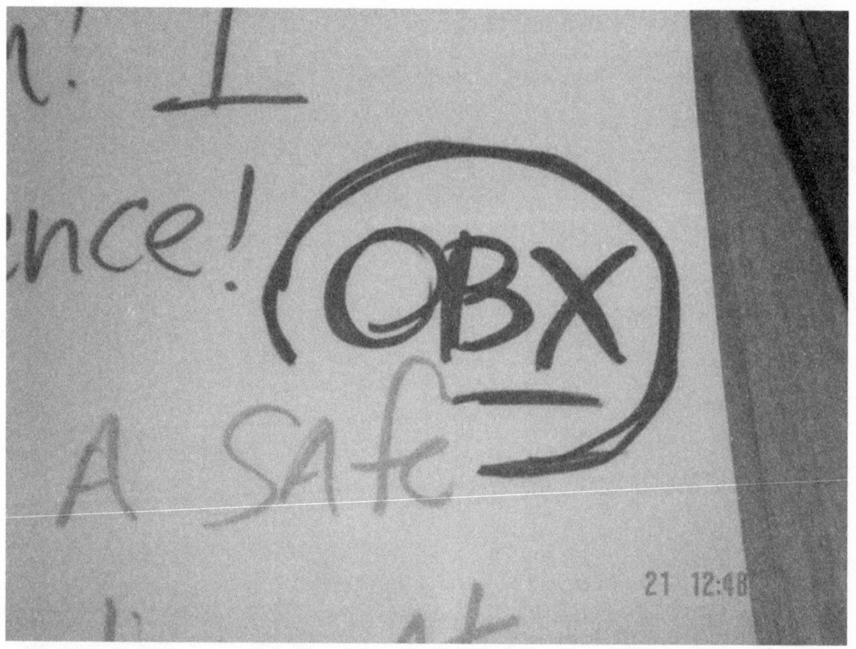

This is a reference to the Outer Banks, the location of the wedding she went to with me.

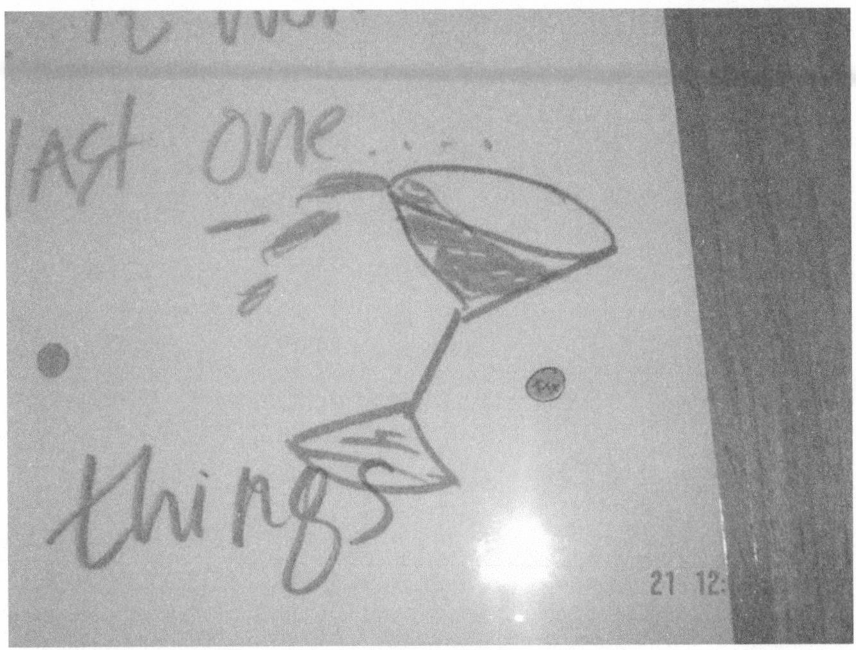

This is of course a drawing of the cosmo that she spilled at that wedding.

This is where she drew her face onto the head of a little chicken. I guess because at the time, I sometimes referred to women as “chicks.”

This is a bucket of coal. This is probably a reference to a time when she did something stupid—I cannot remember what it was specifically was, she did so many stupid things—and I said, "You are dumber than a coal bucket." At least, I think that's what she's referring to. It might also be a reference to what she thought she was getting from Santa that year because, of course, she still believed in him.

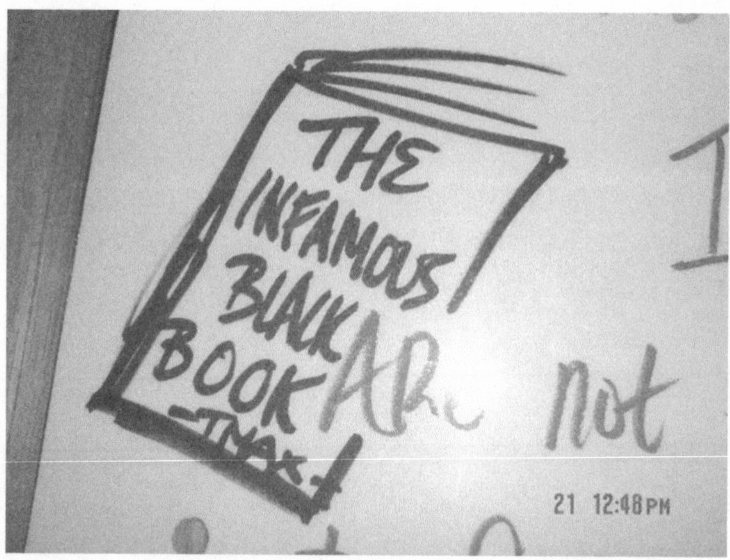

This is a reference to the "book" I wrote called *The Definitive Book of Pick-Up Lines.* I put "book" in quotes because it was just a self-published thing I put together for my law school friends, with all the ridiculous lines we compiled hitting on girls in law school.

And then of course, there is what she actually wrote. You can see it in the picture, but I'll transcribe it too, in case you can't read her pre-pubescent, multi-colored writing:

> Thank you very much for taking me to shoot a gun! I had a mind-blowing experience! I hope you have a safe trip and have a really fun time at the wedding! I'm sure it won't be quite as eventful as the last one . . . (or at least you hope not!)
>
> It is too bad that things are not better between us. Things were so perfect the first 29 days. Now all we do is fight and are mean to each other. You taught me so much and you have made me a much happier and more productive person! My gossip is a lot more juicer because of you!
>
> I wish we were better together, so I guess it's goodbye. I don't want to make you mad anymore.
>
> Katy

As I stood at my car reading this, my first thought was "29 days? Who counts the exact number of days you see someone?" Then I realized I was reading this on a shot-up gun target that had been placed on my car, and thought, "Oh Jesus . . . What have I done?"

Not only did I teach her *how to shoot a gun,* I once had a conversation with this girl after watching a war movie about why the ambushes in the movie were technically incorrect and how to set up a good, L-shaped ambush (by setting-up overlapping fields of fire and stuff like that), AND I described to her, in accurate detail, the basics of how sniping in an urban environment differed from wooded environments, another area that the movie was weak on.

I drove to the airport looking over my shoulder the whole way like a mafia snitch, fully expecting a hail of gunfire to break out at any moment. I must have circled the parking lot at the Fort Lauderdale airport ten times trying to see if anyone was following me.

After I returned to Florida, and a week went by free of any sniper attempts, I let my guard down. It was then that I answered my phone without checking the caller ID, and lo and behold, it was Miss AK-47. She was just as happy and bubbly as ever, and asked me a question:

MissVermont "Hey Tucker! I was calling because I wanted to talk to you about something. You know so much about women and relationships and stuff like that, and I've learned so much from talking to you . . . I was wondering if you could give me advice on how we could get back together."

I swear to God she asked me this. I was flabbergasted.

Tucker "You want advice? Go find a really good psychoanalyst, and get help, because you are fucked up."

She hung up. I would not hear from her for almost two years. But once she came back on my radar, it was with the type of vengeance that can only come from a cunty stage mom from hell, and I would get to know, firsthand, the woman responsible for the creation of this shitstorm of a girl.

Part 3: The Lawsuit

Occurred, May 2003

> *I read a news report*
> *Some lawyer in Florida wanna take us to court*
> *Somebody tell that country ass hick*
> *To go suck a dead man's dick*
> —Geto Boys, "We Can't Be Stopped"

I didn't think about MissVermont again until sometime around January of 2003, when I mentioned something about her on my messageboard. My website had been up for about four months at that point, and I had a small but dedicated readership (for the people who read *AFF*—this is right about the time the TuckerFest party was being planned), so when PWJ, Jojo, and SlingBlade began regaling my fans with their favorite MissVermont anecdotes, everyone asked for the full story.

I resisted at first, until I saw on her website that she was going to do an MTV episode of "MADE", where she would be the pageant coach to a tomboy girl and enter her in a pageant. After seeing that she was still making herself out to be a sober, abstinent pageant girl, I decided to write up my version of our time together.

Now, even though the story I ended up writing was true, it's never that simple. I recognize that the way I see the events in my life is not always precisely the way other people see them. Every story has three truths—my truth, your truth, and the real truth—and I was not foolish enough to think I had a monopoly on all of them. So I emailed the original story to her before I posted it. She didn't respond, so when I put my story up in early 2003, I posted this at the top of the page:

"And to Katy: Even though you haven't responded to the email I sent you, I know you check this site every few weeks. You're welcome to email me with corrections or additions to the story. If I got something wrong or left something out, please let me know and I'll be happy to change it. In fact, if you want to write your own version of our relationship, I swear that I will post it, COMPLETELY UNABRIDGED, right next to mine. This is your opportunity to rebut anything I say here."

Obviously part of my desire to do that was for entertainment purposes, but part of it was also because if I was gonna use her real name, she deserved a chance to respond with her version of the events, in her own words, in the same space I tell my story. That's only fair.

I didn't hear anything. Not even a simple, "Fuck off." I assumed she either didn't care or didn't have anything to add.

Boy, was I wrong.

On May 4th, 2003, I got a frantic voicemail from my mother. She was yammering about some reporter calling her and saying my website had been banned or something like that, none of it made any sense. She left a name and number—some reporter from the *Palm Beach Post*—so I called. The reporter shocked me to the point that I needed her to repeat and explain what she said several times. I still didn't believe it:

MissVermont's lawyer had convinced a judge in Palm Beach County, Florida to issue an ex-parte temporary restraining order against me, forcing me to remove the MissVermont story from my site.

Why is this so shocking? It is what's called a "prior restraint" order, and this was the first time in US LEGAL HISTORY one had been issued against a website. In fact, it was one of the only times it'd even been issued ever, in the long history of the American legal system. A "prior restraint" ruling is the highest level of speech restriction and is issued almost exclusively in cases of national security—for example, if someone wanted to publish the name of an undercover CIA operative in a foreign country. This judge was brazenly ignoring the First Amendment and 200+ years of US legal precedent. This was truly breathtaking.

But don't take my word for it. Check out these selected excerpts from the longer *New York Times* article about the case [all bolding is mine]:

> ". . . Until a Florida judge issued an unusual order last month, Mr. Max's site also contained a long account of his relationship with Ms. Johnson, whom he portrayed, according to court papers, as vapid, promiscuous and an unlikely candidate for membership in the Sobriety Society.

The order, entered by Judge Diana Lewis of Circuit Court in West Palm Beach, forbids Mr. Max to write about Ms. Johnson. It has alarmed experts in First Amendment law, who say that such orders prohibiting future publication, prior restraints, are essentially unknown in American law. Moreover, they say, claims like Ms. Johnson's, for invasion of privacy, have almost never been considered enough to justify prior restraints.

Ms. Johnson's lawsuit also highlights some shifting legal distinctions in the Internet era, between private matters and public ones and between speech and property. **Judge Lewis ruled on May 6, before Mr. Max was notified of the suit and without holding a hearing.** She told Mr. Max that he could not use 'Katy' on his site. Nor could he use Ms. Johnson's last name, full name or the words 'Miss Vermont.'

The judge also prohibited Mr. Max from 'disclosing any stories, facts or information, notwithstanding its truth, about any intimate or sexual acts engaged in by' Ms. Johnson. . ."

". . . This victory should send a clear message to all parasitic smut peddlers who live off the good names of others," [Michael Santucci] said in the release, which also noted that Ms. Johnson 'emphatically denies the story contained on Tucker Max's Web site.'

Mr. Santucci did not respond to an e-mail message asking whether his issuing a news release was at odds with his request to seal the court file on privacy grounds. . ."

". . . That the sites are also used to make money should make no difference in whether Mr. Max may be forbidden to write about Ms. Johnson, said Gregg D. Thomas, an expert in First Amendment law at Holland & Knight in Tampa, Fla. **'This is clearly a suppression of free speech,' Mr. Thomas said of Judge Lewis's order.**

Prior restraints based on invasion of privacy are unusual. 'It has happened perishingly rarely,' said Diane L. Zimmerman, a law professor at New York University and an expert in First Amendment and privacy law. 'When it has happened it has generated enormous controversy. . ."

"**. . . The prohibition on linking to Ms. Johnson's site is 'kooky,' said Susan P. Crawford,** who teaches Internet law at Cardozo School of Law at Yeshiva University. . ."

Fucking crazy, isn't it? It got even more ridiculous. Look at the press release her lawyer sent out just days later (again, all bolding mine—you can just read the bold parts and skip the rest if you want, it's boring BS):

Former Miss Vermont, Katy Johnson, Breaks Silence On Injunction Against 'Depraved Web Site'

BOCA RATON, Fla., June 5 /PRNewswire/ —

The former Miss Vermont and Miss Vermont USA, Katy Johnson, who won a preliminary injunction against a web site that demeans women and promotes character assassination, is speaking out.

According to Ms. Johnson, Tucker Max exploited her image and published scurrilous lies about her on his web site just to sell T-shirts and other merchandise. Last month, a Florida judge ordered a temporary injunction against Max forcing him to take down all references to "Katy Johnson" and "Miss Vermont" on his web site.

"I feel vindicated by the judge's decision, and I hope this suit will put an end to the ugly untruths he parades on this reprehensible web site. Since the lawsuit began, I have been contacted by other victims of his lies who have offered their support," **said Ms. Johnson.**

Ms. Johnson says Max's assertions published on his web site that she is a "whore" and a "prostitute" are malicious, false and hurtful. She vehemently denies the story about her on the web site.

"I never intended to be a champion of privacy rights or become involved in First Amendment issues; to me this is about Right vs. Wrong, and he was wrong to attack my reputation on the Internet for no other reason than his own commercial gain."

Ms. Johnson says that she did not file the lawsuit out of vengeance but to stop further damage to her reputation and others. Her biggest concern was that little girls trying to visit her web site to see the Starrlettes or Miss Vermont web sites for pageant information were being diverted by search engines to Max's depraved web site.

She filed the lawsuit under FL Statutes 540.08, which prevents unauthorized use of name or likeness and provides for punitive damages and royalties, in order to get swift justice through an injunction and conclude the lawsuit quickly. Ms. Johnson says that Max has willfully violated the injunction since it was issued, and she intends to go back to court to find him in contempt. "This person is greatly harming me by the way he is associating my name with his immoral web site and the disgusting products he promotes."

Ms. Johnson, a member of MENSA, is a columnist for Pageantry Magazine and author of "True Beauty: A Sunny Face Means A Happy Heart." She will be appearing on the MTV documentary "MADE" on June 28, as a coach who has one month to turn a tomboy into a beauty queen. Katy's cartoon web site, katyjohnson.com, promotes character for 8 to 12-year-old girls through her Starrlettes comic strip.

And no, I did not make up the part of the press release that reads, "Ms. Johnson, a member of MENSA." I wish I had, because it might be the funniest line in *any* of my books.

But it gets even better. I was served papers a few days later and read the actual lawsuit. All the case materials are online (**www.tuckermax.com/missvermont**), and you can read them yourself if you hate your life. There is a reason I never went to class in law school and people pay lawyers to do this shit—it's boring as fuck. I will try to explain everything in the plainest language possible. She sued me for three different things:

1. Unauthorized use of likeness: She accused me of selling things with her name or likeness on them, without her permission. This was just silly. I did have affiliate links to buy t-shirts on my site, but the shirts themselves had nothing to do with her in any way.

2. Invasion of privacy: This is a common law tort, which accuses me of making private facts about Katy public, by publishing them to the public at large. In plain language, she is saying I told everyone her secrets.

3. Battery: She accuses me of civil battery—hitting her, basically. There were no details to this baseless accusation in the legal filing of course, because it was not only a lie, but it was nothing more than a jurisdictional ploy. Basically, this was their way of trying to make me resolve the case in Florida court instead of having it moved to a court in Illinois (jurisdictional issues are big deals in most lawsuits, but are so tedious if I took the time to explain them to you, you'd burn this book and then try to fight me).

That's it. That's *everything* she sued me for. When I first learned about the lawsuit, I assumed by her statements—like any normal human being would—that she'd be contesting the truth of my story. And honestly, I was kind of excited about that. I had intentionally left out anything even remotely debatable and only put in the events with witnesses or pictures—her behavior at the wedding, her blowing me in the bathroom, the gun target, etc. I was more than willing to defend the truth of my story in a court of law. Then I saw her actual pleading—no mention of libel, defamation, slander . . . there is NOTHING in her lawsuit that actually *contests the truth of the story.*

I repeat for emphasis: The lawsuit NEVER accuses me of saying anything untrue about Katy. In fact, in order for count #2 to be valid, what I say about her *has to be true.* Her lawsuit is, in effect, legally admitting that my story is true, and then taking the position that I didn't have the right to say it.

Katy's lawyer was using a very shrewd legal strategy that allowed them to deny the facts of my case to the press, but never actually put the facts of what happened in front of a court of law. By not suing me for libel, the only issues were technical aspects of the law, and NOT the truth of the story. This strategy is what you would use ONLY if you're trying to hide something and silence a voice you don't want to hear. And though it was within the *letter* of the law, it was so far outside its spirit that the whole thing verged on immoral and unethical chicanery. More importantly, what it meant was that Katy knew what was up, she was just trying to intimidate me into taking my story down.

I'll never forget the moment I came to the realization that this was no longer about truth. This was someone trying to use power and influence in an illegitimate and unethical way to bully me into shutting up, to silence the truth and steal my liberty from me.

What the fuck? I live in America, right? This shit isn't supposed to happen here, is it?

Well, it was happening to me. And if I didn't do something about it, I was going to get fucked. Make no mistake about it, this was a big deal, and this was a serious attack not only on my First Amendment rights, but on anyone who published truth on the internet.

I may have gone to a top ten law school, but this shit was beyond my ability. I needed a great lawyer, one, you know, who actually took the bar. I went to the best internet First Amendment lawyer I could find, a guy named John Carey. He was very interested in the case, discussed it thoroughly with me, and I was impressed. This dude got it. He would be able to help justice prevail. He was even willing to do it at a steep discount, but he wouldn't do it without getting paid something, at least, a $7,000 retainer to start.

I checked my bank account. I had $44. Freedom is not free, indeed.

I was fucked. But my fucking went deeper than my account balance. It went to the core of all my decisions in the two years between when I met MissVermont and when she sued me. Let me explain:

I met MissVermont in the summer of 2001, right after I graduated from Duke and moved to Florida to work for my father. The summer before, I'd hated being a lawyer so much that it only took me three weeks of acting like a complete asshole to get fired (that is the charity auction story from *IHTSBIH*). It didn't take too much longer than that for me to hate the restaurant business and get fired from there as well. The only thing that was different was how and by whom I was fired.

When I got to South Florida, my dad's entire company was fucked up. All the stuff my dad saw was great: the restaurants ran really well, he was making money, customers were happy, etc. But the backend of the business was a total shitshow. Costs were way out of whack and the mid-level employees were thieves and liars who didn't care about the business as much as they did about massaging my dad's ego so they could keep leeching off of him. I figured this out quickly, and realized immediately how to turn the business around. I could get rid of the shitty employees, reconfigure the backend to make everything more efficient, renegotiate contracts with vendors and reduce prices—I could, in effect, add all sorts of value by bringing it into the 21st century.

I made a major error in implementing my plan, one that is totally obvious in retrospect: I TOLD all the toxic middle management thieves all about my great plans. As quickly as I had realized that they were the problem, they figured out that most of my plan would involve either firing them or cutting off their gravy train. I didn't care though; I thought that because my plan was the right one, and my name was on the door, my father would back me over them. [Adding to this scorched earth tactical blunder was the fact that I had done enough reckless shit—like having MissVermont blow me in the bathroom—to give them ammunition to use against me.]

One day my dad sat me down to talk about some recent issues in the restaurant. I thought he was going to discuss a way to at least solve the problems. I was wrong.

Father "Tucker, I'm going to have let you go."

Yes, you read that right. *My father fired me from the family business because he picked his ass-kissing employees over his own son.*

As I sat there and listened to his bullshit rationalizations for why he was doing this, something became crystal clear to me:

The disease does not cause itself. The employees *weren't* the problem. And even though I'd approached this wrong, I wasn't even the problem. The problem was my father. His employees were able to act the way they did because he'd implicitly allowed it for years. Those toxic shitheads knew my father better than me. I thought the best of him, but they understood he actually *wanted* employees who kissed his ass, not people who had ambition to do things the right way. At 25, I was still naive enough to think life and business were about truth; they knew it was really about feeding the egos of those above you. They gave him what he wanted and I didn't, so he protected them and not me.

It was nice to understand this, even if it was a little late, but regardless of how right I may have been, I gotta be honest: It was pretty shitty to have my own dad fire me from the family business. This meant—after also getting fired from my law firm—that I'd now failed at the two things I was supposed to have been training for in college and grad school. That sucked, and those failures forced me to really examine my life, and ask myself some hard questions:

What kind of life did I want to lead? One I loved, one I was proud of and that made me happy . . . or a life that other people told me I was "supposed" to lead but I hated?

What kind of person was I going to be? Just another sheep, another cog in the machine, working a crappy job I couldn't stand . . . or was I going to be the type of person who blazed my own trail and made an awesome life I loved living?

I realized I had a choice to make: swallow my pride, go back to the corporate machine, and try to be a lawyer or a businessman, but this time make sure I acted like a sheep and did it their way . . . or do something where I carved my own path in life and didn't have to eat anyone else's shit. Something I really loved doing.

Looking at it that way, there wasn't really a choice. I *had* to leave that world and go create my own life. It came down to one simple thing for me: Every day I have to wake up and look at myself in the mirror, and if I'm not excited to live the day in front of me, proud of who I am and what I'm spending my time doing . . . then what's the fucking point?

It took a while to figure out what I wanted to do (that's a whole different story), but in August of 2002, I moved to Chicago and started writing full time. I did nothing but dedicate myself to my work. I refused to get a "normal" job to support myself, only doing side things to cover bills (like teaching for Princeton Review). For me, it was sink or swim.

By May 1, 2003—despite a lot of initial setbacks—my site had officially blown up. I had hundreds of thousands of readers, I had been featured on MTV, I had girls coming to me for sex (like it should have been all along). I'd bet everything on myself, taken a series of immense risks, almost failed, and here I was, making it. It was the greatest feeling in the world.

There was only one problem: money. My small savings had run out real fast. This was 2002/2003, remember. People were just starting to get real-world famous for their writing on the Internet, but no one was making any money at it. No shit, it got to the point where I was eating ramen on the days I was lucky enough to eat at all.

With that backstory, you understand my mindset and my financial position in May of 2003. So, on the verge of getting everything I wanted, here comes the MissVermont lawsuit, threatening to take everything away. The most frustrating part was that even though I was right, even though I had truth on my side, it didn't matter. I needed a lawyer to defend that truth, and if I couldn't find the $7,000 to hire him, MissVermont was going to beat me simply by manipulating the law. She was lying, threatening my future as a writer with her flagrant hypocrisy, and she was going to win . . . by default.

But where the fuck do I get $7,000? I had $44 in my bank account. Yeah, tons of people read my writing and knew my name, but none of them were paying me (this was also a few years before my book came out). I had nowhere else to turn, so I did the only thing I could do:

I humiliated myself, and went to my father. I begged him to put up the money for the retainer.

Even though my father had fired me from the family business because he's an insecure narcissist who picked his sycophants over his own son, he's not an evil monster—he understood how fucked I was, and he agreed to help me. But he put a condition on his financial assistance to me:

In return for him paying for my legal defense, I had to promise him I would drop my dreams of being a writer, start studying for the bar, take it, and then go to work as a lawyer.

You see, my dad was fixated on me "doing something" with my life, and the only way he could see that happening was "putting my education to use" by becoming a lawyer. That's one of the main reasons I even went to law school at all—because my dad wanted me to be a lawyer. It fit his image of success for me. When I moved to Chicago to become a writer, he was pissed at me because there was no place for "struggling writer" within his image of success for his son. He did want me to succeed at life—it was just that his notion of success was vastly different from mine, and now he had the leverage he needed to get me to go back into the law, something I had left because I hated it.

In order to save my dream of becoming a writer . . . I had to give my dream up. The irony is so fucking thick it makes me sick.

I took the deal. What choice did I have? Sometimes you have to cut the deal with the devil. It was so fucking depressing, but he paid the retainer, and as usually happens once you take the devil's deal, shit immediately started going right:

I complied with the court order and took "The MissVermont Story" off my website—only because my lawyer insisted—which inspired about 100 other sites to host the story. My original MissVermont story went from what was essentially a completely anonymous story on some random website, to being the most read thing on the Internet for a week or two. By suing me, dumbass Katy Johnson attracted 1,000x more attention to me and my story than it would have gotten on its own. I became a First Amendment hero, to the point where even the ACLU filed an amicus brief on my behalf (essentially saying that my side of the position was the right one).

My lawyers did what they said they would: They smoked Katy's dumbass lawyer. They called his bluff. Since Katy Johnson went on record as saying that this story was so harmful to her reputation, and needed it to be taken down immediately, we filed a brief asking for expedited discovery.

"Discovery" is the portion of a court case where the two sides get to have their lawyers interview the witnesses from the other side and examine all their relevant files. What this meant was that my lawyer would be able to sit down and ask Katy all sorts of questions about the facts of the case—ON THE RECORD. This would mean she would have to tell the truth, under penalty of perjury, about everything I wrote in my story.

So if she denied, say, sucking my dick in the bathroom of Max's Grille, then I would bring in the waiters who walked in on us. Or if she denied anything about the wedding, I'd bring in the guests. It would put every single fact of my story under legal scrutiny—which is what I wanted, because I was telling the truth and she was lying. [And not only that, but my lawyer would ask her about exactly WHY she was no longer at Stetson law school, which would mean—on the record—she'd have to explain the whole story behind her decision to send envelopes of fake anthrax to her own mother.]

As soon as we did that, Katy sent me an email asking me to settle the case. Oh no, honey, I WANT discovery. I WANT you to answer these questions. Let's bring it ALL into the light and bathe in truth.

Pretty predicable what happened next: They dropped their case against me, without a whimper or any bullshit news stories or press releases. Since then, I've heard nothing from Katy or her lawyer.

I won. I fought for my freedom and won.

But that wasn't the last battle I had to fight. I'd promised my dad I would quit this "writing thing" and go take the bar and be a lawyer. For two months, I tried to keep my word to him. I started studying for the bar. I got my bar application and started filling it out. The Illinois Bar application has to be typed or printed out, and I didn't have a printer, so I had to go to the Lincoln Park library and use their typewriters. That's right, MECHANICAL FUCKING TYPEWRITERS.

I'll never forget the day I went there to type out my bar application. Sitting in this tiny, moldy smelling room, as I punched away on this ancient machine, I felt sicker and sicker. Physically ill, like I had been gut-punched. I tried to ignore it, but I couldn't—I ended up vomiting in the trashcan. I didn't have the flu or anything. This was my body sending me an unmistakable message.

I threw away all the bar materials and left the library. I told my dad I wasn't taking the bar, I wasn't going to be a lawyer. I was going to pursue my dream and be a writer, regardless of what he said or did. It was my life to live the way I wanted to live it, right or wrong. I told him I was sorry I went back on my word, but I wasn't going to have *my* life held hostage by *his* desires. I promised I'd pay him back the $7,000 when I could afford to.

He cut me off. He's never given me anything again. The supreme irony is now that I'm a #1 best-selling author and all his friends are fans of my writing, he thinks what I did was a great idea, and he loves to brag about me to his friends. Yeah, OK.

It's funny because my dad was doing to me exactly what Kathleen Johnson was doing to Katy: Both of them were forcing a life on us we didn't want. They tried to make us into something we weren't. But that doesn't work. You can't live a lie—not without destroying yourself. That's probably why I took this fight so personally, why it made me so angry at the time, and why I refused to go back to being a lawyer. Both Kathleen Johnson and my father wanted to shut me up and reinforce their own lies through mine.

But that's not going to happen, not to me at least. I'd rather die standing than live with a boot on my neck. As I write this, it's 2011. I did become a successful writer, my dad got his money back, and MissVermont is . . . well, I don't know what she's doing now. Hopefully for her sake, she's figured out the things I have and found a way to live her own life.

But the offer will always be out there: Katy Johnson, you are welcome to write your version of what happened between us, and I will publish it, unedited, either on my site or in a revised version of this book. I'm as interested to read it as everyone else is.

There was one good thing that came out of her lawsuit. She released a whole raft of hilarious new cartoons based on me. [You can see them along with the rest at the end of this story.]

[This part of the story isn't all that funny, and you can skip it if you want. But I had to write it, and if you're interested in this case, it might be worth it.]

Postscript: Some Speculation

You scream obscenity, but it's publicity
You're all hoes, so don't act like you don't know
Better fuck with somebody else before you get popped
Because we can't be stopped
—Geto Boys, "We Can't Be Stopped"

I know I talked about how angry I was at this lawsuit and how I took it personally because it threatened not only my very existence as a writer, but my struggle to find my identity. That's all true. And I'm still pissed about it, years later.

But here's the thing: At this point in my life, I don't hold any animosity toward MissVermont (Katy Johnson). I don't think she was the reason for the lawsuit. As the months and years went by, more and more facts got filled in and added to the things I already knew, until a clearer picture emerged of what actually caused the lawsuit:

I think Katy was a pawn in this, and that her mom, Kathleen Johnson, was the entire cause of EVERYTHING.

Consider these facts:

- I know it was her mom who made Katy do all the things that Katy did—pageants, charities, cartoons, law school, modeling, everything. The fact that is Katy didn't want to do any of that, but did it because her mom made her, was a constant and recurrent theme in her life. It was like her job was being Kathleen Johnson's daughter, not being herself.

- By the way—Katy's full name is Katy Johnson, Jr. I shit you not. If that isn't the perfect little piece of evidence for the existence of an evil narcissist mother, I don't know what is.

- I know that in the month or so that Katy and I were "dating," her mom went around and bragged to people that Katy was dating Dennis Max's son, and that it was "serious." The people who told me this all said the same thing I did: She didn't say it in a caring way or say anything about what we were like as a couple. It was all about how it reflected on her narcissistic self-image and how Katy was a trophy for her to bestow.

- Re-read that press release. It should immediately be clear that wasn't Katy talking. She can't conjugate verbs in her own native language. Clearly that was from the pen of someone else.

- In the several years following the lawsuit, many people have emailed me and told me all kinds of information about Kathleen. One worked in the offices of Michael Santucci, the lawyer who sued me. That person told me that they never saw Katy once, but that Kathleen was constantly calling and coming into the office and was in charge of every aspect of the lawsuit—she drafted the press releases, she worded Katy's "statements", she did all of it. Another person who emailed me worked for Katy's (now) husband. She must have typed 5,000 words about what a cunt Kathleen Johnson was to her, all stuff that sounded like the woman I met. And another was a girl who went to law school at Stetson with Katy, and basically confirmed all of what Katy told me about the anthrax thing—that it happened, that her mom was the target, that it was her MOM who hushed it up, etc.

So what do these facts mean? What is the conclusion to draw? Here's what I think:

Not only do I believe that everything surrounding the lawsuit was orchestrated by Kathleen Johnson, Sr., I also believe she is an evil, toxic narcissist, and I'd even go so far as to bet that almost every problem in Katy's entire life is directly attributable to her awful mom.

Think about it: What was the purpose of Kathleen Johnson, Sr. filing this lawsuit? Was it to prevent people from talking about her daughter? Was it to prevent people from reading my story? Was it to help solve any of the obvious issues in her daughter's life?

Fuck no. The whole scene was manufactured by Kathleen Johnson, Sr. to protect her identity to her Palm Beach social circle. That's the only explanation that fits the facts.

What other purpose could her actions serve? If the purpose of the lawsuit was to prevent her daughter from being publicly embarrassed, she not only failed, she achieved the opposite result. If she only wanted to silence me, she could have done that WITHOUT calling the press. But she didn't. After all, it was KATY'S MOM who alerted the press about this case. In fact, she went out of her way to humiliate her daughter by INTENTIONALLY having an AP reporter cover the case, splashing the story all over the front page of every newspaper in America.

Why would she do this? What is the motive here? These are not the actions of someone who cares about truth, or even cares about her daughter. These are the actions of a narcissist when she's suffered a narcissistic injury. She ruthlessly attacks and then makes sure that everyone she cares about SEES that she's attacked the truth she doesn't want to face. It's not about reality to a narcissist; it's about perception. That's all she cares about, and that's why the press reporting the lawsuit was more important that the lawsuit itself.

Why do you think Katy did not respond when she saw the story, but the minute that my MTV special came on, and Katy's MOM found out what I had written, she freaked? And look at the way she approached the situation: She didn't email me or call me to try and discern the truth of the accusations. Nope. She convinced Judge Diana Lewis—who incidentally is a personal friend of Kathleen Johnson, Sr.—to issue a prior restraint ruling that was called things like "unprecedented" and "kooky" by every legal scholar who saw it.

Had I never written anything, no one would know any of this negative stuff about Katy. But I did. And I used her real name, because she was a public figure. And though not many people were reading my site at the time, nothing like that stays anonymous for long on the Internet. And once Kathleen, Sr. saw it, I can promise you she had a meltdown—just like she did when she found my boxers in Katy's Explorer.

But this was worse—with the boxers, she was the only one who saw them, so she could hide that. Same with the fake anthrax thing—she could hush that up and hide it. But this story was public. She couldn't hide it. ALL of her friends would see it. That meant that the mom's entire false identity was on the line—I was inflicting a massive narcissistic injury NOT on Katy, but on Kathleen, Sr. If all her friends knew the truth, that Katy was not the trophy that Kathleen claimed she was, Kathleen could no longer maintain her constructed identity of perfect mother to a perfect child.

Katy's mom did not treat Katy like a daughter; she used Katy as an extension of her ego. She dealt with her not as an individual human with her own wants and needs and personality, but as a doll or accessory for her to dress up and display in front of others, whose successes and failures were not her own, but were an extension of Kathleen's. Katy wasn't a person to her mom; she was an employee. That is abuse, plain and simple. Katy may be fucked up, but how can you blame her?

Within the context of having a mom like this, Katy's actions regarding the fake anthrax make perfect sense. I mean, don't get me wrong—it was profoundly fucking stupid to fake a terrorist attack—but can you understand why she subconsciously hates her mom so much? And why she would do something like that, tell me she did it, but not be able to explain *why* she did it?

The saddest thing is that I think the true victim here is Katy. Katy was a young and confused girl, caught between an evil, controlling narcissist mother and a fucking asshole guy (that would be me). Don't get me wrong, she lied to everyone in her life and did some fucked up shit, but like most of us, she was very much a victim of forces beyond her control, and she was too young and inexperienced to understand any of it. And with a mom like that, she didn't have a chance.

Of course I didn't understand ANY of this as it was going on either. Come on—I was 25 years old and at the height of my youthful, drunken, whorish idiocy. I was doing nothing more than reacting to the things in front of me like any 25-year-old guy would. As I write this now, I'm 35. Ten years of experience helps you see a lot of things.

I'm going to end this story with a special message for Kathleen Johnson:

I know you found those boxer-briefs in Katy's car. I know you looked up the citation record and found the tickets in North and South Carolina (I have friends, too). You knew my story was the truth. But you filed that lawsuit anyway. You thought you could use your connections to bully me. You thought I would fold and disappear. You thought that because I was a poor, powerless nobody at the time, you could bury the truth I was exposing and save your bullshit reputation.

Your first lawsuit was so unethical and borderline illegal that I could have come after you in 2003. But I didn't have the resources then. It took everything I had just to win. The last time you came at me, you did it when I was least able to defend myself, and you did it by making your daughter the battleground.

Not this time. I just printed a lot of stuff about YOU. I think it's all true, but some of it might not be. I don't care. I'm printing it anyway. Now you have the chance to come at me again—except this time, you can leave your daughter out of it. Just you versus me. And this time, I'm neither poor nor powerless. Now it'll be a fair fight.

But as you sit there, fuming and raging, fantasizing about how you'll crush me with the lawsuit you're about to file . . . remember the advice of Omar:

"You come at the king, you best not miss."

Because this time, you won't be able to avoid discovery . . . you fucking cunt.

This is supposed to be advice to young pageant girls, and apparently she thinks they need to be TOLD that they can't steal expensive designer clothes. Is petty theft this much of a problem in the junior pageant circuit? And look at Katy's reaction in the last panel—she's got her arms crossed and she's smiling, like she's happy her friend got arrested. What a fucking cunt.

Aren't those girls supposed to be her friends? Why are they talking shit about her? Probably because she was such a cunt when their friend got arrested. She needs to feel better, so she goes to the only thing on earth she knows she's smarter than, better looking than, and thinner than—a fucking cow. Why a cow? Seriously, why not friends or parents or even a dog?? You know Katy, maybe the reason you don't get along with other girls is because your best friend is a goddamn farm animal.

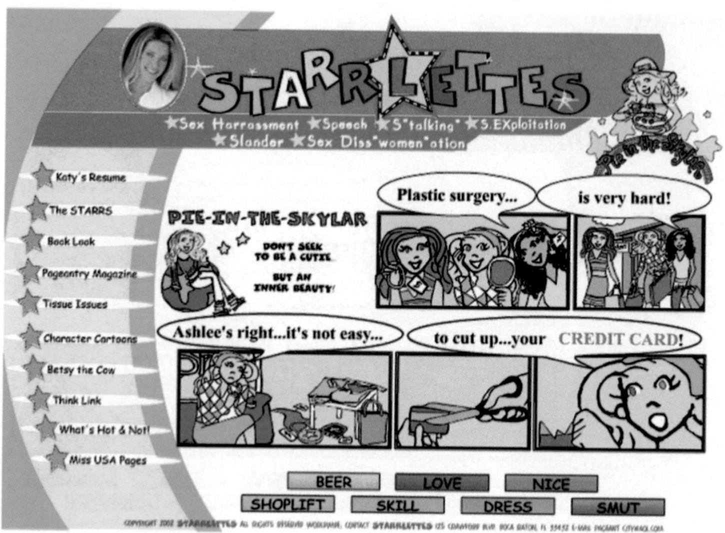

This one is disturbing on many levels. Notice how the characters have flat affects—no expression, just caricatures of emotions. This is what sociopaths are like. More importantly, look at what this cartoon is saying, that the struggle here isn't accepting oneself, it's about destroying the chance to do it. She can't actually use restraint and not spend, she has to remove the opportunity to even use a charge card. It's like saying it's hard to not speed when you have a fast car, so the answer is to drive it into a pole. You can't speed if your car is broken. That's the type of logic you see on Lockup: Raw. I mean, you don't try to help someone stop killing themselves, you just take away their shoelaces. She's admitting she is incapable of taking care of herself, and is nothing more than a ward of whoever pays her bills.

WHY DOES HER EXPRESSION NEVER CHANGE!!!! And honey, purses are just signaling devices to other women about status. They have nothing to do with personality.

What is her talent? Superhuman handjobs? And if this is a talent show, why is the ribbon already on her guitar? She gave such a good handjob the judges just ran up there and stuck it on? You have to go to great lengths to improve—apparently this means posing with a guitar in your bedroom, on a beach, and in a pasture. Don't even get me started on the wordplay.

I guess the point she's making is that a tattoo's not like an unwanted pregnancy—you can't stab it to death to make it go away. I like how the guy apparently has a tattoo of a peace dove—this is a mark of Cain to her? And the guy doesn't say anything? He just sits there are she shits all over him? WTF? He looks suspiciously like a Jew. Like a young Jeff Goldblum. And like he's getting this tattoo against his will in that second frame. What is this, Dachau?

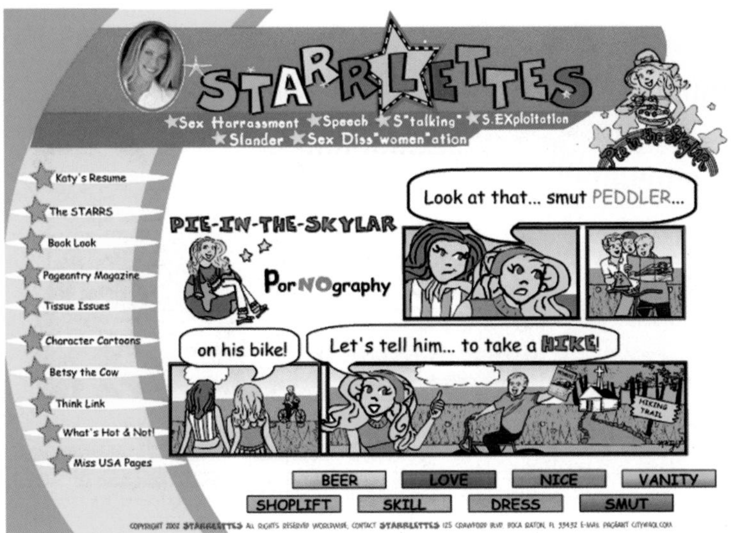

Seriously—who rides a bike to or from a porn store?

Who are these dudes that only have one leg and ride up his ass on the bike? Where are their bikes?

And I mean, if I saw some random guy riding his bike down the street, smiling and waving porn in the air—you wouldn't go party with that dude?

And in case you aren't sure what hike means, she has conveniently put a hiking trail behind him. A hiking trail that goes ten yards, before it dead ends in a church.

I'm no Freud, but do you think it's really coincidence that the colors on the smut are the same as the colors of her shirt and hair? A good artist does that on purpose. She is not a good artist, she's just an idiot.

You don't drink? Only in a cartoon, Katy.

I like how as she says she doesn't drink, she's chillin on his futon with her legs in the air. Yeah, you NEVER do this.

What is the end game here? So some creepy albino with a mullet and red eyes invites you back to his place, and you think this is a good idea. So you decide to sprawl out in your tube top and lecture him about drinking?

Why does she think being Christian means she shouldn't drink wine? DIDN'T JESUS DRINK WINE??? Didn't he say drink wine, because it is my blood??? But apparently in Katy's world, God won't bless wine drinkers. And sorry Katy, humans can't be divine, only Jesus can be.

That's the best part of this cartoon—that the dude is the most pious person. He's the one drinking wine like Jesus says to do, he even says a prayer over it and asks God for his blessing. She refuses to drink the blood of Christ (wine), and then gets her theology completely wrong (humans can't be divine).

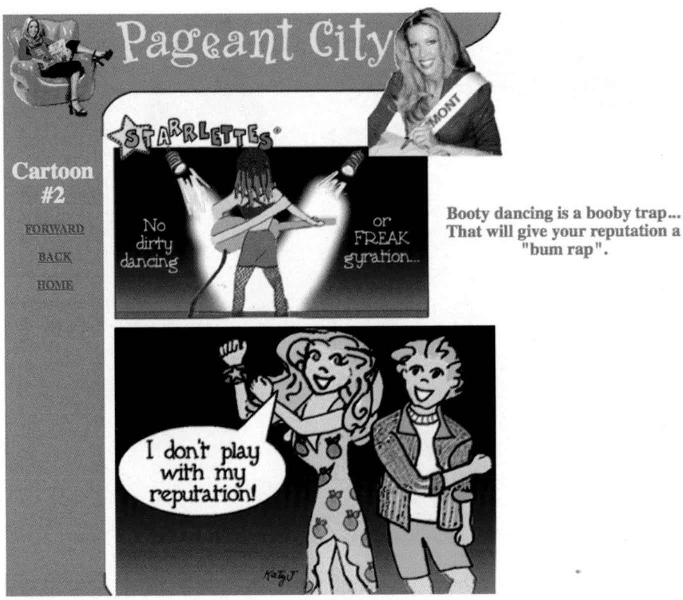
Pageant City
STARRLETTES
Cartoon #2
FORWARD
BACK
HOME
No dirty dancing
or FREAK gyration...
Booty dancing is a booby trap... That will give your reputation a "bum rap".
I don't play with my reputation!

She doesn't play with her reputation, even though her dress is cut basically at her pelvic bone? I guess reality doesn't matter, just what people think about her. That's her reality, whatever her reputation is. But according to the cartoon, she still wants to grind her crotch against a dude's genitals, she just doesn't want to be judged about it.

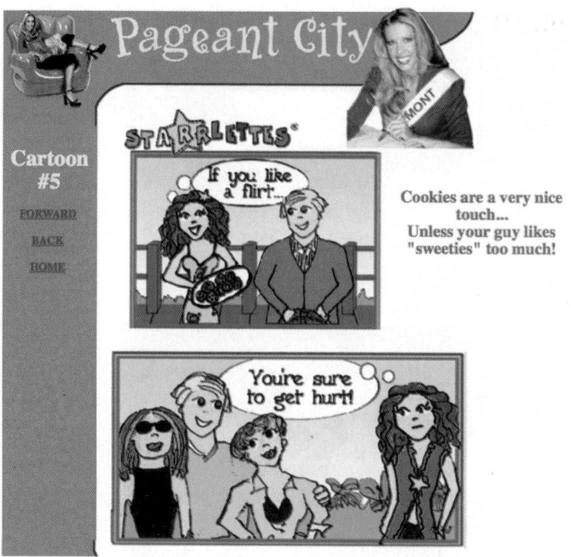

This makes no sense to me. Is she saying that if you like flirtatious guys, then for some reason, cookies are great? Unless he's fucking a ton of other girls, then well, cookies aren't worth a shit. I could've told you that. Cookies aren't as good as sex. And in no case do cookies make a guy like you over girls who put out. Is it me, or did Katy draw the girls he's with to look like black coke whores?

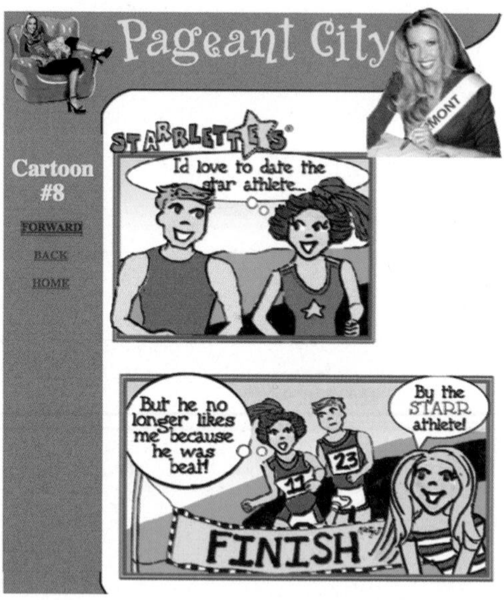

Her message here is that she wants to date a thing ("the star athlete"), not a person. She doesn't say if she likes him as a person, it's like it never even occurs to her. But he no longer likes her because she won? So she's saying not to be better at things than guys you like? And how can he be a star athlete if he can't outrun a girl?

Is she saying that women should wait on guys to make a move? Also, how sexist and regressive—women shouldn't pursue men? Wow. Welcome to the 50's Holly Homemaker.

And excuse me, why exactly do girls have nothing to prove? Is she saying that by dressing like a girl, she's indicating she has a vagina, and her end of the deal is done? It's up to the guy now. Her assumption is that guys engage girls based solely on the fact that they ARE girls. She's saying that because she's wearing a tight top showing her tits and a low cut skirt, you know everything you need to know—she has a vagina. The implication is that that's all she has to offer, and that's why guys should have to make the first move.

What's up with him talking to two girls, having a threesome lined up, and then going up to her because . . . why? She looks like a bigger slut? She's acting like a standoffish bitch? What guy would abandon TWO girls for her?

What about the other two girls? She draws them all pissed off—she's accentuating that her victory is not over only him, but over those girls too. She's saying that they're desperate sluts, so they deserve to be hurt.

And you know what kind of guy relentlessly pursues a standoffish girl? A date rapist. Why? Because he hates women and wants to punish women like this. Proof: He's offering her a taste of his roofie colada in the frame.

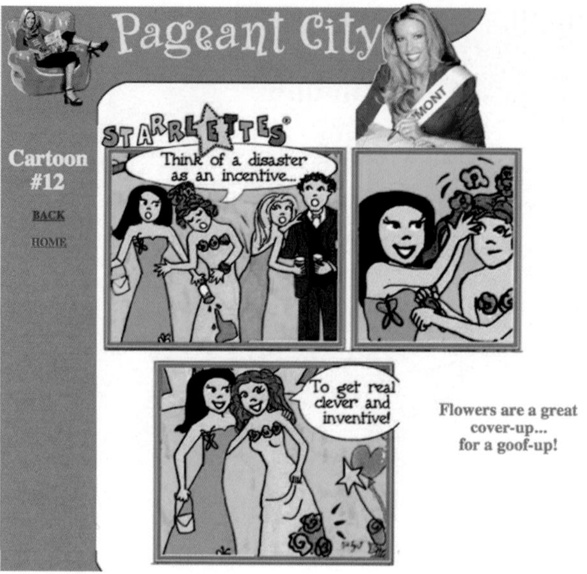

I guess the point is not to clean up the mess, but to cover it and pretend nothing happened. What does that sound like?

First off, if you like a dude and don't kiss him because you want to play bullshit games, there's no guessing—you're a psycho bitch. And even in her own cartoon, where she refuses to even KISS a dude, her tits are BLOWING off the page. I mean, she looks like Mariah Carey singing the national anthem. To her credit though, I wouldn't kiss someone who made that face either.

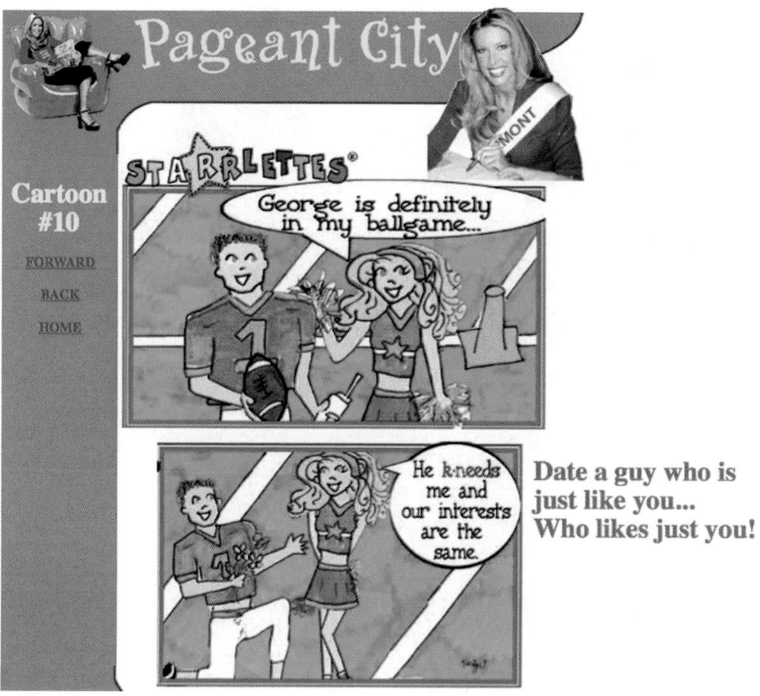

This cartoon is seriously disturbing. Does he kneed her like she is dough? He's a good masseuse? Or does she want a guy who gets on his hands and knees and begs you for shit like a pussy? Or is she saying that she prefers a guy who literally needs her and is so co-dependent with her that he can't leave?

And she says to date a guy who is just like you? So he's a moody, game playing bitch who won't kiss on the first date? She's saying to find a spineless, obsessive loser star athlete, who is completely dependent on you, and will beg you for stuff. But also shares your interests in purses and fashion. So she wants a closeted self-hating homo?

You are who you date? YOU ARE WHO YOU DATE??? She's saying women have no inherent value as human beings, aside from their external status symbols—like purses or who you are dating. She's literally telling a generation of girls that they will be judged on who they can get to date them. So if you're single, you are NOTHING. You have failed as a woman, is that it Katy? This is so offensive to women, I'm offended, and I'm a man. If I showed this cartoon to my daughter, I'd turn myself in for child abuse, that's how awful the message there is.

[And I like how she says "Always hoping for a white knight." White knight. NOT a knight in shining armour. A WHITE knight. You can't take a black knight home to your mother.]

Look at the bill. $500. What a money grubbing whore.

And yeah, we know you don't like to fuck in restaurants, you prefer being taken in the back of a crappy SUV in the parking lot.

Look at how little clothes she has on. She has a heart in her cleavage. She's barely covering her snatch. How can you not think he'll expect sex—he can already smell your vagina.

And the dude looks like he's a castaway, like he was just rescued at sea. Of course he expects sex, he hasn't seen another person in years.

Let's not pretend Katy knows the first thing about anyone ethnic and dispense with this shit right now: No one that color is allowed to play tennis at any of the Palm Beach clubs Katy belongs to.

And I like how it's two brown people together, like she's saying those people should stick to their own kind. What a bitch.

Apparently, it's also hot to swing dance until you break your spine.

You know what's even less hot? Not thinking because you're fucking retarded.

Nice job not letting the guy under the umbrella, you selfish bitch.

I mean . . . do I really need to point out that she drew a cartoon where the girl is getting fucked by a horse?

Look at the horse's face!!! He's thinking, "Damn, this girl took my whole load and smiled about it!"

Tucker Max, Knee Abuser

Occurred, August 2009

I was in NYC for a bunch of business meetings, nothing special. About halfway through one of them, this female lawyer started giving me the most ridiculous "fuck me" vibes I've ever gotten in a business setting. This was a real meeting with a bunch of other people in it, so she wasn't being inappropriate or forward at all—but there was no doubt about what she was doing. She kept shooting me those sly sideways glances while she stroked her hair, she would give genuine smiles to me when we locked eyes—the kind you can't fake, when the eyes smile with the face—and when I was talking, she would either stroke her pen or her arm and stare intently at me.

When a woman goes out of her way to send signals like that, there is only ONE conclusion to draw: She wants to fuck. And not subconsciously—she's hoping you come talk to her. People ask me all the time how I get myself into the situations I write about. Well, how many times have you been in a bar or at a party and you thought someone was shooting you glances like this, but you did nothing, either because you thought it meant nothing or because you were afraid of rejection? I am afraid of riding on motorcycles and angry Persian women holding knives, but when it comes to rejection, I'm fresh out of fucks to give.

As soon as the meeting was over and I'd finished the worthless chit-chat with people who wanted to feel important, I casually pulled her aside:

Tucker "Am I off base, or were you giving me serious 'fuck me' eyes in that meeting?"

I didn't really ask it as a question. She turned bright red. We both knew. I don't know why she was so shocked—I guess no one had ever directly called her out like that before—but after a second I could see in her eyes that she'd mentally switched from "high-powered attorney" mode to "naughty vixen" mode. We were still in an office during business hours, so she maintained decorum.

Vixen "I think this is an issue that merits further discussion. Here's my card, gimme a call. On my cell."

The best part is that she rubbed her finger against my wrist when she handed her business card to me. Come on. I wouldn't have needed this many hints if we were playing Clue. I got it honey: It's the Colonel, with the pipe, in your ass.

We met for drinks later that night. It was a worthless formality; she was barely done with her martini before we were out the door looking for a place to fuck. We were on the Upper West Side, and my hotel was all the way in Soho. She had a good suggestion:

Vixen "I have a key to the Midtown office. Let's go there."

It was a late Friday night, so the place was empty. Law firms are sterile and spooky enough when the cubicle zombies are there, but when they're all gone, they're almost like crypts.

She pulled me into the huge conference room we'd been in earlier.

Vixen "I've always wanted to fuck in here. Now every time I do a deal I can think of your cock inside me."

I had to stop myself from making a lawyers-are-always-fucking-people joke. Too easy.

I take her clothes off, push her on the table on her back and thrust into her. When you see office sex in the movies, it always looks so erotic.

That's Hollywood for you. In real life, office sex is uncomfortable and annoying:

The conference table is just high enough that I have to stand on my tiptoes to get my dick inside her, which is a fucking hassle, but nothing I haven't dealt with before. I'm a professional; I can make it work.

Except I can't, because my calves start to cramp from being on my tiptoes so long. And not little periodic cramps either—these are bad. So bad, that after a few minutes, my legs start to seize up and shake. From the waist down, I look like Michael J. Fox.

So I flip her over onto her hands and knees and climb up on the table to fuck her from behind. OK, this is working . . .

For like thirty seconds. The table is hard oak, and my knees are hurting like a motherfucker. I flip her back over and we go at missionary style. This works great for me, but she starts grimacing in pain. The lacquer on the table is giving her friction burns on her back. So THAT'S where that squeaking noise was coming from.

So we stand up, ON THE CONFERENCE TABLE, and I bend her over and fuck her from behind as she holds onto the PowerPoint projector for balance.

FINALLY, this position works for both of us. It starts getting intense. She doesn't want me to whisper sweet nothings in her ear—no, she's all about me calling her a "filthy whore" and "dirty lawyer slut" and all that type of shit people who repress themselves are into. Whatever.

I'm calling her a tort slut and getting close to cumming, so I start humping really hard. I move to get better leverage and set a wider, sturdier base. I put my right foot to the outside of hers and I'm maneuvering to do the same thing with my left foot when it hits a slick spot of sweat left over from when she was on her back. Everything happened so fast.

My left foot slipped, my right knee buckled, I heard an audible 'pop' and fell off the table in pain, landing on my face. Thankfully their expensive carpet was well padded, but I knew immediately:

I tore my ACL.

I could feel the instability in the joint. And it fucking hurt.

FUUUUUUCK!!

Vixen "Are you OK?"
Tucker [wincing in pain] "Not really."
Vixen "Oh." There was a long pause, and I felt it coming before she even said it, "Are you going to be able to finish? I was so close."

If I hadn't been in so much pain, I think I might have grabbed the stapler and beat her unconscious with it.

I could just fucking gag on the poetic justice of it all:

At 24, I had an opportunity to fuck a senior partner at a prominent Silicon Valley law firm on her conference table. For some inexplicable reason, I turned it down. I wrote an email to my friends about it, got fired from that job as a result, and the email ended up launching me onto the path that led me to writing, and now ten years later at 34, here I am on this senior partner's conference table; this time not as an employee but as a high-profile client. And this time, I took the opportunity fuck her, only to tear my ACL in the process.

You think maybe fate is telling me something?

I limped back to LA and went to see my orthopedist. I already had an orthopedist because two months earlier I'd hurt my knee at the gym. At the time he did an exam and an MRI and gave me these instructions:

Orthopedist "You still have an ACL there, so worst case it's a partial tear, but it's tough to tell from this MRI if you tore it or just strained it. We'll look at it again in a few months and see how it's doing in terms of swelling and joint stability, but things are looking good now."
Tucker "OK, cool."
Ortho "But this is very important—do NOT do ANYTHING strenuous with your legs during that time. No running, no jumping, no kicking, no weight lifting, nothing at all like that. No even light jogging. Upper body stuff is fine, but if you do have a partial tear, you can make it much worse by putting any sort of strain in your knee. Once we know the nature of the injury, then we can structure a rehab protocol."

I get an appointment with him a few days after I got back to LA, and my knee was massively swollen. The MRI showed a complete tear of the ACL, a partial MCL tear, and several microfractures. He was PISSED:

Ortho "Tucker, what did I tell you? So you just ignored me and went and worked out anyway?"
Tucker "No man, I wasn't working out at all."
Ortho "You don't tear an ACL like this walking down the street, Tucker."
Tucker "I know . . . I did it having sex."
Ortho "What?"
Tucker "Look, I'm not excited about my ACL either, but the way I did it is actually kinda funny: I was fucking this lawyer on a conference table and I slipped on some sweat. My knee buckled and I fell off the table. That's how it happened."

You ever do something as a kid that was so outside the realm of normal that your parents just stared at you, completely lost as to how to even react? Well, he gave me that look. The nurse giggling was the only thing that pulled him back into reality:

Ortho "Well, I can't treat you. You are a knee abuser. I am referring you to Dr. Marc Friedman, he is the best orthopedist in Southern California, maybe he can talk to you about what you . . . do."

Are you kidding? I had a doctor *fire me as a patient* because of this incident? What am I supposed to do with that? I guess just add it to the resume:

Tucker Max, *Knee Abuser.*

Sexting with Tucker Max: A/S/Location, Location, Location

Some of the girls who sexted me were into pretending we were in weird, exotic locations, except they always left it to ME to pick the place. Like because I'd written a book about fucking lots of women, all of the sudden I was some kind of connoisseur of imaginary exhibitionism. I didn't understand this at first—not only do you want to have fake sex, but you want to do it in a fake place NOT of your choosing??—and I eventually learned to stop trying. Fools act foolish; that's what they do. You can't actually try to understand them; you just have to go with it.

So I did, and they turned out to be some of the funnier exchanges.

Location, Location, Location #1: Pussy Pussy

smh
YOUR FACE HERE
it doesn't turn you on?
no!!
YOUR FACE HERE
fine, then lets at least make the cat watch
the cat??
YOUR FACE HERE
would you rather we include the cat in our fucking?
what?? no
YOUR FACE HERE
yea me neither
cats are a pain the ass to fuck
you have sex with cats?
YOUR FACE HERE
mostly dead ones
the live ones fight too much
omg—u r kidding right
YOUR FACE HERE

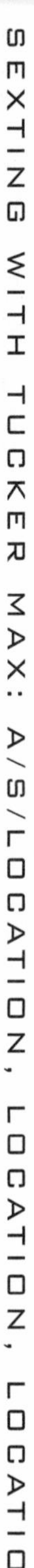

the problem with the dead one is that you gotta wrap it in a plastic bag when u fuck it

that way when it explodes, it doesn't get all over the furniture and smell up the place

the hell?

you ever tried to clean up a dead sex cat? its a doozy

i dont think i want to sext with u anymore

Location, Location, Location #2: Playoff Ready

ive been thinking about sexting with you all day

where are we gunna sext?

on our phone

be serious

let's pretend to be in a library

well have to be quiet

lol thats hot

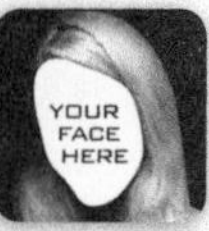

i want you in the stacks like in college

this is a public library

its mostly just crappy dvds and sleeping bums

ugh ok

i want you on some books

ok i have to poop first

you find the sexiest book for us to fuck on

lol how about your book

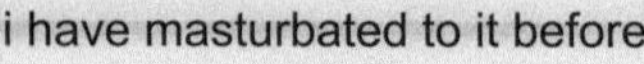

i have masturbated to it before

Im in the bathroom stall

ow. the poop is hurting

now its feeling good

haha ok

there's some kid outside the stall yelling about needing to dookie

HEY SHUT UP KID!! IM SHITTING IN HERE!!

YOUR FACE HERE

lol dont be mean!!

my shit smells

I can hear the kid dry heaving from the smell

YOUR FACE HERE

gross

I hogged the stall for so long, the kid shit his pants and ran crying to his mother

I WIN!!

r u done pooping? I want anal in the library

YOUR FACE HERE

lol

I just took a shit so big that I'm having postpartum depression

YOUR FACE HERE

r u into s&m & stuff? lets do that

not really
im more into ass to mouth
i like that too
YOUR FACE HERE
when I see ass go to mouth in porn, Im totally disgusted
then I cum immediately
i wanna lick your ass
YOUR FACE HERE
i pull you in the bathroom and push your mouth into my ass
i flip my tongue at your asshole
YOUR FACE HERE
YOU HAVE POOP IN YOUR MOUTH!!!
POOP MOUTH!!! DOOKIE TEETH!!
ewwww
YOUR FACE HERE
ahahahah even the bums are laughing at your teeth!
RUDE
YOUR FACE HERE

Location, Location, Location #3: 8 Mile

where r we fucking?
idk
let's sneak into a trailer park and fuck in some bumpkins double wide
ahaha rotflmao!!!
ok lets do it
YOUR FACE HERE
so we're in the trailer park. its shitty lots of broken down cars
trash everywhere
lol is there such thing as a nice trailer park?
let's go into this trailer, the concrete blocks that its on are not rotted
it should support our fucking
lol ur crazy

I grab you by the hair and kiss you

i kiss you back

i rub ur cock thru ur pants its so hard and big

these curtains are really crappy. who designed this place? They should be ashamed of themselves

i pull ur hard cock out and stare at it

i cant stand these floral patterns anymore, so i push you to the bedroom

i lay on the bed and cant wait to get my pants off

UGH! It's the same patterns in here? When did they buy this stuff, 1970?

just cum fuck me!

I grab my cock and dive right into your pussy!

hey—why are children running around in here?

YOUR FACE HERE
?? idk
they got dirty faces and no shoes
they keep yelling about lunch
YOUR FACE HERE
what r u talking about?
These aren't your kids?
YOUR FACE HERE
what kids!! were fucking on the bed
I know, but these damn kids are distracting me!
they keep yelling about wanting push pops and cans of frosting for lunch
YOUR FACE HERE
r we gonna sext or not?
they think you're their mom
are you?
YOUR FACE HERE
no!
since im humping their mom, i think its only fair they get some candy for lunch

give them money or whatevs

this is stupid lets sext

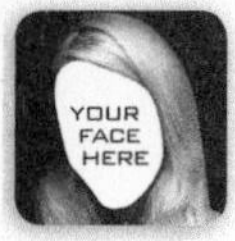

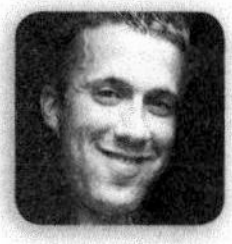

dont you realize the children are our future?

dont you care about your kids?

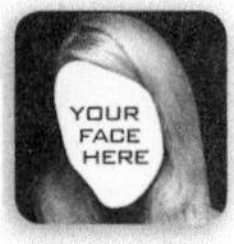

THEY ARE NOT MY KIDS!!

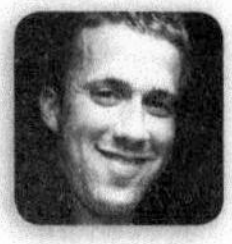

seriously though—who eats frosting straight out of the can?

let's grab one of these kids and give it a good shaking

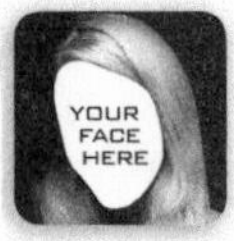

how is this sexy to you?

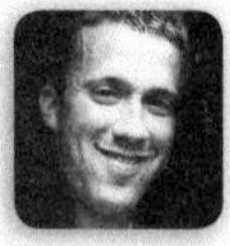

shaking children is pretty much the tops

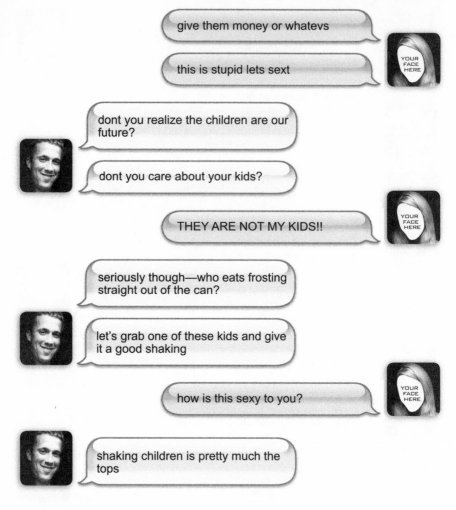

LOCATION, LOCATION, LOCATION #4: THE CLAMBURGLER

Im at my place
YOUR FACE HERE
No dummy, let's sext in public
ok im into public thats hot
We're in McDonalds
no lets be somewhere exciting and exotic
OK, we're at the Rock & Roll McDonalds in Chicago
lol thats not exotic
There's only one of them in the world
lol but why mcdonalds?
I'M HUNGRY AND I WANT TO FUCK IN MCDONALDS!
ok thats weird
lol

I grab your hand and we walk inside. Hey look, there are new items on the dollar menu!

who cares were here to fuck

Look at the a retard mopping. Don't you think it's nice that McDonalds hires the mentally handicapped?

lol

i pull you into the first booth and slide my hand down your pants you are so hard

Don't you think people will see us here?

WHATEVER we find a booth that is secluded

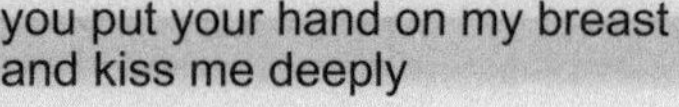

you put your hand on my breast and kiss me deeply

I kiss you back and grab your tits hard

Wait, but should we eat first? I'm kinda hungry

YOUR FACE HERE

no lets fuck im so horny

But if I don't eat Ill have low blood sugar, and I really want to fuck you the best I can

ok fine. but youd better fuck me so hard I can't walk tomorrow

You sound like Emily Dickinson

who?

Just some whore I banged who writes all this poetry about me. LAME

What do you want to eat?

lol

maybe get something we can use with sex, like chocolate syrup

I don't like mixing semen and food

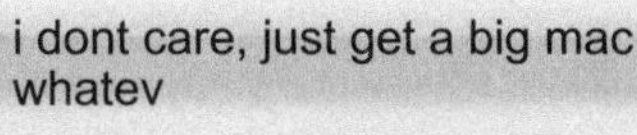

i dont care, just get a big mac whatev

I can't eat a big mac. I eat paleo, no grains

I start to order, but I get distracted. There is a ginger working the register

ginger? like a redhead?

Yes. And he has cornrows. This makes me VERY uncomfortable

lol thats weird

A fat woman comes in. She's so big she has to ride one of those motorized scooters

I say in a deep, mysterious voice, "We've been expecting you."

omg lol that would be halarious

I decide to ask her something Ive always wondered about

-"How do you wipe? I mean, you are clearly too fat to reach your own asshole. Do you tie a rag on a stick?"

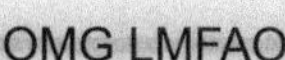

OMG LMFAO

She starts crying and slowly rolls her scooter out

as the handicapped doors open, she lets out a sloppy wet fart

it sounds like someone burping with a mouth full of pudding

lol ur so funny lol

Now Im really turned on

I grab you and pull you into our secret hidden McDonalds booth

I pull your penis out of your pants its so hard i cant resist and start sucking it right away

thats right, suck it good, suck it like its a mcflurry bitch

I massage ur balls and groan as I deep throat you

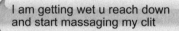

I am getting wet u reach down and start massaging my clit

Your pussy is so wet, it sounds like theres water splashing everywhere

im so wet ur fingers are all in my pussy

It sounds like a waterfall

im so hot ur playing with my clit and pussy and about to make me cum

That sound can't be your pussy juice. I look around.

i want ur cock in me so bad

HEY! The retard janitor is staring at us!

just ignore him, this is so hot

I DONT TAKE NO LIP FROM NO RETARD!

I pull out of you and confront him. I'm a good fighter

wtf?

He tard bellows and attacks me

HELP!

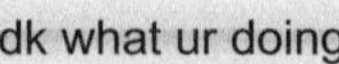

idk what ur doing

????

Too late. He's too strong. He whipped me with his retard strength

lol?

I don't think I can finish now, he really hurt me.

this is the weirdest sexting ever lol

Now he's asking me for candy

Do you have any Jolly Ranchers in your purse?

The Law School Weddings and Bachelor Parties

For years I've known that I'd eventually write a story that detailed all the ridiculous bachelor parties and weddings of my law school friends. I saved this story for as long as I could, because even though basically all my friends have been married or engaged for a while now, I wanted to end it with a bachelor party and wedding story of my own.

Yeah, right.

This is my third book and I'm *still* the only one of my law school friends without a wife. Everyone else even has kids (except Credit). It's time to stop waiting for pigs to fly across the frozen tundra of hell and just drop the story.

El Bingeroso's Bachelor Party, Part 1
Charlotte, NC

Occurred, November 2000

The first bachelor party was for El Bingeroso, before we even graduated from law school. He was having an "official" bachelor party in Kansas

City the following spring, but we didn't really know any of the people who were going to organize that party, so we planned our own surprise bachelor party for just us law school friends. Mainly because we wanted to make sure it was awesome, but also when you're 25, you take every excuse you can to throw a party.

We decided on an overnight trip to Charlotte. GoldenBoy set the whole thing up, rented a van, reserved the hotel rooms, set up the strip club, etc. He also had the brilliant idea that we should all wear the same outfit, like the goofy sluts do for lame bachelorette parties.

His choice of outfit: Light blue button down shirts and khaki pants.

I'm not kidding at all. I have no idea why he wanted to do this. I guess because he was engaged and wasn't going to get laid anyway, he thought we all needed to spend the weekend inside of a Dockers commercial. Nine dudes, all dressed up like poor Catholics on Sunday, assemble at his place and get in the van.

GoldenBoy "OK, because I know things can get out of control with some of you, I spent the extra money for complete coverage."
Tucker "You bought 'walk away' insurance? You're sure?"
GoldenBoy "Oh yes. I went over this extensively with the agent. We're covered for anything, even acts of God."

You don't have to tell me twice!

I stepped back, took an NFL kicker stance, then drove my foot into that van like I was Adam Vinateri. There was a deafening smash as the body panel crumpled into a HUGE dent. I don't know if you've ever kicked the shit out of a van, but if not, I recommend it. Very fun.

Much to my surprise, GoldenBoy freaked out.

GoldenBoy "WHAT THE FUCK ARE YOU DOING?!?"
Tucker "What? You said you had walk away insurance, right?"

GoldenBoy couldn't even respond. He just stood there stuttering, staring at me in enraged disbelief.

Tucker "This isn't even an act of God. It's covered."
Hate "I *told you* not to tell Tucker about the insurance."
Tucker "I don't understand why you're mad, GoldenBoy. Insurance means everything is free!"

There was one more element to this plan: we had to kidnap El Bingeroso. Let me explain:

El Bingeroso's fiancée was very "strict" with him. The reason he's usually the wildest of the group when he goes out is that she requires him to be so docile the other 99.9% of his life (I would never call her controlling or domineering. NEVER). There was no way in hell she was going to let him come with us if she knew we were planning a bachelor party out of town.

First off, he already had an "official" bachelor party planned for the spring (one where *her father and uncle* would be in attendance). Second, she did not get along at all with GoldenBoy (too long to explain why, but it boiled down to petty bullshit). And third, the only reason El Bingeroso got to go on the Austin Road Trip—which we'd just gotten back from a few weeks earlier—was that he pitched it as a "law school bachelor" party to her. He got arrested there, she freaked out, and there were no more weekend trips for El Bingeroso.

And it's not like we could tell El Bingeroso ahead of time that we were going to Charlotte and trust him to make up a good excuse. He was afraid of the woman he was planning to spend the rest of his life with (I don't blame him; despite my fearlessness with any sort of authority, I made it a point to never cross Kristy). The minute she began the fiancée forensics, he would fold and sing like a canary. GoldenBoy decided to wait until the day before to tell him anything, and even then all he said was that we were all going out that night, and to wear a light blue button down with khaki pants.

When we pulled up to his place, all he saw was nine identically-dressed dudes in a white cargo van. He was too confused to fight until we had already dragged him into the van and were driving away. It was like a flashbang grenade of debauchery and bad decisions. Only then did we explain:

El Bingeroso "We're spending the night in Charlotte? Are you kidding?"
Hate "Look around. We're all dressed the same! Do you think this is a joke, asshole?"
El Bingeroso "Kristy is going to be PISSED."
GoldenBoy "We aren't turning around."
El Bingeroso "Fuuuuck . . . gimme a beer. I need to get real drunk before I tell her I won't be home until tomorrow."

GoldenBoy was in charge of making the Charlotte plans. You can tell he's had a girlfriend for a LONG time, because his plan was to have us start at a bar, then go to a strip club, THEN to a night club. Who the fuck puts the strip club anywhere but the END OF THE NIGHT? How does that make any fucking sense?

We start at some random Irish bar. After pounding beers for the entire drive from Durham to Charlotte, plus a few shots in the bar, El Bingeroso finally has the courage to call Kristy. He is outside for at least ten minutes. He comes back in looking like he'd just put down the family dog. Personally.

GoldenBoy "Everything OK man?"
El Bingeroso "No."
Hate "You still getting married?"
El Bingeroso "Probably."
Tucker "I know the solution to this problem!"
El Bingeroso "Line'em up. I need something to drown her disappointment in me."

We did so many Irish Car Bombs, the bartender ran my card, signed me out, and then made us start another tab with a different card. My bill was so high he was afraid the card would get declined and I'd leave without paying. Weird—I'd never met the guy, yet it's like he'd known me my whole life.

It was only like 6pm, so it was still happy hour, and pretty much everyone else in this bar was dressed in business clothes having a post-work drink to relax. We were not. We were in attack mode, looking for targets. And unfortunately for them, a group of young fat secretaries came into the bar and made the calamitous mistake of choosing to stand near us. They chatted away, stuffing their faces with the free happy hour food, oblivious to the fact that the world as they knew it was about to crumble around their cankles, like so many crumbs from the free appetizers they were chowing on.

Hate is normally pretty tolerant of most people—well, he normally holds his anger about people inside himself—but when he gets drunk and ornery, if you prod him the right way, he'll let it out:

Hate "Fat girls should not be friends with other fat girls because all they do is tell each other how cute they look in clothes that are clearly too small for them. This is just offensive to those of us who know what a gym is."
SlingBlade "You have a unique and interesting perspective. I would like to subscribe to your newsletter."
Tucker "Hate, you should go tell it to them. I bet they think short guys are lame."

I was joking, but Hate was so drunk he took me seriously and immediately walked over and started talking to them. This was the first indication that he wasn't just drunk, but FULLY in the tank. He NEVER approaches girls. The second indication came moments later when he stormed right into the middle of the group:

Hate "HEY LADIES! HOW ABOUT YOU JUST STOP EATING FOR A WHILE? HAVE YOU THOUGHT OF THAT?"

Even from a distance, I could tell that the fatties were confused by this short angry person yelling at them. You know how cows get all flustered when they're getting herded by border collies? It was just like that. I quickly scurried over to get in on the fun.

Tucker "My friend is only trying to be helpful. He doesn't like to see people wasting their gym memberships."

Of course, this started a whole heated conversation filled with ridiculous fatty logic and the flimsiest of rationalizations. I can't remember what they said; it was nothing spectacular. They weren't even very good at lying to themselves about why they were fat. One thing I do remember was one of the girls trying to accuse Hate and I of drinking too much. The gall of her!

Fatty1 "You don't think you drink too much?"
Tucker "What does that even mean, 'too much'?"
Fatty1 "How many times have you woken up and had no idea how you got home?"
Tucker "That's not drinking too much, that's called your twenties!"
Fatty2 "I don't like it when guys drink too much."
Tucker "I find that when I drink I become incredibly charming. I do things like yell obscenities at random people, vomit everywhere and break things that don't belong to me. When I get drunk outside, in addition to being abusive and destructive, my charm extends to urinating in inappropriate places, running around with my clothes off and passing out in public parks. That sounds like awesomeness to me."

They weren't convinced, so I thought I'd try to spice everything up by adding more alcohol:

Tucker "Hey bartender, we need shots! And bring extras for the these pregnant girls, they're drinking for two!"

We were ejected from the bar, even though I was the one who got a drink thrown at me. How does that make sense? If I'd known a joke that tame was going to get us kicked out, I'd have just roundhouse kicked one of the girls in her donut hole instead to get my money's worth. Hindsight is always 20/20.

Here we were, kicked out of a bar at 7:30pm on a Friday. GoldenBoy had rented one of those party buses for the night so we could all drink and not have to drive. Unfortunately, it wasn't scheduled to pick us up until 8pm. You'd think this half hour would be a good opportunity to slow down, maybe drink some Gatorade, and pace ourselves.

Yeah, you'd think. We walked to a 7–11, bought a 30-pack, and drank it on the street like a fucking homeless baseball team. You know the night is off to a banging start when you are street-drinking before the sun even goes down.

Ten obnoxious guys, all dressed like Catholics on Sunday, can easily get shitfaced and descend on a strip club without creating too much of a stir . . . at 1am. We got there at 8:30pm. We sit down at our table, and some girls come over and start talking to us. The stripper talking to SlingBlade was kind of a bitch to him, and then got up and left.

Tucker "Dude, how did you not just rip into that stripper?"

He kinda swayed in his seat for a second.

SlingBlade "I'm so drunk, I couldn't find the way to my ass with a flashlight and a map. I don't feel good. In fact, I'll be right back."

Ten minutes later, PWJ comes back from the bathroom.

PWJ "I just walked in the bathroom and heard SlingBlade yelling 'HUH, YEAH, you gotta want it!' What the fuck is wrong with him?"

A few minutes later, SlingBlade comes out holding his abdomen.

SlingBlade "Dude, taking antibiotics and then drinking is a bad idea. I just let loose a symphony of bowel movements, each in different pitches and melodies. It was like a poop xylophone."

The bachelor show for El Bingeroso was pretty conventional. They took him up onstage, poured alcohol down his throat, rubbed their tits in his face, tied him up, hit him with belts and just generally used him to vent their rage against men, before unceremoniously kicking him off the stage.

The other guys dispersed and were getting lap dances or whatever, and I was left to watch El Bingeroso. We were sitting on bar stools by one of the stages, and at this point he was so drunk he had basically reverted to a state of mild retardation. Whenever a stripper came near him, he would reach out to touch her, like a child fascinated by an aquarium of fish. The whole time he was swaying back and forth on his stool, trying to stay on but of course falling off, and then cheering every time I caught him.

El Bingeroso "Woooooooo—YAAAAY!!!!! Hahhahhahahhaha!"

Eventually the bouncer sees this dog and pony show, and tells me that my friend is too drunk and has to leave. Thinking quickly, I used a technique I've used many times to save my drunk friends from getting tossed out of bars:

Tucker "No man, he's not drunk, he's got M.S. You know—Multiple Sclerosis. Normally he's OK, but after a few beers, he can't really sit up well."
Bouncer "Oh shit dude, I didn't realize. Sorry about that. Just keep an eye on him okay? And no more grabbing dancers."
Tucker "Yeah, no problem. I'll do that."

Then I made the major mistake of the night. Because we were all basically shit-canned, and it was only 10:30pm, I figured I needed to get us sobered up for the club we were about to go to. This was 2000, back before ephedrine exploded the heart of a professional baseball player and got banned. I had some ephedrine with me because I would take it when I was really drunk but wanted to keep drinking—real smart, I know, but it's safer than coke at least—so I took a few. Hate and PWJ saw me and asked for one too.

If you've never taken ephedrine, the best way I can explain it is this: Imagine what it's like to drink a bunch of Red Bulls. Add a couple Adderall. Now strap your heart to a car battery and switch it on. That's basically ephedrine (well, several ephedrine. I don't think what we took was the "recommended dose"). Half an hour later, I was ready to run a marathon carrying El Bingeroso on my back like he was Yoda.

El Bingeroso wouldn't take an ephedrine, but the alcohol was catching up to him and so he wanted to eat. This strip club had food, but they were telling me the fucking kitchen was closed.

Tucker "Hate, come over here, I need some help."

His pupils were dilated, fists clenched at his sides, and his nostrils were flared. He looked like Diego Sanchez right before a UFC fight.

Hate "I don't think I could deal with it if someone crossed me right now."
Tucker "OK, we don't need to fight, we just have to find some food for El Bingeroso. See if we can order a pizza or something. I have to stay here and keep him upright."

Hate looked around the club, saw a guy with a plate in front of him that still had food on it. He purposefully strode over.

Hate "EXCUSE ME SIR! ARE YOU DONE WITH YOUR FOOD?"

The guy just kinda stared at him. I think he was wondering if this was the busboy, and if so, why he was yelling at him.

Hate "GIVE UP THE FISH! MY DRUNK FRIEND WOULD LIKE TO EAT IT."

If you're not sure how to get kicked out of a strip club, taking a half-eaten plate of food from another customer will get it done.

We pile back on the drunk shuttle and ask the driver to stop somewhere for food. I guess in Charlotte the phrase "stop somewhere for food" means to pull into a truck stop with a Subway in it. I'm not even kidding. The best part: the Subway was not open. I would've gotten behind the counter and made my own sandwich, but they'd put all the food away. None of this stopped Hate from standing at the counter screaming for sandwiches until some poor old janitor making minimum wage had to explain to him what the "CLOSED" sign meant.

We stuffed a bunch of truck stop hotdogs that looked like wilted horse dicks into El Bingeroso's mouth, and then went downtown to the club where we supposedly had reservations for a table or something. We get there, and of course none of us are on the list except GoldenBoy. He has some friends who are inside at our table, tells us he'll be right back, and goes into the club. Given this set of facts, which one of these would you think was the case:

1. GoldenBoy was going to get his friends to get the rest of us in, or,

2. GoldenBoy decided, in the middle of a bachelor party that he'd organized for one of his best friends, to ditch everyone on the street out and just drink in the club without us.

I think any rational person would assume #1 is the most likely scenario. PWJ didn't. He was convinced GoldenBoy had ditched us. He calls GoldenBoy approximately 35 times in the next four minutes.

Of course he doesn't answer, because he's busy and inside a loud club. Each unanswered call makes PWJ progressively angrier—and because he's drunk and high on ephedrine, he deals with his anger by spiking his phone as hard as he can into the sidewalk outside. It shatters into ten pieces. Hate—who is also drunk and high on ephedrine—sees that and accuses PWJ of being on steroids.

Hate "I knew it! You've been getting too big lately! Roid rage! You're on the juice!"
PWJ "What are you talking about? Fucking GoldenBoy screwed us!!"
Hate "Your lats are too fucking big, that's another sign of juicing!"
PWJ "I rowed crew in college you idiot!"
Hate "Juicer!"

As they scream at each other like feral tomcats, I get fed up and take the other six of us into the bar across the street.

Finally something goes right: There's a bachelorette party at this bar! The easiest way in with a group of girls anywhere is to have something in common with them, and there isn't much more in common than being out to celebrate your friend's last night of freedom. We immediately link up and go through all the introductions, and of course I pay zero attention to anyone's name except the girl who really strikes my fancy.

Tucker "You're the hot one, I'll remember your name."
HotOne "Oh will you?"

We do a few rounds of shots, the girls try to get the bachelor and bachelorette to make out (they won't) and everyone is getting along great. I could tell SlingBlade actually was kinda sick, because he was even being nice to the girls. At some point, HotOne gives me a naughty look and does a "come hither" with her finger. I oblige, totally thinking she's going to tell me to meet her in the bathroom to fuck. She leans in, pulls my ear to her mouth, gives me just the slightest hot breath to tickle me, and seductively whispers:

HotOne "What's my name?"

FUUUUCK!!!! FUCK! FUCK! FUCK!

You know what it's like to "know" something, and then the second you are called out on it, you go completely blank? Yeah, that was me. I racked my brains. I'd said her name to myself earlier so I would remember it; unfortunately that was several drinks earlier. You could've offered me 2004 Google stock and I wouldn't have remembered. This was my chance to lock her pussy up, and I was fucking blowing it like Michael J. Fox playing Operation.

So I played the only card I had: misdirection.

Tucker "Yeah right . . . what's MY name?"

Saved! Her expression gave it away.

Tucker "You don't know it!"
HotOne "Well you don't know mine!"
Tucker "I know your name, but until you know my name, I'm not gonna say it. There are principles involved here."
HotOne "You don't know my name!"
Tucker "I don't just give it away for free. You gotta earn it."

For the next few hours, we fucked with each other:

HotOne "Do you even remember what I just said?"
Tucker "It doesn't matter what you said. If it was important, a man would've said it."

HotOne "Just shut up. Every time you talk, I like you less."
Tucker "I'm sorry, did you say something? I just hear a faint buzzing noise coming from your area. Like a gnat that won't leave."

HotOne "If you talked less, it'd be better. Then I could imagine you have the kind of personality I like."
Tucker "At least I'm good looking. I'm going to have to fuck you from behind and push your face in the pillow, so I can pretend you're a girl I'm attracted to."

HotOne "Your friends say you're a dog. Does that mean if I throw a stick, you'll leave?"

Tucker "It's a good thing for you I blacked out an hour ago and won't remember any of the stupid jokes coming out of your mouth."
HotOne "I'll tell you one thing that won't be coming out of my mouth: Your penis."
Tucker "Oh I know. You're too much of a princess to suck a good dick."
HotOne "I am so good at that!"

If you know ANYTHING about women, you know HotOne and I were destined to fuck. You don't spend that much time pushing buttons, flirting with limits and testing boundaries without knowing that you're about to blow a penis-sized hole through all of them.

The sex was really intense. You know when you have an angry, chemical attraction to someone and you want to pound the shit out of them? That's what we had. We let everything go and fucked like the plane was going down.

At one point, I had her legs over my shoulders jack-hammering her like I was setting a bridge pylon. She had her hands dug into my ass cheeks, pulling me towards her. I came. HARD. So hard that I grunted my orgasm out and shot a snot booger onto her cheek. She didn't notice, as she was just as enraptured as me. I quickly wiped it off her face . . . and spread it on her sheets, which she also didn't notice. Then we passed out.

Flawless victory!

The next morning we fucked again and she got in the shower. This was my chance to win the "what's my name" battle. I looked everywhere for something with her name on it: her purse for a driver's license, her coffee table for mail or magazines. I couldn't find anything. Then it hit me:

Caller ID!

This was 2000, when people still had landlines, so I called a friend's home phone from her home phone:

Tucker "Dude, what name is on the caller ID?"

She came up behind me and put her arms around me, right as he read off the caller ID:

HotOne "You figure my name out yet?"
Tucker "Is it 'Blocked Caller'?"

GoldenBoy's Bachelor Party
Las Vegas, NV

Occurred, March 2001

GoldenBoy only got one bachelor party, so the party combined his frat brothers from UVa with his law school friends from Duke. The best man (his older, married brother) organized it, and decided that we should do GoldenBoy's bachelor party in Las Vegas. OK, I guess. Then he decided we should all stay at the Hard Rock. Fuck.

The Hard Rock had JUST been featured in *Playboy;* every idiot douche and corn-fed Big 12 meathead on earth was now going there. And of course, since we were going on our spring break, which fell in the middle of March, that meant it fell perfectly on the beginning of March Madness, when about 2 million men—and zero women—descend on Vegas.

In summary: The bachelor party will be 25 guys, in a hotel full of guys, in a city full of guys. This is another example of why you *don't let married guys organize bachelor parties.*

I showed up at the Hard Rock early in the day, and honestly wondered if I wasn't in a gay club. It was fucking AWFUL. The ratio was at least 80/20, guys to girls. It was worse than a strip club on Saturday night with a Baptist convention in town. And the pool!! Greased-up guidos everywhere, and the only girls around were working—and I'm not just talking about the cocktail waitresses. Super.

In the face of the obvious disaster that this weekend would be, I did the only thing that made sense: I started drinking heavily and gambling recklessly.

Three hours later, I'm up $400 and have put away about ten vodka Red Bulls, and I think I'm fucking king of the casino. I see four guys covered in UVa gear walking through the casino, clearly some of GoldenBoy's frat brothers from college, so I go up and introduce myself. They have no fucking idea what I'm talking about.

Tucker "So you aren't friends with GoldenBoy?"
Guy "I have never heard that name before."
Tucker "What do you mean you aren't friends with GoldenBoy? Why the fuck would you be wearing so much goddamn UVa stuff at the Hard Rock if you aren't here for his bachelor party?"

I was genuinely mad at them for not knowing him. I was that drunk.

Everyone eventually came in, and both groups linked up for a late dinner. We hadn't really discussed plans for once we got to Vegas, so other than the actual bachelor party itself on Saturday night, there was no itinerary. It became clear that the majority of GoldenBoy's friends were in Vegas to do two things: snort a shitload of coke, and cheat on their girlfriends/wives by fucking a bunch of prostitutes.

This was the weekend I came to explicitly understand something that I'd always felt, but never internalized: Not all guys who "party" are the same. There are basically two types of cool party guys:

1. "Beer and girls": Beer and girls guys are about fun. To them, partying is about spending time with their friends, meeting new people, getting drunk, acting stupid and laughing at the ridiculous shit they do.

Partying is about fun and the enjoyment of life, and there's always a happiness and joy to what they do—I mean, if you aren't enjoying your life, what's the fucking point, right? These are the types of guys who do something productive with their lives, who build stuff or make stuff or create things. Examples of "beer and girls" guys are me, Charles Barkley, Dean Martin, Ferris Bueller, Van Wilder, Adam Carolla, etc.

2. "Coke and hookers": Coke and hookers guys aren't like that. They seem to be similar because they party as well, but in a very different way. There is no joy in their partying. It's about excess, self-destruction and escape. Their partying is about fleeing from reality, drowning their self-loathing in serious substance abuse, and about hurting other people to express their inner rage. They're the type of guys who go work for an investment bank or a corporate law firm and revel in the fact that they screw people for a living. But the reality is that they hate themselves and everything about their lives. The iconic coke and hookers guy is, of course, Charlie Sheen. Other examples would be Joe Francis, every trust fund brat in Hollywood, and pretty much any male character in a Bret Easton Ellis book.

These are obviously arbitrary categories, and just like any artificial category, it's not always a bright line distinction—someone can do coke every now and then, but still be a "beer and girls" type. And someone can hate himself and be a piece of shit to everyone, and still never pay for sex. It's less about the precise details of *how* you party, and more about *why* you party: are you engaging your life, or escaping from it? "Beer and girls" guys engage their lives because they enjoy them. "Coke and hookers" guys escape from their lives because they hate them. That's the essential difference.

If you go out a lot, you understand exactly what I'm talking about. But I think a lot of people who don't go out and have fun miss this basic, fundamental distinction; they just lump everyone together. Even calling someone a "frat" guy doesn't really mean anything—I know tons of frat guys on both sides of the aisle, and the scene at our table that night was a great example.

The law school guys all wanted to go out, get drunk, talk to girls and have fun—what we always do. The UVa guys all wanted to score blow and fuck as many hookers as they could find—it was creepy. Like watching "To Catch A Predator" (except they wanted fucked out whores, not little girls).

We compromised by going our separate ways that night. Not surprisingly, BrownHole—the one "coke and hookers" guy who was somehow in our Duke Law group—went off with the guys who do things that people who hate their lives do, while GoldenBoy and his one other UVa frat brother went to a bar with us.

I'm not sure how, but someone knew of a cool, laid back bar in Vegas. It was in some random casino that was a little off the strip, but we had a fucking blast talking to all kinds of random girls. Some of the highlights:

- This girl I met was nice but naive, and this was just too much for me:

Girl "I believe there is one person for everyone, and we are all just searching for that person."
Tucker "Are you fucking kidding me? There are 6 billion people on earth. Even if you leave out all the Chinese, Indians, and Africans, you're still looking at like 3 billion people. Subtract the women, and that's 1.5 billion men to search through. Even if I am generous and take out all the old people and the kids and the retards and the people who don't speak English, you are still looking at, like, 250 million men. And you are looking for ONE guy out of that whole pool? YOU'RE TOTALLY FUCKED. You're never finding him. I hope you like cats."

- I ended up unintentionally cock-blocking PWJ with this one:

PWJ "So you are into astrology? Interesting. Can you guess my sign?"
CuteGirl "YEAH! Let me see, you are smart, confident but still sweet and compassionate . . . Aquarius?"
PWJ "Right! Wow, very good." I don't know for sure, but I'm pretty sure PWJ is a different sign.

CuteGirl "I know, I have a gift." [turns to me] "I bet I can figure out your sign!"
Tucker "Oh please do."
PWJ "No, I don't think that's such—"
Tucker "So you think you can tell my birth month based on a few general characteristics? As if everyone born in the same month has the same personality?"
CuteGirl "Yeah! Let's see . . . you are aggressive, funny, intellectual . . . Sagittarius?"
Tucker "Nope."
CuteGirl "Leo."
Tucker "Nope."
CuteGirl "Taurus."
Tucker "Nope."
CuteGirl "Virgo?"
Tucker "There are only 12 of them, if you guess enough, you'll eventually get it right."
CuteGirl "Well, it's not an exact science."
Tucker "I can read minds too!"
CuteGirl "Right. OK, what am I thinking right now?"
Tucker "Hmmm . . . you're thinking about tongue fucking my shitpipe."

• Typical SlingBlade:

Girl "So, do you have a girlfriend?"
SlingBlade "Well, sort of, but we're not technically dating."
Girl "So you aren't in love with her?"
SlingBlade "No. They say if you love someone, set them free, so I did. But that girl never came back, so I don't love the girls tied up in my basement anymore, I just appreciate them."

• An enlightening exchange for PWJ:

Tucker "You know you want to hook up with me; just admit it."
Girl "I don't want to just have a one night stand with some random guy I met an hour ago."

Tucker "I don't consider them one night stands. They're auditions for love."
Girl "If you want to have sex with me, we have to already be in love."
Tucker "No, that's not how it works. You provide vaginal access, and in return, I model the awful treatment that your abusive childhood has caused you to interpret as love. That's how it works with fucked up girls."
Girl "I'm not fucked up!"
PWJ "THAT'S how you do it! Now it all makes total sense!"
Tucker "You haven't figured out how that works yet?"
PWJ "Sorry, I wasn't raised in an emotionally abusive household. My parents loved me."

The night ended real late (because of gambling and drinking, not hooking up), so the next day was mainly spent watching basketball and recovering for that night, which was the official bachelor party night. After a relatively calm dinner, GoldenBoy's frat brothers took us to a club before the strip club.

I hate clubs. You know why all clubs are loud and dark? They make it loud because you can't sound stupid if no one can hear you. They make it dark so you can pretend you aren't ugly. The fact is, if your life has meaning, you don't spend time in a Las Vegas night club.

We finally leave and go to the strip club. I was not in a good mood ten seconds before we entered, but once we got inside, I have to tell you, that changed. I've been to a lot of strip clubs in my life, but going to a top 5 Vegas strip club on the Saturday of the beginning of March Madness is like nothing else on earth. I've never seen so many stunningly beautiful women in one place in my life. It was amazing.

And sadly . . . I got right back into a bad mood. Why? Because pretty much every single one of these stunning women were emotionally dead hustlers. This wasn't one of those strip clubs where the girls sit and talk and hang out. These girls were professionals in the truest sense. I'm not even talking about them having sex for money—which I am sure 90%+ of them did—I'm more talking about how they sized up and interacted with guys. For example, at an average strip club under normal circumstances we can always find more than a few strippers who think we're hilarious and want to sit and bullshit with us for a long time. That did not happen at this club. Everything was an explicit financial evaluation; there was no pitter-patter. This was within five minutes of entering the club:

Stripper "Hey, how are you?"
Tucker "You don't know it yet, but my penis is going to end up in your mouth."
Stripper "Honey, for enough money, that can happen."
Tucker "Uh . . . I was kinda making a joke . . ."

Hitting on hookers is as pointless as it gets and no fun at all. And they were ALL hookers. I'm not criticizing per se, but places like that are creepy and annoying to spend time in to me. After I realized this, I mainly just kept to my beer and myself. SlingBlade had some fun with it:

Stripper "What's your name?"
SlingBlade "Did you get a good discount on your fake tits? I would think brick-layers do them for cheap."

Stripper "I'd love to give you a good time."
SlingBlade "I'm genuinely curious: How much would it cost to shit on your chest?"

Stripper "How'd you like some company?"
SlingBlade "I think if you were reduced to your constituent elements, you'd be nothing more than jizz and glitter."

SlingBlade "You're the kind of creature I feared was living under my bed as a kid."
Stripper "You aren't funny. People don't think you're funny."
SlingBlade "Yes, but they don't mistake me for a whore either."

As you can imagine, girls who are hustling to make their $2k a night don't have time for bullshit like that. The Duke guys were unpopular. But the UVa guys were *very* popular, and we didn't see much of them over the course of the night. I'm sure you can figure out why. The very best anecdote:

One of the UVa guys went off to a private room with a stripper/hooker. He was gone for a long time. When he came back, she was still with him, but now they looked like they'd just fucked. He hadn't even wiped the sweat off his forehead. SlingBlade leans in to me:

SlingBlade "She looks like she has a lot of self-esteem."

As they came over and sat down, I knew it was coming, I could see him teeing it up . . . but man when it finally let loose, it was even worse than I thought it would be:

SlingBlade [turns to the stripper/hooker] "If I wanted to measure the amount of semen currently in your vagina, could I use a measuring cup, or would I need a gallon bucket?"
Stripper "WHAT?"
SlingBlade "I bet your vagina smells like a zoo."

We did not have a good trip. The UVa guys sure did though. The next day at breakfast summed up the whole trip:

UVa Guy "Fuck man, I think I forgot to wear a rubber when that stripper was blowing me last night."
Tucker "You wear rubbers for oral sex?"
UVa Guy "With these sorts of hookers, you have to. I got some shit once just from a blowjob. My wife was pissed, she almost left me because she got it too."
Tucker "YOU'RE MARRIED??"

The UVa guy looked at me like it was a stupid question, and scoffed at me to his friends.

UVa Guy "Yeah, of course."

I talk a lot about how people should follow their passion and live the life they want, not the one they think they are supposed to. A lot of what I say in that realm is abstract. This is not—this is exactly what I'm talking about. If you want to be single and bang a ton of girls, just fucking go do it, don't pretend to be something else, like married. I've always lived the life I wanted, I've been happy as a result, and I've never felt the need to do shit like this guy. You don't have to follow my advice . . . but if you don't, you've got a life of fucking hookers in strip clubs behind your wife's back to look forward to.

El Bingeroso's Bachelor Party, Part 2
Kansas City, MO

Occurred, June 2001

El Bingeroso's wedding was on a Sunday, so the "official" bachelor party was scheduled for the Friday night beforehand, in Kansas City, Missouri. Why Kansas City? Well, the wedding was about an hour away in some bumfuck town, and Kansas City was the closest big city. Plus, it was convenient for all of El Bingeroso's and Kristy's extended male family—who were planning to come.

Yeah, you read that right. Uncles, cousins, stepfathers—everyone was going to be there. It was like a hoedown. Now you understand why we wanted to have a real bachelor party earlier in the year.

The night started at some random bar in KC. We were going to meet there, then all get on the drunk bus they rented and go to the strip club. The law school crew and I get to the bar, and of course, it's completely dead except for us. Great. Who doesn't like hanging out at a bar with

20 dudes? Then all of the sudden, El Bingeroso's best friend "Mermaid" walks into the bar . . . with a male midget. This was not expected.

Mermaid "Dude, sorry I only brought a midget, but getting an animal out of the zoo is a pain in the ass."

Well played, my friend.

You'd expect the midget thing would be awesome, right? It wasn't. First off, it was a male midget. Second, he was super lame. He didn't do a little jig or fight any Orcs or anything that you see them do in the movies. We didn't even get to toss him. He just stood around drinking his beer like a normal boring person.

Tucker "I'm not sure what I was expecting from the midget, but . . . this isn't it."
Dirty "Get a picture of the midget punching you in the nuts. Or fisting you. That would be cool."
Hate "Well, I like him. I'm not the shortest guy in the group for once."

This bar was ridiculously boring, and when I get bored, I get destructive. I was planning on just breaking random shit *Road House* style, but El Bingeroso's older brother Buddy had a better idea. He went out to the drunk bus we'd rented, grabbed a porn DVD (it may have been a VHS actually, this was 2001 in the Midwest), went into the AV closet of the bar, and put porn on all the TVs. It was pretty awesome . . . except for the fact that now we were 20 dudes and a midget, without girls . . . watching porn in a bar.

The bar manager got pissed. It was time to go anyway, so we started to get on the drunk bus and head to the strip club. The midget wanted to settle up with Mermaid, which made no sense to me.

Tucker "He's not coming to the strip club with us? You only rented the midget for 90 minutes??"
Mermaid "He was $200 an hour, what am I supposed to do? For that much, I should at least get a handjob."

Midget "I do that, but it's extra."

Midget for the win!! That joke alone was almost worth the money.

The strip club in KC was easily among the worst I've ever seen or heard about. When I walked in, the first stripper I see has stretch marks on her stomach. The second was missing teeth. The third looked like one of the bouncers, except in a bikini. I mean . . . come on.

Dirty "If you can't remember their names, just look at the numbers on the backs of their jerseys. And remember, Offensive Line's numbers are in the 60s and 70s, Defensive Line's are in the 90s."

El Bingeroso's stepfather—who apparently is on his one night out of the year—is not deterred by this catastrophe. In fact, he looks like he's in heaven. He quickly surveys the field, and goes right up to a stripper.

StepCreeper "Alright young lady, those look like some big melons. These hands are registered scales, put'em in here and let me weigh'em, see if they break my personal record."

Without a second thought, she dropped those post-partum milk teats right into his waiting hands. It was that kind of strip club, and it was going to be that kind of bachelor party. Ironically enough, the people we thought would make this a shitty night were the ones going buck wild with the strippers.

The law school group huddled by the bar for safety, and it took a few more beers than normal to venture into the clown car that was the main stage at this club. The only good that came out of it was this conversation I got into with a stripper about dating. She was not very attractive, so of course she was totally into me.

Stripper "You don't have a girlfriend?"
Tucker "Definitely not."
Stripper "So what do you like in a girl? What turns you on?"

Tucker "To me, the sexiest possible thing about a female is if she's totally into me."
Stripper "Haha! What about like dates, what do you like to do?"
Tucker "The ideal first date includes cumming on the chick's back, having her immediately fall asleep, stealing $50 out of her purse, and then sneaking out the window."
Stripper "You're so funny!"
Credit "The funny thing is, he's not joking."
Stripper "I still don't know why you don't have a girlfriend. You seem like boyfriend material."
SlingBlade "HAHHAHHAHAHA—only a stripper could meet Tucker Max and think 'I want to date this man.'"

She insisted on figuring out why I didn't have a girlfriend. And SlingBlade insisted on, well, being himself.

Tucker "I would date a girl, it's just that women are like parking spots: All the good ones are taken, and once you see a great one that you think is available, it turns out to be handicapped."
Stripper "Haha! That's so funny and true!"
SlingBlade "No, women are like parking spots because they're all whores and liars."
Stripper "How does that make any sense?"
SlingBlade "Whatever. Logical consistency is for stupid sluts who dance on tables."
Stripper "I'm not a slut or a whore."
SlingBlade "You may be the whoringest whore who's ever whored."
Stripper [to me] "Um, your friend is kind of a piece of shit."
SlingBlade "Look at yourself. I bet your stepdad won't even fuck you anymore."
Stripper "I don't even have a stepdad!"
SlingBlade "Oh sorry . . . then was it your uncle or your neighbor who touched you when you were 8, hmmph?"
Stripper "No one touched me when I was 8!"
SlingBlade "Well, then what happened? Your mom emotionally broke you through her incessant nagging and withholding love?"

Stripper "My mom is dead, you asshole."
SlingBlade "I say we dig her up, and skull fuck her back to life. That'll teach her to tell you that you aren't good enough!!"

This started at least a half-hour war between the stripper and SlingBlade. I can't even recall the whole conversation, because I was too busy laughing and struggling to take down the machine gun fire of SlingBlade's one liners. These were my favorites:

SlingBlade "Tucker, no wonder she likes you. She has that empty feeling that only fellatio can fill."

SlingBlade "How much would it cost to get you to cry on stage?"

SlingBlade "If you just had one more daddy issue, you could have been a porn star. So close."

SlingBlade "Yes, I'm sure you're only stripping to put yourself through therapy."

SlingBlade "The only thing more obvious about you than your lack of self-esteem, is the fact that your vagina is a quiver for dicks."

SlingBlade "Do you still hear the lambs screaming, Clarice?"

In that period, I probably laughed more than any other time in my life. And even though the stripper was getting really pissed at SlingBlade, no matter how much abuse was heaped on her, she stuck around and kept taking more—just like in most of her relationships. Eventually, she said something particularly stupid, and SlingBlade put a button on the night:

He whispered, "Shhhhhhhhh" at her, then gently placed his finger on her lips and whispered, "You're welcome."

She finally stormed off.

Tucker "That was amazing and brutal at the same time."
SlingBlade "We should go back up to the ship, nuke her from orbit. It's the only way to be sure."

Mermaid comes back from one of the private rooms, and sniffs his fingers.

Mermaid "Oh yeah, I smell like romance."

Mermaid is definitely a coke and hookers guy. Thankfully, the night ended relatively soon after that.

We had one more night to kill before the wedding on Sunday, so we decided to just have a calm, easy night out drinking. And of course, that night ended up being the best one.

We went to a bar that Dirty knew pretty well. It couldn't have been more different from the one the previous night: cool place, lots of energy, and a ton of girls. I picked out our targets almost immediately. A group of loud, drunk girls who were wearing the type of lipstick shades you'd expect to see around the base of a penis.

Tucker "Those girls are naughty."
SlingBlade "They are also ugly."
Tucker "They are not ugly!
SlingBlade "Fine. But they *are* whores."
Tucker "What is wrong with you?"

PWJ, Dirty, and I immediately go over and talk to them.

Tucker "So ladies, I'm new to Kansas City. What should we do here?"
SlingBlade "Tucker is looking for girls with round faces and big foreheads. Do you know any?"

I admit, I laughed. They didn't think it was funny. Try something funnier then:

Tucker "Would you ladies like some beer? It has almost no GHB in it."

Nothing.

Tucker "If you knew how amazing I am, you'd be way more into my drunken advances."

No laughs. These ladies clearly had an underdeveloped sense of humor. Nothing was really working, but big faces aside, these girls had huge tits and were obviously looking to get fucked, so I had to try one last ditch effort with the one I was talking to.

Tucker "So, I just have one more question . . . you wanna get out of here?"
Girl "NO!"

They were so disgusted, they moved to a different part of the bar.

Tucker "Why don't they want to have sex with us?"
PWJ "Tucker, we didn't even pretend we had any interest in them as human beings. Maybe that's why."
Tucker "Does that kind of stuff matter?"
PWJ "Well, yes Tucker, that 'stuff' matters."
Tucker "I don't like that stuff!"

We found another group of girls to talk to. Dirty got us in with this:

Dirty "You ladies look like you read a lot of horse novels."

It was a pretty basic conversation, and one of the girls seemed to think SlingBlade was hot.

Girl "Do you want to dance?"
SlingBlade "No."

She actually laughed at that and they started talking, so I turned back and focused on the girl I was talking to. A few minutes later, I overhear this exchange:

Girl "You aren't very fun to talk to. I'm going back to my friends."
SlingBlade "Thanks for playing, we have some lovely parting gifts for you, like this wonderful feeling of rejection."

Poor SlingBlade.

Tucker "What did you say to her?"
SlingBlade "I don't remember . . . something that included a flurry of profanity."
Tucker "Why do you even talk to girls if you're just going to do this shit?"
SlingBlade "For me, the thrill in meeting new people comes from the fact that I hate everyone I already know. That first thirty seconds before I realize they are just as stupid as everyone else, that's just pure bliss."

PWJ, Dirty, and I kinda got in with this group, and a different girl in the group started talking to SlingBlade. Everything seemed to be going fine, until I felt a tap on my shoulder. It was the girl who'd been talking to SlingBlade. She had a look of distress on her face.

Girl "Your friend called me a blasphemer! Why would he say that?"

I was still laughing when SlingBlade came over to find me. He saw the girl and got a look of disgust on his face.

SlingBlade "You're still here?"
Girl "Why are you so mean to people?"
SlingBlade "That's the only thing that gets me up in the morning. The opportunity to blow someone else's candle out, so that mine can shine that much brighter."
Girl "You like to be mean to people? Why would you do that? What made you so angry?"
SlingBlade "It started when I was 6, and realized the *The Neverending Story* did, in fact, end."
Tucker "No no, there is a real reason he's like this. And it's a woman's

fault. It's not your fault, but he takes it out on all women because he's a fucking dumbshit. Let me explain . . ."

I gathered the entire group of girls together, about five of them, and told them the whole story about him, basically, his high school girlfriend cheated on him and broke his heart and he never recovered (the same story in "Everyone Has 'That' Friend" in *IHTSBIH*).

Because I am an awesome storyteller, by the time I was done all the girls felt genuine sympathy for him, and were actually on his side. He fixed that shit real quick.

Girl1 "That's so sad. I'm sorry."
Girl2 "Did you ever try to get back with your girlfriend?"
SlingBlade "Yes, after she'd had more men in her than a submarine, I was eager to reconcile."
Girl2 "I was just asking."
Girl1 "So you never saw her again after that time in her dorm?"
SlingBlade "Oh no, I hung out with her a lot after that, but only because I hated her. That's the reason I hung out with her, actually—I wanted to get her drunk and insert a two-liter bottle of Coke in her vagina and then leave. I wanted her to wake up and realize what a worthless whore she is."

This conversation was going nowhere—i.e., they weren't going to fuck us—so we decided to head to another bar where a girl PWJ wanted to meet out was drinking with a bunch of her friends. Not really paying attention, I started to walk out of the bar with the glasses in my hand.

Bouncer "You can't take those drinks with you. That's against the rules."
Tucker "No, you don't understand: The rules don't apply to me."

He firmly places his hand on my chest.

Bouncer "You're not leaving with them."

He's a big dude. I think maybe I should obey him. Then I remember that I'm Tucker Max—these drinks are coming with me.

I look into his eyes. He's serious. The scars on his face seal my decision: I will avoid a physical solution. That's fine. I'm smarter than this motherfucker, so I should be able to outsmart him.

I look him in the eye for an extra second, and then pound both drinks as fast as I can. Then I enthusiastically football spike the glasses into the garbage can next to the bouncer, like an offensive lineman who's just scored the only touchdown of his life.

Tucker "I told you I was leaving with those drinks!"

The bouncer just stared at me with a mix of shock and confusion. In that extra second before his brain processed it all into a violent rage, I got the fuck out.

We tried to get into the next bar, but as we were going in, SlingBlade made a joke about the girl coming out. He pointed to her stomach and said:

SlingBlade "When's the baby due?"
Bouncer "You can't talk to girls like that. You can't come in here."

SlingBlade is the only person I've seen who can get kicked out of a bar *before* he even gets into it. Actually, kicked out isn't even the right word. He got kicked *away,* like a gypsy beggar.

PWJ goes in, gets the girl he knows, and we bring her with us to another bar. You should have seen this girl. Was she hot? Yes. Was she such a fucking disaster that even I could see the looming carnage from miles away, like a tsunami of big-tittied self-delusion? Fuck yes.

Because this girl was an insecure nutcase, the first thing out of her mouth to us was to tell us about all the fancy and important shit she'd done. She was a student, a model, a sportscaster, a filmmaker, a non-profit organizer, an astronaut . . . blah, blah, blah. If history has taught us anything, it's that there are only two ways to deal with a tsunami: Make a run for it to higher ground or dive right into its face. Well we'd all had enough to drink by this point that none of us were in any condition to run anywhere. It only took about five minutes of this bullshit before SlingBlade, Dirty, and I laid into her.

Dirty "You're a model? Yeah."
CrazyGirl "I am so a model! I've been in magazines!"
SlingBlade "Were you lying on top of a low-rider?"
CrazyGirl "No! Real magazines!"
SlingBlade "Those are real magazines. That's were I see all the new styles of Dubs."
Tucker "I bet she could model. You know those 'before' pictures in the gastric bypass ads? Someone has to pose for those."
CrazyGirl "I'm not fat!'

That's true—she wasn't fat in the least, I was just saying that to make her crazier. I can be kind of a dick like that.

CrazyGirl "I've been on TV too, you know!"
Dirty "Was this the type of show you pay for with a credit card over the Internet?"
SlingBlade "Technically, porn doesn't count as modeling."
CrazyGirl "No!"
Tucker "I could see it. They use plain looking women in TV commercials, too."
Dirty "She probably starred in a commercial where naughty children are baked into pies."

She got pretty flustered, and the wheels started to come off. It crashed and burned when we got to the reason why PWJ was even fucking her to begin with.

SlingBlade "Well, you're just a joy to hang out with. Christ, I wonder what mood enhancing cocktail PWJ had to dull himself with to stand talking to you long enough for you to let him shoot his load in you."

Tucker "I can just picture it: PWJ all hunched over, sweat glistening off his pasty white nakedness, desperately humping back and forth, his awkwardness making him look kinda of like a crippled dog trying to bury a treat. His hot pink tank top on the floor, his jean shorts around his ankles, face scrunched up right before he cums, so tight you can't see his eyes."
PWJ "SHUT UP YOU'RE FREAKING ME OUT!!!"
CrazyGirl "That's not what it was like!"
SlingBlade "Is it romantic? I bet it is. I bet PWJ looks deeply into your eyes as he uses your vaginal cavity for a masturbatory aid."
Tucker "Did he punch you right after he came? He's into that."
Dirty "That sounds like fun, PWJ. I wanna fuck a girl until she screams in ecstasy and then punch her in the mouth."
CrazyGirl "He didn't do that! He's not into that!"

Of course he isn't into that (I don't think), but they pretty much left the bar after that. If she'd stayed much longer, I'm fairly certain we could have broken her down so completely that she'd emotionally dissociate and attack us right there in the bar. That's usually what happens when narcissists get confronted with a reality that differs from the one they've constructed in their mind.

We eventually start talking to these other girls. Pretty cute, typical young professional girls, a few years out of college, etc. Since they were all in the same sorority together in college, they had that false confidence those types of girls get when they travel in packs. Like hyenas with mascara. I forget what I said that pissed one off, but this exchange is really what got us in:

Girl "Does this work? Going around insulting girls?"
Tucker "They're only insults if you have no sense of humor."

Her friend thought I was hilarious and we hit it off. She was clearly the naughty one of the group, and I was all about it. Somehow we got on the subject of sex, and what these girls counted and what they didn't, how they counted vacation sex and one night stands differently from their "real" number, etc., etc. A totally nondescript conversation, except of course SlingBlade was with me, and this is one of his hot button issues with women.

NaughtyGirl "I'll be right back, I have to go to the ladies' room."
SlingBlade "If you fuck a guy in the bathroom, will it count?"

She scowled at him as she walked off.

SlingBlade "You've outdone yourself with this one, Tucker."
Tucker "What? She's hot."
SlingBlade "Jesus Christ—she's a preposterous whore. Just give her two sour apple martinis, and she'll go supine faster than a boneless cat on heroin. I'm sure you'll love her."

I thought the girl had left, but she was talking to her friends on the other side of me and heard this. She got pissed.

NaughtyGirl "Excuse me! I'm not a whore! Or a slut! Or anything! I have standards!"
SlingBlade "Since you're talking to Tucker, I guess your standard is 'He doesn't hit me after sex'?"
NaughtyGirl "First off, I haven't agreed to sleep with your friend!"
SlingBlade "Oh please. You'd fuck a one-legged homeless man if he had a penis and told you that you were cool."

Apparently, this hit her anger g-spot, because the girl went fucking nuts. She lost her fucking mind at him, screaming and yelling and cursing and all kinds of shit. I honestly can't remember what she said; I just remember it was a flurry of words that were both angry and barely intelligible. I'm fluent in whorespeak and I still missed most of it. I do remember the final exchange, because I laughed so fucking hard I nearly blew a blood vessel in my eye.

Girl "So? What do you have to say for yourself?"
SlingBlade [sarcastically] "You make me feel small inside."

Girl "Good. You deserve it, you fucking piece of shit."
SlingBlade "Sorry, I'm out of silver bullets and holy water. I'm defenseless against you."
Girl "I knew you wouldn't have anything to say, I know guys like you."
SlingBlade "I'm curious—the abortion where your soul should be: Is it filled with human excrement or dog excrement?"

She pretty much had to be physically separated from him at that point, lest a fight break out.

Tucker "Dude, that's the second girl you've driven to the point of violence tonight. You gotta stop that shit."
SlingBlade "If I can't make fun of disgusting whores, then what's the point of America?"

Right around then, Credit, Jojo, and Hate showed up. And they were fucked up. As were we. After two near-fight experiences—with girls, no less—I was pretty much done with trying to get SlingBlade to talk to women, so to entertain ourselves, we decided to play a game called "Expose Yourself." It's exactly what it sounds like. For example, my finest contribution was betting I could walk from our table to the bathroom and back, with my dick out, without anyone noticing. I did it successfully. Everyone laughed. I felt like a god. Then Jojo had to ruin it:

Jojo "Tucker, don't get too excited. Maybe the fact that no one noticed your penis is a bad sign."
Tucker "FUCK YOU!! THIS IS WHY NO ONE LIKES BLACK PEOPLE!!"

We get more and more fucked up, and the ugly girls get more and more attractive, and of course, since I am perpetually horny, I make inroads with a girl who, four hours earlier, I would only have talked to if I needed to pull a plow. And of course, my friends mocked me ruthlessly about it.

Hate "Max, out of all the things you've tried to put your penis in . . . this one is the most unfortunate."
Tucker "There is an upside; I forgot to wear deodorant."

Jojo "How is this different than any other night?
Credit "Max, I lived with you for two years; I'm just happy that you've learned what deodorant is."
Hate "I don't know dude. She's not good . . . at attractiveness. Or skinniness."
Credit "I bet she's good at football."
SlingBlade "That would be the only way I'd pick her. If I was choosing sides for tackle football."

Their arguments were persuasive. She was not attractive.

Tucker "Yeah, it might be time to bail."

Jojo set his drink down in frustration, let out a sigh, then took a deep breath, looked me in the eyes and gave me his very best Morgan Freeman voice:

Jojo "Tucker—there's no such thing as a lukewarm hell."

That instigating motherfucker! He ALWAYS does this to me. Now I HAVE to fuck her—when you're drunk and a mystical Negro tells you to walk a path, you gotta walk it.

Even if it means waking up next to a Missouri sea-donkey on the morning of your friend's wedding, and then escaping from her house without your underwear or any money, so you have to walk the five miles back to your hotel.

El Bingeroso's Wedding
Lawrence, KS

Occurred, June 2001

As crazy and ridiculous as his bachelor party was, El Bingeroso's wedding was pretty normal. It was a huge wedding at a massive chapel with 300+ people. Mermaid, Dirty and Tully had all been given STRICT instructions by many of the wedding-goers to be on their best behavior, and the rest of us were sufficiently scared of El Bingeroso's father that we were unwilling to do anything that might make even the slightest scene.

The reception was pretty basic, and God, were the speeches boring. I mean, wedding speeches are always boring, but these were particularly brutal. Ever been to a third grade piano recital? That's a fucking tweaker rave compared to this shit.

SlingBlade "I would rather watch the amputee Olympics than this."
Tucker "Who are you kidding? The amputee Olympics would be awesome!"
Credit "Is there such a thing?"
PWJ "Yes. It's called the Paralympics."
Tucker "You're kidding. There's an amputee Olympics? How did I not know about this? WHY IS IT NOT ON ESPN!?!?"
Hate "SHHHHHH!"

Since the speeches weren't holding my attention, I became obsessed with coming up with new TV ideas.

Tucker "Seriously, how do blind people know when to stop wiping their asses? There's got to be a TV show idea there. You could do it like "The Price Is Right." Before they took dumps, the blind people would have to

guess how many wipes it would take without going over. Whoever gets closest wins. If they get it exact or within one wipe they win BOTH prizes. The loser gets their living room furniture rearranged."
SlingBlade "Listen to yourself."
Tucker "DUDE—Retard porn! What a great idea! We'll be rich!"
SlingBlade "You're dead to me."

Then El Bingeroso's crazy uncle got up, started rambling about nonsense, and dropped possibly the greatest gem in the history of wedding speeches:

CrazyUncle "Ah, the memories. I can remember it just like it was yesterday, when I taught El Bingeroso the best way to kill a rat is to stick a rusty nail in a 2 × 4 and whack'em with it . . . but that's not what we're here to talk about. El Bingeroso and Kristy, have a good life, Live Long and Prosper."

Then he made the Vulcan sign and started crying. I wanted to stand and applaud.

I assumed that after the speeches, everyone would get drunk and the fun would start. El Bingeroso had assured us that he put his foot down with Kristy and her family about the absolute necessity of having an open bar. Unfortunately he didn't really pay much attention to the details after he won that battle, and as we all know, that's where the devil is.

The "open bar" was a joke. The ways we got fucked were numerous. First, it didn't open until after the speeches. Second, someone decided that the open bar would consist only of domestic light beer, well whiskey, and white wine. I'm not even kidding—those were the *only* choices. Third, there was ONE bar. For 300 people. Fourth, and possibly most ingeniously, the bar was staffed by two kids who'd never actually poured a drink in their lives. When I first went up there and ordered a light beer, I got back a cup of foam.

Bartender "Sorry, this is my first time working the bar."

Tucker "You don't know to hold the cup to the nozzle and tilt it at an angle?"
Bartender "I'm only 18, I can't even drink yet."

Whatever, I was getting free beer, and the bartender was a cute girl, so I wasn't going to complain. Much.

SlingBlade on the other hand, was not as forgiving. He orders a whiskey and ginger ale. This girl does her very best to get the drink right, painstakingly mixing what she thinks are the proper amounts of whiskey and ginger ale, softly inserting a stir stick, and then delicately placing it on a napkin and handing the drink to SlingBlade. This was like only the third mixed drink the girl had made EVER, and since this was the Midwest, she took pride in her work and eagerly awaited SlingBlade's response, hoping for at least a nod of assent on a job well done.

He took one sip. His head tilted to the side and his jaw shifted. Oh no—I know what that look means. In the most sarcastic possible tone, SlingBlade says, "Oh that's great," then slams the ginger ale in the trashcan and walks off. The poor girl looked like someone just stabbed her new kitten.

Tucker "You ruined her whole month."
SlingBlade "She's an idiot."
Tucker "Come on, let's go hit on some girls."
SlingBlade "I'm going to sit at the table by myself. There's not enough liquor here for me to be social."

Sadly, there were very few targets. Most of the attractive single girls there were Kristy's friends from college and she went to one of those schools where women go to get their M.R.S. degrees, so pretty much every one of them had her serious boyfriend/fiancé/husband with her.

There was one girl up for grabs, and from the jump PWJ was all over her. She was his perfect type of girl: big natural tits, very sweet demeanor, kinda rural but not stupid, etc. She had been Kristy's sorority sister in college. Dirty kept talking her up, telling PWJ about how cool she was and that she had a twin, and that he should ask her about her twin. He harped on this over and over: Ask about her twin, her twin will only come out at night, her twin is the one PWJ really wants to hit on. I just assumed Dirty had a threesome with her and her twin, and that was his way of bragging to us—the dude is nicknamed Dirty after all.

Not quite.

After PWJ talks to her for about 30 minutes, he asks her about her twin. She says she doesn't have one. He's kinda confused but lets it go because they're hitting it off. They keep talking and flirting, and then all of the sudden a random bridesmaid comes over and pulls PWJ aside. She talks to him for a minute, then takes the cute girl to the bathroom. PWJ storms over to the table.

PWJ "Where is Dirty? That motherfucker!"
Tucker "What? You looked like you were in."
PWJ "Well, apparently that girl is seriously schizophrenic and just got out of a mental institution, where she's been for like A YEAR. Which coincidentally is the last time she'd had consensual sex. And she doesn't have a twin at all—unless you count her other personality as a separate person. "

I'll admit, I laughed . . . but that was fucked up. I wouldn't even have done that.

I made friends with the cute bartender and she just let me fill up my own beer, so I ended up getting pretty bombed. Homer Simpson said alcohol was the cause of and solution to all of life's problems. That includes standards. The only single girl I could find at the wedding was this one girl who was, well, less than ideal. She was fun to talk to, though, so I bullshitted with her for most of the night. By the end, I was ready to go home with her. Some of my friends were not in agreement with my choice, especially SlingBlade, who was sober and annoyed with everything.

Tucker "At the very least, she's a butterface."
SlingBlade "She insults the term butterface. She's a butternothing."
Tucker "She's good enough for the dick."
SlingBlade "Your dick needs glasses."
Hate "Tucker, he's right. She's ugly."
Tucker "What time is it?"
Hate "2am."
Tucker "Nobody is ugly at 2am."
SlingBlade "You'd think . . . but this one has an ugly that appears to be timeless."
Tucker "Does this girl have any discernible talent, except for the two hanging off her chest? No. Do I care? No."
SlingBlade "She looks like a pot roast."
Tucker "Whatever . . . I'll take one for the team."
Hate "What team??"
Tucker "Isn't Credit trying to fuck her friend?"
SlingBlade "Listen to what you're saying."
Hate "This one put the 'ugly' in 'ugly.'"
Tucker "HEY! FUCK YOU BOTH! It's my dick and I'll put it wherever I want!"

I woke up the next morning with one of those awful kicked-in-the-head hangovers you get from cheap light beer. I looked over at the "girl," and thanked god she hadn't rolled herself into a spooning position because when I took all of her in as a healthy, sober man who loved his life and his limbs, I finally understood where the term "coyote ugly" came from.

GoldenBoy's Wedding
Outer Banks, NC

Occurred, July 2001

You've already read this story—it's the wedding I took MissVermont to in "The (almost banned, now complete) Miss Vermont Story." So yeah, that wedding probably takes the cake for the craziest of the group.

JonBenet's (sort of) Bachelor Party
Tampa, FL

Occurred, January 2002

After a six-month period that saw graduation from law school, two bachelor parties, and two weddings, we settled into our real lives and our post-school jobs. And, to put it bluntly: real life sucked. One day, JonBenet sent this particularly depressing email to the group:

> I hate to whine, but it is the only thing I really excel at, so:
>
> Is anyone else still at the fucking office? I'm sitting here in the conference room trying to concentrate hard enough to overcome my involuntary muscle control so I can force my heart to stop beating. The world would be a better place if I did not wake up tomorrow. I demonstrated the slightest aptitude for mathematics at work and now I have been designated firm math guru and get the lamest assignments in the his-

tory of the legal profession. The best years of my life are way behind me. I could have gone to West Point and could be killing terrorists right now. Instead, I am basically gay.

Of course we all tried to cheer him up. Not by talking about our emotions or trying to understand the real cause of our depression—be serious; that's what women do. Women reinforce social bonds by complimenting each other (but not really meaning it), whereas we men socialize by insulting each other (but not really meaning it). So that's what we did.

Credit's email:

> I'm not sure how long I'm going to last in the legal profession either. I just went through a week of training, which included the dreaded 'Effective Public Speaking' workshop. Interestingly enough, sweating profusely while muttering to yourself is not one of their classic styles of public speaking. My firm has now cut off all access to Espn.com for the foreseeable future. Tech support has told me to stop calling them trying to bypass the block of the site.

My response:

> You aren't the only one seriously depressed. I never realized how much I liked school, and how incredibly different it is from the real world, until I actually got fully into the real world. For example, in academia, being mean, rude, and crass to people has no consequences, except that people you don't even like anyway talk shit about you. Whatever, fuck'em if they can't take a joke. In real life, being mean, rude, and crass to people has VERY REAL consequences, like having employees quit because you constantly berate them.

An example of my day:

> 9:00am: Wake up. Bitch about having to get up early. Throw water on my body. Put on whatever clothes smell least offensive.

9:06: Call a random employee at home. Tell them they suck and are close to being fired. Hang up on them as they attempt to respond. Feel immediately better.

9:15: Walk down to the restaurant and try to pretend I am interested, and not just biding my time until I either feel the sweet release of death or become a star for some unknown reason.

9:18: Grab a random employee, and tell them that this could be their last day if they don't quit stealing. Ignore their lamentations to the contrary.

9:24: Call one of our liquor or food vendors. Tell them their products aren't fit for consumption by starving jackals. Tell them I don't ever want to see them in my establishment again unless they drop prices 2% across the board.

Of course, SlingBlade came over the top and trumped us all with the best email:

All of these problems are well and good, but we already knew Jon-Benet was a whiny little girl. I think we should be more concerned with the new Supreme Court ruling that states aren't allowed to execute retards. This baffles me. And how does this happen? I can't imagine the retard lobby is too effective. How does their legal memo read:

Section 1: Kiling us am bad, it hurts . . . no likey it. Bunnies are pritty. Lissen too me, i have a daploma.

Section 2: Oh dear, I just pooed myself. I was going to fire off a legal missive of fearful import, but now my oversized pants are choked with poo. Please no die.

Staring reality in the face, we did the only thing a group of immature mid-twenty-something guys could do besides mock each other over email—we planned to get together and drink. El Bingeroso lived in Tampa at the time, and he informed us of a yearly party in Tampa called "Gasparilla," which is basically Tampa's version of Mardi Gras. We were all solidly in.

Two weeks before we were supposed to go to Gasparilla, out of nowhere, JonBenet tells us he got engaged to the girl he was dating. We all congratulated him and decided that now the party would double as a bachelor party.

Then, at 9pm on the Monday before we were all supposed to leave, we got this email from JonBenet:

> I was in this morning at 7:00am doing meaningless shit after missing a 12-hour drinking/Madden session with my friends. Nobody at my firm likes me. I do not have time to support my alcohol problem. My fiancée gives shitty head and talks way too much. My favorite strip club just promulgated a rule forbidding all "contact" with the entertainers. I am sure my car has a flat tire. I have to cancel my Gasparilla tickets to sit on conference calls where everyone seems to understand what the fuck is going on except me. My law firm is a dirty sweatshop and I was clearly tricked by the summer program. I haven't had anal in five years. I'm losing my sex drive. And I'm done.
>
> I want to die,
>
> JonBenet
>
> PS—Honest to God, she unilaterally purchased and hung curtains in my living room last week. Son of a . . . what have I done?

And with that, JonBenet bailed on the weekend that was supposed to be about both our depression and his engagement. I think there is a joke to make there, but thinking about it makes me too sad to try. Oh well. It's not like we can't get drunk and act like assholes without him.

We all get in late on Friday, so we just relax that night. I get my ass up early the next morning, ready to drink, and wake up everyone who was staying with us at El Bingeroso's house.

Tucker "Let's go, motherfuckers. Time to crack the first one. These beers aren't going to throw themselves up."

Kristy and her friends had set themselves up for the night at a really nice resort hotel, so they wouldn't have to be around all the drunk idiots in Tampa for Gasparilla. Like her husband and his friends, namely me. She packed up and left about noon, but not before giving a stern lecture to El Bingeroso.

Kristy "This isn't going to be one of those nights, is it? Where you just drink a lot, and everyone laughs at you when you get into all kinds of trouble."
El Bingeroso "No, no. It'll be fine."
Tucker "What? Getting in trouble is the whole point of drinking! Well, that and having anonymous sex with women."

El Bingeroso's house was right on a main pedestrian street, and because it was a holiday, there were a ton of people walking by. We were grilling out and drinking on the front lawn all day, so of course we invited every female who was even mildly attractive to join us.

All of this was amazing to one of El Bingeroso's neighbors, this guy Dan, whose wife was friends with Kristy and was going with her. He was super nice, but kind of a nerd, and his wife definitely owned his balls. I don't think he'd even heard of day drinking before, so when I handed him a beer as his wife drove off, he acted like a naughty kid getting chocolate behind his parents' backs. When I started inviting girls walking by the house to drink with us, and some accepted and joined us, the dude thought I was some sort of mad genius. And when I started fucking with them, and they were clearly into it, the dude looked at me like I'd invented fire.

I didn't hear this, but later on that night he said to El Bingeroso:

Dan "Hey El Bingeroso, I really like your friend Tucker, he's really cool."
El Bingeroso "Wow . . . I've never heard that before. Normally, people say

things like 'what the fuck is wrong with your friend?' or, 'Your friend slept with my wife,' but never, 'Your friend is really cool.'"

I knew a girl in Tampa who was pretty hot and I'd always had a good time with, and since she lived close to El Bingeroso, I invited her to come over, bring some friends, and drink with us before going to the parade. Part of the reason I liked her was that I was living in Boca Raton at the time, and by that point I'd lost my perspective on what made a good woman. SlingBlade had not. Living in DC, he'd only gotten angrier about women.

He immediately hated everything about her: her designer clothes, her uppity attitude, her wealthy pedigree, everything. Then I made the mistake of telling him that she was married to some guy who paid no attention to her, and would come to Boca to fuck me because they were going through their divorce. I was too drunk to really think about the result from setting his anger match to her emotional gasoline. It didn't take long, about an hour, before she found me by the grill, distraught.

UppityWhore "Um . . . your friend came over, then he said I was dirty and left. What's wrong with him? Why would he say that?"
Tucker "You must not know SlingBlade. That's his way of saying he likes you."
UppityWhore "And he said my friend was fat!"
Tucker "Maybe fat is a bit harsh . . . but she is definitely stumpy. She kinda looks like someone carved her out of a tree with a chainsaw."
UppityWhore "WHAT!"

SlingBlade walks over, and she whirls on him in a rage.

UppityWhore "Who do you think you are? You can't judge me!"
SlingBlade "Oh we're well past that point. I'm just trying to decide what precisely to judge you for."
UppityWhore "How about if I started judging you? How would you like that?"

SlingBlade "Hold on, let me get this straight—you're married? Right now?"
UppityWhore [pauses in frustration, because she knows he's right] "Technically, but it's more complicated than—"
SlingBlade "And you're sleeping with Tucker. Right?"

She doesn't respond, she just clenches her jaw. I'll hit this softball if you don't want to, honey.

Tucker "I'd say that we're horse-fucking, but close enough."
SlingBlade "Precisely. I feel very confident judging the fact that you are a cheating tramp."
UppityWhore "You don't know all the facts! You're just a . . . computer nerd in a Superman shirt!"
SlingBlade "So says the slut who is cuckolding her husband."
UppityWhore "Tucker, your friend is an asshole and I hate him and want him to leave."
SlingBlade "Go throw rocks at school buses, you whore."

It still makes me laugh that this girl thought I would ditch one of my best friends for her. Be serious. I like pussy, but I'd sooner rub my penis on the hot grill than let this girl tell me what to do. She and her friends were unceremoniously sent packing.

That meant it was time for us to go to the parade so I could find a different girl to horse-fuck. Because El Bingeroso told us that Gasparilla was a costume party, I brought a costume with me: the same scrubs I wore to the DC Halloween party. I decided to put them on.

I have no idea why I wore them, let alone kept them on. I looked fucking ridiculous walking around in stolen nurse scrubs. I blame alcohol. In fact, I was the only one who even dressed up, unless you count the Superman shirt SlingBlade had on. Or the fact that Credit changed from his normal white wife-beater into his more formal maroon wife-beater.

Gasparilla is held in Tampa's bar district, a place called Ybor City. If you've never been it's like a mini-Bourbon Street with less culture and more disgusting hookers. The parade starts at the beginning of Ybor City and winds around for like two miles as huge crowds stand on each side of the street.

We're walking to find a good spot, when I see a target I can't pass up: A street preacher. Every time a bunch of people are gathered around to drink and have fun, you can usually expect some religious nutcase to want to ruin it for everyone. Gasparilla is no different. He was rambling about all kinds of lunacy about why we're all bad for doing things that feel good:

Tucker "Excuse me—how is it you know that all of this stuff you're saying is true?"
Zealot "I read it in the Bible. It's all right here in the Bible," he slaps the Bible he has in his hand.
Tucker "But what's wrong with just drinking and having fun?"
Zealot "It ain't in da Bible, and this book is our law. It's our guide to the world!"
Tucker "Yeah, that makes sense. After all, I know that the Man with the Yellow Hat is friends with a mischievous little monkey, because it's in *Curious George.*"

The dude went eerily silent. Either he didn't know who Curious George was, or he was just that taken aback. Then he started out real low, and began elevating his speech until he was screaming at the top of his lungs.

Zealot "God will strike you down! Be a sinner if YOU WANT, THAT JUST MEANS **MORE ROOM IN HEAVEN FOR ME!**"
Tucker "There is no God! We're just soulless bags of meat, doomed to toil in misery!"

I was so drunk, I was arguing religion with a street preacher. Welcome to Gasparilla.

So many people come out to this thing that they set up bleachers on the sidewalk for everyone to watch the parade. We find a place to stand, and it starts out the way most parades start: with bands and other boring shit. To pass the time, Dan explains the history of Gasparilla to us along with its traditions and all the other Wikipedia shit I would probably care about if I were lame like him. At this point, I'm starting to get upset with the parade. Not enough attention is being paid to me. Then a float comes by, and the people on it are throwing beads into the crowd.

Tucker "There are moving floats? Like in a real parade?"
Dan "Yeah. You know, it's called the Knight PARADE for a reason."
Tucker "So this is basically the same as a Mardi Gras parade, with people riding the floats and throwing beads?"
Dan "Yeah, pretty much."
Tucker "Why aren't we on a float throwing beads?"

Dan explains that Gasparilla is organized by these things called "krewes" that are ostensibly charities, but sound to me like drinking clubs for people who like to use charity to show everyone how much money they have. In other words, people who think they're better'n me. He says that you have to be in a krewe to ride on a float, and that the memberships are very limited and strictly controlled and he's hoping to get invited into one someday, and blah blah blah—I don't care about your fucking problems, buddy.

Tucker "I'm getting on a float, and I'm throwing beads at girls."
Dan "No, Tucker, that's not possible."
Tucker "No, I don't think YOU understand. I am Tucker Max. I am getting on a float. I'll make sure to toss you with some beads when we come by."

No one is drunk enough to come with me. Fuck'em. They've given up on life. Not me. I'm not going to let these assholes keep me from my destiny. I'm going to throw beads at naked breasts.

I find an alley behind the street that's parallel to the parade, and start running down it, in the opposite direction of the parade. I'm jumping over trashcans, dodging feral cats . . . it takes fucking forever, but I finally come out the end. There it is: The staging area for the floats. There are like ten floats still waiting to go. It's beautiful.

But I'm just some drunk shithead dressed in scrubs. How the fuck am I going to get on the float? I think about it for a second, and then an obvious solution comes to me. I go straight up to the guy who looks like he's in charge, and act like I own the place.

Tucker "Hey man, I fell off my float and while I was busy getting up, the cops came by and wouldn't let me catch up to it. Some bullshit about keeping the parade route clear of people—whatever, you know how they are at Gasparilla. They told me to just jump on another float. Can you help me out here?"
Guy "Oh yeah, no problem man. Just hop on this one going out now."

He talked to someone who was in charge of that float, and he came right down and welcomed me.

Guy "Hey man, welcome aboard. Here are some beads, help us throw these out."

I didn't even have to yell "show me your tits" before girls in the crowd started lifting up their shirts for beads. This was more than enough entertainment to occupy me until the float got to the bleachers where my friends were standing. I got right in the front of the float, so they couldn't miss me.

Tucker "WHO'S NOT GETTING ON A FLOAT MOTHERFUCKER?!?!?!? WHERE YOU AT NOW BITCH?!?!??!"

This was way before I started writing for a living, so up to that point in my life, I had never seen another grown man want, so completely, to live inside my skin. That changed when I saw the look on Dan's face. Neither "shocked" nor "incredulous" is the right adjective. I think maybe "astonished" or "awestruck" is more accurate. The rest of my friends just shook their heads and sighed. They've seen this movie enough to not be thrown off by plot twists.

Of course once I was past them, I got bored. Watching a bunch of semi-toothed corpulent rednecks fight for plastic trinkets can be fun, but there was no way it was going to hold my notoriously limited attention. I decide to play a game called "Hurt People With Beads." The average spectator watched float after float pass by with costumed people softly tossing beads into a crowd eagerly jostling for another band of plastic balls. They were not prepared for my Beads of Death. Instead of just tossing them out, I started rifling them as hard as I could at everyone within range. The scoring for my game is simple: 1 point for every person who gets visibly pissed, 3 points for drawing blood, 5 points if you knock someone over. If you can knock someone out, that's 100 points and game over. You are the King of the Parade.

I had nearly pulled off a 5-point shot when I accidentally hit one of the parade organizers in the head. She got PISSED. 1 point!

She ran up to the float:

Organizer "If you do that again, we aren't inviting you back next year!!"
Tucker "Fuck you bitch, I wasn't even invited THIS year!"

I thought that was a pretty funny joke. But yeah, I was kicked off the float pretty quickly after that.

It took a while, but I eventually linked back up with my all my friends. Jojo had a friend who'd set us up with a VIP table at a club in YBor City. I normally hate "bottle service" type clubs, but I was so drunk I'd forgotten most of what I hated. And one of the advantages of clubs like that is they attract the types of girls who think being in the VIP with bottle service is cool, and those girls tend to end the night with my penis in their mouth.

Three girls ended up at our table. One was very hot, and obviously naughty, one was very attractive but somewhat reserved, and the third was OK—and of course she was the one completely into me, and the one who had quite obviously "called" me to her hotter friends. Great. Hot naughty girl announces to the table that she not only likes girls, but that she wants to hook up with a girl. In the VIP area. This can definitely be arranged. SlingBlade, who normally hates all women, is so drunk he agrees to escort this woman around the club while I focus on my girl.

She tells me she is in college. It takes me about three seconds to realize that she not only has a mediocre face, but a mediocre intellect as well.

Tucker "So, what are your plans for after graduation?"
Girl "I'm majoring in pre-law. I hope to go to law school when I graduate."
Tucker "You're going to fit in well at a low ranking law school."
Girl "What's that supposed to mean?"
Tucker "Exactly."

Even Credit got in on the action, hitting on the other quiet girl.

Credit "Do you like my wife beater? It's maroon instead of white."
QuietGirl "A wife-beater? That's awful. You can't describe clothes like that. What if I told you I was wearing a nigger-hanging shirt?"
Tucker "Those exist? Where can I buy one of those nigger-hanging shirts?"
QuietGirl "You can't say that!"
Tucker "We have a very annoying black friend, Jojo. He's over there. Go talk to him for awhile, you'll understand why I want one of those shirts."

At some point I have to go piss. This club has the type of bathrooms that are one at a time, and there's a line for the men's room. I am not a patient person. I test the women's bathroom door. It's open, and no one's in there. Don't mind if I do.

I come out of the bathroom refreshed and ready to go back at it. There's a girl waiting in line now, who looks at me with an expression like she just smelled piss somewhere it shouldn't be.

RandomBitch "You know, the sign on the door says 'Women.'"
Tucker "Well, then you shouldn't go in there since you're a 'Cunt.'"

From this point forward, I have only the haziest memories of what happened at the club. I do know I drank a lot. I seem to remember Hate being a creeper with girls. And though I would like to forget it, I ended up making out with the marginal girl in front of everyone.

But not just making out. It was apparently like something off the cover of a really bad romance novel. I was rubbing her face, being all affectionate, kissing her like I was trying to lick all the icing off a cupcake—I don't know. I'm sticking to the excuse that I have no memory. Writing this story, I emailed Credit to ask if he remembered this incident:

"Oh yeah, I remember that kiss. I don't know what you were saying to her, but she had her gut hanging out of a shirt that was two sizes too small, which made the kiss even more ridiculous. Hate, El Bingeroso, and I left the club before those girls, so I'm not sure why they left. I know that SlingBlade was talking to one of them until he got too drunk. Then he cut his hand on a broken bottle and was just sitting in the corner of the bar staring at it. I remember Jojo saying that he asked SlingBlade what happened with the girl and he was so catatonic he just lifted his hand to show the cut."

My next (relatively) clear memory is us out on the street, heading home. I was still hammered, SlingBlade was comatose, and Jojo was frustrated trying to babysit us and find a cab at the same time. So Jojo decides to leave me on a park bench with SlingBlade, telling me:

Jojo "I'm going to find a cab. SIT HERE and DON'T move. I'll bring the cab here and pick you two up once I get the cab."
Tucker "OK."

You probably think that I eventually got up and left. I didn't. I sat there just like Jojo told me to, with absolutely no intention of leaving. Even despite the fact that Jojo was gone so long that I'd almost forgotten why I was even with SlingBlade on this park bench to begin with. At some point, a pick-up truck with two guys in the front seat pulled up. One of them leaned out and randomly yelled:

Redneck "Hay, yew a docter?"

I look around. Where the fuck is this doctor he's yelling at?

Redneck "HAY! Hay man—you thar—iz yew a doctor?"

He's talking to me? Why? Oh yeah—I have scrubs on!

Tucker "Uh, yeah, maybe. Why?"
Redneck "Can yew look at ma friend in the back thar, we thank he might be ded."

I walk over to the truck, and sure enough, there's some dude lying in the bed, completely motionless.

Tucker "OK, sure. Can you guys give me and my friend a ride to [El Bingeroso's suburb]?"
Redneck "Sure, hop on in."

I get SlingBlade into the truck, and then check the passed-out guy's pulse. Well, I did what I assume is check his pulse; all I really did was imitate what they do on medical TV shows and put my fingers on his wrist. I thought I felt something, so I gave a very confident diagnosis.

Tucker "He is alive. What happened?"

I was totally bombed, but I will never forget his response as long as I live:

Redneck "He tried ta roofie this girl's drank, but he ended up dranking the beer hisself by accident."

I guess it was a long drive, because I passed out. I know this because I had the "WHAT THE FUCK??!?!" moment that comes when you wake up in the exposed bed of a pick-up truck while traveling 80 mph down an interstate at 5am, lying next to your best friend and *a failed date rapist.* I distinctly remember thinking to myself:

"Tucker, your actual life choices have led to this."

Yes, apparently they have.

PWJ's Bachelor Party Montreal

Occurred, April 2005

The next bachelor party wasn't for three years. It was for PWJ, the first of the group to get engaged to a girl he met after law school. By this point everyone had been in their jobs for a while and was making money (I was even starting to see success with writing; that started after the Gasparilla bachelor party). We could go somewhere cool and fun. For some reason, PWJ thought this meant we should go to Montreal.

Though I love teasing Canadians, for the most part I like Canada. Great beer, everything's cheap (or at least it was back then), the people are nice, and the girls tend to be attractive and slutty—the best mix of attributes. But of all cities to pick in Canada—Vancouver, Toronto, even Calgary or Ottawa—why pick Montreal?? The only bastion of French people in North America, and we're going there on purpose?

The only good part of the flight was when I was in line at customs, and the old guy in front of me was getting harassed about something trivial by the French-Canadian customs idiot. He said something about his papers not being in order and the old guy responded, “Yeah, well son, I didn’t need a visa when I landed at Okinawa, and I don’t see why I need one now.” It was awesome. I wanted to start chanting, “USA! USA!”

Once in Montreal, I found out immediately why PWJ picked it: There were hot girls EVERYWHERE. Hot girls working at the airport. Hot girls driving buses. They have so many hot girls in Montreal, they let them do menial labor jobs: I saw hot girls WORKING ON ROAD CREWS. I’m not remotely kidding—I saw them with my own eyes. TWO of them. One was shoveling asphalt, the other was holding a sign. And they were both HOT.

The first night in town was really tame because most of the guys didn’t show up until really late. The next night though, the official bachelor party night, was great.

We started with dinner at some Japanese place. Because SlingBlade grew up poor, he’d never learned how to use chopsticks. We made fun of him as he cycled through all the various beginner chopstick mistakes. He eventually just went with the most rudimentary method: holding one in each hand like a shovel, and using them to awkwardly scoop the food into his mouth. After he FINALLY got the first piece of tempura fish into his mouth, he yelled across the restaurant:

SlingBlade “BONZAI! I have mastered your choppity sticks!!”
Tucker “Dude, that’s not even remotely the right way to use chopsticks. Look at me, the way I do it, with both sticks in one hand.”
SlingBlade “Fuck them. They’re a conquered culture. I don’t need to learn their inferior ways. Get me a fork, and be quick about it!”

One of my favorite parts of the weekend actually happened at dinner. Some guys didn’t really know PWJ’s fiancée, so he was explaining what was cool about her. PWJ is a total car nerd, and earlier that year bought a shitty, broken down 1965 Mustang that he had grandiose plans to restore. One of the things he mentioned about his fiancée was the fact that she loved classic cars, and would help him with his Mustang.

Tucker "I still don't know why you're obsessed with that ridiculous penis car of yours."
PWJ "A classic car is not a penis car! It's different. Look—"
SlingBlade "Blah blah blah . . . shut up. It's the same."
PWJ "No, it's not, listen to me—"
SlingBlade "PWJ, I can't wait for the day your Mustang is all fixed up and you take it for your first drive. You'll be cruising around, top down, wind sweeping through your receding hairline, beady eyes squinting against the sun, thinking about all the chicks you could pull with this if only you were single. Then, when you're stopped at a red light, another old red Mustang will pull up. Sitting in it will be a 45-year-old guy, totally bald on top but with a salt and pepper pony tail pulled from his side hair, grey '80s-era Oakleys with a red band keeping them on his head, Tommy Bahama shirt unable to hide the sweat stains on his copious paunch, one of those pine tree things hanging from his mirror. He will look over at you, smile, give a thumbs-up, and say, 'Niiiiice car, man.' With that, your little 'this isn't a penis car' fantasy will come crashing into the reef of reality and unceremoniously sink. I can't wait."

[The good news is that, as I write this in 2011, PWJ has sold his Mustang and no longer harbors any stupid penis car fantasies. Apparently, the reality of multiple children was the reef his fantasy sank on.]

GoldenBoy had been to Montreal a few months before for the bachelor party of one of his undergrad "coke and hookers" UVa buddies, and so he knew the lay of land pretty well. He set us up at a strip club he said was amazing. We arrive, and from the outside, it looks about as shady as a non-ghetto strip club can look. Like something Larry Flynt would own—awful, gaudy neon (even for a strip club), tattered signs, trash all over the place. And perhaps worst of all, it had the most ridiculous strip club name I've ever seen in a Western nation. I think it was called "Club Super Sex." We were very skeptical to say the least.

Tucker "GoldenBoy, what the fuck? I thought we went over this in Vegas—the nasty hookers are for your UVa friends, not us. I don't want to pay for a Canadian to suck my dick."

GoldenBoy "Trust me Tucker, this place is great."
SlingBlade "Not all Canadians suck dick . . . some of them just put it in their mouths and hold it there for awhile."

Yeah . . . he was right, I was wrong. Hot was everywhere. The strippers were hot. The bartenders were hot. The cocktail waitresses were hot. Even the fucking coat check girl was hot. And from what I could tell, it wasn't just a front for a brothel. These girls were real human beings.

Small problem: Most of them were French.

Actually, that's wrong. They were French-Canadian, which is even worse than real French. French-Canadians are so shitty, neither real Canadians nor real French want to claim them. Can you imagine getting rejected by BOTH of those groups? At that point, it's time to find a rope and end it. I've had ugly fat girls turn me down before, and I've never felt as rejected as a French-Canadian.

We all start making the basic French jokes everyone always makes, and then my asshole friends have to go and ruin the fun.

Hate "Tucker, aren't you part French-Canadian?"

Tucker "Fuck off, Hate."
Credit "Wait, you told me about this once—what was your grandmother's last name?"
Tucker "The fact that I have a grandmother whose maiden name is Cormier is not relevant to this discussion."

Everyone laughs at me, of course.

GoldenBoy "I don't know Tucker, sounds like you're one of them."
Tucker "No! My grandfather won her in a game of cards. It's different."
SlingBlade "Blood in, blood out."
Tucker "GENETICS ARE NOT DESTINY!"

[You have no idea how much I tried to leave my Quebec ancestry out of this little part of the story, but my friends would not have it. When PWJ read over the story, he said, "Dude I was on pain pills this whole trip because it was right after my surgery, so there is a lot of detail I can't really remember, but THAT I remember very, very clearly." Fuck him.]

Right as we got there, the bachelor from another bachelor party was getting up on stage for his bachelor thing. At the beginning, it looked pretty normal, the strippers bringing him on stage, teasing him, tying him up . . . and then it took a real bad turn. Little did we know, this was the type of strip club where you needed a safe word. They got real serious whips and chains, tied him up with Gitmo restraints, and FUCKED. HIM. UP. Not like a normal stripper just venting her suppressed rage—these girls were S&M professionals, and this was some serious abuse porn. It was like watching the Rodney King tape, except this guy didn't have it coming.

When they were done, the bachelor was visibly exhausted. He staggered off the stage, fell to his knees, and vomited blood everywhere. Well, it was almost certainly red wine—you know, because he was a stupid French-Canadian—but still, he was in bad shape. We talked to the waitress about this, and apparently, this was standard procedure at this club, nothing unusual.

Tucker "GoldenBoy, you didn't tell us about this."
GoldenBoy "I don't really remember it being like this. I was real drunk though."
PWJ "Guys, I'm thinking I'll skip that portion of the bachelor party."

After seeing that, none of us had the gall to push PWJ into doing it, so we skipped that part and just got PWJ a bunch of dances.

Because this was a pretty fancy place, there was an attendant in the bathroom. I hate those guys, but in America they are generally pretty nice and leave you alone if you don't engage them. I guess it's different in

Montreal. After I finished pissing, I was walking out, and the dude starts in on me:

Attendant "Aren't you going to wash your hands?"
Tucker "My penis is clean, my hands are clean, I didn't piss on my hands—that means I don't need to wash them."
Attendant "That doesn't sound right to me."
Tucker "You work in a fucking bathroom. I don't think I'm gonna take advice from you."

After a few drinks, I decided to prepare my buddies for the show that was about to start. Not a strip show, mind you. This was a show I was orchestrating: I'd invited a bunch of girls to come and hang out with us. They were all girls I'd never met, but who had emailed me through my site when I announced I was coming to Montreal.

Tucker "Alright guys, the first set of girls should be showing up any minute."
Hate "I'll believe it when I see it."

This was 2005, so by now the dynamic between all of us from law school was starting to change. From about 2000 to about 2004, I was sort of the black sheep of the group. Where everyone else had taken the normal career path and just choked down all the bullshit being a lawyer requires, I was the one who got fired from my summer associate job and was effectively kicked out of the legal profession. As they progressed in their careers, I was the one who got fired by my dad from the family business. As they started to get married and get serious about family, I was the one who kept partying and went on this ridiculous "I want to be a writer" wild goose chase. As they started to make real money, I was the poorest of the group, the one who didn't have a job, the one who looked like he was going nowhere.

But around 2005, it started to turn around. I was making money off my website. My friends were starting to get questions about me from random people they worked with who'd read my website. I had a book coming out the next year. And girls were starting to come to me to hook up, instead of me having to do the normal guy thing, and work to get them.

I'd told them some of these girls we were coming out. Of course they were skeptical. They still thought this writing thing was stupid bullshit, and that I would eventually have to give it up and get some sort of conventional job, like the rest of the sheep.

And then, three girls showed up to the strip club. Two of them were pretty, and all of them were looking for me. They even got us a really good table up front. Almost immediately, a bunch of the strippers came. At first I thought it was because they thought I was hot or knew who I was or something. Yeah right, like a fucking French-Canadian can read English. Nope, the girls who came with us knew like half the strippers that worked there.

Tucker "How do you know all these girls? Do you work here?"
Girl "No, not at all. We, uh, just go to school with them."
SlingBlade "Jesus Christ."
Tucker "HAHHAHAHAHAHAHA."
Hate "Riiiiiiiight."
Tucker "You can just tell us the truth, we don't give a shit. I'll fuck you either way, it's just if you work here, I need to know so I can get more condoms."
Girl "I swear! They all go to school with us!"
GoldenBoy "So you're telling me that the whole 'stripper in school' thing is not a myth?"
SlingBlade "Next they'll be telling us that they're real humans beings, and not simply objects for our vile lust."

Then two more girls came looking for me. I was talking to one of them, when the last girl who told me she was coming finally showed up. By herself . . . and she was stunning. Ridiculously hot. She introduced herself:

Frenchie "Allo, are you Tucka?"

Thickest Quebec accent ever. Instant turn off. I look at her again, up and down. She's the hottest girl in this whole place, strippers included.

Tucker "You wore deodorant, right? OK, you're sitting next to me."

Fuck it, I don't care if she talks like her tongue is stapled to the roof of her mouth. Hot trumps frog.

She ended up being a really cool girl, and all of us had a great time. With seven guys and six girls, the ratio was great, the beer was very delicious, and the girls turned out to be pretty cool. Even the girls who came out to fuck me and realized I was fucking the Frenchie didn't get pissed; they just hit on my friends. Considering most girls think my law school friends are not only nicer than me, but also better looking, this worked out great.

One of the girls was . . . a bit slow. She told us she was half Irish and half Mexican. We immediately dubbed her "MexiMick."

SlingBlade "You're half Irish, half Mexican? Wonderful. So you're drunk AND lazy."
MexiMick "We aren't drunk or lazy! Everyone in my family has a job!"
SlingBlade "Oh please. The legacy of both of those cultures is alcoholism and carbohydrates."

MexiMick was the least attractive of the group, which naturally gave Credit the best shot. He wasn't doing well on his own, so we convinced her that Credit was Mexican and she should hook up with him for cultural unity. Dude is as Jewish as matzo ball soup. Not smart, she was.

MexiMick "He is kinda cute."
Credit "It must be the salsa stains on my shirt that make me so attractive."
SlingBlade "For someone who cleans all day, you sure are messy."
Tucker "YOU LEAVE MY GARDNER ALONE."

Hate "I might believe Credit is Mexican, but never that he'd do yard work. He has the motivation of a broken vending machine."
MexiMick "Leave him alone, he's nice! I think he's a good Mexican!"
Tucker "Credit is a terrible Mexican! I bet I speak more Mexican than Credit: Taco, burrito, enchilada, quesadilla!"
MexiMick "Hey, there's no such language as Mexican! It's called Spanish!"
SlingBlade "And here I was wondering why everyone thought you were dumb."
Tucker "Credit, look at all these tables that need to be bussed. Get to work! ¡Ándale ándale, arriba, arriba!"

At some point, a stripper with a thick accent came over and made the mistake of talking to SlingBlade.

FrenchStripper "Allo. You are very sexy."
SlingBlade "You look like you'd be sticky to touch."
FrenchStripper "You want dance? You like hummingbird move, yes?"
SlingBlade "I like my own move. Prematurely ejaculating and then crying myself to sleep. I call it the Double Starburst."
FrenchStripper "What is 'premature ejaculating'?"

The Frenchie with me translated for her, but she just looked confused. She had three names tattooed on her arm. So I asked the obvious question.

Tucker "What are those tattoo names of? Your kids?"
FrenchStripper "Yes, my children."
SlingBlade "You have kids? Wonderful. Parlez-vous social services?"

Through her laughter, my Frenchie translated again. I guess the stripper got it this time, because she left. No wonder my books have been translated into over 25 languages, and still not French.

I thought I was with the hottest girl in the strip club. Then this ridiculous girl walked by holding a tray of drinks.

Hate "Wow. Look at her. Why is she waiting tables and not stripping?"

SlingBlade "Because her father loved her?"
Tucker "No, he just didn't sexually abuse her. If he loved her, she'd be working at Cheesecake Factory."

Some of the girls we were with knew the hot cocktail waitress, and told us she was in school with them, so they got her to come over. I order our table a tray of shots—Thug Passion, to fuck with my friends. And I make a point of telling her to hit on SlingBlade when she came back.

HotWaitress "That guy? I hear he's been kinda mean to some of the girls."
Tucker "That's just his social mask. Underneath it, he's actually a sweet teddy bear, I promise."

She comes back, we do our shots, and she delivers in a way I'd never have expected.

HotWaitress "So why are you so mean to everyone?
SlingBlade "I'm not mean to everyone. Just stupid people. So I'll probably be mean to you."
HotWaitress "I'm not stupid."
SlingBlade "EVERYONE IS STUPID EXCEPT FOR ME."
HotWaitress "I'm smart. I'm as smart as you."
SlingBlade "You're as smart as me? Look, just because you can beat a meth-addicted French stripper at checkers doesn't make you smart. It just makes you the tallest midget."
HotWaitress "I could say the same thing about you. Being mean doesn't make you smart either."
SlingBlade "Oh, sweet irony. I wish you were smart enough to understand what the word irony means, so you could get that joke."
HotWaitress "I know what irony is."
SlingBlade "HAHHAHAAH! Oh please—PLEASE—explain to us as to what irony is."
HotWaitress "It's when something is not what you expect it to be. Like you mean the opposite of what you're saying."

STUNNED SILENCE.

This girl might be a fucking idiot, she might have number of problems, but make no mistake about it—she was right. That IS the **real** definition of irony, not the synonym for "coincidence" that idiot hipsters use it for when they want to sound like they know something.

Tucker "OH MY GOD THAT WAS AMAZING!!!"
HotWaitress "I told you I was smart!"

Everyone cracked up. SlingBlade just sat there steaming. It was awesome. The best part was that in the middle of us cracking up, he reached for his drink, but was so rattled that he knocked it over and it spilled all over himself. He just sat there, staring at the empty glass, vodka and club soda soaking his lap.

SlingBlade "Even God is laughing at me right now."

Turns out this girl actually WAS in school with those girls, and she was also an English major and a comedian. Nice. Canadian strip clubs are not like American ones—you can't automatically assume the girls working there are fucked up, because Canadians, especially French-Canadians, have a much healthier attitude towards sex than Americans. Who would've thought?

As the night went on, I tipped her crazy money to come back and keep fucking with SlingBlade, and though it got a little animated at times, it was obvious these two were a little into each other. I tried to get him to admit this to himself.

Tucker "She's hot and cool, and she does seem kinda smart. You should hook up with her."
SlingBlade "Zero percent chance."
Tucker "Dude, she's hot. I'd fuck her till I passed out."
SlingBlade "You'd fuck the exhaust pipe on her car. The only way I could

bring myself to fuck her was, if immediately afterward, I got to beat her skull in with a brick."
Tucker "I've never seen a girl impact you like this dude. And I think she's flirting with you too, if you'd stop being a dick and play your cards right, I bet you get something here."
SlingBlade "Here is the list of people I would fuck before her: 1. Hitler, 2. Osama Bin Laden, 3. a stray dog infected with mange. Do I need to go on?"

I was still laughing at his ridiculousness when she came back to the table. She said to me, right in front of him:

HotWaitress "Your friend is really funny. I like him."
Tucker "You like him? You can take him home with you if you want. We don't want him any more."
HotWaitress "I don't know, he's kind of mean. He is cute though." [to SlingBlade] "So what would you do if I took you home with me?"
SlingBlade "Knock you unconscious and steal everything in your house."

Of course he was saying it as a joke, but most people don't get his jokes. She got it and laughed. This girl was so cool, she even got his ridiculous sense of humor.

HotWaitress "I think your friend here is a Muppet. He has no body hair, no sex drive, and he's always making snide comments."
SlingBlade "Bitch please. I've stepped over better looking girls than you trying to find a quiet place to masturbate."
HotWaitress "You can masturbate now? Is your mom proud that you're finally able to maintain an erection?"
SlingBlade "I'm going to take a steaming dump in your vagina."
HotWaitress "I guess that's what I would do if I was mad I couldn't stay hard."

WOOOOOO!! I mean . . . I was in shock. You don't understand—I've known SlingBlade for 10+ years. He is a comedic genius. I've never seen anyone not named Tucker Max (or Jojo) keep up with him in a battle of insults for more than three lines. Everyone eventually runs out; he just keeps going.

Yet, here was this girl, who works in a STRIP CLUB IN MONTREAL, not just hanging in, but giving it back to him. Hard.

You have no idea how much I wanted these two to hook up. She was definitely flirting with him at this point. I would have done anything to make it happen. And I tried everything I could. Unfortunately, this was not a movie; this was real life. He just bailed. There's not even a good ending the story. He just fucking left and went back to his hotel. It was so heartbreaking.

[Incidentally, this is one of the reasons that, in the movie based on my first book, Nils and I developed the story arc that had the SlingBlade character hook up with the funny stripper—if he wouldn't fuck her in real life, I was going to make him fuck her in the land of make believe.]

As the night wore on and we got even more fucked up, Hate got creepier. Not really a shock with him—even though he's the nicest dude out of all us, sometimes he just comes off creepy. It got to where Hate was just staring at the girls. Like, 'I'm watching you jump rope in the schoolyard from my bedroom window through a telephoto lens' staring. At one point he leaned over and said to me in the loudest stage whisper ever:

Hate "One of these girls is going home with me."

Not even two minutes later, the group of three girls got up to "go to the bathroom" and disappeared. A minute later, I got this text:

"we were going back to your hotel, but your friend freaks us out sorry"

Yeah, Hate can do that. No problem. I ended up going home with the stunning French girl who I was planning to fuck anyway.

The problem was, I was so drunk, I needed to eat first. She took me to some late-night place to get this stuff called "poutine." If you've never heard of it, I'll try to explain: It's french fries with brown gravy and chunks of tasteless white cheese on top. I've had it sober since then, and it's disgusting. But when you add it to a stomach that has nothing but beer and cognac shots in it, it's so delicious you eat two of them.

Of course, the consequences are not as delicious:

In the middle of sex, you succumb to an alcohol/carb coma, and pass out, still hard, inside of a French-Canadian girl. I'm pretty sure this is exactly how the French beat the English at the Siege of Fort William Henry during the French and Indian War.

PWJ's Wedding
Lexington, KY

Occurred, June 2005

Weirdly enough, PWJ ended up getting engaged to a girl from the city I grew up in, Lexington, Kentucky (lived there from 8 to 16). Not only that, but they decided to get married in Lexington as well.

For this wedding, I was actually in the wedding party, which meant I had to get a tux. I'm not used to this procedure—I'm normally assigned a seat as far away from the wedding party as possible—so I didn't realize I was supposed to not only get measured for my tux in Chicago (where I lived at the time), but I was also supposed to go back to the store when it was ready and pick it up and *bring it with me* to Kentucky.

Whoops.

Apparently me not picking up my tux in Chicago was a huge deal, or so one would assume from the frantic calls and voicemails left on my phone. I didn't really listen to them. But it all worked out. Thankfully PWJ used one of the tux stores that is everywhere and had a location in Lexington, and because he's cheap, he picked out a tux package that's common, so the Lexington store had my size in stock. I picked it up Friday when I landed, problem solved.

Since it was a late wedding on Saturday, we all decided beforehand to go out drinking that Friday night after the rehearsal. Everyone was looking forward to it. Everyone but El Bingeroso, who was jumping out of his fucking skin with anticipation. He was super eager to go out and rip shit up for one specific reason: Kristy was not in Lexington. Because of her job or something I don't care about, she wasn't coming in until Saturday morning. This meant El Bingeroso could get supremely fucked up, something that was increasingly rare now that he had settled into married life. At the rehearsal dinner, he explained a normal night out:

> You want to hear what my life is like now? A few months ago, my 'fun time' was supposed to be hanging out with this guy from the office and his wife. He seemed like a cool guy at the office and Kristy got along with his wife, so I thought it would be fun.
>
> I get us tickets to this late-night beer thing at Busch Gardens. There are no kids there so it's just adults and beer everywhere for the night and is supposed to be awesome. Once we get there, they tell me they 'don't really drink that much.' They're newlyweds, about 28. They suck more than you can imagine, and I feel misled by the guy's superficial cool guy act at the office. I'm pissed, and visibly becoming restless with the evening, conversation, everything—so I begin to drink. Copiously. I decide to shotgun two 'yards' of beer, those giant tall glasses, made for white trash guys who go to the carnival and don't realize they just paid 8 bucks for basically 14 oz. of beer, but it's tall so they figure they got more. They are shocked that someone can drink that much that fast.
>
> Waiting in line for 30 minutes for the rides was bad enough, but listening to the wife was basically killing me. I try to act like I'm sleeping, leaning on the railings, anything so I don't have to listen to her fucking stories about how she is a preschool teacher. Oh your kids are so cute, tell me more about their fucking finger paintings and dollies!

I interrupt her and decide to launch into my collection of Scottish jokes. I'm cracking myself up. I end the monologue by telling a joke that ends "not so good doc, she bit three inches off my penis, shit in my face, and my neighbor came out of the closet with his hands up." I nearly choke I'm laughing at myself so hard, but when I look up, Kristy has a nervous look on her face and the couple is looking at each other with the kind of expression they would have if a dirty bum approached them and asked them to wash his asshole.

Undeterred, I tell them I want to go on the Tilt-A-Whirl [ed note: a ride that involves lots of spinning]. They are unsure of my stomach's capability of successfully maneuvering the ride. I assure them that I'm a tank, built for rock fights and state fairs. No laughter.

We get on the ride, and I began to feel the uncontrollable impulse to vomit six pounds of beer and three pounds of pizza. I yell out, half-joking, 'I think I'm gonna puke!', and the woman totally loses her cool. She literally starts to freak out. Not in preschool anymore are you?

I didn't puke, but miraculously the couple wanted to leave after that. On the way home, they stopped to check the oil in their car, and wipe the front windshield. At midnight on a Saturday. I wanted to get out of the car and kick this guy in the nuts.

THAT is now my life. So fuck all of you, we're going out drinking tonight.

Can't argue with that.

After we finish all the toasts to PWJ and his bride, and we get sufficiently drunk on the open bar, everyone decides to not waste time at a normal bar, that it's a strip club night. PWJ tells us about a strip club that he went to when they came to Lexington to check out the wedding spot. Me, PWJ, SlingBlade, El Bingeroso, Hate, and GoldenBoy head off.

I drive one car, and PWJ drives another. As we are walking to our cars, Hate half-jokingly asks me the question that would define the night:

Hate "Tucker, you get insurance on your rental?"
Tucker "Are you kidding? How many bachelor parties have we done—is there any way I wouldn't get walk away insurance?"
El Bingeroso "You have insurance!"
Tucker "Yes motherfucker, of course."

El Bingeroso does a little crow hop, and throws the champagne glass in his hand as hard as he can into the back windshield of my rental car. It shatters so hard, it fucking atomizes.

El Bingeroso "WOOOOOOOOO!! Let's go get drunk motherfuckers!!"
Hate "Oh yeah!"
GoldenBoy "Hold on, I owe you one too!"

And of course, GoldenBoy proceeds to kick the shit out of the door panels of my Ford Taurus rental. They are surprisingly resilient, and much to his frustration, he basically does nothing but leave a tiny little scuff.

Tucker "HAHHAHA—you pussies can't even hurt a rental car?"

File that under "arrogance" and cross-reference it with "foreshadowing."

Once we get to the strip club, PWJ huddles us together outside and gives us a very calm, strict warning about his night:

PWJ "OK, so I've been here once before. This place is a bit . . . redneck. Let's not get out of hand here guys, OK? And remember: I HAVE TO GO TO MY WEDDING TOMORROW. That is the most important thing here."
Tucker "PWJ, I apologize for everything I am about to do tonight."
SlingBlade "So, PWJ, let me get this straight—I'm NOT allowed to punch any of the girls?"
PWJ [let's out a long sigh] "At least wait until I've left, OK?"

The place looks fairly pedestrian from the outside, like any strip club in any southern town, but once inside, it is a whole different story. I have been to BYOB strip clubs in rural Louisiana that were nicer inside than this place. This place looked like a truck stop Arby's with a Planned Parenthood in the back.

Not to mention the girls. Oh man. It was straight out of a southern ethnography. Outside of the major cities in the South, there are really only three types of southern girls who are single:

1. Really pretty, but way too young.

2. Hot, in their prime, ready to fuck . . . but already with multiple kids and/or divorced.

3. Old and worn out.

This is because if you're a woman raised in the South, you either get married and have kids, or you get out of your podunk town and move to a real city as soon as you can.

Well, this strip club had all three of these types of women. The disparities were so weird it was jarring. There'd be one girl who could not have been more than 18 or 19, and was absolutely SMOKING hot, but you could tell she was raised in such a disastrously abusive and shitty home that she was destined to end up dying in a trailer park meth lab explosion. Across the room there'd be the 25-year-old stripper who has what could have been an amazing face if she'd grown up with even basic nutritional standards, but instead is covered with the acne scars and wrinkles that come from after a decade of drinking cheap beer, smoking cigarettes, eating nothing but processed sugar and fried foods, and popping out three kids by two different dads. Not to mention the old ones, that I guess are there to remind of you why every city has an animal shelter. Ever been to one of those restaurants that calls itself "fusion" but doesn't really know what it wants to be so it ends up just smashing three totally different cuisines together in no logical way? It was like that, except the food had no clothes on.

We sat down, got some drinks from the cocktail waitress—no joke, she was missing at least one MOLAR—and it became immediately obvious that we were not the usual type of crowd that came to this place. This was for two reasons:

1. A bunch of strippers descended on us, thinking we'd be easy marks, and,

2. We were the only ones who weren't dressed in Dickies and work boots.

The first stripper who came over was completely batshit. Not even remotely sane. So of course she wants to talk to SlingBlade. You would assume he would light a girl like that up. Nope. He just sat there, polite but distant, not really saying anything, nodding his head as she went on and on, rapid-fire style. Eventually, SlingBlade reached for a cocktail napkin, wrote something on it, and slid it to me. It said:

"Go for help"

I tried to engage her in conversation, to either misdirect her or maybe even buy a dance for PWJ or something. She was having none of it. This girl was LASER focused on SlingBlade, who wasn't doing or saying anything, he was just sitting there like a patient boyfriend. Finally, she gets called to the main stage to dance and leaves, making him promise not to go anywhere.

Tucker "Dude—what was that? I've never seen you hold back with a girl like that."
SlingBlade "I was afraid she'd stab me."
Tucker "Come on dude, she's not that bad."
SlingBlade "Hell hath no fury like a woman with borderline personality disorder, attachment issues, and low-level dementia."

He moved positions at the table so that he was now with his back to the wall, in between me on one side and Hate on the other. She didn't come back over; she just glared at me the rest of the night, like I'd stolen her boyfriend. Creepy.

As some other stripper came up and tried to hustle me for a dance, I noticed a tattoo on the back of her neck. It's a name, "Nick," written in some retarded form of calligraphy.

Tucker "Is that your boyfriend?"
Stripper "Yeah."
Tucker "So if I give you a tip, will it just go to tricking out Nick's Camaro?"
Stripper "Nick doesn't drive a Camaro."
Tucker "An IROC?"
Stripper "NO!"
Tucker "A Mustang? What does he drive?"
Stripper "My truck."
Tucker "HE DOESN'T EVEN HAVE HIS OWN CAR!"
SlingBlade [condescendingly] "Let me take you away from all this. You are so beautiful; you deserve better than Nick. Don't you realize how many men want to love you?"
Stripper "We have a great relationship, he's just between jobs!"
SlingBlade "Between jobs. That's so precious. Did Nick pick that phrase up from CNBC while you're at work?"
Tucker "How long have you been dating him?"
Stripper "Since high school."
Tucker "And how many kids do you have with him?"
Stripper "Two."
SlingBlade "Wow."
Tucker "So you got knocked up by your high school boyfriend, and now you work at a titty bar to support him, while he sits at home and plays video games."

She didn't respond immediately, which says everything. Laughter everywhere.

Stripper "It's not what it sounds like."
Tucker "It sounds like you need a new boyfriend."

SlingBlade [still condescendingly] “I’ll be that man. I’ll even love your kids like they’re mine. I’ll be your knight in shining white Mustang.”
Stripper “Well, that’s your opinion, and you know opinions are like assholes, right? Everyone’s got one.”
Tucker “Opinions are NOT like assholes. You can’t shove your dick in an opinion.”
Stripper “Whatever. I’ll be right back, I’m going to the powder room.”
SlingBlade “You don’t need more whore paint, you’re beautiful just the way you are!”

At one point, two different strippers were trying to get me to pay for dances. I told them that they had to play rock paper scissors for it. They actually did it, so I got a few dances for PWJ from the winner. Afterwards, somehow we started talking about anal. The stripper was into it. SlingBlade was not.

Stripper “You don’t like anal? You’re missing a big part of life there, buddy.”
SlingBlade “Yes, I was in the middle of an especially vigorous masturbation session back at the hotel, and I thought to myself, ‘you know SlingBlade, you need more anal in your life.’”
Stripper “Anal is fun, I like it.”
Tucker “I gotta agree with her on this. What’s the saying: Beer is like anal—you don’t know you won’t like it unless you do it so much you pass out.”

I’m not exactly sure when he did this, and I definitely cannot tell you why he did this, but at some point Hate left the strip club and went next door, bought like five pints of Jack Daniels, came back into the strip club, and passed them out to all of us to drink.

Tucker “Dude, they have alcohol here.”
Hate “They aren’t bringing it fast enough for me and El Bingeroso.”

Pretty quickly after that, shit got out of hand. I was staying pretty sober because I was driving, but Hate and El Bingeroso were not. Hate bought a dance from a girl, and while she was rubbing her ass in his face, he smacked her butt. It was HARD. It was bad. Even I thought it was out of line. You wanna hit a stripper, that's fine, but you have to make sure she's OK with it and work out the price.

And of course, El Bingeroso is hootin' and hollerin' and carryin' on, and before I know it, in a strip club stuffed with illegal Mexican immigrants, union factory workers, and farmers, all the bouncers were watching us. And not even being subtle about it. There were five big dudes, standing within 20 feet of our table, staring at us.

Right around this point was when I think PWJ ended up bailing. He even snuck out quietly, he was that afraid of getting arrested the night before his wedding. Then, one of the bouncers sees something.

Bouncer "Hey, what is this? Is this a Jack Daniels bottle?"
Hate "That's what it looks like."
Bouncer "You can't bring these in here! Whose is this?"
Hate "I have no idea, they were here when we got here."

Hate argued with the guy for at least ten minutes about the bottles being there when we sat down. He had him convinced that we were just victims of circumstance, and the dude was going to buy us a round of shots as an apology, when El Bingeroso decided to get up on a chair, pull a JD bottle from his blazer pocket, and take a swig in front of everyone while screaming at the top of his lungs:

El Bingeroso "YYYEEEEEEEEEEEEEE-HHHAAAAAAAAAAAAAAAAA AAHHHHHH!!!!"

And that was that. SlingBlade left with PWJ, so it was me, El Bingeroso, Hate, and GoldenBoy who would be driving back in my car. I'd stayed pretty sober, so I was fine. Out in the parking lot, El Bingeroso was not. He was having problems walking, ping-ponging off of cars, garbage cans, people, everything. That is, he was having problems until the sight of my rental car clicked in, and a series of bachelor party-related memories triggered an adrenaline rush that propelled him on a straight line sprint in cowboy boots that ended with him kicking one of the door panels on my rental car as hard as he could. Apparently trying to kick a field goal with a Ford Taurus is a lot like playing pool—the drunker you are, the better you are—because he put a huge fucking HOLE in the side of the door panel.

Tucker "Dude . . . "
GoldenBoy "Shut up you asshole, you have walk away insurance!!"

Hello karma, and fuck off.

We finally get El Bingeroso to stop kicking the car and get inside of it. He gets in the car, but he doesn't calm down. He's in the back next to GoldenBoy and Hate is up front with me. He rips the headrest off Hate's seat, and starts using it like a hammer to break the rear passenger window. Well, auto glass is difficult to break, and after a couple of minutes of exhausting and unsuccessful work, El Bingeroso gives up. He drops the headrest, then leans his head against Hate's seat.

El Bingeroso "I don't feel good."
GoldenBoy "Tucker, pull over!"
Hate "YOU FUCKING PUSSY! YOU HOLD THAT SHIT IN!"
El Bingeroso "I'm gonna puke!!"
GoldenBoy "Pull over Tucker, pull over! HURRY!"
Tucker "Hold on, hold on!"
Hate "DON'T YOU PUKE YOU PUSSY! DON'T YOU FUCKING DO IT!"

Strangely, he went silent for a second. There was no "puke" scream. Then I clearly heard the distinctive splash of vomit. A LOT of vomit. Like when you pour out a five-gallon bucket from the top of a ladder.

GoldenBoy "Too late."
Hate "YOU FUCKING PUSSY! EAT IT UP YOU PUSSY!!!"
El Bingeroso "I don't feel good."

Because Kristy wasn't coming until the next day, El Bingeroso didn't even get a room for Friday night. I had a double, so he passed out in the other bed in my hotel room. I made sure he lay face down with his head over the edge of the bed, put a trashcan beneath it, and went to sleep.

Since I didn't drink much that night, the next morning I woke up relatively early. I got up, checked El Bingeroso's trashcan—there was pretty much nothing but drool in it—and then went to pee.

As I walked back from the bathroom, I saw something on the floor, right at the edge of the El Bingeroso's bed: A big, round black ball of . . . something. I looked at it and looked at it, I even got down on my knees and got up real close to it, because I honestly could not figure out what it was—picture a big meatball sitting there on the floor, but hard and dry. PWJ called me:

Tucker "Yeah, El Bingeroso's still asleep . . . no vomit in the trash, but there is something on the floor by the end of his bed . . . that's got to be vomit I guess . . . I mean, it has to be vomit, it can't be poop . . . I mean, it's right here on the edge of the bed, and there's no trail of anything to the bathroom or any liquid around it and it's all dry . . . has to be vomit, or food I guess."

Hearing my conversation, El Bingeroso starts to wake up, pauses, then shoots up in bed in utter confusion:

El Bingeroso "Where am I? Why am I naked!"
Tucker "Uhh . . . you're naked?"

This was pretty awkward. Neither of us really knew what to say at that point; I'd had no idea he was naked until he said it, because he was under the covers. He couldn't figure out why his clothes were off.

El Bingeroso "What happened?"
Tucker "You don't remember?"
El Bingeroso "No!"
Tucker "Anything?"
El Bingeroso "I remember throwing a champagne glass at your car."

I recount the whole night to him as I throw a towel at him.

El Bingeroso "Wow. I did all that? I was out of control."
Tucker "And then there's this on the floor over here. I guess you decided to throw up off the edge of bed instead of into the trash can I set out for you."

He took a shower and, after finding his clothes tangled in the covers of his bed, got dressed. Apparently he had taken them off in the middle of the night. Then he started to clean up the puke at the end of the bed.

El Bingeroso "Uhh . . . Tucker . . . I don't think this is puke."

Let me tell you something: There is nothing more disturbing than a pile of shit where it doesn't belong.

Tucker "Wait a minute. Wait wait wait. That is **poop**? YOU TOOK A SHIT ON THE FLOOR!"
El Bingeroso "I guess so. This is definitely poop."
Tucker "How . . . why . . . oh my God . . . it all makes sense. That's why you didn't have clothes on this morning—you took them off in the middle of the night to take a shit! But why did you shit on the floor?!?!"

He just gave me a sad, pitiful look. I lost it.

Tucker "The bathroom is FIVE FEET AWAY!! And why is it right off the edge of the bed? Look at the shit—it's like, three inches from the bed! So let me get this straight: you woke out of your drunken stupor, realized you had to take a shit, took your clothes off, but decided that the bathroom was too far, so you copped a squat on the edge of your bed, balancing yourself as you squeezed out a huge turd, then just got back under the covers and went to sleep? And you don't remember any of it???"
El Bingeroso [sheepish shrug] "Sorry?"

These are my friends. As he was cleaning it up, he still had the gall to ask a favor.

El Bingeroso "Hey, can we not tell Kristy about this?"

Forget Kristy, I'm telling the WORLD about that shit.

The wedding was pretty basic. I can't remember anything at all noteworthy or funny happening before or during the ceremony. It was just a very nice, normal wedding. And PWJ's wife either didn't have any hot single friends, or didn't invite them to the wedding, because there was literally not one unattached woman between the ages of 21 and 51 there to hit on at the reception. No big deal, that's why God invented alcohol—AND FULL OPEN BARS. After the wedding I met up with some friends from high school, and then we got REALLY housed.

The next day was far more eventful than the wedding.

I woke up feeling like I needed to apologize to everyone I've ever met. There was a small Hispanic woman shaking me, I had french fries in my mouth, and I was lying in the hallway of my hotel with a room service tray next to me. I never really figured out if it was room service that *I* ordered, or if it was someone else's. Let's just say it was mine. Either way, I woke up in the hallway outside my room, with food still in my mouth that had come off a room service tray. Classy.

I crawled into my room and plopped down on the bed at like 6:30am. At 10:30, my phone rang, waking me up. I had a 5pm flight, and I was WAY too hung over to board a plane. So I decided on the most obvious solution: at 11:01am, I rolled into the convenient store.

Tucker "We can buy beer at 11am on Sunday, right?"
Clerk "Yeah . . . sure."

I grabbed a sixer and a gallon of water and strode over the counter.

Clerk "Uhh . . . why do you have a tuxedo on?"
Tucker "Wedding."

Clerk "Starting early?"
Tucker "No, the wedding was yesterday. I'm on my way to return the tux."

I wish I had a picture of his facial expression. You'd have thought I farted on a toddler.

I drove to the mall and sat in the parking lot alternating drinking beer and water, until noon when everything opened. They had barely unlocked the door when I stumbled into the tuxedo store.

Employee "Can I help you?"
Tucker "I need to return my tux."

She looked at me confused for a second, and then it clicked.

Employee "The one you have on?!?"
Tucker "Yeah."
Employee "You're . . . you're still *wearing* the tux."
Tucker "So? Is that like, bad or something? I'm not supposed to wash it, am I?"
Employee "No . . . but, well . . . what clothes are you going to put on?"
Tucker "You don't have, like, stuff for me to wear out?"
Employee [look of complete shock and disgust] "No."
Tucker "Oh . . . well . . . I'm in a mall, I'll just go buy something."

I was still really hung over, so it wasn't until I was paying for my new clothes at the sporting goods store that I realized what had transpired. Initially, I was kinda confused by her reaction. It literally didn't even occur to me as I was doing it that wearing the tux when I was going to give it back would be an issue. At the store, I asked her about this.

Tucker "Does this not happen often?"
Employee "In the seven years I've been working here, you're the first person to ever bring the tux back while still wearing it."
Tucker "Really?"

Employee "Oh yeah. That is definitely a first. I've never even heard of this happening."

I then proceeded to eat enough fast food to kill a small child, and drove back to the hotel to pick up Hate and go to the airport. The car STUNK. If you've never smelled day-old vomit that's been cooking in a parked car—don't. We had to put all the windows down just to drive it. At the airport I dropped the car off at the rental place, and Hate was already laughing.

Hate "Max, I don't care what kind of insurance you have, there is no way they're letting you out of this. No chance."
Tucker "I'll be fine."

At the drop off place, I am behind like three other cars getting checked in, so I just leave my keys in it and walk into the airport. I go through check-in and like ten feet from security, over the loud speaker we hear:

"Tucker Max, Tucker Max, please report to the Budget counter immediately. Tucker Max, to the Budget counter. Thank you."

Hate "AHAHHAH—Oh boy Max, I knew it! I knew they weren't going to like that. I'm coming back with you, I want to see this showdown."

We get to the counter, and the woman has a look of shock on her face.

Agent "Are you Mr. Max?"
Tucker "Yep. What's the problem?"
Agent "The car is destroyed. There is vomit on the floor, the headrest is missing and there is a *hole* in the door! How did this happen?"
Tucker "I don't know. I have insurance, right?"
Agent "Well, yes, but if it's intentional, it's not covered."
Tucker "It's not intentional. Can I go now?"
Agent "No, we need a police report or something."
Tucker "I'm confused. I told you I have no idea how any of it happened.

It just appeared. There is nothing to report to the police. And I have walk away insurance, right, so it's covered, right?"
Agent "Well . . . yes."
Tucker "It's not walk away insurance, if I can't just *walk away,* is it?"

She was so aghast at this, she didn't say anything. So I walked away.

The Death of SlingBlade
Phoenix, AZ

Occurred, July 2007

If you've read my first two books, you know all about SlingBlade. I have a lot of funny and interesting friends, but that dude is on a different level. He's not only funny and smart as hell, but he also sees the world in a different way from the rest of us. This is the email SlingBlade sent telling us he was getting married:

> So I assume that those of you who are married and thus purchased a diamond for your wife are aware of how evil and corrupt the diamond cartel is. I was not. Apparently, diamonds are almost worthless other than the value attached to them by the silly tramps that DeBeers has brainwashed into thinking 'diamond equals love.' Congratulations, ladies, your quest for the perfect princess cut not only supports terrorism and genocide, but has managed to destroy an entire continent.
>
> Speaking of blood diamonds, what the hell is going on here? Everyone is upset about African children losing their limbs? Perhaps I missed their concern about these same children during the Rwandan genocide. Here's a solution: Stop buying diamonds. No no, the avarice of the entitled whore cannot be contained.

> And if blood diamonds are so fucking bad, why can't I buy them at a discount? Or at least get them with a death certificate or an appendage or some sort of cogent backstory that might indicate an actual meaning to this useless little cube of carbon. Clearly the diamond market is broken on multiple levels.
>
> In an entirely unrelated matter, I am now engaged.

SlingBlade's bachelor party and wedding were, well, I'm not sure how to describe them. So I won't. There is not really even a story to tell here, just a series of barely correlated events:

- There was no bachelor party. SlingBlade is a recalcitrant misanthrope, didn't want to deal with any of the typical bachelor party bullshit, and doesn't have any friends close enough to him to set it up anyway. It's not that people don't like him enough to do it—I would have set up his bachelor party in a heartbeat—it's that he didn't talk to any of us about it. One day out of the blue, we just got an invitation to his wedding.

- The wedding was in Phoenix. To a girl that none of us had ever met. Or really even heard him talk about. I saw a picture, and she was very pretty, but that's about it.

- The wedding was at a crappy hotel, with basically no reception after. Why? SlingBlade asked his fiancée what her family could contribute to the wedding. She gave him a number. That became the precise cost of the wedding. He's that cheap. I could write a whole other story just about how cheap that motherfucker is, but that example pretty much sums it up.

- When I got to the hotel, there was a sign up about the two other groups that were also at the hotel that weekend. I swear to God one was a Special Olympics group and the other was some sort of homosexual organization. SlingBlade's wedding was sharing the hotel with fags and retards; one group wasn't allowed to get married, the other group couldn't spell it.

- Since SlingBlade's wedding didn't really have a wedding party, and he let other people handle all the wedding details (his precise instructions were "I'll wear a tux and show up and say 'I do' and that's it"), the rehearsal dinner the night before didn't include anyone except for some family and one friend. There were only about 30 people at the wedding to begin with.

- This did not sit well with me. I gave SlingBlade and his wife cash as their wedding gift (I did this with all my friends; it's the best gift). But I took the amount I was going to give them, and subtracted out the cost of the meal from the night before the wedding, when they were at the rehearsal dinner.

- I met SlingBlade's wife the day of the wedding. She seemed like a very nice, sweet woman, and she was truly hot—a legit five-star.

- The wedding ceremony was held overlooking the pool. During the day. When a bunch of gay guys were hanging around. Making out in the background. Of the wedding ceremony.

- It was just a weird, strange wedding all around. But that's not why I called this section "The Death of SlingBlade." I did that because the marriage has worked out great for him. He's still very much happily married, has two kids that he adores and dotes over, and he's happier than I've ever known him to be. The guy who was such a misfit that he had to talk in a SlingBlade voice at bars in order to talk to girls—he's dead. This is all great for him as a person, but this kinda sucks a bit for me, because he's nowhere near as funny as he used to be when he was depressed and angry. When I talk to him now, he makes jokes about punishing the weeds in his garden. Hence, the death of SlingBlade.

But you know what—he's my friend and I'd rather see him happy and unfunny, than depressed and hilarious, so good for him, seriously. I still have never hung out with his wife (because of his job, they live very far away from the rest of us), but I think, based on the thank-you note she wrote me, that SlingBlade married a woman who is appropriate for him:

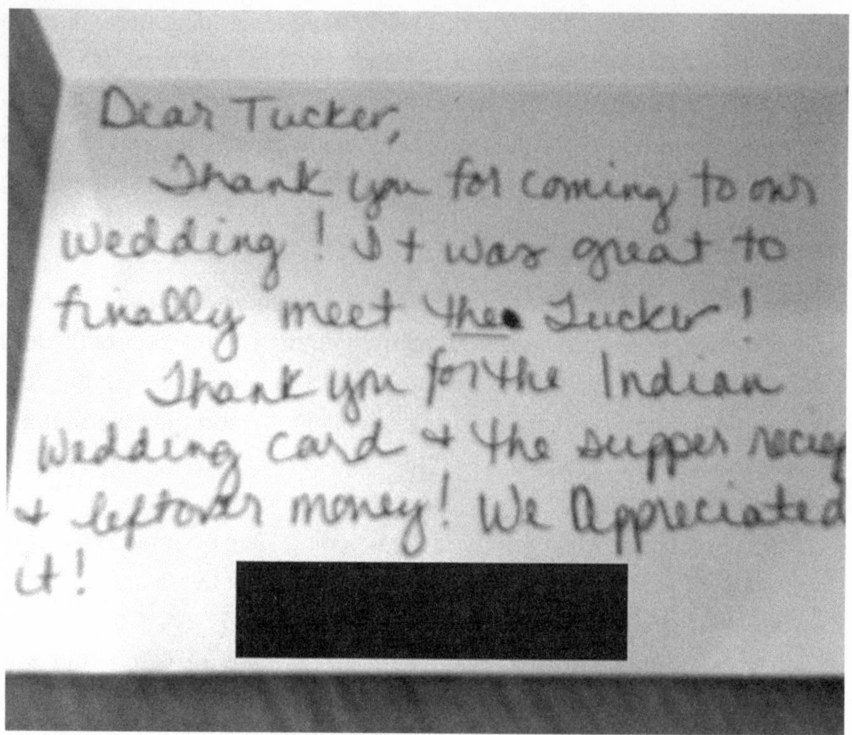
Dear Tucker,
Thank you for coming to our wedding! It was great to finally meet the Tucker!
Thank you for the Indian wedding card + the supper recei[illegible] + leftover money! We appreciated it!

Hate's Bachelor Party
Tampa, FL

Occurred, October 2007

Hate's bachelor party was fine, but wasn't like the others. Part of the problem was, since it was 6+ years after we all graduated, everyone had kids or other conflicts with their jobs and most couldn't make it. The only law school friends who could were me and El Bingeroso, and we didn't know most of the other people he had coming to his bachelor party.

There is no in-between when it comes to mixing groups at a bachelor party. It either works seamlessly or fails miserably (e.g., GoldenBoy's Vegas bachelor party). Hate had become not just a lawyer, but basically a fucking ambulance chaser. As a result, some of his friends at this bachelor party were the types of guys who buy boats on the local lake to get girls. You know the types—the ones who have white blazers in their closet. That they wear on out in public. When it's NOT Halloween. I don't generally mix well with those types of guys, so it was a strange dynamic all weekend, and as a result, there was nothing funny or ridiculous to write about.

The only reason I'm even putting this in here is that traveling between bars, I got a ride from the greatest cab driver of all time. There was a new rap song playing on the radio. I was drunk, of course, and I wanted to hear it.

Tucker "Yo, turn that shit up man."

I guess he didn't hear me, because he just kept driving. I looked at his name on his taxi license, and it was something African and unpronounceable.

Tucker "Hey Prince Akeem, hey Prince of Zamunda, turn that shit up."

He turned and looked at me, and in a thick African accent, said:

Cabbie "Hey Lisa MacDowell, shut the fuck up!"

GREATEST CAB DRIVER EVER!!

I tipped the guy $50 when he dropped me off.

Hate's Wedding
Pittsburgh, PA

Occurred, April 2008

Hate's wedding was possibly the most boring wedding of all time. Which probably means it was a great wedding for the couple and the families, but no one really cares about that shit, especially not me. The wedding was so boring there were only a few things worth writing about:

I was talking to some random girl who was a friend of the bride. She was super mediocre in every way, but she seemed to like me, so that meant she had at least one good quality. Great, except who ever got a boner thinking about the silver lining?

Girl "What do you do for a living?"
Tucker "I don't know. Have a lot of vacant sex with morally questionable women and get drunk every day."
Girl "That's not a job."
Tucker "That's what you think! My life is proof of your incorrectness!"

I went on to explain my book, website, etc., and she was fascinated by the fact that I was in my 30's and unmarried. She was that type of girl.

Girl "Don't you want kids? Do you even like kids?"
Tucker "Oh yeah, I love kids. I want to have a bunch more."
Girl "You have a kid? No you don't."
Credit "He does have a few kids . . . they're just all in the dumpster behind Planned Parenthood."

I not only convinced this girl that I had a son, I got her to believe that I was trying out all kinds of new experiments on him to see what happened as a result.

Girl "Experiments? Like what?"

Tucker "Well, let's see. I bought him a cat, waited until he bonded with it, then the next time he was bad, I took the cat out back with a shotgun, and told him, 'If you won't clean your room, someone has to pay for your insubordination.' Then I took the cat behind the shed and shot the gun off in the air a few times, until I could hear him collapse in tears. Then I let the cat go and it ran off, scared as shit. He promised to never let his room get dirty, and by God, it's worked. He's afraid to even leave his rug on the floor!"

Girl "OH MY GOD!! HOW COULD YOU DO THAT??"

Tucker "Well, his room has to stay clean doesn't it? You know of a better way to get him to understand the seriousness of the issue?"

Girl "That is so wrong!"

SlingBlade "Sounds reasonable to me."

Well, once I realized she was taking me seriously, I really went nuts with the bullshit:

"I do all sorts of classical conditioning with him. For example, I have a foghorn I set off every time he takes a bite of any food. You should see his little spoon shake as he raises every bite of Frosted Flakes to his lips."

Or my personal favorite:

"One day when he was at school, I took all his action figures and hung them from the ceiling with nooses around their necks. I pinned notes on them with tags. Some were ominous like, 'You're next' or 'Only the beginning,' but some were nonsensical, like 'Fish are delicious.' I swore to him that I had no idea who did it. I told him that it was probably the demons in his closet, and they must be getting sick of his shit, and he should probably be careful at night. He cried a lot over that. I don't think he slept for a week."

By the end of the conversation, she was in tears. I don't mean this figuratively. She thought all these ridiculous lies were true, and she was crying, thinking about the poor child who was enduring all this abuse. I almost felt bad for her. Then I remembered that I'm an asshole and she's an idiot, so instead I laughed at her.

Sadly, that was not the end of the mediocre girl parade. Some of us went out drinking in Pittsburgh after the wedding, and though I have met hot girls in Pittsburgh before, they must have all been hanging out with the Steelers that night, because none were out at the bar we went to.

At some point, two girls approached me and started hitting on me. I always feel bad for mediocre girls who hit on me. On one hand, I like it that they have the courage to actually take things into their own hands with a guy and not just passively wait for guys to come to them. That's sexy, and I want to encourage more of that behavior in women.

On the other hand . . . these girls looked like something I'd draw with my left hand. I don't mean to be a dick (that's a lie), but come on ladies: Do you really not have any notion of where you fit in the hook-up hierarchy?

Of course, alcohol and rationalization can solve that problem, so I talk to them for a while. The one girl who was way more into me, MediocreGirl, kept asking me questions about myself, and I kept making goofy jokes. The other girl, BitchyGirl, had a look on her face like she'd just smelled poop, and got progressively more annoyed with the situation. Then MediocreGirl asked me another question about myself, and it happened:

Tucker "But enough about me. Let's talk about you. What do you think about me?"
BitchyGirl "Oh that's great, why don't we just focus even more on you! Why don't you tell us about your stupid books!!"

The funny thing was, I didn't know they had recognized me, and I hadn't mentioned one thing about my books or anything like that. MediocreGirl was trying to slow play me, but BitchyGirl hated me too much to let it ride. What a golden opportunity for entertainment. When the universe sends you signs like this, you don't punch a gift whore in the mouth.

Tucker "Uh oh. I think you need to see a doctor, your Down Syndrome is acting up again."
BitchyGirl "Oh that's real original."
Tucker "So people call you retarded a lot? Maybe that means something."
BitchyGirl "What's next, you going to call me an idiot?"
Tucker "Well, I generally go with 'fucking idiot,' but we can stick with just plain 'idiot' if you prefer."
BitchyGirl "Oh you're so funny aren't you, every girl wants to fuck you, you're just the greatest guy of all time, MAKE ME PUKE!"
Tucker "I don't know why you're mad. If you're going to be an idiot, you may as well be the fucking type."

I think the fact that I remained totally calm and smiling pissed her off the most.

BitchyGirl "You can fuck off and DIE!"
Tucker "Just some advice: You're not really hot enough to talk about fucking."
BitchyGirl "Whatever! You don't even dress well!!!"
Tucker "I know, I shoulda bought an outfit, but I paid my light bill instead."

Everyone laughed, except the two girls. They were just completely confused. I guess they don't listen to Project Pat in Pittsburgh.

There was all sorts of drama after that between BitchyGirl and MediocreGirl, but I didn't pay attention. I thought they had gone, when MediocreGirl came back over. She made some apology, whatever.

MediocreGirl "I still want to hang out with you."
Tucker "Great. I assume we're going to fuck right?"
MediocreGirl "What?!? No!"
Tucker "Then there's not really any reason for us to hang out."
MediocreGirl "What? Why not? I think you'd be fun to talk to, to hang out, witty banter, all that stuff."
Tucker "If you aren't fucking, I'd rather shit my house keys than hang out with you."

MediocreGirl "Can't a girl just hang out with you and not have sex?"
Tucker "Of course. I have a ton of platonic female friends. It's just that YOU are not going to be one. Unless I'm putting my penis in you, there is no other value to you. You bring nothing else to the table."
MediocreGirl "Look, all I want is to talk to you, pick your brain, see what you're like, you know, stuff like that."
Tucker "See, what you're talking about is why hanging out with ME would be fun for YOU. It doesn't explain anything about why it'd be fun for ME. You don't bring banter. You aren't witty. You aren't funny. There is nothing to pick from your brain. You're looking for *me* to entertain *you.* A relationship is an exchange, not a one-way street. Look beyond your own personal desires for a second and understand what you bring to the exchange—*nothing.* Except a wet hole."
MediocreGirl "I AM very funny and interesting! All my friends say so!!"
Tucker "You mean like that stupid bitchy girl who just left? Great judge of character."
MediocreGirl "More than her!"

Ironically, by telling her she wasn't interesting, I had made it into an interesting conversation. But I've been down that road before; the half-life on explaining idiocy to an idiot is short.

Tucker "Look, I gave you the chance to be interesting, and you failed at that. I gave you the chance to be slutty, and you failed at that. You're out of chances."
Girl "Well you missed your chance to get with me!!"
Tucker "This is like a pile of dogshit telling me that I missed out on stepping in it. I think I'll be OK, thanks."

Funny enough, I think that statement pretty much describes the whole city of Pittsburgh.

Tucker's Bachelor Party and Wedding

Nowhere

Neither of these has happened. Not even close.

I'm sort of pissed that I don't have a bachelor party or wedding of my own to write about. Of course, I don't even have a girlfriend, much less a fiancée or a wife, which is a fairly important part of the whole bachelor party/wedding apparatus.

I'll eventually get married, but when I think about it, I seriously doubt I'll even have a bachelor party. What's the point? I don't need a last night of freedom. What could I do that I haven't already done? Most importantly, what do I even have left that *I want* to do?

Nothing. My 15-year run of drunken excess and sexual revelry was the most amazing bachelor party ever. I've lived all of that type of lifestyle I want to live. If I felt like I needed a bachelor party on top of it, it would probably mean I wasn't done with that part of my life yet.

But I am done with it.

Which is why the time has come for the final chapter . . .

Epilogue: The Retirement

There's a certain feeling you get
when you're real and you spit
and people are feelin' your shit.
This is your moment
and every single minute you spend
trying to hold onto it
cause you may never get it again.
So while you're in it
try to get as much shit as you can
and when your run is over
just admit when it's at it's end.
—Eminem

When I got to the literary world, it was like a great big pussy, just waiting to get fucked—and I stepped up and fucked the ever loving shit out of it. As I sit here putting the finishing touches on this book, it's September 2011—exactly nine years to the month since I launched TuckerMax.com. I've cherished almost every moment of this past decade. All the successes I've achieved are humbling and amazing to me; they surpassed every dream I had for myself when I started. In the nine years since I started, I've entertained countless people, sold millions of books, invented a new literary genre, and had a movie made about my life. And I haven't even turned 36 yet.

This is not to say I haven't made mistakes or done stupid things I wish I hadn't. Of course I've done things I regret—how could I not?—but I wouldn't change anything, even the setbacks and failures I've had to endure. Good always comes with bad, and both have been beneficial in their own way.

But as awesome as my last nine years writing these stories has been, I think it's time for me to move on. There are a lot of reasons, but the big one is pretty simple:

This is not who I am anymore.

When I first started in 2002, I was writing stories about the way my life was *at that moment.* But over the last couple years, I've realized that I don't do all the funny but stupid shit I did when I was 25 anymore, and I find myself writing about the way my life *used to be.* I'm not the same person I was when I started writing these stories, and I don't live the same life I did then—so it no longer makes sense for me to keep writing that way.

Plus, even though I had a blast and I racked up some great stories, you've read them all now. With the publishing of this book, I've told all the great fratire style stories I have about drinking, partying, and fucking.

Given that, I think it makes sense for me to step off this stage and leave fratire behind, forever.

Three final things:

1. I'm only done with fratire, not with writing or life: I am retiring from fratire, but I am NOT "retiring" in the sense that I am done with life. I'm not going to lay on a beach and count my money, or stop drinking or having sex with girls I like, or stop doing the things I love doing—that's bullshit. I will NEVER stop being who I want to be. I'm not done as a writer either. I have a shit ton more things I want to write about (in fact, I'm already working with Nils Parker on an advice book that'll come out soon), I'm just done writing the "Tucker Max" style stories that I made famous. These stories invented the "fratire" genre, but my run in it is over; it's up to someone else to pick up the fratire torch and carry it to new places.

2. Thank you: I want to thank all of you. Seriously, I cannot express enough how much all the support from you people has meant to me. You aren't really a writer until someone pays to read your work, and millions of you have paid your hard earned money to read my writing, and that is awesome. I sincerely thank each and every one of you who supported me (and make sure you get your free copy of *Sloppy Seconds,* which is my tangible thanks to my fans).

3. More to say about retirement, just not here: I have a lot more thoughts about retiring, my career, fratire, etc, but most of them are self-indulgent, weepy bullshit, so I'm not putting them here. My books have always first and foremost been about laughter and entertainment, and that's how I want to keep it. The deeper, emotional, self-reflective parts of my life are very important to me, but I've never really put them in my books, and there's no reason to change that now. If you care about the rest of my thoughts on this subject and want to read them, I've posted them on my website: **www.tuckermax.com /retirement.**

Thank you all again for supporting me. I hope you've had as much fun reading about this aspect of my life as I had living it.

"We should all be so lucky as to go out like that—knowing our limitations, knowing we have reached the apex of our career, and leaving on our own terms."

—Gregg Doyle

"I believe one thing holds it all together. Everything I've ever done was with excitement, because I wanted to do it, because I loved doing it."

—Ray Bradbury

Acknowledgments

Since I knew I had another book coming out shortly, I didn't do any acknowledgements for *Assholes Finish First.* Consider this a combined thanks for that book, this book, and *Sloppy Seconds:*

Nils Parker: His editing is so crucial to my work, I'm not sure I can overstate its importance. He doesn't write my books, but without his substantial input, suggestions, joke help and editing advice, there is no doubt in my mind that the last two books would have been no where near as good as they are. So many of "my" iconic jokes and lines are stolen from him, I gave him *a percentage of the profits from this book*—and I STILL think I got the better part of the deal. I've said this for years: He's a better writer than I am, possibly the best writer I know, and I'm lucky to be able to work with him.

Erin Tyler (Bunny): Erin has done so much more than just help me with my writing; she has helped me with my life more than anyone ever, including my parents, and much of my success as an artist and a human is due to the simple fact that she's my friend. I deserve the credit for my success, but honestly, but without her helping me, I might not have had *any* success at all. To say I'm lucky to have her in my life is such an understatement as to be laughable; like saying Scottie Pippen "had a role" in all those Bulls championship teams.

Above, I said Nils is "possibly" the best writer I know. I hedged that statement because of Erin; she's his only competition for #1. Erin has been working on her own books that will come out eventually, and I want to be on record right now as saying they are already way better than mine. I predict they'll not only outsell mine by a large margin, but will be embraced by the world and become true classics that people love and read for generations. I am the bigger star today—but that's only because the world hasn't read her books yet.

Jeremie Ruby-Strauss: Jeremie has been my editor through all four of my books. I've never worked with anyone else, partially because he's so fucking good at his job, but possibly also because no one can work with me. I'm not an easy person to deal with sometimes, but Jeremie handles me like a seasoned pimp. I think the best proof of what a great editor Jeremie is lies in the results: go pick up the acknowledgements sections of all the major, out-of-left-field best sellers over the past decade. There is one name you'll see over and over—Jeremie Ruby-Strauss. This is not an accident. He's one of the best, if not *the* best, out there.

Of course I have to thank all my law school friends—PWJ, SlingBlade, Hate, Jojo, Credit, El Bingeroso, GoldenBoy and JonBenet. Without them, none of this would have been possible. As a group, they are funnier than me, smarter than me, cooler than me, and probably even more fun to hang out with than me. I'm the famous one simply because I wrote all this stuff down, not because I was any better at it.

I have to give a mention to my long time agent, Byrd Leavell, if for no other reason than the fact that he's had to endure, by his estimate, over 20,000 book proposals sent to him from people claiming to be some version of "the next Tucker Max." He's never signed one of them—but he has signed some of the best new original writers out there, and if you think you're one of those, he's the guy to talk to. There are not many agents who really understand new media and where publishing is going in the future, but I guarantee you, Byrd is one of them (mainly because he's smart enough to listen to what I tell him).

Definitely have to thank Kathleen O'Hurley (@Slashleen), who gave me the inspiration for many of my favorite lines in the book. Also thanks to Jason Mustian (@jasonmustian), who gave me a ton of funny jokes, even though he's a dirty Brooklyn hipster.

My assistant Ian Claudius did a great job helping put this book and *AFF* together. He doesn't deserve any credit for how good it is, but he did do all the shitty work that sucks to do, but has to be done. And my copy editor on this book, Emily Reynolds, is the first copy editor I've ever worked with that actually did a good job.

I forgot to thank Elliot Throne in *IHTSBIH,* which was an egregious oversight. He knows how important he's been to my success. Without his help at a crucial time, none of this might have ever happened.

Other people who directly contributed to the stories in this book or in *AFF,* either by jogging my memory about details, suggesting changes, or otherwise adding something to make my last two books better:

Paul Ardaji ("Junior" in the stories), Michael Soloway, Doug Polster, Matt Berry, Ben Corman, Jeff Waldman, Ryan Holiday, Lorraine Schwartz, Luke Heidelberger, Charlie Hoehn, Mike Boulerice (KungFu Mike). I would put my dog in the acknowledgements because she's sat at my feet as I've written almost every word of my books, but that's ridiculous. She only cares about marrow bones and tennis balls, not this bullshit.

I'm sure I'm forgetting a ton of people. What do you want from me, compassion and empathy? Have you READ my books? Now get the fuck out of here and go make your own stories.